David
May

W9-CKC-089

CLEANNESS

Noah's Ark

MS Cotton Nero A.X., f. 56a
(reproduced by permission of the British Library)

OLD AND MIDDLE ENGLISH TEXTS

General Editor: G. L. BROOK

Cleanness

Edited by

J. J. ANDERSON

MANCHESTER UNIVERSITY PRESS

BARNES & NOBLE BOOKS · NEW YORK

Published by Manchester University Press
Oxford Road, Manchester M13 9PL

UK ISBN 0 7190 0665 1

USA

HARPER & ROW PUBLISHERS INC
BARNES & NOBLE IMPORT DIVISION

US ISBN 0 06 490178 5

Printed in Great Britain at the Alden Press, Oxford

CONTENTS

PREFACE

In this edition I have sought chiefly to provide a good conservative text of *Cleanness* and to elucidate the difficult language of the poem in glossary and notes. The text has been transcribed from the facsimile of MS Cotton Nero A.x. published by the Early English Text Society, and checked against the manuscript in the British Library. Where the ink is badly faded in the manuscript, ultra-violet photographs have been used as an aid to reading. In both text and apparatus I have taken advantage of published work on the poem, including of course the editions of Morris, Menner, and Gollancz, but at the same time I have tried to look at every problem afresh.

I am very grateful to the many people who have helped me, in large and small ways, in the work of editing. In particular, Professor W. Rothwell has willingly consulted his materials for the forthcoming Anglo-Norman Dictionary in response to a stream of queries from me, and I owe several new interpretations and etymologies to him. Professor G. L. Brook, the General Editor of the Old and Middle English Texts series, has borne delays with patience and has given me useful criticism. The publisher and his staff at the Manchester University Press have always been efficient and considerate. Thanks are also due to Professor R. Allen Brown and B. T. Batsford Ltd. for permission to reproduce two drawings from Professor Brown's book, *English Castles*, to Mr M. C. Seymour and Oxford University Press for permission to quote from Mr Seymour's edition of *Mandeville's Travels*, © Oxford University Press, 1967, to the Council of the Early English Text Society for allowing me to use the facsimile published by the Society as the basis of my text, and to the British Library Board for giving me access to the manuscript and for supplying me with ultra-violet photographs.

J. J. A.

ABBREVIATIONS

AN	Anglo-Norman
BT, BT Suppl.	Bosworth–Toller, *An Anglo-Saxon Dictionary*, with Supplement
Cant. Tales	*The Canterbury Tales*, ed. F. N. Robinson
Cl.	*Cleanness*
Cursor M	*Cursor Mundi*, ed. R. Morris
CVC	Cleasby–Vigfusson–Craigie, *An Icelandic–English Dictionary*
Da.	Danish
Dest. Troy	*The Geste Historiale of the Destruction of Troy*, ed. G. A. Panton and D. Donaldson
Du.	Dutch
EDD	*The English Dialect Dictionary*
EETS OS, ES	Early English Text Society Original Series, Extra Series
ES	*Englische Studien*
Gen. and Ex.	*The Middle English Genesis and Exodus*, ed. O. Arngart
GGK	*Sir Gawain and the Green Knight*
Godef., Godef. Compl.	Godefroy, *Dictionnaire de l'Ancienne Langue Française*, with Complément
JEGP	*Journal of English and Germanic Philology*
L	Latin
LG	Low German
MÆ	*Medium Ævum*
Mand. T	*Mandeville's Travels*, Cotton version, ed. M. C. Seymour
MDu.	Middle Dutch
ME	Middle English
MED	*Middle English Dictionary* (Michigan)
MFlem.	Middle Flemish
MHG	Middle High German
ML	Medieval Latin
MLG	Middle Low German
MLN	*Modern Language Notes*
MLR	*Modern Language Review*
MnE	Modern English
MP	*Modern Philology*
MScots	Middle Scots
Mustanoja	*A Middle English Syntax*, I
N & Q	*Notes and Queries*

Neophil.	*Neophilologus*
Nhb.	Northumbrian
Norw.	Norwegian
ODa.	Old Danish
OE	Old English
OED	*The Oxford English Dictionary*
OF	Old French
OI	Old Icelandic
ON	Old Norse
ONF	Old Northern French
OSw.	Old Swedish
Pat.	*Patience*
Piers P	*Piers Plowman*, A-text ed. G. Kane, B- and C-texts ed. W. W. Skeat
PL	*Patrologia Latina*
PMLA	*PMLA*: Publications of the Modern Language Association of America
Prov.	Provençal
Rom. Rose	*Le Roman de la Rose*, ed. É. Langlois
Siege Jerus.	*The Siege of Jerusalem*, ed. E. Kölbing and Mabel Day
SN	*Studia Neophilologica*
Sw.	Swedish
TL	Tobler–Lommatzsch, *Altfranzösisches Wörterbuch*
u.-v.	ultra-violet (see p. 11)
Wars Alex.	*The Wars of Alexander*, ed. W. W. Skeat

INTRODUCTION

Cleanness is one of four poems in MS Cotton Nero A.x., Art. 3, in the British Library; the others are *Pearl*, *Patience*, and *Sir Gawain and the Green Knight*.[1] None of these poems exists in any other manuscript. The text of *Cleanness* occupies folios 57a–82a;[2] it is preceded by *Pearl*, and followed by *Patience* and *Sir Gawain*. There are two full-page illustrations to the poem, on folios 56a and 56b. The first of these depicts the Ark (with only seven aboard instead of the biblical eight), the second is of Daniel expounding the writing on the wall to Belshazzar and his queen. For most of *Cleanness* the manuscript is in good condition and the writing is easy to make out, but occasionally it is faded to the point of illegibility, notably down the left-hand margin of folio 60a. The scribe's hand is a clear, compact 'Gothic minuscule', with few unusual features. Compared with the other poems in the manuscript, *Cleanness* appears to have more than its share of scribal errors,[3] and bad patches, suggestive of undue haste or wandering attention, are more noticeable.[4] From time to time a second hand is in evidence, usually simply retracing the original, but sometimes altering or adding a letter or word; this hand is also present in the other poems in the manuscript, though less often than in *Cleanness*. The second hand may be identified by a darker ink (though not infallibly, as the original ink varies in shade), and by the forms of the letters, some of which differ markedly from those of the original scribe.

On grounds of language, style, subject-matter, and general imaginative outlook, it is probable that the four poems are by the one poet, whose name is not known. The dialect of *Cleanness*, as of the other poems in the manuscript, is recognisably North-West Midland, and the presumption is that the author lived in or near this area. The poems were evidently written in the latter half of the fourteenth century; in *Cleanness*, the poet draws upon *Mandeville's Travels*, written *c.* 1357, and the handwriting of the manuscript is dated by C. E. Wright as not later than 1400.[5] Any more precise date for *Cleanness*, or for any of the poems, must be speculative.

The manuscript of *Cleanness* contains thirteen large initial capitals, in blue and red. The poem begins with an eight-line capital, there is one of four lines at line 557, and another of four lines, after a single-line space, at line 1157. The other large capitals are of three lines. The four-line capital at line 1157 is of the same kind as the capitals which have been taken to mark the major structural divisions in *Sir Gawain*, and it marks the beginning of a major episode in *Cleanness*, the story of the fall of Jerusalem and Belshazzar's feast. The four-line capital at line 557 is not so prominent, but it seems likely that it too is intended to mark the beginning of a main episode, that of the destruction of Sodom and Gomorrah. That the poet has a threefold structure in mind is clear from line 1805: 'Þus vpon Þrynne wyses I haf yow Þro schewed', and the 'Þrynne wyses' must refer to the three main stories, those of the Flood, Sodom and Gomorrah, and Belshazzar's feast. The three-line capitals do not appear to be of major structural importance, but they are not used haphazardly. Most mark a formal division in the biblical text, and the others are probably there to indicate a division of some significance for the poem.[6]

In all four poems in the manuscript a small slanting double line appears regularly in the left-hand margin. Apart from lines beginning with large capitals, which leave no room for it, and a few other instances where it may be obscured, the mark appears beside the first, thirteenth, and every subsequent twelfth line in *Pearl*, beside every long line immediately after a 'wheel' in *Sir Gawain*, and beside the first, fifth, and every subsequent fourth line in *Cleanness* and *Patience*. In *Pearl* and *Sir Gawain* the marginal mark always coincides with the beginning of a stanza, as the stanzas are defined by the formal metrical schemes of those poems. It seems reasonable, therefore, to take it that the marginal mark is meant to coincide with the first line of a stanza also in *Cleanness* and *Patience*, though in these poems there is no metrical confirmation of stanza division. The thought in these poems, however, does seem to be shaped consistently into the four-line units; it may overspill from one stanza to another, occasionally for several stanzas at a time,[7] but the quatrain pattern always reasserts itself. It is noteworthy that the thirteen large initial capitals in the manuscript of *Cleanness*, and the five in *Patience*, all occur in fourth lines where one would expect the marginal mark to be. In *Cleanness* it is only in lines 1541-85 that the marginal marks actually run counter to the sense; but the quatrains, though displaced, are still there.[8] The scribe may have made a copying error at around line 1541, perhaps retaining a line which had been cancelled in his original and thereby displacing the quatrains, though the marginal marks continue mechanically. The situation recalls that in *Patience* 513-15, where the scribe seems to have copied three extra lines without this affecting the sequence of marginal marks every four lines. In *Cleanness* the scribe seems to have realised and recovered his error—perhaps simply by leaving out a line—at around line 1589, after which the marginal marks once more accord with the sense. The displacement is corrected in the present edition by printing lines 1541-5 and 1586-90 as five-line stanzas and lines 1591-2 as a two-line stanza.

The poems have no titles in the manuscript. The title *Cleanness* was adopted for his 1864 edition by Richard Morris, who used the first word of the poem, as he did also for *Pearl* and for *Patience*. In 1906, C. G. Osgood, in the preface to his edition of *Pearl*, proposed *Purity* as a better title. Others continued to refer to the poem as *Cleanness*, however, until Menner, without further explanation, accepted Osgood's title for his edition of 1920. Gollancz's edition, a year later, appeared as *Cleanness*. Since Menner's edition, usage has been evenly divided. 'Cleanness' has the advantage of being the poet's word; he uses 'purity' only once. Nor is 'purity' an entirley acceptable modern equivalent of the poet's 'cleanness', for its sense is relatively narrow and abstract. 'Cleanness' has a wider range of senses, physical as well as abstract, which the poet exploits to the full. The word itself is the focus of his meaning.

The meaning of 'cleanness' is not defined, but rather is allowed to emerge slowly in the course of the poem. Fundamental to 'cleanness' is respect for God. The poet emphasises the perfect respect shown by Noah, Abraham, and (apart from his one lapse) Nebuchadnezzar, who are the poem's three chief examples of cleanness in man. Conversely, uncleanness is always bound up with lack of respect for God. In a sense, all sin is unclean, as all sin has an element of such disrespect, and it is therefore proper that the sinner, whatever his sin, should be deprived of the beatific vision, which is the reward offered by the sixth beatitude (cf. lines 177–92). But disrespect for God is more prominent in some sins than in others, and it is most flagrant in those sins which involve not merely a refusal to accept God's laws, but a wilful rejection of His grace, a spurning of His gifts to men. Thus the 'filth of the flesh' of Noah's world and of Sodom and Gomorrah involves a wilful rejection of God's greatest physical gift, which is like the bliss of Paradise (line 704). For their part, Zedekiah and Belshazzar abuse God's spiritual gifts, Zedekiah by turning away from the Covenant which God has established with Abraham for the benefit of the Jewish race, Belshazzar by his contemptuous use (called 'filth' in lines 1721, 1798) of the sacred vessels which God in His mercy has accepted as instruments of direct spiritual communication between Himself and man; this is the sin of the false priests at the beginning of the poem. For a man to be cleansed of sin by penance from the priest, and then to slip back into evil ways again, is likewise to abuse the sacraments and to reject God's mercy (lines 1133–44). In the parable of the wedding feast, the point about those who refuse the invitation is that they are *privileged* to be invited, and still refuse: 'More to wyte is her wrange þen any wylle gentyl' (76). The man who goes to the feast in dirty clothes, i.e. in a state of sin, also flouts God's act of charity. Such behaviour towards one's creator and benefactor is unnatural, an aspect of uncleanness which is brought out particularly in the image of the Dead Sea; Christ, who in the central section of the poem exemplifies perfect cleanness, is 'kyng of nature' (1087). Uncleanness is the sin of ultimate contempt for God and His order, and as such it is the sin which, more than any other, provokes Him to uncontrollable fury.

The structure of the poem is as complex as its meaning. The three main stories are prefaced and linked by other matter from which they cannot easily be detached, and which gives the poem more of a continuous flow than the poet's concluding remark about his 'þrynne wyses', taken at its face value, might indicate. Moreover, a network of implied connections between passages is superimposed on the linear progression of the poem. Thus the opening example of the false priests and their misuse of God's 'gere' is paralleled by Belshazzar's misuse of God's 'guere' later. There is also a connection with the idolatry of Zedekiah, the defilement of God's food by Lot's wife, and the inner corruption of the men who lived before the Flood. There is a contrastive relation, too, with the scrupulous religious observances of Noah and Abraham. In the poem's linear structure, the episode of the fall of Satan functions as an example, along with the fall of man, of sin punished in moderation, in contrast to the 'filth of the flesh' of Noah's world, which God punishes pitilessly. But there is also a clear non-linear relation, underlined by specific verbal echoes, between the fall of Satan and the fall of Nebuchadnezzar. The wedding feast at the beginning of the poem looks forward not only to Belshazzar's feast at the end, but also to the meals provided for God by Abraham and Lot—all are symbolic occasions on which man's respect for God is put to the test and judged. There are many such non-linear relations, and they are important to the development of the poem's themes.

The poet's narratives are founded firmly on the Vulgate Bible. Menner[9] points out that about three-fifths of the poem's lines go back more or less directly to the Vulgate, which the poet must have had in front of him as he composed. Many of these lines translate the original Latin very closely. At the same time the poet frequently alters the emphasis of his original in various ways. The most obvious is by elaboration of the biblical narrative, as in the description of the wedding feast, the flight from the Flood, and the Temple vessels at Belshazzar's feast. The poet uses this technique of elaboration for his most spectacular effects. Less obviously, the poet will compress or omit a biblical detail if it is inappropriate in the context of the poem, or for purposes of narrative economy. Thus the conclusion of the wedding feast parable in Matt. XXII. 14: 'Multi enim sunt vocati, pauci vero electi' is omitted as being out of keeping with the argument of the poem, and the biblical detail that it is Sarah's fear which prompts her to lie to God (Gen. XVIII. 15) is omitted probably because it would conflict with the domestic tone of this scene in *Cleanness*. The third flight of the dove (Gen. VIII. 12) is irrelevant to the poet and is left out, and Lot's two hesitations, in Gen. XIX. 16 and 18–19, become one in the poem.

Apart from the Vulgate, the only certainly identifiable sources of narrative detail in *Cleanness* are *Mandeville's Travels*,[10] used chiefly in the descriptions of the Dead Sea and the vessels at Belshazzar's feast, and *Le Roman de la Rose*, drawn on once and referred to by name in line 1057. The poet makes free use of apocryphal and legendary material which gathered round the biblical text. Certain details in *Cleanness* recall the *Cursor Mundi*, but there is no evidence of a direct connection between the two poems.

The idea of moral and spiritual cleanness is important in the other three poems in the manuscript, as well as in *Cleanness*. Cleanness is an aspect of 'trawþe' in *Sir Gawain*, of holy innocence in *Pearl*, of patient acceptance of God's will in *Patience*. In all the poems there is a particular interest in penance as the means whereby the sinner is to be cleansed of his sins, and it is in connection with the doctrine of penance, and particularly in the penitential literature of the later middle ages, that the idea of cleanness/uncleanness is most fully discussed by theologians and homilists, usually with reference to the sixth beatitude.[11] The parable of the wedding feast is a subject for sermons for Easter Day, which was the one day in the year when all Christians, having first cleansed themselves by penance, were expected to take communion. The sermons develop the garment imagery of the parable; the preachers exhort men to come to the altar in the clean garments of charity and penance, as opposed to the foul garments of sin.[12] The view that cleanness is a matter of faith and respect for God as well as of physical purity is fundamental in penitential writing.[13] More specifically, the poet's link between 'filth of the flesh' and Belshazzar's sacrilege may owe something to St Paul's idea of the body as God's temple, e.g. in 1 Cor. III. 16–17 (cf. 1 Cor. VI. 19): 'Nescitis quia templum Dei estis, et Spiritus Dei habitat in vobis? Si quis autem templum Dei violaverit, disperdet illum Deus. Templum enim Dei sanctum est, quod estis vos.' Writers on the virtue of cleanness often use St Paul's imagery.[14] *Cleanness* is in several ways close in spirit to the Epistle of Jude and the Second Epistle of Peter, much of which is taken over from Jude. In urging purity of life and faith upon their fellow-Christians the authors of the epistles, like the poet, see disrespect for God's law as an important part of uncleanness. God punishes the unrighteous, and especially those 'qui post carnem in concupiscentia immunditiae ambulant, dominationemque contemnunt, audaces, sibi placentes, sectas non metuunt introducere blasphementes' (2 Pet II. 10).[15] The link between fleshly sin and spotted garments occurs in Jude 23: 'odientes et eam, quae carnalis est, maculatam tunicam'. The Book of Revelation also makes this link. In Rev. II. 12–III. 6, immorality, in the two aspects of sexual licence and idol-worship, is seen as a danger to the churches, and is symbolised by soiled garments, while those who have conquered their passions wear white garments. In Rev. XIX. 7–8, the bride of the Lamb comes to the marriage feast adorned in bright white linen, which is the righteous deeds of the saints.[16] In 2 Pet. III. 14, Christians are urged to be 'immaculati et inviolati' in expectation of the Lord's coming. The point that to slip back into sin is worse than never to have escaped from it (cf. *Cleanness* 1133–44) is found in 2 Pet. II. 20–1, though it is common in writings on penance. The epistles of Peter and Jude also suggest part of the narrative framework of *Cleanness*. In 2 Pet. II. 1–9, the three examples of the swift destruction ('celerem perditionem') which falls upon the unclean and rebellious are the fall of the angels, the Flood (the epistle emphasises the preservation of Noah for his righteousness), and the fall of Sodom and Gomorrah (with emphasis on the preservation of Lot). Narrative sequences based on these episodes in Genesis (and usually including, like *Cleanness*, the fall of man) are of course commonly used in the middle ages to exemplify God's punishment of His rebellious creation. Only the poet, however, puts the Genesis sequence together with the story of Zedekiah, Nebuchadnezzar (a standard example of the saving power of penance), and Belshazzar (a standard example of God's punishment of sacrilege). In both theme and narrative the poet creates a new synthesis, while making full use of the resources of tradition.

NOTES

[1] For information on the general features of the manuscript, and the few facts that we have concerning its history, see Gollancz's Introduction to the EETS facsimile of the manuscript.

[2] This is according to the generally-accepted ink numbering on the manuscript. According to the pencil renumbering, the folios are 61a–86a.

[3] For instance, the scribe writes the same word twice (a representative type of scribal error which is usually quite unambiguous) twelve times in *Cleanness* (1812 lines), eleven times in *Sir Gawain* (2530 lines), twice in *Patience* (531 lines), and three times in *Pearl* (1212 shorter lines).

[4] E.g. in ff. 77a–77b (ll. 1440–511).

[5] *English Vernacular Hands from the Twelfth to the Fifteenth Centuries* (Oxford, 1960), p. 15.

[6] Formal division in biblical text: l. 125, Matt. XXII. 11, beginning of wedding garment episode, not in Luke; 249, beginning of Gen. VI; 345, beginning of Gen. VII; 601, beginning of Gen. XVIII; 781, beginning of Gen. XIX; 1357, beginning of Dan. V. Other: 193, introduction to story of Noah; 485, God's covenant with Noah; 689, God's threat to destroy Sodom and Gomorrah; 893, the destruction of the cities.

[7] This happens mostly in passages of rapid action (e.g. *Cleanness* 401–24, 945–60), where it enhances the narrative urgency.

[8] Cf. Gollancz, *Cleanness*, p. x.

[9] *Purity*, p. xxxix.

[10] The poet undoubtedly knew *Mandeville's Travels* in an early French text, probably the Insular version (ed. G. F. Warner, *The Buke of John Maundevill*, London, 1889); see C. F. Brown, *PMLA* XIX. 149–53, and cf. notes to ll. 1014 and 1026. But the poet may also have read the work in English; cf. notes to ll. 927 and 1048. In the present edition, the Cotton version, in English, is cited (ed.

M. C. Seymour, *Mandeville's Travels,* Oxford, 1967), and discrepancies between this and the Insular version which may be of significance for the poem are noted.

[11] For a full treatment of the relation of *Cleanness* to penitential literature see J. B. Zavadil, 'A study of meaning in *Patience* and *Cleanness*' (unpublished dissertation, Stanford University, 1962).

[12] See the sermons for Easter Day in Trinity College MS B. 14. 52 (ed. R. Morris, EETS OS 53, pp. 92–101), and in Mirk's Festial (ed. T. Erbe, EETS ES 96, pp. 129–32).

[13] So in *The Book of Vices and Virtues,* a fourteenth-century translation of the French *Somme le Roi,* those 'þat kepeþ clennesse of herte and of body' are blessed, for 'þei ben clensed of derkenesse and errour as forȝens vnderstondyng, and of tecches of synne as forȝens here wille' (ed. W. N. Francis, EETS OS 217, p. 270). The poet's 'filth of the flesh' is usually dealt with by homilists under the heading of lechery, which had established status as one of the seven deadly sins. In *The Book of Vices and Virtues,* unnatural sexual acts, which attract God's greatest anger and are epitomised by the sin of Sodom and Gomorrah, are the fourteenth and last branch of lechery (p. 46).

[14] See e.g. the section on 'clennesse' in the thirteenth-century *Vices and Virtues* (ed. F. Holthausen, EETS OS 89, pp. 122–5). Jerome's commentary on the sixth beatitude, repeated by later commentators, is: 'Quos non arguit conscientia ulla peccati. Mundus mundo corde conspicitur: templum Dei non potest esse pollutum' (*PL* 26, col. 35).

[15] Cf. Jude 8: 'Similiter et hi carnem quidem maculant, dominationem autem spernunt, majestatem autem blasphement'.

[16] This last passage in particular recalls the parable of the wedding feast. Cf. the thirteenth-century *Vices and Virtues*: 'Wel him ðe is clene iþrowen [by tears of repentance], and hafð ðat faire scrud of charite all besett mid ȝimstanes of gode werkes! He mai cumen, mid gode(s) fultume, in to ðe bredale to-fore ðe bredgume, and mid him wuniȝen on michele merhðe and on michele ædinesse' (p. 95).

BIBLIOGRAPHY

FACSIMILE OF MS COTTON NERO A.X., ART. 3

Pearl, Cleanness, Patience, and Sir Gawain, reproduced in facsimile from MS Cotton Nero A.x. in the British Museum, with Introduction by I. Gollancz. EETS OS 162, London, 1923.

EDITIONS OF 'CLEANNESS'

Gollancz, I., *Cleanness,* 2 vols. London, 1921, 1933. Reissued in one vol. with prose translation by D. S. Brewer, London, 1974.

Menner, R. J., *Purity.* Yale Studies in English No. 61, New Haven, 1920.

Morris, R., *Early English Alliterative Poems.* EETS OS 1, London, 1864; 2nd ed. 1869. Contains *Pearl, Cleanness,* and *Patience.*

——, *Specimens of Early English.* Oxford, 1867. Also with W. W. Skeat, *Specimens of Early English,* Part II, Oxford, 1872; rev. ed. 1894. Lines 235–544, 947–72, 1009–51.

TRANSLATIONS OF 'CLEANNESS'

Gardner, J., *The Complete Works of the Gawain-Poet.* Chicago, 1965.

Stone, B., *The Owl and the Nightingale, Cleanness, St Erkenwald.* London, 1971.

Weston, Jessie L., *Romance, Vision, and Satire.* Boston, 1912. Lines 1357–812.

Williams, Margaret, *The Pearl-Poet.* New York, 1967.

STUDIES OF 'CLEANNESS'

Ackerman, R. W., 'Pared out of paper: *Gawain* 802 and *Purity* 1408', *JEGP* LVI (1957), 410–17.

Bateson, H., 'The text of *Cleanness*', *MLR* XIII (1918), 377–86.

——, 'Three notes on the Middle English *Cleanness*', *MLR* XIX (1924), 95–101.

Binz, G., Review of Menner's edition, *Literaturblatt für germanische und romanische Philologie,* XLII (1921), cols 376–9.

Bödtker, A. T., '*Covacle,* not *conacle*', *MLN* XXVI (1911), 127.

Brett, C., 'Notes on *Cleanness* and *Sir Gawayne*', *MLR* X (1915), 188–95.

Clark, J. W., 'Observations on certain differences in vocabulary between *Cleanness* and *Sir Gawain*', *Philological Quarterly,* XXVIII (1949), 261–73.

Emerson, O. F., 'A note on Middle English *Cleanness*', *MLR* X (1915), 373–4.

——, 'Middle English *Clannesse*', *PMLA* XXXIV (1919), 494–522.

——, Review of Menner's edition, *JEGP* XX (1921), 229–41.

Foley, M. M., 'A bibliography of *Purity* (*Cleanness*), 1864–1972', *Chaucer Review*, VIII (1973–4), 324–34.

Fowler, D. C., 'Cruxes in *Cleanness*', *MP* LXX (1973), 331–6.

Gollancz, I., 'The text of *Cleanness*', *MLR* XIV (1919), 152–62.

Holthausen, F., 'Zu dem mittelenglischen Gedicht *Cleanness*', *Archiv für das Studium der neueren Sprachen und Literaturen*, CVI (1901), 349.

——, Review of Menner's edition, *Anglia Beiblatt*, XXXIV (1923), 136–8.

Kelly, T. D. and J. T. Irwin, 'The meaning of *Cleanness*: parable as effective sign', *Medieval Studies*, XXXV (1973), 232–60.

Luttrell, C. A., 'Baiting of bulls and boars in the Middle English *Cleanness*', *N & Q* CXCVII (1952), 23–4.

——, '*Cleanness* and the Knight of the Tour Landry', *MÆ* XXIX (1960), 187–9.

Menner, R. J., Review of vol. I of Gollancz's edition, *MLN* XXXVII (1922), 355–62; of vol. II, *MLN* I (1935), 336–8.

Morse, Charlotte C., 'The image of the vessel in *Cleanness*', *University of Toronto Quarterly*, XL (1970–1), 202–16.

Ohlander, U., 'A passage in *Cleanness*: a note on Middle English construction change', *Göteborgs Högstolas Årsskrift*, LVI (1950), 313–23.

Thomas, P. G., 'Notes on *Cleanness*', *MLR* XVII (1922), 64–6, and *MLR* XXIV (1929), 323–4.

Williams, D. J., 'A literary study of the Middle English poems *Purity* and *Patience*'. Unpublished dissertation, Oxford, 1965.

Zavadil, J. B., 'A study of meaning in *Patience* and *Cleanness*'. Unpublished dissertation, Stanford University, 1962.

EDITIONS AND STUDIES RELATING TO 'CLEANNESS'

Anderson, J. J., ed., *Patience*. Manchester, 1969.

Bateson, H., 'Looking over the left shoulder', *Folk-Lore* XXXIV (1923), 241–2.

Brewer, D. S., 'Courtesy and the *Gawain*-poet', in *Patterns of Love and Courtesy: Essays in Memory of C. S. Lewis*, ed. J. Lawlor (London, 1966), 54–85.

——, 'The *Gawain*-poet; a general appreciation of four poems', *Essays in Criticism*, XVII (1967), 130–42.

Brown, C. F., 'The author of *The Pearl*, considered in the light of his theological opinions', *PMLA* XIX (1904), 115–53. Includes 'Note on the dependence of *Cleanness* on the *Book of Mandeville*', 149–53.

Chapman, C. O., 'Virgil and the *Gawain*-poet', *PMLA* LX (1945), 16–23.

——, *An Index of Names in Pearl, Purity, Patience, and Gawain*. Cornell, 1951.

Day, Mabel, 'The weak verb in the works of the *Gawain*-poet', *MLR* XIV (1919), 413–15.

——, 'Strophic division in Middle English alliterative verse', *ES* LXVI (1931–2), 245–8.

Ekwall, E., 'Zu Patience 143', *ES* XLIX (1915–16), 483–4.

Emerson, O. F., 'Legends of Cain, especially in Old and Middle English', *PMLA* XXI (1906), 831–49.

——, 'Some notes on The Pearl', *PMLA* XXXVII (1922), 52–93.

Everett, Dorothy, *Essays on Middle English Literature*. Oxford, 1955.

Gollancz, I., '*Pearl, Cleanness, Patience*, and *Sir Gawain*', in *The Cambridge History of English Literature*, I (Cambridge, 1907), 320–34.

Gordon, E. V., ed. *Pearl*. Oxford, 1953.

Gordon, E. V. and C. T. Onions, 'Notes on the text and interpretation of *Pearl*', *MÆ* I (1932), 126–36, and *MÆ* II (1933), 165–88.

Gradon, Pamela, *Form and Style in Early English Literature*. London, 1971.

Hoffman, D. L., ' "Renischsche Renkes" and "Runisch Sauez" ', *N & Q* CCXV (1970), 447–9.

Hulbert, J. R., 'Quatrains in Middle English alliterative poems', *MP* XLVIII (1950–1), 73–81.

Kaluza, M., 'Stropische Gliederung in der mittelenglischen rein alliterirenden Dichtung', *ES* XVI (1892), 169–80.

Kottler, B. and A. Markman, *A Concordance to Five Middle English Poems*. Pittsburgh, 1966.

Luttrell, C. A., 'The *Gawain* group: cruxes, etymologies, interpretations', *Neophil.* XXXIX (1955), 207–17, and *Neophil.* XL (1956), 290–301.

——, 'A *Gawain* group miscellany', *N & Q* CCVII (1962), 447–50.

McLaughlin, J. C., *A Graphemic–Phonemic Study of a Middle English Manuscript*. The Hague, 1963.

Markman, A., 'A computer concordance to Middle English texts', *Studies in Bibliography*, XVII (1964), 55–75.

Moorman, C. F., *The Pearl Poet*. New York, 1968.

Muscatine, C., *Poetry and Crisis in the Age of Chaucer*. Notre Dame, 1972.

Neilson, G., *Huchown of the Awle Ryale, the Alliterative Poet*. Glasgow, 1902.

Oakden, J. P., *Alliterative Poetry in Middle English*, 2 vols. Manchester, 1930, 1935.

Spearing, A. C., '*Patience* and the *Gawain*-poet', *Anglia*, LXXXIV (1966), 305–29.

——, *The Gawain-poet*. Cambridge, 1971.

Sunden, K. F., 'The etymology of ME. *trayþ(e)ly* and *runisch, renisch*', *SN* II (1929), 41–55.

Thomas, J., *Die alliterierende Langzeile des Gawayn-Dichters*. Jena, 1908.

Thomas, M. C., *Sir Gawayne and the Green Knight*. Zurich, 1883.

Tolkien, J. R. R. and E. V. Gordon, eds, *Sir Gawain and the Green Knight*. Oxford 1925; 2nd ed., rev. N. Davis, 1967.

Vantuono, W., '*Patience, Cleanness, Pearl* and *Gawain*: the case for common authorship', *Annuale Medievale*, XII (1971), 37–69.

NOTE ON THE EDITED TEXT

The text is printed in quatrains, it is divided into three sections on the basis of the large illuminated capitals which begin lines 1, 557, and 1157 in the manuscript, and it indicates the occurrence of the other large capitals in the manuscript (see pp. 1–2). The spelling of the manuscript is reproduced, except for editorial emendations. The long *i* of the manuscript is printed as *j* (*J*) when consonantal, and as *i* (*I*) when vocalic. Capitalisation, punctuation, and word division are according to modern usage. Abbreviations, most of which offer no difficulty, are expanded silently. The curl above *o* is here expanded invariably to *ur*, though the scribe may have intended *r* in some instances, particularly in *four* 756, *fourferde* 560, *vmbeþour* 1384. The abbreviation q, which may represent either *quoþ* or *quod*, is here expanded to *quoþ* (cf. *coþe*, *Sir Gawain* 776), and *wᵗ*, which is found written out as both *with* and *wyth*, is here expanded to *with*. The curved stroke sometimes found after *gh* (and once after *l* in *wyrl* 475) is treated as a mere flourish; note *innoghe* 1303, which has the curved stroke in the manuscript after the *gh*, where expansion to *e* is hardly possible.

The footnotes indicate features of interest in the manuscript text, and attempt to explain readings which are not straightforward. *From u.-v.* or *from offset* means that a reading which is unclear or illegible in both the original manuscript and the EETS facsimile is at least reasonably clear in ultra-violet photographs supplied to the editor by the British Library, or in offsets which in some places in the manuscript the wet ink has left on the opposite page. The footnotes also indicate emendations of the original which are adopted in the edited text.

[CLEANNESS]

[I]

CLANNESSE who-so kyndly cowþe comende, f. 57a
And rekken vp alle þe resounȝ þat ho by riȝt askeȝ,
Fayre formeȝ myȝt he fynde in forþering his speche,
And in þe contrare kark and combraunce huge. 4

For wonder wroth is þe wyȝ þat wroȝt alle þinges
Wyth þe freke þat in fylþe folȝes hym after,
As renkeȝ of relygioun þat reden and syngen
And aprochen to hys presens, and presteȝ arn called. 8

Thay teen vnto his temmple and temen to hymseluen;
Reken with reuerence þay rychen his auter;
Þay hondel þer his aune body, and vsen hit boþe.
If þay in clannes be clos, þay cleche gret mede, 12

Bot if þay conterfete crafte and cortaysye wont,
As be honest vtwyth and inwith alle fylþeȝ,
Þen ar þay synful hemself, and sulped altogeder
Boþe God and his gere, and hym to greme cachen. 16

He is so clene in his courte, þe kyng þat al weldeȝ,
And honeste in his housholde, and hagherlych serued
With angeleȝ enourled in alle þat is clene
Boþe withinne and withouten, in wedeȝ ful bryȝt. 20

Nif he nere scoymus and skyg and non scaþe louied,
Hit were a meruayl to much, hit moȝt not falle.
Kryst kydde hit hymself in a carp oneȝ,
Þer as he heuened aȝt happeȝ and hyȝt hem her medeȝ. 24

Me myneȝ on one amonge oþer, as Maþew recordeȝ,
Þat þus of clannesse vncloseȝ a ful cler speche:
'Þe haþel clene of his hert hapeneȝ ful fayre,
For he schal loke on oure lorde with a loue chere.' 28

As so saytȝ, to þat syȝt seche schal he neuer
Þat any vnclannesse hatȝ on, auwhere abowte;
For he þat flemus vch fylþe fer fro his hert
May not byde þat burre, þat hit his body neȝe. 32

---

2 s of askeȝ *probably altered from* k 3 *MS* forerīg
26 *First s of* clannesse *altered from* ȝ 32 *MS* neȝen

Forþy hyȝ not to heuen in hatereȝ totorne,
Ne in þe harlateȝ hod and handeȝ vnwaschen.
For what vrþly haþel þat hyȝ honour haldeȝ
Wolde lyke if a ladde com lyþerly attyred,   36

When he were sette solempnely in a sete ryche,   f. 57b
Abof dukeȝ on dece, with dayntys serued?
Þen þe harlot with haste helded to þe table
With rent cokreȝ at þe kne, and his clutte trascheȝ,   40

And his tabarde totorne, and his toteȝ oute,
Oþer ani on of alle þyse, he schulde be halden vtter,
With mony blame ful bygge, a boffet peraunter,
Hurled to þe halle dore and harde þeroute schowued,   44

And be forboden þat borȝe, to bowe þider neuer,
On payne of enprysonment and puttyng in stokkeȝ;
And þus schal he be schent for his schrowde feble,
Þaȝ neuer in talle ne in tuch he trespas more.   48

And if vnwelcum he were to a worþlych prynce,
ȝet hym is þe hyȝe kyng harder in heuen;
As Maþew meleȝ in his masse of þat man ryche
Þat made þe mukel mangerye to marie his here dere,   52

And sende his sonde þen to say þat þay samne schulde,
And in comly quoyntis to com to his feste:
'For my boles and my boreȝ arn bayted and slayne,
And my fedde fouleȝ fatted with sclaȝt;   56

My polyle þat is penne-fed, and partrykeȝ boþe,
Wyth scheldeȝ of wylde swyn, swaneȝ, and croneȝ,
Al is roþeled and rosted ryȝt to þe sete;
Comeȝ cof to my corte, er hit colde worþe.'   60

When þay knewen his cal þat þider com schulde,
Alle excused hem by þe skyly he scape by moȝt.
On hade boȝt hym a borȝ, he sayde by hys trawþe:
'Now turne I þeder als tyd þe toun to byholde.'   64

Anoþer nayed also and nurned þis cawse:
'I haf ȝerned and ȝat ȝokkeȝ of oxen,
And for my hyȝeȝ hem boȝt, to bowe haf I mester;
To see hem pulle in þe plow aproche me byhoueȝ.'   68

33 ȝ of hyȝ from u.-v.   50 heuen, MS her euen
64 turne, MS tne

'And I haf wedded a wyf,' so wer hym þe þryd,
'Excuse me at þe court, I may not com þere.'
Þus þay droȝ hem adreȝ with daunger vchone,
Þat non passed to þe place, þaȝ he prayed were.   72

Thenne þe ludych lorde lyked ful ille,   f. 58a
And hade dedayn of þat dede—ful dryȝly he carpeȝ.
He saytȝ: 'Now for her owne sorȝe þay forsaken habbeȝ;
More to wyte is her wrange þen any wylle gentyl.   76

Þenne gotȝ forth, my gomeȝ, to þe grete streeteȝ,
And forsetteȝ on vche a syde þe cete aboute
Þe wayferande frekeȝ, on fote and on hors,
Boþe burneȝ and burdeȝ, þe better and þe wers.   80

Lapeȝ hem alle luflyly to lenge at my fest,
And bryngeȝ hem blyþly to borȝe as barouneȝ þay were,
So þat my palays platful be pyȝt al aboute;
Þise oþer wrecheȝ iwysse worþy noȝt wern.'   84

Þen þay cayred and com þat þe cost waked,
Broȝten bachlereȝ hem wyth þat þay by bonkeȝ metten,
Swyereȝ þat swyftly swyed on blonkeȝ,
And also fele vpon fote, of fre and of bonde.   88

When þay com to þe courte, keppte wern þay fayre,
Styȝtled with þe stewarde, stad in þe halle,
Ful manerly with marchal mad for-to sitte,
As he watȝ dere of degre dressed his seete.   92

Þenne seggeȝ to þe souerayn sayden þerafter:
'Lo, lorde, with your leue, at your lege heste
And at þi banne we haf broȝt, as þou beden habbeȝ,
Mony renischche renkeȝ, and ȝet is roum more.'   96

Sayde þe lorde to þo ledeȝ: 'Layteȝ ȝet ferre,
Ferre out in þe felde, and fecheȝ mo gesteȝ;
Wayteȝ gorsteȝ and greueȝ, if ani gomeȝ lyggeȝ;
What kyn folk so þer fare, fecheȝ hem hider.   100

Be þay fers, be þay feble, forloteȝ none,
Be þay hol, be þay halt, be þay on-yȝed,
And þaȝ þay ben boþe blynde and balterande cruppeleȝ,
Þat my hous may holly by halkeȝ by fylled.   104

72 *MS* plate   86 n *of* metten *altered from* ȝ
104 *Last two strokes of* m *of* may *altered from* a

For certeȝ þyse ilk renkeȝ þat me renayed habbe,
And denounced me noȝt now at þis tyme,
Schul neuer sitte in my sale my soper to fele,
Ne suppe on sope of my seve, þaȝ þay swelt schulde.'   108

Thenne þe sergaunteȝ at þat sawe swengen þeroute,   f. 58b
And diden þe dede þat demed as he deuised hade,
And with peple of alle plyteȝ þe palays þay fyllen;
Hit weren not alle on wyueȝ suneȝ, wonen with on fader.   112

Wheþer þay wern worþy oþer wers, wel wern þay stowed,
Ay þe best byfore and bryȝtest atyred,
Þe derrest at þe hyȝe dese, þat dubbed wer fayrest,
And syþen on lenþe biloogh ledeȝ inogh;   116

And ay a segge soberly semed by her wedeȝ.
So with marschal at her mete mensked þay were;
Clene men in compaynye forknowen wern lyte,
And ȝet þe symplest in þat sale watȝ serued to þe fulle,   120

Boþe with menske and with mete and mynstrasy noble,
And alle þe laykeȝ þat a lorde aȝt in londe schewe;
And þay bignne to be glad þat god drink haden,
And vch mon with his mach made hym at ese.   124

NOW inmyddeȝ þe mete þe mayster hym biþoȝt
Þat he wolde se þe semble þat samned was þere,
And rehayte rekenly þe riche and þe pouer,
And cherisch hem alle with his cher, and chaufen her joye.   128

Þen he boweȝ fro his bour into þe brode halle,
And to þe best on þe bench, and bede hym be myry,
Solased hem with semblaunt and syled fyrre,
Tron fro table to table and talkede ay myrþe.   132

Bot as he ferked ouer þe flor he fande with his yȝe
Hit watȝ, not for a halyday honestly arayed,
A þral pryȝt in þe þrong, vnþryuandely cloþed,
Ne no festiual frok, bot fyled with werkkeȝ.   136

Þe gome watȝ vngarnyst with god men to dele,
And gremed þerwith þe grete lorde, and greue hym he þoȝt.
'Say me, frende,' quoþ þe freke, with a felle chere,
'Hov wan þou into þis won in wedeȝ so fowle?   140

108 *MS* þaȝ þaȝ   117 *MS* soerly
119 *Second* y *of* compaynye *altered from* i, *as 'dot' shows*
127 *MS* poueu + er *abbrev.*

Þe abyt þat þou hatʒ vpon, no halyday hit menskeʒ;
Þou, burne, for no brydale art busked in wedeʒ.
How watʒ þou hardy þis hous for þyn vnhap neʒe,
In on so ratted a robe, and rent at þe sydeʒ? 144

Þow art a gome vngoderly in þat goun febele; f. 59a
Þou praysed me and my place ful pouer and ful nede,
Þat watʒ so prest to aproche my presens hereinne.
Hopeʒ þou I be a harlot, þi erigaut to prayse?' 148

Þat oþer burne watʒ abayst of his broþe wordeʒ,
And hurkeleʒ doun with his hede, þe vrþe he biholdeʒ;
He watʒ so scoumfit of his scylle, lest he skaþe hent,
Þat he ne wyst on worde what he warp schulde. 152

Þen þe lorde wonder loude laled and cryed,
And talkeʒ to his tormenttoureʒ: 'Takeʒ hym,' he biddeʒ,
'Byndeʒ byhynde at his bak boþe two his handeʒ,
And felle fettereʒ to his fete festeneʒ bylyue; 156

Stik hym stifly in stokeʒ, and stekeʒ hym þerafter
Depe in my doungoun þer doel euer dwelleʒ,
Greuing and gretyng and gryspyng harde
Of teþe tenfully togeder, to teche hym be quoynt.' 160

Thus comparisuneʒ Kryst þe kyndom of heuen
To þis frelych feste þat fele arn to called;
For alle arn laþed luflyly, þe luþer and þe better,
Þat euer wern fulʒed in font þat fest to haue. 164

Bot war þe wel, if þou wylt, þy wedeʒ ben clene,
And honest for þe halyday, lest þou harme lache;
For aproch þou to þat prynce of parage noble,
He hates helle no more þen hem þat ar sowle. 168

Wich arn þenne þy wedeʒ þou wrappeʒ þe inne,
Þat schal schewe hem so schene, schrowde of þe best?
Hit arn þy werkeʒ wyterly þat þou wroʒt haueʒ,
And lyned with þe lykyng þat lyʒe in þyn hert, 172

Þat þo be frely and fresch fonde in þy lyue,
And fetyse of a fayr forme to fote and to honde,
And syþen alle þyn oþer lymeʒ lapped ful clene;
Þenne may þou se þy sauior and his sete ryche. 176

For fele fauteʒ may a freke forfete his blysse,
Þat he þe souerayn ne se; þen for slauþe one,
As for bobaunce and bost and bolnande priyde,
Þroly into þe deueleʒ þrote man þryngeʒ bylyue; 180

For couetyse and colwarde and croked dede3,   f. 59b
For monsworne and menscla3t and to much drynk,
For þefte and for þrepyng vnþonk may mon haue,
For roborrye and riboudrye and resoune3 vntrwe,   184

And dysheriete and depryue dowrie of wydoe3,
For marryng of maryage3 and mayntnaunce of schrewe3,
For traysoun and trichcherye and tyrauntyre boþe,
And for fals famacions and fayned lawe3.   188

Man may mysse þe myrþe þat much is to prayse
For such vnþewe3 as þise, and þole much payne,
And in þe creatores cort com neuer more,
Ne neuer see hym with sy3t, for such sour tourne3.   192

BOT I haue herkned and herde of mony hy3e clerke3,
And als in resoune3 of ry3t red hit myseluen,
Þat þat ilk proper prynce þat paradys welde3
Is displesed at vch a poynt þat plyes to scaþe;   196

Bot neuer 3et in no boke breued I herde
Þat euer he wrek so wyþerly on werk þat he made,
Ne venged for no vilte of vice ne synne,
Ne so hastyfly wat3 hot for hatel of his wylle,   200

Ne neuer so sodenly so3t vnsoundely to weng,
As for fylþe of þe flesch þat foles han vsed;
For, as I fynde, þer he for3et alle his fre þewe3,
And wex wod to þe wrache for wrath at his hert.   204

For þe fyrste felonye þe falce fende wro3t,
Whyl he wat3 hy3e in þe heuen, houen vpon lofte,
Of alle þyse aþel aungele3 attled þe fayrest,
And he vnkyndely as a karle kydde a reward.   208

He se3 no3t bot hymself, how semly he were,
Bot his souerayn he forsoke and sade þyse worde3:
'I schal telde vp my trone in þe tramountayne,
And by lyke to þat lorde þat þe lyft made.'   212

With þis worde þat he warp þe wrake on hym ly3t;
Dry3tyn with his dere dom hym drof to þe abyme.
In þe mesure of his mode his met3 neuer þe lasse;
Bot þer he tynt þe type dool of his tour ryche.   216

Þa3 þe feloun were so fers for his fayre wede3,   f. 60a
And his glorious glem þat glent so bry3t,
As sone as dry3tyne3 dome drof to hymseluen,
Þikke þowsande3 þro þrwen þeroute;   220
  220 Þi of Þikke from u.-v.

Fellen fro þe fyrmament fendeȝ ful blake,
Sweued at þe fyrst swap as þe snaw þikke,
Hurled into helle-hole as þe hyue swarmeȝ.
Fylter fenden folk forty dayeȝ lencþe,   224

Er þat styngande storme stynt ne myȝt;
Bot as smylt mele vnder smal siue smokeȝ for þikke,
So fro heuen to helle þat hatel schor laste,
On vche syde of þe worlde aywhere ilyche.   228

Þis hit watȝ a brem brest and a byge wrache;
And ȝet wrathed not þe wyȝ, ne þe wrech saȝtled,
Ne neuer wolde for wylnesful his worþy God knawe,
Ne pray hym for no pite, so proud watȝ his wylle.   232

Forþy þaȝ þe rape were rank, þe rawþe watȝ lyttel;
Þaȝ he be kest into kare, he kepes no better.
Bot þat oþer wrake þat wex, on wyȝeȝ hit lyȝt,
Þurȝ þe faut of a freke þat fayled in trawþe,   236

Adam inobedyent, ordaynt to blysse,
Þer pryuely in paradys his place watȝ devised,
To lyue þer in lykyng þe lenþe of a terme,
And þenne enherite þat home þat aungeleȝ forgart.   240

Bot þurȝ þe eggyng of Eue he ete of an apple
Þat enpoysened alle pepleȝ þat parted fro hem boþe,
For a defence þat watȝ dyȝt of dryȝtyn seluen,
And a payne þeron put and pertly halden.   244

Þe defence watȝ þe fryt þat þe freke towched,
And þe dom is þe deþe þat drepeȝ vus alle;
Al in mesure and meþe watȝ mad þe vengiaunce,
And efte amended with a mayden þat make had neuer.   248

BOT in þe þryd watȝ forþrast al þat þryue schuld;
Þer watȝ malys mercyles and mawgre much scheued.
Þat watȝ for fylþe vpon folde þat þe folk vsed
Þat þen wonyed in þe worlde withouten any maysterȝ.   252

222 S of Sweued from offset; w not entirely clear
224 Fylter from u.-v. and offset   225 Er from offset
226 Bot from u.-v. and offset   228 On from u.-v. and offset
229 Þ of Þis from u.-v.   230 MS & ȝet from u.-v. and offset
233 MS lyttlel   248 MS & from u.-v. and offset
250 Þ of Þer from u.-v. and offset   251 þ of þat from u.-v.
252 Þ of Þat from u.-v.

Hit wern þe fayrest of forme and of face als,   f. 60b
Þe most and þe myriest þat maked wern euer,
Þe styfest, þe stalworþest þat stod euer on fete,
And lengest lyf in hem lent of ledeȝ alle oþer.   256

For hit was þe forme foster þat þe folde bred,
Þe aþel auncetereȝ suneȝ þat Adam watȝ called,
To wham God hade geuen alle þat gayn were,
Alle þe blysse boute blame þat bodi myȝt haue.   260

And þose lykkest to þe lede þat lyued next after;
Forþy so semly to see syþen wern none.
Þer watȝ no law to hem layd bot loke to kynde,
And kepe to hit and alle hit cors clanly fulfylle.   264

And þenne founden þay fylþe in fleschlych dedeȝ,
And controeued agayn kynde contrare werkeȝ,
And vsed hem vnþryftyly vchon on oþer,
And als with oþer, wylsfully, upon a wrange wyse.   268

So ferly fowled her flesch þat þe fende loked
How þe deȝter of þe douþe wern derelych fayre,
And fallen in felaȝschyp with hem on folken wyse,
And engendered on hem ieaunteȝ with her japeȝ ille.   272

Þose wern men meþeleȝ and maȝty on vrþe,
Þat for her lodlych laykeȝ alosed þay were;
He watȝ famed for fre þat feȝt loued best,
And ay þe bigest in bale þe best watȝ halden.   276

And þenne eueleȝ on erþe ernestly grewen,
And multyplyed monyfolde inmongeȝ mankynde,
For þat þe maȝty on molde so marre þise oþer
Þat þe wyȝe þat al wroȝt ful wroþly bygynneȝ.   280

When he knew vche contre coruppte in hitseluen,
And vch freke forloyned fro þe ryȝt wayeȝ,
Felle temptande tene towched his hert;
As wyȝe wo hym withinne werp to hymseluen: 284

'Me forþynkeȝ ful much þat euer I mon made;
Bot I schal delyuer and do away þat doten on þis molde,
And fleme out of þe folde al þat flesch wereȝ,
Fro þe burne to þe best, fro bryddeȝ to fyscheȝ.   288

Al schal doun and be ded and dryuen out of erþe   f. 61a
Þat euer I sette saule inne, and sore hit me rweȝ
Þat euer I made hem myself; bot if I may herafter,
I schal wayte to be war her wrencheȝ to kepe.'   292

Þenne in worlde watȝ a wyȝe wonyande on lyue,
Ful redy and ful ryȝtwys, and rewled hym fayre;
In þe drede of dryȝtyn his dayeȝ he vseȝ,
And ay glydande wyth his God his grace watȝ þe more. 296

Hym watȝ þe nome Noe, as is innogh knawen;
He had þre þryuen suneȝ, and þay þre wyueȝ;
Sem soþly þat on, þat oþer hyȝt Cam,
And þe jolef Japheth watȝ gendered þe þryd. 300

Now God in nwy to Noe con speke
Wylde wrakful wordeȝ, in his wylle greued:
'Þe ende of alle kyneȝ flesch þat on vrþe meueȝ
Is fallen forþwyth my face, and forþer hit I þenk. 304

With her vnworþelych werk me wlateȝ withinne;
Þe gore þerof me hatȝ greued and þe glette nwyed;
I schal strenkle my distresse and strye al togeder,
Boþe ledeȝ and londe and alle þat lyf habbeȝ. 308

Bot make to þe a mancioun, and þat is my wylle,
A cofer closed of tres clanlych planed;
Wyrk woneȝ perinne for wylde and for tame,
And þenne cleme hit with clay comly withinne, 312

And alle þe endentur dryuen daube withouten.
And þus of lenþe and of large þat lome þou make:
Þre hundred of cupydeȝ þou holde to þe lenþe,
Of fyfty fayre ouerþwert forme þe brede, 316

And loke euen þat þyn ark haue of heȝþe þrette,
And a wyndow wyd vponande wroȝt vpon lofte,
In þe compas of a cubit kyndely sware,
A wel dutande dor don on þe syde. 320

Haf halleȝ þerinne and halkeȝ ful mony,
Boþe boskeȝ and boureȝ and wel bounden peneȝ;
For I schal waken vp a water to wasch alle þe worlde,
And quelle alle þat is quik with quauende flodeȝ. 324

Alle þat glydeȝ and gotȝ and gost of lyf habbeȝ,   f. 61b
I schal wast with my wrath, þat wons vpon vrþe;
Bot my forwarde with þe I festen on þis wyse,
For þou in reysoun hatȝ rengned and ryȝtwys ben euer: 328

312 *MS* wᵗime   318 vponande, *MS* vpon
324 *MS* þat þat, *line through second* þat

Þou schal enter þis ark with þyn aþel barneȝ,
And þy wedded wyf with þe þou take,
Þe makeȝ of þy myry suneȝ—þis meyny of aȝte
I schal saue of monneȝ sauleȝ, and swelt þose oþer.   332

Of vche best þat bereȝ lyf busk þe a cupple;
Of vche clene comly kynde enclose seuen makeȝ,
Of vche horwed in ark halde bot a payre,
For-to saue me þe sede of alle ser kyndeȝ;   336

And ay þou meng with þe maleȝ þe mete ho-besteȝ,
Vche payre by payre, to plese ayþer oþer.
With alle þe fode þat may be founde frette þy cofer,
For sustnaunce to yowself and also þose oþer.'   340

Ful grayþely gotȝ þis godman and dos Godeȝ hestes,
In dryȝ dred and daunger, þat durst do non oþer.
Wen hit watȝ fettled and forged and to þe fulle grayþed,
Þenn con dryȝttyn hym dele dryȝly þyse wordeȝ: 344

'NOW Noe,' quoþ oure lorde, 'art þou al redy?
Hatȝ þou closed þy kyst with clay alle aboute?'
'Ȝe, lorde, with þy leue,' sayde þe lede þenne,
'Al is wroȝt at þi worde, as þou me wyt lanteȝ.'   348

'Enter in þenn,' quoþ he, 'and haf þi wyf with þe,
Þy þre suneȝ withouten þrep, and her þre wyueȝ;
Besteȝ, as I bedene haue, bosk þerinne als,
And when ȝe arn staued styfly, stekeȝ yow þerinne.   352

Fro seuen dayeȝ ben seyed I sende out bylyue
Such a rowtande ryge þat rayne schal swyþe,
Þat schal wasch alle þe worlde of werkeȝ of fylþe;
Schal no flesch vpon folde by fonden on lyue,   356

Outtaken yow aȝt in þis ark staued,
And sed þat I wyl saue of þyse ser besteȝ.'
Now Noe neuer stynteȝ—þat niȝt he bygynneȝ—
Er al wer stawed and stoken as þe steuen wolde.   360

Thenne sone com þe seuenþe day, when samned wern alle,   f. 62a
And alle woned in þe whichche, þe wylde and þe tame.
Þen bolned þe abyme and bonkeȝ con ryse;
Waltes out vch walle-heued in ful wode stremeȝ.   364

Watȝ no brymme þat abod vnbrosten bylyue;
Þe mukel lauande logh to þe lyfte rered.
Mony clustered clowde clef alle in clowteȝ,
Torent vch a rayn ryfte and rusched to þe vrþe,   368

359 *MS* stysteȝ   niyȝt, *MS* niyȝ

Fon neuer in forty daye3, and þen þe flod ryses,
Ouerwalte3 vche a wod and þe wyde felde3;
For when þe water of þe welkyn with þe worlde mette,
Alle þat deth mo3t dry3e drowned þerinne.   372

Þer wat3 moon for-to make when meschef was cnowen,
Þat no3t dowed bot þe deth in þe depe streme3.
Water wylger ay wax, wone3 þat stryede,
Hurled into vch hous, hent þat þer dowelled.   376

Fyrst feng to þe fly3t alle þat fle my3t;
Vuche burde with her barne þe byggyng þay leue3
And bowed to þe hy3 bonk þer brentest hit wern,
And heterly to þe hy3e hylle3 þay aled on faste.   380

Bot al wat3 nedle3 her note, for neuer cowþe stynt
Þe ro3e raynande ryg, þe raykande wawe3,
Er vch boþom wat3 brurdful to þe bonke3 egge3,
And vche a dale so depe þat demmed at þe brynke3.   384

Þe moste mountayne3 on mor þenne were no more dry3e,
And þeron flokked þe folke for ferde of þe wrake.
Syþen þe wylde of þe wode on þe water flette;
Summe swymmed þeron þat saue hemself trawed,   388

Summe sty3e to a stud and stared to þe heuen,
Rwly wyth a loud rurd rored for drede;
Hare3, hertte3 also, to þe hy3e runnen,
Bukke3, bausene3, and bule3 to þe bonkke3 hy3ed,   392

And alle cryed for care to þe kyng of heuen;
Recouerer of þe creator þay cryed vchone.
Þat amounted þe mase, his mercy wat3 passed,
And alle his pyte departed fro peple þat he hated.   396

Bi þat þe flod to her fete flo3ed and waxed,   f. 62b
Þen vche a segge se3 wel þat synk hym byhoued;
Frende3 fellen in fere and faþmed togeder,
To dry3 her delful deystyne and dy3en alle samen;   400

Luf loke3 to luf, and his leue take3,
For-to ende alle at one3 and for euer twynne.
By forty daye3 wern faren, on folde no flesch styryed
Þat þe flod nade al freten with fe3tande wa3e3;   404

For hit clam vche a clyffe cubites fyftene,
Ouer þe hy3est hylle þat hurkled on erþe.
Þenne mourkne in þe mudde most ful nede
Alle þat spyrakle inspranc—no sprawlyng awayled—   408

385 were, *MS* wat3   395 *MS* þe masse þe mase

Saue þe haþel vnder hach and his here straunge,
Noe þat ofte neuened þe name of oure lorde,
Hym aȝtsum in þat ark, as aþel God lyked,
Þer alle ledeȝ in lome lenged druye.   412

Þe arc houen watȝ on hyȝe with hurlande goteȝ,
Kest to kytheȝ vncouþe þe clowdeȝ ful nere;
Hit waltered on þe wylde flod, went as hit lyste,
Drof vpon þe depe dam—in daunger hit semed,   416

Withouten mast oþer myke oþer myry bawelyne,
Kable oþer capstan to clyppe to her ankreȝ,
Hurrok, oþer hande-helme hasped on roþer,
Oþer any sweande sayl to seche after hauen.   420

Bot flote forthe with þe flyt of þe felle wyndeȝ;
Whederwarde-so þe water wafte, hit rebounde.
Ofte hit roled on rounde and rered on ende;
Nyf oure lorde hade ben her lodeȝmon, hem had lumpen harde. 424

Of þe lenþe of Noe lyf to lay a lel date:
Þe sex hundreth of his age and none odde ȝereȝ,
Of secounde monyth þe seuenteþe day ryȝteȝ,
Towalten alle þyse welle-hedeȝ and þe water flowed,   428

And þryeȝ fyfty þe flod of folwande dayeȝ.
Vche hille watȝ þer hidde with yþeȝ ful graye;
Al watȝ wasted þat þer wonyed þe worlde withinne,
Þer euer flote, oþer flwe, oþer on fote ȝede.   432

That roȝly watȝ þe remnaunt þat þe rac dryueȝ,   f. 63a
Þat alle gendreȝ so ioyst wern ioyned wythinne.
Bot quen þe lorde of þe lyfte lyked hymseluen
For-to mynne on his mon his meth þat abydeȝ,   436

Þen he wakened a wynde on wattereȝ to blowe;
Þenne lasned þe llak þat large watȝ are;
Þen he stac vp þe stangeȝ, stoped þe welleȝ,
Bed blynne of þe rayn—hit batede as fast.   440

Þenne lasned þe loȝ, lowkande togeder,
After harde dayeȝ wern out an hundreth and fyfte.
As þat lyftande lome luged aboute
Where þe wynde and þe weder warpen hit wolde,   444

427 seuenteþe, *MS* seuēþe   430 *MS* yreȝ
432 on *interlined*   433 *catchword* þat roȝly watȝ

Hit saȝtled on a softe day, synkande to grounde;
On a rasse of a rok hit rest at þe laste,
On þe mounte of Ararach, of Armene hilles,
Þat oþerwayeȝ on Ebrv hit hat þe Thanes.   448

Bot þaȝ þe kyste in þe crageȝ were closed to byde,
Ȝet fyned not þe flod, ne fel to þe boþemeȝ;
Bot þe hyȝest of þe eggeȝ vnhuled wern a lyttel,
Þat þe burne bynne borde byhelde þe bare erþe.   452

Þenne wafte he vpon his wyndowe and wysed þeroute
A message fro þat meyny, hem moldeȝ to seche.
Þat watȝ þe rauen so ronk, þat rebel watȝ euer;
He watȝ colored as þe cole, corbyal vntrwe.   456

And he fongeȝ to þe flyȝt and fanneȝ on þe wyndeȝ,
Haleȝ hyȝe vpon hyȝt to herken typyngeȝ;
He croukeȝ for comfort when carayne he fyndeȝ,
Kast vp on a clyffe þer costes lay drye.   460

He hade þe smelle of þe smach and smoltes þeder sone,
Falleȝ on þe foule flesch and fylleȝ his wombe,
And sone ȝederly forȝete ȝisterday steuen,
How þe cheuetayn hym charged þat þe kyst ȝemed.   464

Þe rauen raykeȝ hym forth þat reches ful lyttel
How alle fodeȝ þer fare, elleȝ he fynde mete;
Bot þe burne bynne borde, þat bod to hys come,
Banned hym ful bytterly, with bestes alle samen.   468

He scheȝ anoþer sondeȝmon and setteȝ on þe doue,   f. 63b
Bryngeȝ þat bryȝt vpon borde, blessed and sayde:
'Wende, worþelych wyȝt, vus woneȝ to seche.
Dryf ouer þis dymme water; if þou druye fyndeȝ,   472

Bryng bodworde to bot, blysse to vus alle.
Þaȝ þat fowle be false, fre be þou euer.'
Ho wyrles out on þe weder on wyngeȝ ful scharpe,
Dreȝly alle alonge day þat dorst neuer lyȝt.   476

And when ho fyndeȝ no folde her fote on to pyche,
Ho vmbekesteȝ þe coste and þe kyst secheȝ.
Ho hitteȝ on þe euentyde and on þe ark sitteȝ;
Noe nymmes hir anon and naytly hir staueȝ.   480

447 *MS* mararach   449 *MS* wern   458 Haleȝ *from u.-v.*
460 *MS* costese   469 *MS* doūe   475 *MS* wyrl + *curved stroke*

Noe on anoþer day nymmeȝ efte þe dove,
And byddeȝ hir bowe ouer þe borne efte bonkeȝ to seche;
And ho skyrmeȝ vnder skwe and skowteȝ aboute
Tyl hit watȝ nyȝe at þe naȝt, and Noe þen secheȝ.   484

ON ark on an euentyde houeȝ þe dowue;
On stamyn ho stod and stylle hym abydeȝ.
What! ho broȝt in hir beke a bronch of olyue,
Gracyously vmbegrouen al with grene leueȝ.   488

Þat watȝ þe syngne of sauyte þat sende hem oure lorde,
And þe saȝtlyng of hymself with þo sely besteȝ.
Þen watȝ þer joy in þat gyn, where jumpred er dryȝed,
And much comfort in þat cofer þat watȝ clay-daubed.   492

Myryly on a fayr morn, monyth þe fyrst,
Þat falleȝ formast in þe ȝer, and þe fyrst day,
Ledeȝ loȝen in þat lome, and loked þeroute
How þat wattereȝ wern woned and þe worlde dryed.   496

Vchon loued oure lorde, bot lenged ay stylle,
Tyl þay had typyng fro þe tolke þat tyned hem þerinne.
Þen Godeȝ glam to hem glod þat gladed hem alle,
Bede hem drawe to þe dor, delyuer hem he wolde.   500

Þen went þay to þe wykket, hit walt vpon sone;
Boþe þe burne and his barneȝ bowed þeroute;
Her wyueȝ walkeȝ hem wyth, and þe wylde after,
Þroly þrublande in þronge, þrowen ful þykke.   504

Bot Noe of vche honest kynde nem out an odde,   f. 64a
And heuened vp an auter and halȝed hit fayre,
And sette a sakerfyse þeron of vch a ser kynde
Þat watȝ comly and clene—God kepeȝ non oþer.   508

When bremly brened þose besteȝ and þe breþe rysed,
Þe sauour of his sacrafyse soȝt to hym euen
Þat al spedeȝ and spylleȝ; he spekes with þat ilke,
In comly comfort ful clos and cortays wordeȝ: 512

'Now, Noe, no more nel I neuer wary
Alle þe mukel mayny-molde for no manneȝ synneȝ;
For I se wel þat hit is sothe þat alle seggeȝ wytteȝ
To vnþryfte arn alle þrawen with þoȝt of her hertteȝ,   516

481 MS doveue   515 seggeȝ, MS māneȝ

And ay hatʒ ben and wyl be ʒet fro her barnage;
Al is þe mynde of þe man to malyce enclyned.
Forþy schal I neuer schende so schortly at ones
As dysstrye al for maneʒ synne, dayeʒ of þis erþe.   520

Bot waxeʒ now and wendeʒ forth and worþeʒ to monye;
Multyplyeʒ on þis molde, and menske yow bytyde.
Sesouneʒ schal yow neuer sese of sede ne of heruest,
Ne hete ne no harde forst, vmbre ne droʒþe,   524

Ne þe swetnesse of somer, ne þe sadde wynter,
Ne þe nyʒt, ne þe day, ne þe newe ʒereʒ,
Bot euer renne restleʒ—rengneʒ ʒe þerinne.'
Þerwyth he blesseʒ vch a best and bytaʒt hem þis erþe.   528

Þen watʒ a skylly skyualde, quen scaped alle þe wylde;
Vche fowle to þe flyʒt þat fyþereʒ myʒt serue,
Vche fysch to þe flod þat fynne couþe nayte,
Vche beste to þe bent þat bytes on erbeʒ.   532

Wylde wormeʒ to her won wryþeʒ in þe erþe,
Þe fox and þe folmarde to þe fryth wyndeʒ,
Herttes to hyʒe heþe, hareʒ to gorsteʒ,
And lyouneʒ and lebardeʒ to þe lake ryftes.   536

Herneʒ and hauekeʒ to þe hyʒe rocheʒ,
Þe hole-foted fowle to þe flod hyʒeʒ,
And vche best at a brayde þer hym best lykeʒ;
Þe fowre frekeʒ of þe folde fongeʒ þe empyre.   540

Lo, suche a wrakful wo, for wlatsum dedeʒ,   f. 64b
Parformed þe hyʒe fader on folke þat he made;
Þat he chysly hade cherisched he chastysed ful hardee,
In devoydynge þe vylanye þat venkquyst his þeweʒ.   544

Forþy war þe now, wyʒe, þat worschyp desyres
In his comlych courte þat kyng is of blysse,
In þe fylþe of þe flesch þat þou be founden neuer,
Tyl any water in þe worlde to wasche þe fayly.   548

For is no segge vnder sunne so seme of his crafteʒ,
If he be sulped in synne þat sytteʒ vnclene,
On spec of a spote may spede to mysse
Of þe syʒte of þe souerayn þat sytteʒ so hyʒe.   552

For þat schewe me schale in þo schyre howseʒ
As þe beryl bornyst byhoueʒ be clene,
Þat is sounde on vche a syde and no sem habes,
Withouten maskle oþer mote, as margerye-perle.   556

520 MS sӯne *interlined in second hand*   532 MS þat þat

[II]

SYÞEN þe souerayn in sete so sore forþoȝt
Þat euer he man vpon molde merked to lyuy.
For he in fylþe watȝ fallen, felly he uenged,
Quen fourferde alle þe flesch þat he formed hade.   560

Hym rwed þat he hem vprerde and raȝt hem lyflode,
And efte þat he hem vndyd, hard hit hym þoȝt;
For quen þe swemande sorȝe soȝt to his hert,
He knyt a couenaunde cortaysly with monkynde þere,   564

In þe mesure of his mode and meþe of his wylle,
Þat he schulde neuer for no syt smyte al at oneȝ,
As to quelle alle quykeȝ, for qued þat myȝt falle,
Whyl of þe lenþe of þe londe lasteȝ þe terme.   568

Þat ilke skyl for no scaþe ascaped hym neuer;
Wheder wonderly he wrak on wykked men after,
Ful felly for þat ilk faute forferde a kyth ryche,
In þe anger of his ire þat arȝed mony.   572

And al watȝ for þis ilk euel, þat vnhappen glette,
Þe venym and þe vylanye and þe vycios fylþe
Þat bysulpeȝ manneȝ saule in vnsounde hert,
Þat he his saueour ne see with syȝt of his yȝen.   576

Þus alle illeȝ he hates as helle þat stynkkeȝ;   f. 65a
Bot non nuyeȝ hym, on naȝt ne neuer vpon dayeȝ,
As harlottrye vnhonest, heþyng of seluen;
Þat schameȝ for no schrewedschyp, schent mot he worþe!   580

Bot sauour, mon, in þyself, þaȝ þou a sotte lyuie,
Þaȝ þou bere þyself babel, byþenk þe sumtyme
Wheþer he þat stykked vche a stare in vche steppe yȝe,
Ȝif hymself be bore blynde, hit is a brod wonder,   584

And he þat fetly in face fettled alle eres,
If he hatȝ losed þe lysten, hit lyfteȝ meruayle;
Trave þou neuer þat tale, vntrwe þou hit fyndeȝ.
Þer is no dede so derne þat ditteȝ his yȝen;   588

Þer is no wyȝe in his werk so war ne so stylle
Þat hit ne þraweȝ to hym þro er he hit þoȝt haue;
For he is þe gropande God, þe grounde of alle dedeȝ,
Rypande of vche a ring þe reynyeȝ and hert.   592

577 Þus, MS þat   581 MS sauyo+ur abbrev.
584 MS hȳ sele   586 MS he he

And þere he fyndeȝ al fayre a freke wythinne,
Þat hert honest and hol, þat haþel he honoureȝ,
Sendeȝ hym a sad syȝt, to se his auen face,
And harde honyseȝ þise oþer and of his erde flemeȝ.   596

Bot of þe dome of þe douþe for dedeȝ of schame,
He is so skoymos of þat skaþe he scarreȝ bylyue;
He may not dryȝe to draw allyt bot drepeȝ in hast,
And þat watȝ schewed schortly by a scaþe oneȝ.   600

OLDE Abraham in erde oneȝ he sytteȝ,
Euen byfore his hous dore, vnder an oke grene.
Bryȝt blykked þe bem of þe brode heuen;
In þe hyȝe hete þerof Abraham bideȝ.   604

He watȝ schunt to þe schadow vnder schyre leueȝ;
Þenne watȝ he war on þe waye of wlonk wyȝeȝ þrynne;
If þay wer farande and fre and fayre to beholde,
Hit is eþe to leue by þe last ende.   608

For þe lede þat þer laye þe leueȝ anvnder,
When he hade of hem syȝt he hyȝeȝ bylyue,
And as to God þe goodmon gos hem agayneȝ,
And haylsed hem in onhede, and sayde: 'Hende lorde,   612

Ȝif euer þy mon vpon molde merit disserued,   f. 65b
Lenge a lyttel with þy lede, I loȝly biseche;
Passe neuer fro þi pouere, ȝif I hit pray durst,
Er þou haf biden with þi burne and vnder boȝe restted.   616

And I schal wynne yow wyȝt of water a lyttel,
And fast aboute schal I fare your fette wer waschene;
Restteȝ here on þis rote and I schal rachche after
And brynge a morsel of bred to baume your hertte.'   620

'Fare forthe,' quoþ þe frekeȝ, 'and fech as þou seggeȝ;
By bole of þis brode tre we byde þe here.'
Þenne orppedly into his hous he hyȝed to Sare,
Comaunded hir to be cof and quyk at þis oneȝ: 624

'Þre metteȝ of mele menge, and ma kakeȝ;
Vnder askeȝ ful hote happe hem byliue;
Quyl I fete sumquat fat, þou þe fyr bete,
Prestly, at þis ilke poynte, sum polment to make.'   628

He cached to his cov-hous and a calf bryngeȝ,
Þat watȝ tender and not toȝe, bed tyrue of þe hyde,
And sayde to his seruaunt þat he hit seþe faste;
And he deruely at his dome dyȝt hit bylyue.   632

620 MS ba + 4 minims + e

Þe burne to be bare-heued buskeȝ hym þenne,
Clecheȝ to a clene cloþe and kesteȝ on þe grene,
Þrwe þryftyly þeron þo þre þerue-kakeȝ,
And bryngeȝ butter wythal and by þe bred setteȝ. 636

Mete messeȝ of mylke he merkkeȝ bytwene,
Syþen potage and polment in plater honest;
As sewer in a gvd assyse he serued hem fayre,
Wyth sadde semblaunt and swete, of such as he hade. 640

And God as a glad gest mad god chere,
Þat watȝ fayn of his frende and his fest praysed;
Abraham, al hodleȝ, with armeȝ vpfolden,
Mynystred mete byfore þo men þat myȝtes al weldeȝ. 644

Þenne þay sayden as þay sete samen alle þrynne,
When þe mete watȝ remued and þay of mensk speken:
'I schal efte hereaway, Abram,' þay sayden,
'Ȝet er þy lyueȝ lyȝt leþe vpon erþe; 648

And þenne schal Sare consayue and a sun bere, f. 66a
Þat schal be Abrahameȝ ayre, and after hym wynne
With wele and wyth worschyp þe worþely peple
Þat schal halde in heritage þat I haf men ȝarked.' 652

Þenne þe burde byhynde þe dor for busmar laȝed,
And sayde sotyly to hirself Sare þe madde:
'May þou traw for tykle þat þou terme moȝteȝ,
And I so hyȝe out of age, and also my lorde?' 656

For soþely, as says þe wryt, hit wern of sadde elde,
Boþe þe wyȝe and his wyf, such werk watȝ hem fayled;
Fro mony a brod day byfore ho barayn ay had bene,
Þat selue Sare withouten sede into þat same tyme. 660

Þenne sayde oure syre þer he sete: 'Se! so Sare laȝes,
Not trawande þe tale þat I þe to schewed.
Hopeȝ ho oȝt may be harde my hondeȝ to work?
And ȝet I avow verayly þe avaunt þat I made; 664

I schal ȝeply aȝayn and ȝelde þat I hyȝt,
And sothely sende to Sare a soun and an hayre.'
Þenne swenged forth Sare and swer by hir trawþe
Þat for lot þat þay laused ho laȝed neuer. 668

652 *MS* ȝark   654 *MS* sothly   655 *MS* tōne
657 hit, *MS* he   659 had bene, *MS* byene

'Now innogh, hit is not so,' þenne nurned þe dryʒtyn,
'For þou laʒed aloʒ, bot let we hit one.'
With þat þay ros vp radly as þay rayke schulde,
And setten toward Sodamas her syʒt alle at oneʒ.   672

For þat cite þerbysyde watʒ sette in a vale,
No myleʒ fro Mambre mo þen tweyne,
Where-so wonyed þis ilke wyʒ þat wendeʒ with oure lorde,
For-to tent hym with tale and teche hym þe gate.   676

Þen glydeʒ forth God, þe godmon hym folʒeʒ;
Abraham heldeʒ hem wyth, hem to conueye
In towarde þe cety of Sodamas þat synned had þenne
In þe faute of þis fylþe; þe fader hem þretes,   680

And sayde þus to þe segg þat sued hym after:
'How myʒt I hyde myn hert fro Habraham þe trwe,
Þat I ne dyscouered to his corse my counsayl so dere,
Syþen he is chosen to be chef chyldryn fader,   684

Þat so folk schal falle fro to flete alle þe worlde,   f. 66b
And vche blod in þat burne blessed schal worþe?
Me bos telle to þat tolk þe tene of my wylle,
And alle myn atlyng to Abraham vnhaspe bilyue.   688

'THE grete soun of Sodamas synkkeʒ in myn ereʒ,
And þe gult of Gomorre gareʒ me to wrath;
I schal lyʒt into þat led and loke myseluen
If þay haf don as þe dyne dryueʒ on lofte.   692

Þay han lerned a lyst þat lykeʒ me ille,
Þat þay han founden in her flesch of fauteʒ þe werst;
Vch male matʒ his mach a man as hymseluen,
And fylter folyly in fere on femmaleʒ wyse.   696

I compast hem a kynde crafte and kende hit hem derne,
And amed hit in myn ordenaunce oddely dere,
And dyʒt drwry þerinne, doole alþer-swettest;
And þe play of paramoreʒ I portrayed myseluen,   700

And made þerto a maner myriest of oþer.
When two true togeder had tyʒed hemseluen,
Bytwene a male and his make such merþe schulde come,
Wel-nyʒe pure paradys moʒt preue no better.   704

Elleʒ þay moʒt honestly ayþer oþer welde,
At a stylle stollen steuen vnstered wyth syʒt,
Luf-lowe hem bytwene lasched so hote
Þat alle þe meschefeʒ on mold moʒt hit not sleke.   708

692 MS if   703 MS conne

Now haf þay skyfted my skyl and scorned natwre,
And hentteȝ hem in heþyng an vsage vnclene;
Hem to smyte for þat smod smartly I þenk,
Þat wyȝeȝ schal be by hem war worlde withouten ende.'   712

Þenne arȝed Abraham, and alle his mod chaunged,
For hope of þe harde hate þat hyȝt hatȝ oure lorde.
Al sykande he sayde: 'Sir, with yor leue,
Schal synful and sakleȝ suffer al on payne?   716

Weþer euer hit lyke my lorde to lyfte such domeȝ,
Þat þe wykked and þe worþy schal on wrake suffer,
And weye vpon þe worre half þat wrathed þe neuer?
Þat watȝ neuer þy won þat wroȝteȝ vus alle.   720

Now fyfty fyn frendeȝ wer founde in ȝonde toune,   f. 67a
In þe cety of Sodamas, and also Gomorre,
Þat neuer lakked þy laue, bot loued ay trauþe,
And reȝtful wern and resounable and redy þe to serue,   724

Schal þay falle in þe faute þat oþer frekeȝ wroȝt,
And ioyne to her iuggement her iuise to haue?
Þat nas neuer þyn note, vnneuened hit worþe,
Þat art so gaynly a God and of goste mylde.'   728

'Nay, for fyfty,' quoþ þe fader, 'and þy fayre speche,
And þay be founden in þat folk of her fylþe clene,
I schal forgyue alle þe gylt þurȝ my grace one,
And let hem smolt al unsmyten smoþely at oneȝ.'   732

'Aa! blessed be þow,' quoþ þe burne, 'so boner and þewed,
And al haldeȝ in þy honde, þe heuen and þe erþe;
Bot, for I haf þis talke, tatȝ to non ille
Ȝif I mele a lyttel more, þat mul am and askeȝ.   736

What if fyue faylen of fyfty þe noumbre,
And þe remnaunt be reken, how restes þy wylle?'
'And fyue wont of fyfty,' quoþ God, 'I schal forȝete alle,
And wythhalde my honde for hortyng on lede.'   740

'And quat if faurty be fre and fauty þyse oþer?
Schalt þow schortly al schende and schape non oþer?'
'Nay, þaȝ faurty forfete, ȝet fryst I a whyle,
And voyde away my vengaunce, þaȝ me vyl þynk.'   744

713 *MS* chaūge
732 y *of* unsmyten *first formed erroneously on last stroke of* m
739 wont *interlined*

Þen Abraham obeched hym and loȝly him þonkkeȝ:
'Now sayned be þou, sauiour, so symple in þy wrath.
I am bot erþe ful euel and vsle so blake,
For-to mele wyth such a mayster as myȝteȝ hatȝ alle.   748

Bot I.haue bygonnen wyth my God, and he hit gayn þynkeȝ;
Ȝif I forloyne as a fol, þy fraunchyse may serue.
What if þretty þryuande be þrad in ȝon touneȝ?
What schal I leue of my lorde, if he hem leþe wolde?'   752

Þenne þe godlych God gef hym onsware:
'Ȝet for þretty in þrong I schal my þro steke,
And spare spakly of spyt, in space of my þeweȝ,
And my rankor refrayne four þy reken wordeȝ.'   756

'What for twenty,' quoþ þe tolke, 'vntwyneȝ þou hem þenne?'   f. 67b
'Nay, ȝif þou ȝerneȝ hit, ȝet ȝark I hem grace.
If þat twenty be trwe, I tene hem no more,
Bot relece alle þat regioun of her ronk werkkeȝ.'   760

'Now, aþel lorde,' quoþ Abraham, 'oneȝ a speche,
And I schal schape no more þo schalkkeȝ to helpe.
If ten trysty in toune be tan in þi werkkeȝ,
Wylt þou mese þy mode and menddyng abyde?'   764

'I graunt,' quoþ þe grete God, 'Graunt mercy,' þat oþer;
And þenne arest þe renk and raȝt no fyrre.
And Godde glydeȝ his gate by þose grene wayeȝ,
And he conueyen hym con with cast of his yȝe.   768

And als he loked along þere as oure lorde passed,
Ȝet he cryed hym after with careful steuen:
'Meke mayster, on þy mon to mynne if þe lyked,
Loth lengeȝ in ȝon leede, þat is my lef broþer.   772

He sytteȝ þer in Sodomis, þy seruaunt so pouere,
Among þo mansed men þat han þe much greued;
Ȝif þou tyneȝ þat toun, tempre þyn yre
As þy mersy may malte, þy meke to spare.'   776

Þen he wendeȝ his way, wepande for care,
Towarde þe mere of Mambre, mornande for sorewe;
And þere in longyng al nyȝt he lengeȝ in wones,
Whyl þe souerayn to Sodamas sende to spye.   780

752 of, *MS* if   777 *MS* wendeȝ wendeȝ
778 mornande, *MS* wepande   sorewe *written over original word in second hand*

HIS sondes into Sodamas watʒ sende in þat tyme,
In þat ilk euentyde, by aungels tweyne,
Meuande mekely togeder as myry men ʒonge,
As Loot in a loge dor lened hym alone,   784

In a porche of þat place pyʒt to þe ʒates,
Þat watʒ ryal and ryche, so watʒ þe renkes seluen.
As he stared into þe strete, þer stout men played,
He syʒe þer swey in asent swete men tweyne.   788

Bolde burneʒ wer þay boþe, with berdles chynneʒ,
Royl rollande fax to raw sylk lyke,
Of ble as þe brere-flour, where-so þe bare scheweed.
Ful clene watʒ þe countenaunce of her cler yʒen;   792

Wlonk whit watʒ her wede, and wel hit hem semed;   f. 68a
Of alle featureʒ ful fyn, and fautleʒ boþe;
Watʒ non aucly in ouþer, for aungels hit wern,
And þat þe ʒep vnderʒede þat in þe ʒate sytteʒ.   796

He ros vp ful radly and ran hem to mete,
And loʒe he louteʒ hem to, Loth, to þe grounde;
And syþen soberly: 'Syreʒ, I yow byseche
Þat ʒe wolde lyʒt at my loge and lenge þerinne.   800

Comeʒ to your knaues kote, I craue at þis oneʒ;
I schal fette yow a fatte your fette for-to wasche;
I norne yow bot for on nyʒt neʒe me to lenge,
And in þe myry mornyng ʒe may your waye take.'   804

And þay nay þat þay nolde neʒ no howseʒ,
Bot stylly þer in þe strete, as þay stadde wern,
Þay wolde lenge þe long naʒt, and logge þeroute;
Hit watʒ hous innoʒe to hem þe heuen vpon lofte.   808

Loth laþed so longe wyth lyflych wordeʒ,
Þat þay hym graunted to go, and gruʒt no lenger.
Þe bolde to his byggyng bryngeʒ hem bylyue,
Þat watʒ ryally arayed, for he watʒ ryche euer.   812

Þe wyʒeʒ wern welcom as þe wyf couþe;
His two dere doʒtereʒ deuoutly hem haylsed,
Þat wer maydeneʒ ful meke, maryed not ʒet,
And þay wer semly and swete and swyþe wel arayed.   816

783 MS meuand meuande   785 p of place apparently altered from l
795 MS autly   812 watʒ (1st) supplied

Loth þenne ful ly3tly loke3 hym aboute,
And his men amonestes mete for-to dy3t:
'Bot þenkke3 on hit be þrefte, what þynk so 3e make,
For wyth no sour ne no salt serue3 hym neuer.'   820

Bot 3et I wene þat þe wyf hit wroth to dyspyt,
And sayde softely to hirself: 'Þis vnsauere hyne
Loue3 no salt in her sauce, 3et hit no skyl were
Þat oþer burne be boute, þa3 boþe be nyse.'   824

Þenne ho sauere3 with salt her seue3 vchone,
Agayne þe bone of þe burne þat hit forboden hade,
And als ho scelt hem in scorne þat wel her skyl knewen.
Why wat3 ho, wrech, so wod? Ho wrathed oure lorde.   828

Þenne seten þay at þe soper, wern serued bylyue,   f. 68b
Þe gestes gay and ful glad, of glam debonere,
Wela wynnely wlonk, tyl þay waschen hade,
Þe trestes tylt to þe wo3e, and þe table boþe.   832

Fro þe segge3 haden souped and seten bot a whyle,
Er euer þay bosked to bedde, þe bor3 wat3 al vp,
Alle þat weppen my3t welde, þe wakker and þe stronger,
To vmbely3e Lothe3 hous þe lede3 to take.   836

In grete flokke3 of folk þay fallen to his 3ate3;
As a scowte-wach scarred so þe asscry rysed;
With kene clobbe3 of þat clos þay clater on þe wowe3,
And wyth a schrylle scharp schout þay schewe þys worde: 840

'If þou louye3 þy lyf, Loth, in þyse wones,
3ete vus out þose 3ong men þat 3ore-whyle here entred,
Þat we may lere hym of lof, as oure lyst bidde3,
As is þe asyse of Sodomas to segge3 þat passen.'   844

Whatt! þay sputen and speken of so spitous fylþe;
What! þay 3e3ed and 3olped of 3estande sor3e,
Þat 3et þe wynd and þe weder and þe worlde stynkes
Of þe brych þat vpbradye3 þose broþelych worde3.   848

Þe godman glyfte with þat glam and gloped for noyse;
So scharpe schame to hym schot, he schrank at þe hert.
For he knew þe costoum þat kyþed þose wreche3;
He doted neuer for no doel so depe in his mynde.   852

822 *MS* vnfau+er *abbrev.*+e h *of* hyne *apparently altered from* þ
839 clater, *MS* clat3   840 *MS* þyse

'Allas!' sayd hym þenne Loth, and lyȝtly he ryseȝ,
And boweȝ forth fro þe bench into þe brode ȝates.
What! he wonded no woþe of wekked knaueȝ
Þat he ne passed þe port þe peril to abide.   856

He went forthe at þe wyket and waft hit hym after,
Þat a clyket hit cleȝt clos hym byhynde.
Þenne he meled to þo men mesurable wordeȝ,
For harloteȝ with his hendelayk he hoped to chast: 860

'Oo, my frendeȝ so fre, your fare is to strange;
Dotȝ away your derf dyn, and dereȝ neuer my gestes.
Avoy! hit is your vylaynye, ȝe vylen yourseluen;
And ȝe ar iolyf gentylmen, your iapeȝ ar ille.   864

Bot I schal kenne yow by kynde a crafte þat is better;   f. 69a
I haf a tresor in my telde of tow my fayre deȝter,
Þat ar maydeneȝ vnmard for alle men ȝette;
In Sodamas, þaȝ I hit say, non semloker burdes.   868

Hit arn ronk, hit arn rype, and redy to manne;
To samen wyth þo semly þe solace is better;
I schal biteche yow þo two þat tayt arn and quoynt,
And laykeȝ wyth hem as yow lyst, and leteȝ my gestes one.'   872

Þenne þe rebaudeȝ so ronk rerd such a noyse,
Þat aȝly hurled in his ereȝ her harloteȝ speche:
'Wost þou not wel þat þou woneȝ here a wyȝe strange,
An outcomlyng, a carle?—we kylle of þyn heued!   876

Who joyned þe be iostyse, oure iapeȝ to blame,
Þat com a boy to þis borȝ, þaȝ þou be burne ryche?'
Þus þay probled and þrong and þrwe vmbe his ereȝ,
And distresed hym wonder strayt with strenkþe in þe prece,   880

Bot þat þe ȝonge men so ȝepe ȝornen þeroute,
Wapped vpon þe wyket and wonnen hem tylle,
And by þe hondeȝ hym hent and horyed hym withinne,
And steken þe ȝates ston-harde wyth stalworth barreȝ.   884

Þay blwe a boffet in blande þat banned peple,
Þat þay blustered as blynde as Bayard watȝ euer.
Þay lest of Loteȝ logging any lysoun to fynde,
Bot nyteled þer alle þe nyȝt for noȝt at þe last.   888

856 *MS* pil

Þenne vch tolke ty3t hem þat hade of tayt fayled,
And vchon roþeled to þe rest þat he reche mo3t;
Bot þay wern wakned awrank þat þer in won lenged,
Of on þe vglokest vnhap euer on erd suffred.   892

RUDDON of þe day-rawe ros vpon v3ten,
When merk of þe mydny3t mo3t no more last.
Ful erly þose aungele3 þis haþel þay ruþen,
And glopnedly, on Gode3 halue, gart hym vpryse.   896

Fast þe freke ferke3 vp, ful ferd at his hert;
Þay comaunded hym cof to cach þat he hade:
'Wyth þy wyf and þy wy3e3 and þy wlonc de3tters,
For we laþe þe, sir Loth, þat þou þy lyf haue.   900

Cayre tid of þis kythe, er combred þou worþe,   f. 69b
With alle þi here vpon haste, tyl þou a hil fynde;
Founde3 faste on your fete, bifore your face lokes,
Bot bes neuer so bolde to blusch yow bihynde.   904

And loke 3e stemme no stepe, bot streche3 on faste;
Til 3e reche to a reset, rest 3e neuer;
For we schal tyne þis toun and trayþely disstrye,
Wyth alle þise wy3e3 so wykke wy3tly devoyde,   908

And alle þe londe with þise lede3 we losen at one3;
Sodomas schal ful sodenly synk into grounde,
And þe grounde of Gomorre gorde into helle,
And vche a koste of þis kyth clater vpon hepes.'   912

Þen laled Loth: 'Lorde, what is best?
If I me fele vpon fote þat I fle mo3t,
Hov schulde I huyde me fro hym þat hat3 his hate kynned,
In þe brath of his breth þat brenne3 alle þinke3?   916

To crepe fro my creatour and know not wheder,
Ne wheþer his fooschip me fol3e3 bifore oþer bihynde!'
Þe freke sayde: 'No foschip oure fader hat3 þe schewed,
Bot hil3y heuened þi hele fro hem þat arn combred.   920

Nov wale þe a wonnyng þat þe warisch my3t,
And he schal saue hit for þy sake þat hat3 vus sende hider;
For þou art oddely þyn one out of þis fylþe,
And als Abraham þyn eme hit at himself asked.'   924

891 *MS* al wrank, *l crossed out with vertical wavy line in original ink*
892 *MS* vnhap þat eu+er *abbrev.*   915 hym, *MS* hem
921 wale *appears to have* e *formed on a second* l *which is crossed out with vertical wavy line in original ink*
924 þyn eme *probably original, but* broþ+er *abbrev. written over last four letters in second hand; first stroke of* n, *and final* e, *are visible*

'Lorde, loued he worþe,' quoþ Loth, 'vpon erþe!
Þer is a cite herbisyde þat Segor hit hatte;
Herevtter on a rounde hil hit houeȝ hit one.
I wolde, if his wylle wore, to þat won scape.'   928

'Þenn fare forth,' quoþ þat fre, 'and fyne þou neuer,
With þose ilk þat þow wylt, þat þrenge þe after,
And ay goande on your gate wythouten agayn-tote;
For alle þis londe schal be lorne longe er þe sonne rise.'   932

Þe wyȝe wakened his wyf and his wlonk deȝteres,
And oþer two myri men þo maydeneȝ schulde wedde;
And þay token hit as tayt and tented hit lyttel,
Þaȝ fast laþed hem Loth, þay leȝen ful stylle.   936

Þe aungeleȝ hasted þise oþer and aȝly hem þratten,   f. 70a
And enforsed alle fawre forth at þe ȝateȝ.
Þo wern Loth and his lef, his luflyche deȝter;
Þer soȝt no mo to sauement of cities aþel fyue.   940

Þise aungeleȝ hade hem by hande out at þe ȝateȝ,
Prechande hem þe perile, and beden hem passe fast:
'Lest ȝe be taken in þe teche of tyraunteȝ here,
Loke ȝe bowe now bi bot, boweȝ fast hence.'   944

And þay kayre ne con and kenely flowen;
Erly, er any heuen-glem, þay to a hil comen.
Þe grete God in his greme bygynneȝ on lofte
To wakan wedereȝ so wylde—þe wyndeȝ he calleȝ,   948

And þay wroþely vpwafte and wrastled togeder,
Fro fawre half of þe folde, flytande loude;
Clowdeȝ clustered bytwene, kesten vp torres,
Þat þe þik þunder-þrast þirled hem ofte.   952

Þe rayn rueled adoun, ridlande þikke,
Of felle flaunkes of fyr and flakes of soufre,
Al in smolderande smoke, smachande ful ille,
Swe aboute Sodamas and hit sydeȝ alle,   956

Gorde to Gomorra þat þe grounde laused,
Abdama and Syboym—þise ceteis alle faure
Al birolled wyth þe rayn, rostted and brenned,
And ferly flayed þat folk þat in þose fees lenged.   960

For when þat þe helle herde þe houndeȝ of heuen,
He watȝ ferlyly fayn, vnfolded bylyue;
Þe grete barreȝ of þe abyme he barst vp at oneȝ,
Þat alle þe regioun torof in riftes ful grete,   964

926 Þer, MS þē   e of cite perhaps altered from y   935 tayt, MS tyt

And clouen alle in lyttel cloutes þe clyffeȝ aywhere,
As lauce leueȝ of þe boke þat lepes in twynne.
Þe brethe of þe brynston bi þat hit blende were,
Al þo citees and her sydes sunkken to helle. 968

Rydelles wern þo grete rowtes of renkkes withinne,
When þay wern war of þe wrake þat no wyȝe achaped;
Such a ȝomerly ȝarm of ȝellyng þer rysed,
Þerof clatered þe cloudes, þat Kryst myȝt haf rawþe. 972

Þe segge herde þat soun to Segor þat ȝede, f. 70b
And þe wenches hym wyth þat by þe way folȝed;
Ferly ferde watȝ her flesch þat flowen ay ilyche,
Trynande ay a hyȝe trot þat torne neuer dorsten. 976

Loth and þo luly-whit, his lefly two deȝter,
Ay folȝed here face, bifore her boþe yȝen;
Bot þe balleful burde, þat neuer bode keped,
Blusched byhynden her bak þat bale for-to herkken. 980

Hit watȝ lusty Lothes wyf, þat ouer her lyfte schulder
Ones ho bluschet to þe burȝe; bot bod ho no lenger
Þat ho nas stadde a stiffe ston, a stalworth image,
Also salt as ani se—and so ho ȝet standeȝ. 984

Þay slypped bi and syȝe hir not þat wern hir samen-feres,
Tyl þay in Segor wern sette, and sayned our lorde;
Wyth lyȝt loueȝ vplyfte þay loued hym swyþe,
Þat so his seruauntes wolde see and saue of such woþe. 988

Al watȝ dampped and don and drowned by þenne;
Þe ledeȝ of þat lyttel toun wern lopen out for drede
Into þat malscrande mere, marred bylyue,
Þat noȝt saued watȝ bot Segor þat sat on a lawe, 992

Þe þre ledeȝ þerin, Loth and his deȝter.
For his make watȝ myst, þat on þe mount lenged
In a stonen statue þat salt sauor habbes,
For two fautes þat þe fol watȝ founde in mistrauþe: 996

On, ho serued at þe soper salt bifore dryȝtyn,
And syþen ho blusched hir bihynde, þaȝ hir forboden were.
For on ho standes a ston, and salt for þat oþer,
And alle lyst on hir lik þat arn on launde bestes. 1000

Abraham ful erly watȝ vp on þe morne,
Þat alle naȝt much niye hade nomen in his hert,
Al in longing for Loth leyen in a wache;
Þer he lafte hade oure lorde he is on lofte wonnen. 1004

981 her, *MS* he   1002 *MS* no mon

He sende toward Sodomas þe sy3t of his y3en,
Þat euer hade ben an erde of erþe þe swettest,
As aparaunt to paradis þat plantted þe dry3tyn;
Nov is hit plunged in a pit like of pich fylled.   1008

Suche a roþum of a reche ros fro þe blake,   f. 71a
Aske3 vpe in þe ayre and vselle3 þer flowen,
As a fornes ful of flot þat vpon fyr boyles,
When bry3t brennande bronde3 ar bet þeranvnder.   1012

Þis wat3 a uengaunce violent þat voyded þise places,
Þat foundered hat3 so fayr a folk and þe folde sonkken.
Þere fyue citees wern set nov is a see called,
Þat ay is drouy and dym, and ded in hit kynde;   1016

Blo, blubrande, and blak, vnblyþe to ne3e,
As a stynkande stanc þat stryed synne,
Þat euer of synne and of smach smart is to fele.
Forþy þe derk dede see hit is demed euermore.   1020

For hit dede3 of deþe duren þere 3et;
For hit is brod and boþemle3, and bitter as þe galle,
And no3t may lenge in þat lake þat any lyf bere3,
And alle þe coste3 of kynde hit combre3 vchone.   1024

For lay þeron a lump of led and hit on loft flete3,
And folde þeron a ly3t fyþer and hit to founs synkke3.
And þer water may walter to wete any erþe,
Schal neuer grene þeron growe, gresse ne wod nawþer.   1028

If any schalke to be schent wer schowued þerinne,
Þa3 he bode in þat boþem broþely a monyth,
He most ay lyue in þat lo3e, in losyng euermore,
And neuer dry3e no dethe to dayes of ende.   1032

And as hit is corsed of kynde, and hit cooste3 als,
Þe clay þat clenges þerby arn corsyes strong,
As alum and alkaran, þat angre arn boþe,
Soufre sour and saundyuer and oþer such mony;   1036

And þer walte3 of þat water, in waxlokes grete,
Þe spumande aspaltoun þat spysere3 sellen.
And suche is alle þe soyle by þat se halues,
Þat fel fretes þe flesch and festres bones.   1040

1015 þere fyue *probably original, but* þer faur + *curved stroke overwritten in
second hand;* þ, f *unretouched; traces of original final* e *in* þere, *and* y *in* fyue, *are
visible*   is *interlined in second hand*
1038 *MS* spuniande (i '*dotted*')   1040 *MS* festred

And þer ar tres by þat terne of traytoures,
And þay borgounez and beres blomez ful fayre,
And þe fayrest fryt þat may on folde growe,
As orenge and oþer fryt and apple-garnade,   1044

Al so red and so ripe and rychely hwed   f. 71b
As any dom myȝt deuice, of dayntyeȝ oute;
Bot quen hit is brused oþer broken oþer byten in twynne,
No worldeȝ goud hit wythinne, bot wyndowande askes.   1048

Alle þyse ar teches and tokenes to trow vpon ȝet,
And wittnesse of þat wykked werk, and þe wrake after
Þat oure fader forþered for fylþe of þose ledes;
Þenne vch wyȝe may wel wyt þat he þe wlonk louies.   1052

And if he louyes clene layk þat is oure lorde ryche,
And to be couþe in his courte þou coueytes þenne,
To se þat semly in sete and his swete face,
Clerrer counsayl con I non bot þat þou clene worþe.   1056

For Clopyngnel in þe compas of his clene Rose,
Þer he expouneȝ a speche to hym þat spede wolde
Of a lady to be loued: 'Loke to hir sone
Of wich beryng þat ho be, and wych ho best louyes;   1060

And be ryȝt such in vch a borȝe, of body and of dedes,
And folȝ þe fet of þat fere þat þou fre haldes.
And if þou wyrkkes on þis wyse, þaȝ ho wyk were,
Hir schal lyke þat layk þat lyknes hir tylle.'   1064

If þou wyl dele drwrye wyth dryȝtyn þenne,
And lelly louy þy lorde and his leef worþe,
Þenne confourme þe to Kryst, and þe clene make,
Þat euer is polyced als playn as þe perle seluen.   1068

For loke, fro fyrst þat he lyȝt withinne þe lel mayden,
By how comly a kest he watȝ clos þere,
When venkkyst watȝ no vergynyte, ne vyolence maked,
Bot much clener watȝ hir corse God kynned þerinne.   1072

And efte when he borne watȝ in Beþelen þe ryche,
In wych puryte þay departed, þaȝ þay pouer were.
Watȝ neuer so blysful a bour as watȝ a bos þenne,
Ne no schroude-hous so schene as a schepon þare,   1076

1051 *MS* forferde   1056 *MS* coũseyl coũseyl
1071 *MS* when he venkkyst, *line through* he

Ne non so glad vnder God as ho þat grone schulde;
For þer watȝ seknesse al sounde þat sarrest is halden,
And þer watȝ rose reflayr where rote hatȝ ben euer,
And þer watȝ solace and songe wher sorȝ hatȝ ay cryed.   1080

For aungelles with instrumentes of organes and pypes,   f. 72a
And rial ryngande rotes, and þe reken fyþel,
And alle hende þat honestly moȝt an hert glade,
Aboutte my lady watȝ lent, quen ho delyuer were.   1084

Þenne watȝ her blyþe barne burnyst so clene
Þat boþe þe ox and þe asse hym hered at ones;
Þay knewe hym by his clannes for kyng of nature,
For non so clene of such a clos com neuer er þenne.   1088

And ȝif clanly he þenne com, ful cortays þerafter,
Þat alle þat longed to luþer ful lodly he hated;
By nobleye of his norture he nolde neuer towche
Oȝt þat watȝ vngoderly oþer ordure watȝ inne.   1092

Ȝet comen lodly to þat lede, as laȝares monye,
Summe lepre, summe lome, and lomerande blynde,
Poysened and parlatyk and pyned in fyres,
Drye folk and ydropike, and dede at þe laste.   1096

Alle called on þat cortayse and claymed his grace;
He heled hem wyth hynde speche of þat þay ask after;
For what-so he towched also tyd tourned to hele,
Wel clanner þen any crafte cowþe devyse.   1100

So clene watȝ his hondelyng vche ordure hit schonied,
And þe gropyng so goud of God and man boþe
Þat for fetys of his fyngeres fonded he neuer
Nauþer to cout ne to kerue with knyf ne wyth egge.   1104

Forþy brek he þe bred blades wythouten,
For hit ferde freloker in fete in his fayre honde,
Displayed more pryuyly when he hit part schulde
Þenne alle þe toles of Tolowse moȝt tyȝt hit to kerue.   1108

Þus is he kyryous and clene þat þou his cort askes;
Hov schulde þou com to his kyth bot if þou clene were?
Nov ar we sore and synful and sovly vchone,
How schulde we se, þen may we say, þat syre upon throne?   1112

Ȝis, þat mayster is mercyable, þaȝ þou be man fenny,
And al tomarred in myre whyl þou on molde lyuyes;
Þou may schyne þurȝ schryfte, þaȝ þou haf schome serued,
And pure þe with penaunce tyl þou a perle worþe.   1116

Perle praysed is prys þer perre is schewed, f. 72b
Þaȝ ho not derrest be demed to dele for penies;
Quat may þe cause be called bot for hir clene hwes,
Þat wynnes worschyp abof alle whyte stones? 1120

For ho schynes so schyr þat is of schap rounde,
Wythouten faut oþer fylþe, ȝif ho fyn were;
And wax ho euer in þe worlde in weryng so olde,
Ȝet þe perle payres not whyle ho in pyese lasttes. 1124

And if hit cheue þe chaunce vncheryst ho worþe,
Þat ho blyndes of ble in bour þer ho lygges,
No-bot wasch hir wyth wourchyp in wyn, as ho askes;
Ho by kynde schal becom clerer þen are. 1128

So if folk be defowled by vnfre chaunce,
Þat he be sulped in sawle, seche to schryfte;
And he may polyce hym at þe prest, by penaunce taken,
Wel bryȝter þen þe beryl oþer browden perles. 1132

Bot war þe wel, if þou be waschen wyth water of schryfte,
And polysed als playn as parchmen schauen,
Sulp no more þenne in synne þy saule þerafter,
For þenne þou dryȝtyn dyspleses with dedes ful sore, 1136

And entyses hym to tene more trayþly þen euer,
And wel hatter to hate þen hade þou not waschen;
For when a sawele is saȝtled and sakred to dryȝtyn,
He holly haldes hit his, and haue hit he wolde. 1140

Þenne efte lastes hit likkes, he loses hit ille,
As hit were rafte wyth vnryȝt and robbed wyth þewes.
War þe þenne for þe wrake, his wrath is achaufed,
For þat þat ones watȝ his schulde efte be vnclene. 1144

Þaȝ hit be bot a bassyn, a bolle oþer a scole,
A dysche oþer a dobler þat dryȝtyn oneȝ serued,
To defowle hit euer vpon folde fast he forbedes,
So is he scoymus of scaþe þat scylful is euer. 1148

And þat watȝ bared in Babyloyn in Baltaȝar tyme,
Hov harde vnhap þer hym hent, and hastyly sone,
For he þe vesselles avyled þat vayled in þe temple
In seruyse of þe souerayn sumtyme byfore. 1152

Ȝif ȝe wolde tyȝt me a tom, telle hit I wolde, f. 73a
Hov charged more watȝ his chaunce þat hem cherych nolde
Þen his fader forloyne, þat feched hem wyth strenþe,
And robbed þe relygioun of relykes alle. 1156

1118 ho, MS hȳ 1123 ho *supplied*

[III]

D ANYEL in his dialoke3 devysed sumtyme,
As 3et is proued expresse in his profecies,
Hov þe gentryse of Juise and Jherusalem þe ryche
Wat3 disstryed wyth distres and drawen to þe erþe.　　　1160

For þat folke in her fayth wat3 founden vntrwe,
Þat haden hy3t þe hy3e God to halde of hym euer;
And he hem hal3ed for his, and help at her nede
In mukel meschefes mony þat meruayl were to here.　　　1164

And þay forloyne her fayth and fol3ed oþer goddes,
And þat wakned his wrath and wrast hit so hy3e
Þat he fylsened þe faythful in þe falce lawe
To forfare þe falce in þe faythe trwe.　　　1168

Hit wat3 sen in þat syþe þat 3edethyas rengned
In Juda, þat iustised þe Iuyne kynges;
He sete on Salamones solie, on solemne wyse,
Bot of leaute he wat3 lat to his lorde hende.　　　1172

He vsed abominaciones of idolatrye,
And lette ly3t bi þe lawe þat he wat3 lege tylle.
Forþi oure fader vpon folde a foman hym wakned;
Nabigodeno3ar nuyed hym swyþe.　　　1176

He pursued into Palastyn with proude men mony,
And þer he wast wyth werre þe wones of þorpes;
He her3ed vp alle Israel and hent of þe beste,
And þe gentylest of Judee in Jerusalem biseged,　　　1180

Vmbewalt alle þe walles wyth wy3es ful stronge,
At vche a dor a do3ty duk, and dutte hem wythinne;
For þe bor3 wat3 so bygge, baytayled alofte,
And stoffed wythinne with stout men to stalle hem þeroute.　　　1184

Þenne wat3 þe sege sette þe cete aboute;
Skete skarmoch skelt, much skaþe lached;
At vch brugge a berfray on basteles wyse,
Þat seuen syþe vch a day asayled þe 3ates.　　　f. 73b

Trwe tulkkes in toures teueled wythinne,
In bigge brutage of borde bulde on þe walles.
Þay fe3t and þay fende of and fylter togeder
Til two 3er ouertorned, 3et tok þay hit neuer.　　　1192

1164 were *supplied*　　　　　　　　　　1178 *MS* wyth with

At þe laste, vpon longe, þo ledes wythinne,
Faste fayled hem þe fode, enfaminied monie;
Þe hote hunger wythinne hert hem wel sarre
Þen any dunt of þat douthe þat dowelled þeroute.   1196

Þenne wern þo rowtes redles in þo ryche wones;
Fro þat mete watȝ myst, megre þay wexen;
And þay stoken so strayt þat þay ne stray myȝt
A fote fro þat forselet to forray no goudes.   1200

Þenne þe kyng of þe kyth a counsayl hym takes,
Wyth þe best of his burnes, a blench for-to make.
Þay stel out on a stylle nyȝt er any steuen rysed,
And harde hurles þurȝ þe oste er enmies hit wyste.   1204

Bot er þay atwappe ne moȝt þe wach wythoute,
Hiȝe skelt watȝ þe askry þe skewes anvnder.
Loude alarom vpon launde lulted watȝ þenne;
Ryche, ruþed of her rest, ran to here wedes;   1208

Hard hattes þay hent and on hors lepes;
Cler claryoun crak cryed on lofte.
By þat watȝ alle on a hepe hurlande swyþee,
Folȝande þat oþer flote, and fonde hem bilyue,   1212

Ouertok hem as tyd, tult hem of sadeles,
Tyl vche prynce hade his per put to þe grounde.
And þer watȝ þe kyng kaȝt wyth Calde prynces,
And alle hise gentyle foriusted on Ierico playnes,   1216

And presented wern as presoneres to þe prynce rychest,
Nabigodenoȝar, noble in his chayer;
And he þe faynest freke þat he his fo hade,
And speke spitously hem to, and spylt þerafter.   1220

Þe kynges sunnes in his syȝt he slow euervchone,
And holkked out his auen yȝen heterly boþe,
And bede þe burne to be broȝt to Babyloyn þe ryche,
And þere in dongoun be don, to dreȝe þer his wyrdes.   f. 74a

Now se! so þe souerayn set hatȝ his wrake.
Nas hit not for Nabugo ne his noble nauþer
Þat oþer depryued watȝ of pryde, with paynes stronge,
Bot for his beryng so badde agayn his blyþe lorde.   1228

For hade þe fader ben his frende þat hym bifore keped,
Ne neuer trespast to him in teche of mysseleue,
To colde wer alle Calde and kythes of Ynde—
Ȝet take Torkye hem wyth, her tene hade ben little.   1232

1225 *MS* so u + er *abbrev.* + ay

Ʒet nolde neuer Nabugo þis ilke note leue
Er he hade tyrued þis toun and torne hit to grounde.
He ioyned vnto Jerusalem a gentyle duc þenne—
His name watȝ Nabuȝardan—to noye þe Iues.   1236

He watȝ mayster of his men and myȝty himseluen,
Þe chef of his cheualrye his chekkes to make.
He brek þe bareres as bylyue, and þe burȝ after,
And enteres in ful ernestly in yre of his hert.   1240

What! þe maysterry watȝ mene, þe men wern away;
Þe best boȝed wyth þe burne þat þe borȝ ȝemed;
And þo þat byden wer so biten with þe bale hunger
Þat on wyf hade ben worþe þe welgest fourre.   1244

Nabiȝardan noȝt forþy nolde not spare,
Bot bede al to þe bronde vnder bare egge.
Þay slowen of swettest semlych burdes,
Baþed barnes in blod and her brayn spylled,   1248

Prestes and prelates þay presed to deþe,
Wyues and wenches her wombes tocoruen
Þat her boweles outborst aboute þe diches,
And al watȝ carfully kylde þat þay cach myȝt.   1252

And alle swypped vnswolȝed of þe sworde kene,
Þay wer cagged and kaȝt on capeles al bare,
Festned fettres to her fete vnder fole wombes,
And broþely broȝt to Babyloyn þer bale to suffer,   1256

To sytte in seruage and syte þat sumtyme wer gentyle;
Now ar chaunged to chorles and charged wyth werkkes,
Boþe to cayre at þe kart and þe kuy mylke,
Þat sumtyme sete in her sale syres and burdes.   f. 74b

And ȝet Nabuȝardan nyl neuer stynt,
Er he to þe tem! ple tee wyth his tulkkes alle;
Betes on þe barers, brestes vp þe ȝates,
Slouen alle at a slyp þat serued þerinne,   1264

Pulden prestes bi þe polle and plat of her hedes,
Diȝten dekenes to deþe, dungen doun clerkkes,
And alle þe maydenes of þe munster maȝtyly hokyllen
Wyth þe swayf of þe sworde þat swolȝed hem alle.   1268

Þenne ran þay to þe relykes as robbors wylde,
And pyled alle þe apparement þat pented to þe kyrke,
Þe pure pyleres of bras pourtrayd in golde,
And þe chef chaundeler, charged with þe lyȝt,   1272

1234 *MS* tuyred   1243 so, *MS* fo

Þat ber þe lamp vpon lofte þat lemed euermore
Bifore þe sancta sanctorum, þer selcouth watȝ ofte.
Þay caȝt away þat condelstik and þe crowne als,
Þat þe auter hade vpon, of aþel golde ryche,   1276

Þe gredirne and þe goblotes garnyst of syluer,
Þe bases of þe bryȝt postes and bassynes so schyre,
Dere disches of golde and dubleres fayre,
Þe vyoles and þe vesselment of vertuous stones.   1280

Now hatȝ Nebuȝardan nomen alle þyse noble þynges,
And pyled þat precious place and pakked þose godes;
Þe golde of þe gaȝafylace, to swyþe gret noumbre,
Wyth alle þe vrnmentes of þat hous, he hamppred togeder.   1284

Alle he spoyled spitously in a sped whyle
Þat Salomon so mony a sadde ȝer soȝt to make.
Wyth alle þe coyntyse þat he cowþe clene to wyrke
Deuised he þe vesselment, þe vestures clene;   1288

Wyth slyȝt of his ciences, his souerayn to loue,
Þe hous and þe anournementes he hyȝtled togedere.
Now hatȝ Nabuȝardan nummen hit al samen,
And syþen bet doun þe burȝ and brend hit in askes.   1292

Þenne wyth legiounes of ledes ouer londes he rydes,
Herȝeȝ of Israel þe hyrne aboute;
Wyth charged chariotes þe cheftayn he fyndes,
Bikennes þe catel to þe kyng þat he caȝt hade,   f. 75a

Presented him þe presoneres in pray þat þay token,
Moni a worþly wyȝe whil her worlde laste,
Moni semly syre soun, and swyþe rych maydenes,
Þe pruddest of þe prouince, and prophetes childer,   1300

As Ananie and Aȝarie and als Miȝael,
And dere Daniel also, þat watȝ deuine noble,
With moni a modey moder chylde mo þen innoghe.
And Nabugodenoȝar makes much ioye,   1304

Nov he þe kyng hatȝ conquest and þe kyth wunnen,
And dreped alle þe doȝtyest and derrest in armes,
And þe lederes of her lawe layd to þe grounde,
And þe pryce of þe profetie presoners maked.   1308

1273 b of ber *badly formed, perhaps altered from* w
1274 *MS* þsancta   1291 *MS* nūnēd
1295 rged *of* charged *from* u.-v.   *MS* fynde
1296 *catchword* Bikennes þe catel

Bot þe ioy of þe iuelrye, so gentyle and ryche,
When hit watȝ schewed hym so schene, scharp watȝ his wonder;
Of such vessel auayed, þat vayled so huge,
Neuer ȝet nas Nabugodenoȝar er þenne.   1312

He sesed hem wiþ solemnete, þe souerayn he praysed
Þat watȝ aþel ouer alle, Israel dryȝtyn;
Such god, such gounes, such gay vesselles
Comen neuer out of kyth to Caldee reames.   1316

He trussed hem in his tresorye in a tryed place,
Rekenly, wyth reuerens, as he ryȝt hade;
And þer he wroȝt as þe wyse, as ȝe may wyt hereafter,
For hade he let of hem lyȝt hym moȝt haf lumpen worse.   1320

Þat ryche in gret rialte rengned his lyue;
As conquerour of vche a cost he cayser watȝ hatte,
Emperour of alle þe erþe, and also þe saudan,
And als þe god of þe grounde watȝ grauen his name.   1324

And al þurȝ dome of Daniel, fro he deuised hade
Þat alle goudes com of God, and gef hit hym bi samples,
Þat he ful clanly bicnv his carp bi þe laste;
And ofte hit mekned his mynde, his maysterful werkkes.   1328

Bot al drawes to dyȝe with doel vpon ende;
Bi a haþel neuer so hyȝe, he heldes to grounde;
And so Nabugodenoȝar, as he nedes moste,
For alle his empire so hiȝe, in erþe is he grauen.   f. 75b

Bot þenn þe bolde Baltaȝar, þat watȝ his barn aldest,
He watȝ stalled in his stud, and stabled þe rengne
In þe burȝ of Babiloyne, þe biggest he trawed,
Þat nauþer in heuen ne on erþe hade no pere.   1336

For he bigan in alle þe glori þat hym þe gome lafte,
Nabugodenoȝar, þat watȝ his noble fader;
So kene a kyng in Caldee com neuer er þenne.
Bot honoured he not hym þat in heuen wonies,   1340

Bot fals fantummes of fendes formed with handes,
Wyth tool out of harde tre, and telded on lofte,
And of stokkes and stones, he stoute goddes callȝ,
When þay ar gilde al with golde and gered wyth syluer.   1344

And þere he kneles and calleȝ and clepes after help;
And þay reden him ryȝt, rewarde he hem hetes,
And if þay gruchen him his grace, to gremen his hert,
He cleches to a gret klubbe and knokkes hem to peces.   1348

1315 *MS* gomes   1329 *MS* vpn   1336 on, *MS* no   1339 *MS* neū

Þus in pryde and olipraunce his empyre he haldes,
In lust and in lecherye and loþelych werkkes,
And hade a wyf for-to welde, a worþelych quene,
And mony a lemman neuer þe later þat ladis wer called.　　1352

In þe clernes of his concubines and curious wedeȝ,
In notyng of nwe metes and of nice gettes,
Al watȝ þe mynde of þat man on misschapen þinges,
Til þe lorde of þe lyfte liste hit abate.　　1356

THENNE þis bolde Baltaȝar biþenkkes hym ones
To vouche on avayment of his vayneglorie;
Hit is not innogh to þe nice al noȝty þink vse,
Bot if alle þe worlde wyt his wykked dedes.　　1360

Baltaȝar þurȝ Babiloyn his banne gart crye,
And þurȝ þe cuntre of Caldee his callyng con spryng,
Þat alle þe grete vpon grounde schulde geder hem samen,
And assemble at a set day at þe saudans fest.　　1364

Such a mangerie to make þe man watȝ auised
Þat vche a kythyn kyng schuld com þider;
Vche duk wyth his duthe, and oþer dere lordes,
Schulde com to his court to kyþe hym for lege,　　f. 76a

And to reche hym reuerens and his reuel herkken,
To loke on his lemanes and ladis hem calle.
To rose hym in his rialty rych men soȝtten,
And mony a baroun ful bolde, to Babyloyn þe noble.　　1372

Þer bowed toward Babiloyn burnes so mony,
Kynges, cayseres ful kene, to þe court wonnen,
Mony ludisch lordes þat ladies broȝten,
Þat to neuen þe noumbre to much nye were.　　1376

For þe bourȝ watȝ so brod, and so bigge alce,
Stalled in þe fayrest stud þe sterreȝ anvnder,
Prudly on a plat playn, plek alþer-fayrest,
Vmbesweyed on vch a syde with seuen grete wateres;　　1380

With a wonder wroȝt walle, wruxeled ful hiȝe,
With koynt carneles aboue, coruen ful clene,
Troched toures bitwene, twenty spere lenþe,
And þiker þrowen vmbeþour with ouerþwert palle.　　1384

Þe place þat plyed þe pursaunt wythinne
Watȝ longe and ful large, and euer ilych sware,
And vch a syde vpon soyle helde seuen myle,
And þe saudans sete sette in þe myddes.　　1388

1358 *MS* vayne gorie

Þat watȝ a palayce of pryde, passande alle oþer,
Boþe of werk and of wunder, and walled al aboute;
Heȝe houses withinne, þe halle to hit med;
So brod bilde, in a bay, þat blonkkes myȝt renne.   1392

When þe terme of þe tyde watȝ towched of þe feste,
Dere droȝen þerto and vpon des metten,
And Baltaȝar vpon bench was busked to sete;
Stepe stayred stones of his stoute throne.   1396

Þenne watȝ alle þe halle flor hiled with knyȝtes,
And barounes at þe side-bordes bounet aywhere,
For non watȝ dressed vpon dece bot þe dere seluen,
And his clere concubynes in cloþes ful bryȝt.   1400

When alle segges were þer set, þen seruyse bygynnes;
Sturne trumpen strake, steuen in halle;
Aywhere by þe wowes wrasten krakkes,
And brode baneres þerbi, blusnande of gold.   f. 76b

Burnes berande þe bredes vpon brode skeles,
Þat were of sylueren syȝt, and seues þerwyth;
Lyfte logges þerouer and on lofte coruen,
Pared out of paper and poynted of golde;   1408

Broþe baboynes abof, besttes anvnder,
Foles in foler flakerande bitwene,
And al in asure and ynde enaumayld ryche;
And al on blonkken bak bere hit on honde.   1412

And ay þe nakeryn noyse, notes of pipes;
Tymbres and tabornes tulket among,
Symbales and soneteȝ sware þe noyse,
And bougounȝ busch batered so þikke.   1416

So watȝ serued fele syþe þe sale alle aboute,
With solace at þe sere course, bifore þe self lorde.
Þer þe lede and alle his loue lenged at þe table,
So faste þay weȝed to him wyne, hit warmed his hert,   1420

And breyþed vppe into his brayn and blemyst his mynde,
And al waykned his wyt, and wel-neȝe he foles;
For he wayteȝ on wyde, his wenches he byholdes,
And his bolde baronage aboute bi þe woȝes.   1424

1390 *MS* walle   1402 *MS* sturnen   1405 *MS* þe þe
1406 *MS* seued, *perhaps* er *abbrev. over* v   1408 *MS* glolde

Þenne a dotage ful depe drof to his hert,
And a caytif counsayl he caȝt bi hymseluen.
Maynly his marschal þe mayster vpon calles,
And comaundes hym cofly coferes to lauce,   1428

And fech forþ þe vessel þat his fader broȝt,
Nabugodenoȝar, noble in his strenþe,
Conquerd with his knyȝtes and of kyrk rafte
In Iude, in Ierusalem, in gentyle wyse: 1432

'Bryng hem now to my borde, of beuerage hem fylles;
Let þise ladyes of hem lape, I luf hem in hert.
Þat schal I cortaysly kyþe, and þay schin knawe sone,
Þer is no bounte in burne lyk Baltaȝar þewes.'   1436

Þenne towched to þe tresour þis tale watȝ sone,
And he with keyes vncloses kystes ful mony;
Mony burþen ful bryȝt watȝ broȝt into halle,
And couered mony a cupborde with cloþes ful quite.   f. 77a

Þe iueles out of Ierusalem with gemmes ful bryȝt
Bi þe syde of þe sale were semely arayed;
Þe aþel auter of brasse watȝ hade into place,
Þe gay coroun of golde gered on lofte.   1444

Þat hade ben blessed bifore wyth bischopes hondes,
And wyth besten blod busily anoynted,
In þe solempne sacrefyce þat goud sauor hade
Bifore þe lorde of þe lyfte, in louyng hymseluen,   1448

Now is sette for-to serue Satanas þe blake,
Bifore þe bolde Baltaȝar, wyth bost and wyth pryde.
Houen vpon þis auter watȝ aþel vessel,
Þat wyth so curious a crafte coruen watȝ wyly.   1452

Salamon sete him seuen ȝere and a syþe more,
With alle þe syence þat hym sende þe souerayn lorde,
For-to compas and kest to haf hem clene wroȝt.
For þer wer bassynes ful bryȝt of brende golde clere,   1456

Enaumaylde with aȝer, and eweres of sute;
Couered cowpes foul clene, as casteles arayed,
Enbaned vnder batelment, with bantelles quoynt,
And fyled out on fygures of ferlyle schappes.   1460

1429 forþ þe, *MS* forþe   1452 so, *MS* fo
1453 seuen *blotted, but* s, n, *and part of second* e *visible*
1460 on, *MS* of

Þe coperounes of þe couacles þat on þe cuppe reres
Wer fetysely formed out in fylyoles longe;
Pinacles pyȝt þer apert þat profert bitwene,
And al bolled abof with braunches and leues, 1464

Pyes and papeiayes purtrayed withinne,
As þay prudly hade piked of pomgarnades;
For alle þe blomes of þe boȝes wer blyknande perles,
And alle þe fruyt in þo formes of flaumbeande gemmes, 1468

Ande safyres and sardiners and semely topace,
Alabaundeirynes and amarraunȝ and amastised stones,
Casydoynes and crysolytes and clere rubies,
Penitotes and pynkardines, ay perles bitwene. 1472

So trayled and tryfled a-trauerce wer alle,
Bi vche bekyr ande bolle, þe brurdes al vmbe;
Þe gobelotes of golde grauen aboute,
And fyoles fretted with flores and fleeȝ of golde. f. 77b

Vpon þat avter watȝ al aliche dresset;
Þe candelstik bi acost watȝ cayred þider sone,
Vpon þe pyleres apyked þat praysed hit mony,
Vpon hit baseȝ of brasse þat ber vp þe werkes. 1480

Þe boȝes bryȝt þerabof, brayden of golde,
Braunches bredande þeron, and bryddes þer soten
Of mony kyndes, of fele kyn hues,
As þay with wynge vpon wynde hade waged her fyþeres. 1484

Inmong þe leues of þe launces lampes wer grayþed,
And oþer louflych lyȝt þat lemed ful fayre,
As mony morteres of wax, merkked withoute
With mony a borlych best al of brende golde. 1488

Hit watȝ not wonte in þat wone to wast no serges,
Bot in temple of þe trauþe trwly to stonde,
Bifore þe sancta sanctorum, þer soþefast dryȝtyn
Expouned his speche spiritually to special prophetes. 1492

Leue þou wel þat þe lorde þat þe lyfte ȝemes
Displesed much at þat play in þat plyt stronge,
Þat his iueles so gent wyth iaueles wer fouled,
Þat presyous in his presens wer proued sumwhyle. 1496

1461 *MS* cauacles   1470 *MS* amaffised
1474 *MS* bekyrande þe bolde   1479 Vpon *from u.-v.*
1485 launces *supplied*   1486 f *of* louflych *apparently altered from* e
1491 þer *supplied*   1492 spiritually *is expanded from MS* spũally

Soberly in his sacrafyce summe wer anoynted,
Þurȝ þe somones of himselfe þat syttes so hyȝe;
Now a boster on benche bibbes þerof
Tyl he be dronkken as þe deuel, and dotes þer he syttes.　　　　1500

So þe worcher of þis worlde wlates þerwyth
Þat in þe poynt of her play he poruayes a mynde;
Bot er harme hem he wolde in haste of his yre,
He wayned hem a warnyng þat wonder hem þoȝt.　　　　1504

Nov is alle þis guere geten glotounes to serue,
Stad in a ryche stal, and stared ful bryȝt.
Baltaȝar in a brayd: 'Bede vus þerof!
Weȝe wyn in þis won! Wassayl!' he cryes.　　　　1508

Swyfte swaynes ful swyþe swepen þertylle,
Kyppe kowpes in honde kyngeȝ to serue;
In bryȝt bolleȝ ful bayn birlen þise oþer,
And vche mon for his mayster machches alone.　　　　f. 78a

Þer watȝ rynging on ryȝt of ryche metalles
Quen renkkes in þat ryche rok rennen hit to cache;
Clatering of couacleȝ þat kesten þo burdes
As sonet out of sauteray songe als myry.　　　　1516

Þen þe dotel on dece drank þat he myȝt,
And þenne arn dressed dukeȝ and prynces,
Concubines and knyȝtes, bi cause of þat merthe;
As vchon hade hym in helde, he haled of þe cuppe.　　　　1520

So long likked þise lordes þise lykores swete,
And gloryed on her falce goddes and her grace calles,
Þat were of stokkes and stones, stille euermore;
Neuer steuen hem astel, so stoken is hor tonge.　　　　1524

Alle þe goude golden goddes þe gauleȝ ȝet neuenen,
Belfagor, and Belyal, and Belssabub als,
Heyred hem as hyȝly as heuen wer þayres;
Bot hym þat alle goudes giues, þat God þay forȝeten.　　　　1528

For þer a ferly bifel þat fele folk seȝen;
Fyrst knew hit þe kyng, and alle þe cort after;
In þe palays pryncipale, vpon þe playn wowe,
In contrary of þe candelstik, þat clerest hit schyned,　　　　1532

1506 MS bryȝtȝ　　　　　　1515 MS clat + er abbrev. + iȝ
1516 MS sau + er abbrev. + ay　　1524 MS is

Þer apered a paume, with poyntel in fyngres,
Þat watȝ grysly and gret, and grymly he wrytes;
Non oþer forme bot a fust faylande þe wryste
Pared on þe parget, purtrayed lettres.   1536

When þat bolde Baltaȝar blusched to þat neue,
Such a dasande drede dusched to his hert
Þat al falewed his face and fayled þe chere;
Þe stronge strok of þe stonde strayned his ioyntes.   1540

His cnes cachches to close and cluchches his hommes,
And he with plattyng his paumes displayes his leres,
And romyes as a rad ryth þat roreȝ for drede,
Ay biholdand þe honde til hit hade al grauen,
And rasped on þe roȝ woȝe runisch saueȝ.   1545

When hit þe scrypture hade scraped wyth a scrof penne,
As a coltour in clay cerues þo forȝes,
Þenne hit vanist verayly and voyded of syȝt;   f. 78b
Bot þe lettres bileued ful large vpon plaster.   1549

Sone so þe kynge for his care carping myȝt wynne,
He bede his burnes boȝ to þat wer bok-lered,
To wayte þe wryt þat hit wolde, and wyter hym to say:
'For al hit frayes my flesche, þe fyngres so grymme.'   1553

Scoleres skelten þeratte þe skyl for-to fynde,
Bot þer watȝ neuer on so wyse couþe on worde rede,
Ne what ledisch lore ne langage nauþer,
What typyng ne tale, tokened þo draȝtes.   1557

Þenne þe bolde Baltaȝar bred ner wode,
And bede þe cete to seche segges þurȝout
Þat wer wyse of wychecrafte, and warlaȝes oþer
Þat con dele wyth demerlayk and deuine lettres.   1561

'Calle hem alle to my cort, þo Calde clerkkes,
Vnfolde hem alle þis ferly þat is bifallen here,
And calle wyth a hiȝe cry: "He þat þe kyng wysses
In expounyng of speche þat spredes in þise lettres,   1565

And makes þe mater to malt my mynde wythinne,
Þat I may wyterly wyt what þat wryt menes,
He schal be gered ful gaye in gounes of porpre,
And a coler of cler golde clos vmbe his þrote.   1569

1542 *MS* leŕs   1546 *MS* strof   1559 *MS* ede
1566 *MS* make

He schal be prymate and prynce of pure clergye,
And of my þreuenest lordeȝ þe þrydde he schal,
And of my reme þe rychest to ryde wyth myseluen,
Outtaken bare two, and þenne he þe þrydde." '   1573

Þis cry watȝ vpcaste, and þer comen mony
Clerkes out of Caldye þat kennest wer knauen,
As þe sage sathrapas þat sorsory couþe;
Wycheȝ and walkyries wonnen to þat sale,   1577

Deuinores of demorlaykes þat dremes cowþe rede,
Sorsers of exorsismus, and fele such clerkes.
And alle þat loked on þat letter, as lewed þay were
As þay had loked in þe leþer of my lyft bote.   1581

Þenne cryes þe kyng and kerues his wedes;
What! he corsed his clerkes and calde hem chorles;
To henge þe harlotes he heȝed ful ofte;   f. 79a
So watȝ þe wyȝe wytles he wed wel ner.   1585

Ho herde hym chyde to þe chambre þat watȝ þe chef quene;
When ho watȝ wytered bi wyȝes what watȝ þe cause,
Suche a chaungande chaunce in þe chef halle,   1588
Þe lady, to lauce þat los þat þe lorde hade,
Glydes doun by þe grece and gos to þe kyng.

Ho kneles on þe colde erþe and carpes to hymseluen
Wordes of worchyp wyth a wys speche: 1592

'Kene kyng,' quoþ þe quene, 'kayser of vrþe,
Euer laste þy lyf in lenþe of dayes!
Why hatȝ þou rended þy robe for redles hereinne,
Þaȝ þose ledes ben lewed lettres to rede,   1596

And hatȝ a haþel in þy holde, as I haf herde ofte,
Þat hatȝ þe gostes of God þat gyes alle soþes?
His sawle is ful of syence saȝes to schawe,
To open vch a hide þyng of aunteres vncowþe.   1600

Þat is he þat ful ofte hatȝ heuened þy fader
Of mony anger ful hote with his holy speche;
When Nabugodenoȝar watȝ nyed in stoundes,
He devysed his dremes to þe dere trawþe.   1604

He keuered hym with his counsayl of caytyf wyrdes;
Alle þat he spured hym in space he expowned clene,
Þurȝ þe sped of þe spyryt þat sprad hym withinne
Of þe godelest goddeȝ þat gaynes aywhere.   1608

1579 of, MS &   1593 a of kayser apparently altered from y

For his depe diuinite and his dere sawes,
Þy bolde fader Baltaȝar bede by his name,
Þat now is demed Danyel of derne coninges,
Þat caȝt watȝ in þe captyuide in cuntre of Iues.   1612

Nabuȝardan .hym nome, and now is he here,
A prophete of þat prouince and pryce of þe worlde.
Sende into þe cete to seche hym bylyue,
And wynne hym with þe worchyp to wayne þe bote;   1616

And þaȝ þe mater be merk þat merked is ȝender,
He schal declar hit also as hit on clay standes.'
Þat gode counseyl at þe quene watȝ cached as swyþe;
Þe burne byfore Baltaȝar watȝ broȝt in a whyle.   f. 79b

When he com bifore þe kyng and clanly had halsed,
Baltaȝar vmbebrayde hym, and 'Leue sir,' he sayde,
'Hit is tolde me bi tulkes þat þou trwe were
Profete of þat prouynce þat prayed my fader,   1624

Ande þat þou hatȝ in þy hert holy connyng,
Of sapyence þi sawle ful, soþes to schawe;
Goddes gost is þe geuen þat gyes alle þynges,
And þou vnhyles vch hidde þat heuen-kyng myntes.   1628

And here is a ferly byfallen, and I fayn wolde
Wyt þe wytte of þe wryt þat on þe wowe clyues,
For alle Calde clerkes han cowwardely fayled.
If þou with quayntyse conquere hit, I quyte þe þy mede.   1632

For if þou redes hit by ryȝt and hit to resoun brynges,
Fyrst telle me þe tyxte of þe tede lettres,
And syþen þe mater of þe mode mene me þerafter,
And I schal halde þe þe hest þat I þe hyȝt haue,   1636

Apyke þe in porpre cloþe, palle alþer-fynest,
And þe byȝe of bryȝt golde abowte þyn nekke;
And þe þryd þryuenest þat þrynges me after,
Þou schal be baroun vpon benche, bede I þe no lasse.'   1640

Derfly þenne Danyel deles þyse wordes:
'Ryche kyng of þis rengne, rede þe oure lorde!
Hit is surely soth, þe souerayn of heuen
Fylsened euer þy fader and vpon folde cheryched,   1644

1618 *MS* stande   1619 *MS* as as
1621 s *of* halsed *altered from some other letter, perhaps* ȝ

Gart hym grattest to be of gouernores alle,
And alle þe worlde in his wylle, welde as hym lykes.
Who-so wolde wel do, wel hym bityde,
And quos deth so he deȝyre, he dreped als fast;　　　1648

Who-so hym lyked to lyft, on lofte watȝ he sone,
And quo-so hym lyked to lay, watȝ loȝed bylyue.
So watȝ noted þe note of Nabugodenoȝar;
Styfly stabled þe rengne, bi þe stronge dryȝtyn.　　　1652

For of þe hyȝest he hade a hope in his hert
Þat vche pouer past out of þat prynce euen;
And whyle þat watȝ cleȝt clos in his hert,
Þere watȝ no mon vpon molde of myȝt as hymseluen.　　　1656

Til hit bitide on a tyme towched hym pryde,　　　f. 80a
For his lordeschyp so large and his lyf ryche;
He hade so huge an insyȝt to his aune dedes
Þat þe power of þe hyȝe prynce he purely forȝetes.　　　1660

Þenne blynnes he not of blasfemy, on to blame þe dryȝtyn;
His myȝt mete to Goddes he made with his wordes:
"I am god of þe grounde, to gye as me lykes,
As he þat hyȝe is in heuen, his aungeles þat weldes.　　　1664

If he hatȝ formed þe folde and folk þervpone,
I haf bigged Babiloyne, burȝ alþer-rychest,
Stabled þerinne vche a ston in strenkþe of myn armes;
Moȝt neuer myȝt bot myn make such anoþer."　　　1668

Watȝ not þis ilke worde wonnen of his mowþe
Er þenne þe souerayn saȝe souned in his eres:
"Now, Nabugodenoȝar, innoȝe hatȝ spoken.
Now is alle þy pryncipalte past at ones,　　　1672

And þou, remued fro monnes sunes, on mor most abide,
And in wasturne walk, and wyth þe wyldc dowelle,
As best byte on þe bent of braken and erbes,
With wroþe wolfes to won, and wyth wylde asses."　　　1676

Inmydde þe poynt of his pryde departed he þere
Fro þe soly of his solempnete—his solace he leues,
And carfully is outkast to contre vnknawen,
Fer into a fyr fryth þere frekes neuer comen.　　　1680

1649 watȝ *from u.-v.*　　　1650 loȝed *from u.-v.*
1654 of þat prynce euen *from u.-v.*
1664 þat weldes *touched up and corrected by second hand; original* e *visible by*
u.-v. under superscript t *of* þᵗ
1669 mowþe *followed by* one *in second hand*

His hert heldet vnhole, he hoped non oþer
Bot a best þat he be, a bol oþer an oxe;
He fares forth on alle faure, fogge watȝ his mete,
And ete ay as a horce when erbes were fallen.   1684

Þus he countes hym a kow, þat watȝ a kyng ryche,
Quyle seuen syþeȝ were ouerseyed someres, I trawe.
By þat mony þik thyȝe þryȝt vmbe his lyre,
Þat alle watȝ dubbed and dyȝt in þe dew of heuen;   1688

Faxe fyltered and felt flosed hym vmbe,
Þat schad fro his schulderes to his schyre-wykes,
And twentyfolde twynande hit to his tos raȝt,
Þer mony clyuy as clyde hit clyȝt togeder.   1692

His berde ibrad alle his brest to þe bare vrþe,
His browes bresed as breres aboute his brode chekes;   f. 80b
Holȝe were his yȝen and vnder campe hores,
And al watȝ gray as þe glede, with ful grymme clawes,   1696

Þat were croked and kene as þe kyte paume.
Erne-hwed he watȝ and al ouerbrawden,
Til he wyst ful wel who wroȝt alle myȝtes,
And cowþe vche kyndam tokerue and keuer when hym lyked.   1700

Þenne he wayned hym his wyt þat hade wo soffered,
Þat he com to knawlach and kenned hymseluen.
Þenne he loued þat lorde, and leued in trawþe
Hit watȝ non oþer þen he þat hade al in honde.   1704

Þenne sone watȝ he sende agayn, his sete restored;
His barounes boȝed hym to, blyþe of his come;
Haȝerly in his aune hwe his heued watȝ couered,
And so ȝeply watȝ ȝarked and ȝolden his state.   1708

Bot þou, Baltaȝar, his barne and his bolde ayre,
Seȝ þese syngnes with syȝt and set hem at lyttel,
Bot ay hatȝ hofen þy hert agaynes þe hyȝe dryȝtyn,
With bobaunce and with blasfamye bost at hym kest,   1712

And now his vessayles avyled in vanyte vnclene,
Þat in his hows hym to honour were heuened of fyrst.
Bifore þe barounȝ hatȝ hom broȝt, and byrled þerinne
Wale wyne to þy wenches in waryed stoundes.   1716

1690 First e of schulderes *has vertical stroke through it*; r *touched up and obscured*
1696 *MS* clawres   1697 *MS* pa + 4 *minims* + e
1703 o *of* loued *apparently altered from* e   1711 *MS* dryȝtn

Bifore þy borde hatȝ þou broȝt beuerage in þede
Þat blyþely were fyrst blest with bischopes hondes,
Louande þeron lese goddeȝ þat lyf haden neuer,
Made of stokkes and stoneȝ þat neuer styry moȝt.   1720

And for þat froþande fylþe, þe fader of heuen
Hatȝ sende into þis sale þise syȝtes vncowþe,
Þe fyste with þe fyngeres þat flayed þi hert,
Þat rasped renyschly þe woȝe with þe roȝ penne.   1724

Þise ar þe wordes here wryten, withoute werk more,
By vch fygure as I fynde, as oure fader lykes:
Mane, techal, phares, merked in þrynne,
Þat þretes þe of þyn vnþryfte vpon þre wyse.   1728

Now expowne þe þis speche spedly I þenk:
Mane menes als much as maynful Gode   f. 81a
Hatȝ counted þy kyndam bi a clene noumbre,
And fulfylled hit in fayth to þe fyrre ende.   1732

To teche þe of techal, þat terme þus menes:
Þy wale rengne is walt in weȝtes to heng,
And is funde ful fewe of hit fayth dedes;
And phares folȝes for þose fawtes, to frayst þe trawþe.   1736

In phares fynde I for soþe þise felle saȝes:
Departed is þy pryncipalte, depryued þou worþes;
Þy rengne rafte is þe fro and raȝt þe is Perses;
Þe Medes schal be maysteres here, and þou of menske schowued.'   1740

Þe kyng comaunded anon to cleþe þat wyse
In frokkes of fyn cloþ, as forward hit asked;
Þenne sone watȝ Danyel dubbed in ful dere porpor,
And a coler of cler golde kest vmbe his swyre.   1744

Þen watȝ demed a decre bi þe duk seluen;
Bolde Baltaȝar bed þat hym bowe schulde
Þe comynes al of Calde þat to þe kyng longed,
As to þe prynce pryuyest preued þe þrydde,   1748

Heȝest of alle oþer, saf onelych tweyne,
To boȝ after Baltaȝar in borȝe and in felde.
Þys watȝ cryed and knawen in cort als fast,
And alle þe folk þerof fayn þat folȝed hym tylle.   1752

1722 *MS* hatȝ sende hatȝ sende   1744 *MS* cloler
1746 *MS* baltaȝa

Bot how-so Danyel watȝ dyȝt, þat day ouerȝede;
Nyȝt neȝed ryȝt now with nyes fol mony;
For daȝed neuer anoþer day þat ilk derk after,
Er dalt were þat ilk dome þat Danyel deuysed.   1756

Þe solace of þe solempnete in þat sale dured,
Of þat farand fest, tyl fayled þe sunne.
Þenne blykned þe ble of þe bryȝt skwes,
Mourkenes þe mery weder, and þe myst dryues;   1760

Þorȝ þe lyst of þe lyfte, bi þe loȝ medoes,
Vche haþel to his home hyȝes ful fast,
Seten at her soper and songen þerafter;
Þen foundeȝ vch a felaȝschyp fyrre at forþ naȝtes.   1764

Baltaȝar to his bedd with blysse watȝ caryed;
Reche þe rest as hym lyst, he ros neuer þerafter;   f. 81b
For his foes in þe felde, in flokkes ful grete,
Þat longe hade layted þat lede, his londes to strye,   1768

Now ar þay sodenly assembled at þe self tyme;
Of hem wyst no wyȝe þat in þat won dowelled.
Hit watȝ þe dere Daryus, þe duk of þise Medes,
Þe prowde prynce of Perce, and Porros of Ynde,   1772

With mony a legioun ful large, with ledes of armes,
Þat now hatȝ spyed a space to spoyle Caldeeȝ.
Þay þrongen þeder in þe þester on þrawen hepes,
Asscaped ouer þe skyre watteres and scaled þe walles,   1776

Lyfte laddres ful longe and vpon lofte wonen,
Stelen stylly þe toun er any steuen rysed.
Withinne an oure of þe niyȝt an entre þay hade,
Ȝet afrayed þay no freke—fyrre þay passen,   1780

And to þe palays pryncipal þay aproched ful stylle.
Þenne ran þay in on a res, on rowtes ful grete;
Blastes out of bryȝt brasse brestes so hyȝe,
Ascry scarred on þe scue, þat scomfyted mony.   1784

Segges slepande were slayne er þay slyppe myȝt;
Vche hous heyred watȝ withinne a honde-whyle.
Baltaȝar in his bed watȝ beten to deþe,
Þat boþe his blod and his brayn blende on þe cloþes.   1788

The kyng in his cortyn watȝ kaȝt bi þe heles,
Feryed out bi þe fete and fowle dispysed,
Þat watȝ so doȝty þat day and drank of þe vessayl;
Now is a dogge also dere þat in a dych lygges.   1792

1756 el *of* Danyel *interlined in second hand*   1776 *MS* scaþed

For þe mayster of þyse Medes on þe morne ryses,
Dere Daryous þat day, dyȝt vpon trone;
Þat cete seses ful sounde, and saȝtlyng makes
Wyth alle þe barounȝ þeraboute, þat bowed hym after.   1796

And þus watȝ þat londe lost for þe lordes synne,
And þe fylþe of þe freke þat defowled hade
Þe ornementes of Goddeȝ hous þat holy were maked.
He watȝ corsed for his vnclannes and cached þerinne,   1800

Done doun of his dyngnete for dedeȝ vnfayre,
And of þyse worldes worchyp wrast out for euer,   f. 82a
And ȝet of lykynges on lofte letted, I trowe;
To loke on oure lofly lorde late bitydes.   1804

Þus vpon þrynne weyss I haf yow þro schewed
Þat vnclannes tocleues in corage dere
Of þat wynnelych lorde þat wonyes in heuen,
Entyses hym to be tene, telled vp his wrake.   1808

Ande clannes is his comfort, and coyntyse he louyes,
And þose þat seme arn and swete schyn se his face.
Þat we gon gay in oure gere þat grace he vus sende,
Þat we may serue in his syȝt þer solace neuer blynneȝ.   1812

Amen.

1–4 'He who was able to praise cleanness appropriately, and reckon up all the justifications that are hers as of right, might expect to find excellent examples to further his discourse, and in doing the contrary [i.e. denigrating cleanness] great trouble and difficulty'.

1 **kyndly.** The main sense appears to be 'appropriately, fittingly', but 'by his nature' and 'courteously' ('Cleanness' is a lady) may also apply.

2 **ho.** There is a widespread medieval tradition of personifying moral virtues as ladies. Cf. *Pat.* 30, where the virtues of the Beatitudes, including 'miry Clannesse', are 'Þyse ladyes'.

10 **rychen.** Edd. print *rechen*, but the second letter, obscured by a smudge, is more like *y* than *e*. If *rychen* is correct, an appropriate sense would be that found in *GGK* 2206: 'Þat gere, as I trowe, / Is rychèd ['prepared'] at Þe reuerence me, renk, to mete'.

15–16 'Then they (themselves) are sinful, and both God and His vessels are utterly defiled, and they drive Him to anger'; *ar* is taken with *sulped* as well as with *synful* (cf. Thomas, *MLR* XVII. 64). The priests defile the sacrament, and hence God Himself. *Gere* is vague, but may mean simply the vessels used in administering the sacrament (the word is used of God's vessels in line 1505). The idea that priests in particular need to be spiritually clean, because they serve at God's table, is a contemporary commonplace; see e.g. *The Book of Vices and Virtues* (EETS OS 217), p. 261. Menner solves the syntactical difficulty by emending *Boþe* to *Loþe* and taking *sulped* to refer to the priests; he translates: '. . . they hate God and all that pertains to him'. But the poet's point seems to be not that the priests hate God, but that they are hateful to God. Gollancz emends *sulped* to *sulpen*.

17–18 *Clene (in)* and *honeste (in)* may have the sense 'scrupulous (with respect to)' as well as 'clean (in, amongst)'; the meaning of the lines seems to be that God is both clean in Himself and insists on cleanness in those around Him.

23 The *carp* is the Sermon on the Mount, especially the Beatitudes. Cf. *Pat.* 9–28, where all eight of the Beatitudes are quoted, closely paraphrasing Matt. v. 3–10.

24 Cf. *Pat.* 11: 'A3t happes he hem hy3t, and vcheon a mede'.

27–8 The sixth beatitude; Matt. v. 8 has: 'Beati mundo corde quoniam ipsi Deum videbunt'. The translation in *Pat.* 23–4 is: 'Þay ar happen also þat arn of hert clene, / For þay her sauyour in sete schal se with her y3en'.

28 **loue.** Probably a variant of *lo3(e)*, *lowe* 'low'; the spelling is unusual for this MS, but cf. e.g. *louyly* 'lawful', *Pearl* 565, beside usual spellings *lawe*, *laghe*, etc. (*laue* in *Cl.* 723). *MED* s. loue adj., sense 5d.(a) gives another instance of the phrase *with a low chere* 'with humble bearing' (*Dest. Troy* 1778), also 'of louh chere'.

29–32 'That is to say that the man who has any uncleanness on him, anywhere about him, shall never come to that sight; for He who drives all filth far from his heart may not endure the shock of its coming near His person', lit. '. . . may not endure the shock, that it [filth] should come near His person'.

29 **as so sayt3.** This unique phrase is explained by S. Nevanlinna (*Neuphilologische Mitteilungen* LXXV. 584) as a corruption of the common 'as who saith'; but the *so*, rather than being a corruption of *who*, may be from ON phrases of the type *þat segir svá*.

32 **ne3e.** MS *ne3en*, with the *n* probably picked up from *vnwaschen* two lines further on.

40 **trasche3.** Probably 'old shoes', as suggested by *OED* s. Trash, *sb.* The first example of trash in *OED*, apart from this instance, is from Skelton, *c.* 1518, in the sense 'rubbish'. But *trash* 'old, worn-out boot, shoe, or slipper' is well attested in the modern dialects of the East Lancashire, West Yorkshire, and Cheshire area; see *EDD* s. trash, *v.* and *sb.*, sense 9, and trasher, *sb.* and *v.* The participial adjective *clout(ed)* 'patched' is used regularly of shoes in ME., as in the quotation from the *Paston Letters* in *MED* (s. clouten v., sense 1): 'Her bald batts and her clot schon'.

42 **halden vtter.** The appropriate sense 'thrown out' belongs to ME *helden*, not (as edd.) *holden; helden out* 'throw out' (water, ashes etc.) is common. Forms of the past tense and past participle often show confusion with *holden;* see *MED* s. helden v.

48 W. W. Skeat, *Notes on English Etymology* (Oxford, 1901), p. 289, explains: '"in tale or in touch", i.e. by word or deed', and his explanation is accepted by Menner and Gollancz. But there is no warrant for his sense of *touch*, and in any event the context seems to require a reference to garments. *Talle*, OF *ta(i)lle*, regularly means 'bodily appearance, shape', as in *Cursor M* 11855: 'Yee se he has na mans taill [*var.* tale]'. *Towch* in its three occurrences as a noun in *GGK* appears to have the basic meaning 'small part, detail' (of something larger); thus 'burst of music' (*GGK* 120), 'allusion' (*GGK* 1301), 'term of an agreement' (*GGK* 1677). The sense of *Cl.* 48 may therefore be: 'though he should never again offend either in general appearance or in detail of dress'.

50 **heuen.** MS *her euen;* perhaps the scribe was confused by the *here* two lines further on.

51 **As Maþew mele3 in his masse.** The reference is to Matt. XXII. 1–14 (but the poet also uses Luke XIV. 16–24). Cf. *Pearl* 497–8: 'As Mathew mele3 in your messe / In sothful gospel of God almy3t', and *Pat.* 9–10: 'I herde on a halyday, at a hy3e masse, / How Mathew melede þat his mayster his meyny con teche.' In *Pearl*, and particularly in *Cl.*, *masse* seems to have developed the meaning 'gospel read at mass'.

53 **þat þay samne schulde** 'that men should assemble', apparently a rare indefinite use of *þay* (Mustanoja, pp. 225–6). Cf. Luke XIV. 17: 'dicere invitatis ut venirent'.

55 **bayted** 'baited (by dogs)' in order to improve the flavour of the meat by forcing the animals to exert themselves. The practice is attested, usually for bulls but also for boars, from the fourteenth to the late seventeenth century; see Luttrell, *N & Q* CXCVII. 23–4, and F. C. Morgan, *N & Q* CXCVII. 107.

56 **fatted with scla3t** 'fattened for slaughter'. *With* is apparently used adversatively, in the sense 'in anticipation of', in the same way as *against* (*MED* s. ayen(e)s prep., sense 8. (a)).

59 **ro þeled.** Obscure; the form occurs again in line 890, and also in *Parlement of the Thre Ages* 261 (EETS OS 246): 'Then this renke alle in rosett rothelede [*var.* ratild] thies wordes'. The three contexts require three different meanings, and at least two separate verbs may be involved. For *Cl.* 59, Gollancz compares modern dialect *rozzle* 'heat, warm, scorch' (*EDD* s. rozzle, *v.*), which is probably based ultimately on L *russus* 'red' (another meaning of the modern dialect word is 'redden by drink'). *Ro þeled* may be a parallel formation based on ON *rjóðr*, OE *rēod*, ultimately L *rūfus* 'red'. For line 890, the sense of ON *riðlask* 'rock, waver, reel to and fro' would be appropriate; if the word in *Parlement of the Thre Ages* is the same, the sense there might be 'speak wildly'.

ry3t to þe sete 'ready for men to sit down', lit. 'right to the sitting down (at table)'; cf. *OED* s. Seat, *sb.*, sense 1: 'The action of sitting. Also an assembly at a banquet'. Menner and Gollancz take *sete* as a unique substantival use of the adjective *sete* 'fitting, excellent'. Menner translates the phrase as 'appetizingly', Gollancz as 'right to the proper point'.

61 **þat þider com schulde.** I.e. '(those) who were invited'.

62 **Alle** is evidently thought of first as plural (*hem*), then as singular (*he*).

skyly. Probably a variant of *skill* in the sense 'reason' (*OED* s. Skill, *sb.*¹, sense 3.b.), hence 'pretext, excuse'. Luttrell (*Neophil.* xl. 297) draws attention to the form *skely* in the Dublin MS of *Wars Alex.* 1575: *Scopulus, be some skely þe scriptur it calls* 'the scripture calls it Scopulus, for some reason'. The Ashmole MS has *skill* instead of *skely*. The variant form may be based on ON *skilja*, or it may simply have *y* for *e* (Gollancz).

63 **bor3** is instead of *toun* (line 64, and Wyclif), translating *villam* in Luke XIV. 18 (cf. the Authorised Version's 'piece of ground'). *Toun* is Wyclif's usual word for L. *villa*. The sense 'property, estate' covers both *bor3* and *toun* in the poem.

66 **3at.** Apparently unparalleled as a past participle of *geten* 'get', although *gat* is common as a past tense form in ME. *3at* here and *3ete* 842 have initial palatal consonant (from OE) for the alliteration.

69 **wer hym** 'defended himself', hence 'excused himself', from OE *werian*, reflexive uses of which are common in OE and ME. There are other instances of strong past tense forms of this verb in later ME, and cf. the past tense form *wer* (OE *werian* 'wear') in *Pearl* 205.

71 **droȝ hem adreȝ** 'drew back', a common alliterating phrase. See *MED* s. dri(e n. (2), sense 3. (a).

73 **ludych.** The usual definition of this word is 'of a land, of a people'; see e.g. *MED* s. ledish adj. (2). This is certainly the meaning in line 1556, but possibly the word sometimes has a more general sense as a commendatory epithet. *MED* notes that the Otho MS of Laȝamon has 'Gwennaifer þe leodisse cwene' where the earlier Caligula MS has 'wuneliche cwene'. The sense 'princely, noble' would suit the contexts in *Cl.* 73, 1375; the noun *lede* can mean 'prince' (OE *lēod* m.) as well as 'people' (OE *lēod* f., *lēode* pl.).

76 **wylle gentyl** 'gentile wilfulness' (*OED* s. Will, *sb.*¹, sense 9). The wilfulness of those who have refused the invitation is the more to blame in that they are God's people.

77 **streeteȝ** 'roads, highways' outside the city (Matt. XXII. 9: 'exitus viarum') rather than 'streets' in the city (Luke XIV. 21: 'plateas et vicos civitatis'); this part of the parable (lines 73–84) is based more on Matthew than Luke, and in any event certain details in the poem (*wayferande frekeȝ* 79, *by bonkeȝ* 86) suggest the countryside rather than the town.

78 **forsetteȝ.** Edd., *OED*, and *MED* take *þe cete* as object (Menner glosses 'beset', Gollancz 'surround'), but it gives slightly easier sense to take *þe wayferande frekeȝ* as object: 'and waylay travellers on every side of the city'.

79 **on fote and on hors.** This formula sometimes implies a contrast between the poor and the well-off, as it probably does here. But it is often used without any such implication; cf. 'ryde oþer renne' meaning simply 'go' in *Pat.* 52.

83 'So that every part of my palace will be filled to overflowing'.
    platful. So MS; edd. read *plat ful* (*plat* 'quite'), but cf. MS *stafful* 'cram-full', *GGK* 494.
    pyȝt. For the sense, cf. *OED* s. Pitch, *v.*¹, sense 9.a., where two instances from ME and early MnE are given of the phrase 'pitched full of' meaning 'filled full of'.

85 'Then they went to and fro, rousing the countryside', lit. '... those who roused the countryside'. Elsewhere in ME *cayred and com* is a formula for 'went', as in *kayred and com (to)*, also *caryed and com (to, out of)* in *St Robert of Knaresborough* (*MED* s. cairen v. and carien v.). But Menner is probably right to see an opposition between *cayred* 'went' and *com* 'came' in the phrase used absolutely, as here. Menner translates *þat þe cost waked* as 'those who guarded the country'.

92 'A man's place at table being assigned him according to his rank'.

96 **renischche.** This word, which is peculiar to ME alliterative poetry, remains obscure in spite of much discussion. The first vowel is spelt *u* (*runisch* 1545) as well as *e*, perhaps also *oy*, if *roynyshe* in *St Erkenwald* 52 is the same word. The range of meanings implied by the contexts is 'strange, outlandish, rough'. From the semantic point of view H. L. Savage's suggestion (*St*

Erkenwald, Yale, 1926, note to line 52) of a connection with OE (*ge*)*rȳne* (also *rūn*) 'mystery, dark saying' is promising; a sense-development from 'mysterious, strange' to 'outlandish, rough' is readily understandable, and is found in OE *uncūþ*. Several of the instances of the ME. word which are usually glossed 'rough, fierce' also imply outlandishness; e.g. *GGK* 304, 432, 457, where the word is applied to the behaviour of the Green Knight, and *Pat.* 191, where the sailors, of outlandish race and religion, speak 'runyschly' to Jonah. With reference to the *runisch sauez* of *Cl.* 1545, it is worth noting that in OE *gerȳne* and *rūn* are used specifically of the writing on the wall at Belshazzar's feast (BT s. *ge-rȳne*, and *rūn*, sense IV). ME forms in *e* may go back to OE *gerēne* beside *gerȳne*.

98 **Ferre.** Gollancz emends to *Ferkez*, taking it that the scribe has mistakenly repeated a word; but the repetition is perfectly possible, and cf. *fer* and *fyr* used close together in line 1680. The double *r* may indicate the comparative, as in *ferre* in the previous line, but the form *ferre* has positive sense in *GGK* 1093.

106 **denounced** 'proclaimed' (Gollancz), hence 'borne witness to, acknowledged', perhaps 'honoured'. The sense-development can be paralleled in OF, though not in ME; cf. 'Aouret l'ont et denonciet', with reference to the three kings adoring the infant Jesus (quoted by TL s. denoncier *vb.*).

110 'And they carried out the task, making proclamation as he had ordained', lit. '... those who made proclamation ...'; see *OED* s. Deem, *v.*, sense 10. The construction is like that of line 85, which is concerned with the servants' first foray. Morris and Menner supply *is* after *þat*, Gollancz supplies *watz*.

112 The import is probably merely that they were not all of one family, i.e. they were many and varied.

116 **biloogh** 'below', i.e. below the high dais. This is the first recorded occurrence of the word. The form looks odd, but cf. *loghe* 'low', *GGK* 1373; *oo* is used to indicate a long vowel (see p. 109).

117 'And each man looked dignified in his dress'.

ay a 'each' (Menner), the primary sense of *ay* here being 'in each instance'. There is a similar use of *ay* in *GGK* 128: 'Ay two had disches twelue'. *Her* later in the line should strictly be *his*, but the plural is not uncommon in ME after a singular indefinite subject containing a plural idea, as with *vch-on* in lines 497–8.

soberly. Menner tries to justify MS *soerly* as an adjective from ON *saurligr* 'unclean', comparing *sorze* 'filth' in line 846 and *Pat.* 275. But, apart from the difficulty of the form, such an interpretation runs counter to the general drift of these lines, which is that the wedding guests, whether high-born or low-born, are all respectable, in contrast to the one guest who is singled out for rebuke later. Menner objects that *soberly* is not recorded as an adjective, but *-ly* is of course a usual adjectival termination, and cf. Chaucer's *General Prologue* (*Cant. Tales* I. 289): 'A clerk ther was ... looked holwe, and therto sobrely'. Gollancz, following Emerson (*PMLA*

XXXIV. 496) emends more extensively to *& ay as segges seerly* ('severally').

119–20 'Well-bred men in that company were by no means neglected, and yet the most lowly man in the hall was served unstintingly'.

119   **forknowen** 'neglected' (Gollancz), a unique sense; the *for-* prefix is here understood to imply 'the notion of passing by, abstaining from, or neglecting' (*OED* s. For-, *pref.*¹, sense 3), as in e.g. ME *forheden* 'fail to heed, neglect'. Menner glosses 'recognise, perceive', another unique sense, and one which is not so apposite in context, for the company is made up of men of high as well as of low rank (line 115, etc.).

127   **pouer.** MS *poueu* + *er* abbrev. The scribe has repeated the sequence *ue*, a common kind of error in this MS. Emerson (*MLR* XXXIV. 497) compares the form *pouer* in *Pearl* 1075.

134–6 '(That) there was a fellow not properly dressed for a festival, poorly clothed in the midst of the throng; (he wore) no festive garment, but (one) stained by labours'.

134   **hit watȝ.** For the meaning 'there was' see quotations in *MED* s. hit pron., sense 4b.(b), e.g. *GGK* 1251: 'Bot hit ar ladyes innoȝe'.

136   **werkkeȝ** 'labour(s)', also 'evil deeds, sins'.

143   The usual phrase is *ben hardy to*+infin., and edd. supply *to* before *neȝe*. But a usage without *to*, by analogy with *dare*, is understandable.

145   **vngoderly.** A form found also in line 1092, but apparently nowhere else in ME. The sense 'bad, vile', suggested by the contexts, is that of ME *ungoodly*, of which it may be a variant. Emerson (*PMLA* XXXIV. 510) and Menner compare the form *goder* (OE *gōdre*, f. dat.), found in the common ME phrase *goder hele* 'fortunately'.

146   'You set a very poor and meagre value on me and my house'. Edd. emend MS *nede* to *gnede* (OE *gnēd-, gnēþe* 'niggardly'), but *nede* is found elsewhere as an adjective with sense close to that required here; cf. *Cursor M* (Trinity MS) 2448: *her pasture þo wex al nede* 'then their pasture grew very scanty'. For the use of *praysed* with an adjective, cf. the quotation from *Laud Troy Book* in *MED* s. ap(p)reisen v.: 'Here hodes ... worth michel gode thei were apraysed'. There appears to be a similar use of *vayled* in *Cl.* 1311: *þat vayled so huge*, and cf. line 1117 (note).

148   'Do you take me for a beggar, (that you expect me) to admire your garment?'

159   **gryspyng.** Gollancz emends to *gryspytyng* (OE *gristbitung*), but the shortened form is also found in Mirk's Festial; see *MED* s. grispen.

168   **sowle.** Probably the same word as *sovly* 1111, of obscure origin. There is a ME verb *sowlen* 'make dirty', which *OED* (s. Sowl, *v.*¹) relates to West Flemish *sowelen, suwelen*. Cf. ME *solwy* 'dirty' and *solwen* 'make dirty'.

172   **And lyned with þe lykyng** 'and (which you have) lined with the good disposition of your heart'. The verb (previously read as

lyued 'lived') carries on the identification of *wede3* and *werke3*, the lining of the garment corresponding to the good disposition (*lykyng*) which may not be visible but which nevertheless lies behind a man's good actions. The whole sentence moves freely between concrete and abstract meaning.

173 **Þo.** Sc. the *werke3/wede3*.

185 The infinitives are used as verbal nouns: 'and (for) misappropriating and stealing widows' dowers'.

192 **sour** 'vile'. Menner compares ON *saurr* 'filth' and regards *sour* 'bitter' 1036 as a different word (OE *sur*). But it is probable that both go back to OE *sur*, for which *OED* (s. Sour, *a.* and *sb.*[1], sense 4) gives 'extremely distasteful or disagreeable, bitter, unpleasant' as senses current in ME; so also Luttrell, *Neophil.* XXXIX. 216.

197 'But I have not yet found written down in any book . . .'.

201 **vnsoundely to weng.** I.e. 'to take drastic vengeance'.

204 **wod to þe wrache** 'furiously eager, furious, for vengeance'. Cf. La3amon (Caligula MS) 859: 'Swa wod he was to fehte'.

211 **þe tramountayne** 'the north', primarily 'the north pole-star'; no other ME instance of the word is recorded in *OED*, but *sterre Transmontane* occurs in *Mand. T* (p. 132). Satan traditionally had his seat in the north (ultimately from Isaiah XIV. 13).

215–16 'Nevertheless, His blow was in keeping with the moderation of His nature; He struck down on that occasion only the tenth part of His splendid entourage'. The poet appears to think that God would have been justified in punishing more than a tenth of His angels. The verb has to be supplied in line 215; in line 216, *Bot* is displaced from its natural position after *tynt*. The phrase *In þe mesure of his mode* occurs again in line 565.

215 **met3.** Edd. 'mildness, pity', a noun, otherwise unknown, from *mesen* v., OF *amesir* 'moderate, assuage'; the verb is used in line 764, and cf. *amesyng* 'gentleness', *Pat.* 400. *OED* (s. Mes) conjectures more plausibly that the word means 'blow', representing OF *mes* 'proper distance or range for shooting' (this is *OED*'s definition for the other English instances), also 'shot, cast, throw' (of an arrow, stone, etc.); see TL s. mes *s.m.*, col. 1561. Cf. *kest* 'blow', primarily 'cast', *GGK* 2298.

216 **tour.** Gollancz must be right in taking this as an aphetic form of OF *ato(u)r* 'entourage, retinue'. According to a well-established tradition (reflected in e.g. the OE *Genesis*) God created ten orders of angels, one of which was lost in the Fall; its place was to be taken by mankind (cf. line 240).

222 **Sweued,** if it is the correct reading, is probably best taken as *OED*'s Sweve, *v.* 'sink to rest, subside', etc., here used as an alliterative synonym for 'fall', although the latest examples in *OED* are from La3amon.

224 **forty.** In *Piers P*, B-text, I. 119 and in Milton the angels fall for nine days. The figure forty is found in the account of the fall of the angels in *Cursor M* 510, where it is stated, on the supposed

authority of Bede, that to travel from earth to Heaven would take seven thousand seven hundred years at the rate of forty miles a day.

226 **smylt.** Obscure; perhaps a participial adjective from MDu., MLG *smilten*, a variant of *smelten* 'smelt', here in the developed sense 'refined'. But this would be the earliest recorded instance of the word in English; *OED*'s first instance (in the form of the noun *smelter*) is dated 1455. For the sense, cf. that recorded for the modern verb in the dialects of Cumberland, Yorkshire, and Cheshire by *EDD* (s. Smelt, *v.* and *sb.*¹): 'Preparing lime by mixing it with water, and pouring it through a sieve, to remove impurities'. Menner conjectures an OE **smyltan*, cf. *smilting, smelting* 'amber'.

228 **worlde.** Here 'universe', equivalent to L *mundus*. Cf. the quotation from *Interlude of the Four Elements* (1519) in *OED* s. World, *sb.*, sense 9: 'The yerth as a poynt or center is sytuate / In the myddes of the worlde'.

230–1 'And yet the man [i.e. God] did not become angry, nor did the wretch make his peace, or ever wish to acknowledge his glorious God, on account of his wilfulness.'

231 **for wylnesful** 'on account of being wilful, for wilfulness'. The unique form *wylnesful* is probably best explained as an adjective formed on OE *gewilnes* 'desire' in the same way that ME *wilful* is formed on OE *will(a)* 'desire'.

233 **rape.** Edd. take this as a variant of *rappe* 'rap, blow' (probably of imitative origin), but more exact sense is given by ON *hrap* 'falling down, ruin'; the related verb *hrapa* 'fall headlong, fall in ruin' is used of Satan's fall in the Icelandic version of Luke x. 18: 'Eg sá Satan svo sem eldingu hrapa af himni'. The ME verb occurs in *GGK* in the sense 'hasten', and *rapely* 'quickly, rashly' occurs in *GGK* and *Pearl*. The noun occurs elsewhere in ME in the sense 'haste' (*OED* s. Rape, *sb.*¹).

245 **defence.** Here with the force of 'prohibited thing'; cf. the OF concrete sense 'prohibited place' (Godef. s. defens s.m.).

249 'But in the third (vengeance), everything that had life was destroyed'.

256–8 'And (they were) the most long-lived of all men. For they were the first offspring that the earth bred, sons of the noble forefather named Adam'.

260 **blysse boute blame** 'blameless pleasure', meaning especially unperverted sexual pleasure.

261 'And those who lived immediately after him [Adam] were most like him'.

264 **cors.** *Co(u)rs of kynde* 'course (or way) of nature, natural function(s)' etc. is a standard ME phrase (see *MED* s. cours n., sense 10; s. kinde n., senses 3.(a), 5a.(a), 7.(c)).

265–8 'Usque ad septimem generationem filii Seth fuerunt boni; sed postmodum viri abusi sunt viris, et mulieres mulieribus' (Higden, *Polychronicon*, ed. Babington and Lumby, vol. II, p. 230). Cf. also *Gen. and Ex.* 527–38.

267 **vsed hem** 'practised them' (the *contrare werke3* of line 266). Menner and Gollancz take the verb as reflexive, 'had sexual intercourse', although *OED* (s. Use, *v.*, sense 10.b.) gives no examples of reflexive use of the verb in this sense.

268 **oþer.** Presumably the *fende* of the next line.

269–72 Cf. *Mand. T*, p. 160: 'And that tyme the fendes of Helle camen many tymes and leyen with the wommen . . . and engendred on hem dyuerse folk, as monstres and folk disfigured . . . geauntes . . .'. The interpretation of 'filii Dei' in Gen. VI. 2 as *fendes* may go back to Augustine, who raises the possibility of such an interpretation in *De Civitate Dei*, XV. 23. The usual patristic explanation of Gen. VI. 2 (also found in Augustine) is that the 'filii Dei' are the descendants of Seth, and the 'filias hominum' the descendants of Cain.

275 **þat fe3t loued best.** Lines 274–6 expand the last part of Gen. VI. 4. Cf. *Gen. and Ex.* 546, where the giants born to the daughters of men are 'Migti men and figti'.

279 **þise oþer** 'the others', i.e. mankind, as opposed to the giants who corrupt mankind.

283–4 A close paraphrase of Gen. VI. 6: 'Et tactus dolore cordis intrinsecus'. L *dolor* can mean both 'grief' and 'anger', and both aspects are brought out by the poet: 'Fierce, distressing anger entered His heart; as one anguished inwardly He said to Himself . . .'. In his portrayal of a God with human emotions, the poet takes his lead from Genesis itself. *Werp* (*warp*) in the sense 'speak, say' usually occurs in the phrase *warp word(s)*, as in lines 152, 213, and elsewhere in the poems of the *Gawain*-group. But the verb may be used on its own in this sense, as in the quotation from Wyntoun in *OED* (s. Warp, *v.*, sense 11). Menner puts a comma after *wy3e* 284 and glosses *werp* as 'rushed', but it is not easy to make sense of this; presumably Menner intends some such translation as 'as though in a man, inner woe rushed to His heart'.

287 **al þat flesch were3.** Gen. VI. 17: 'omnem carnem'.

296 **ay glydande wyth his God.** Gen. VI. 9: 'cum Deo ambulavit'.

297 The impersonal construction with *nome* follows an OE usage: 'Brettisc cyning, þām wæs nama Natanleod' (BT Suppl. s. nama, sense 1).

304 **Is fallen forþwyth my face** 'has come before me'; Gen. VI. 13 has 'venit coram me'. The preposition *forþwyth* replaces *before* in the common phrase *before the face of* 'in front of, in the presence of' (*MED* s. façe n., sense 5.(b)). Perhaps the poet picks up *face* from the next phrase in Gen. VI. 13: 'repleta est terra iniquitate a facie eorum'.

307 **strenkle** 'sprinkle, scatter, put forth', for 'disperdam' in Gen. VI. 13 (Wyclif 'scater', later version 'distrye'). The choice of verb is suggestive, perhaps implying the power of the Flood to cleanse sin (cf. line 355), for *strenkle* (or *strinkle*) often has the specific sense 'sprinkle with holy-water'; the noun *strenkle* always means 'holy-water sprinkler'.

distresse 'power', a usual OF sense (TL s. destrece *s.f.*), and one which is probably to be found in the quotation from the Parliament Rolls in *MED* (s. distresse n., sense 1.(d.)): '[a town] destroyed and wastid be over flowing and gret distres of the Water of the Sea'; *MED* gives the meaning 'damage' here. Gollancz glosses *distresse* in the technical legal sense 'seizure of chattels', but this does not go very well with *strenkle*. Menner (evidently followed by *MED*) translates: 'I shall dispel my grief . . .', which is possible, though the meaning of *strenkle* is strained.

308 **lede3 and londe** 'people and land', for Gen. VI. 13: 'eos cum terra'.

310 **cofer** 'coffer', *kyst(e)* 'chest', and *whichche* 'chest' are all used in this section of the poem for Vulgate *arca* 'the Ark'. The words reflect the primary meaning of L *arca* 'chest, box' (for valuables etc.).

313 **endentur** 'notched jointing' (of the ship's timbers). The sense is deduced from the context and is not found elsewhere, but cf. Wyclif's *endentyngis* translating L *commissuras* 'joints' in 1 Chron. XXII. 3 (see quotation in *MED* s. endenting ger.).

316-17 'Make the width exactly fifty [cubits] across, and see to it that your Ark has a height of exactly thirty'.

318 **vponande.** MS *vpon*; the emendation is due to Gollancz, who compares *wel dutande dor* in line 320. The scribe must have been confused by the *vpon* later on in the line. Noah opens the window when he sends out the raven (line 453, following Gen. VIII. 6).

319 'Exactly a cubit square'.

322 **boske3.** This can hardly mean 'bushes' (Menner). If genuine, it may be a variant of *bos* 'cow-house' (line 1075); cf. ML *boscar* in this sense.

325 **gost of lyf.** Gen. VI. 17: 'spiritus vitae'.

328 **þou in reysoun hat3 rengned** 'you have lived by reason'; for the sense of *rengned*, cf. the quotation from Wyclif in *OED* (s. Reign, *v.*, sense 2, b.): 'Also generaly prelatis regnen in symonye'.

332 **of monne3 saule3** 'from amongst mankind', lit. 'from amongst human souls', with *saule* in the sense of 'person, being', as *ame* is commonly in OF.

333-5 Evidently a conflation of Gen. VI. 19 (cf. VII. 9, 15) and VII. 2.

342 **þat durst do non oþer** 'not daring to do otherwise'.

354-5 'A most violent storm, with heavy rain [lit. that will rain heavily], that will cleanse all the world of deeds of filth'.

363 The *abyme* is not the ocean but the depths of the earth below both land and sea, as in line 963—the poet has in mind Gen. VII. 11 (see next note). Therefore *bonke3 con ryse* is best translated as 'the land rose up', i.e. under pressure from the springs below. Cf. *Cursor M* 1767-8, based on the same verse in Genesis: 'Þe see to ris, þe erth to riue, / Þe springes cum ouer-all utedriue'.

364 **Waltes out vch walle-heued.** Cf. line 428: *Towalten alle þyse welle-hede3*. The phrases translate Gen. VII. 11: 'rupti sunt omnes fontes abyssi magnae'. Menner emends *walle-heued* to *welle-heved*,

but *walle* is a genuine variant, found in West Midland and Northern texts, and going back to OE *wælla* beside *wella*.

368 'Every cataract burst open and poured to the earth'.

rayn ryfte. Probably not 'break in rain-cloud' (edd.), but 'rain-sluice', i.e. 'cataract', for 'cataractae' in Gen. VII. 11. *OED* (s. Cataract, *sb.*, sense 1) defines the biblical word as 'the "flood-gates" of Heaven, viewed as keeping back the rain'. The word *ryfte* suggests the gaps or sluices in the flood-gates through which the water pours.

369–408 With this account of the Flood cf. the elaboration in *Cursor M* 1761–1802, which likewise emphasises, though in a more moralistic way, the terror of men and animals as they try to save themselves.

372 **þat deth moȝt dryȝe** 'subject to death'.

375 **wylger.** Obscure, but possibly a variant of *wylder*; cf. the verb *awilgeð* 'becomes wild' beside *awildeþ* in *Ancrene Wisse* (several examples in *MED* s. awilden, -ien v.).

379 Cf. MS 'þe bonk . . . wern' in *Pat.* 343–4; it appears that the poet regarded *bonk* as a possible plural form, alongside the usual *bonkeȝ*.

381 Cf. *Pat.* 220: 'Bot al watȝ nedles note'.

383–4 'Until each valley was brimful to the tops of its slopes, and all the deepest dales were overflowing at the brink', lit. '. . . that were filled up at the brink'.

385 'The greatest mountains on earth were then no longer secure'.

were. MS *watȝ* is probably on account of the singular *mor* immediately preceding; for a similar error, cf. line 449.

dryȝe 'secure', primarily 'strong, enduring', etc. Edd. take the form as a variant of *drye* 'dry', but elsewhere in *Cl.* and in the MS generally this word is always spelt *dr(u)ye*, and *dryȝ(e)* adj. always represents OI *drjúgr*.

395 **þat amounted þe mase** 'that was pointless', lit. 'that amounted to vanity', repeating the sentiment of line 381: 'al watȝ nedleȝ her note'. Edd. take *þe mase* to mean 'confusion'; thus Menner: 'so that the state of confusion increased', and Gollancz: 'So that the confusion proclaimed [i.e. was equivalent to] His mercy had passed'. But elsewhere in ME the phrase *þe mase* means 'delusion, vanity, disappointment' (*OED* s. Maze, *sb.*, sense 1). MS *þe masse þe mase* is clearly dittographic; *mase* is retained as being the usual form.

403 If this line follows the Vulgate (Gen. VII. 17), then *on folde* goes not with *faren* (as edd.) but with *styryed*.

404 **feȝtande.** Probably 'turbulent', the idea being that waves in a rough sea fight each other; cf. the quotation from Mannyng's *Chronicle* in *MED* (s. fighten v., sense 4): 'Þe se gan fighte, þe wawes ros'.

406 **hurkled.** The basic meaning of the verb is 'crouch, cower', and it is often used of animals; cf. MLG *hurken* 'squat'. In line 150 the word means 'hang down (the head)'. The present context suggests a weakened alliterative sense such as 'was set, stood'.

408 **Alle þat spyrakle inspranc** 'everything in which sprang the

breath of life'; cf. Gen. VII. 22, also Gen. II. 7: 'Formavit igitur Dominus Deus hominem de limo terrae, et inspiravit in faciem ejus spiraculum vitae'.

411 **Hym aȝtsum** 'him as one of eight, him and seven others' (acc. dat. after *saue* 409). The construction goes back to OE, which has the numeral in the genitive. The OE meaning is either 'one with a company of eight' (the commonest meaning in ME), or 'one of a company of eight', as in *Beowulf* 3123 (ed. Klaeber): 'Se ācīgde syfone . . . ēode eahta sum'. For further OE examples see BT s. sum, *indef. prn.*, sense I. (1)(b). ME has another similar usage with ordinal numerals, for which see *OED* s. Some, *indef. pron.*, sense A.3.

419 **hurrok.** Evidently a fitting, as again in *Pat.* 185; B. Sandahl (*Middle English Sea Terms*, I, Uppsala, 1951, 126–7) suggests a rudder-band. See further Anderson, *Pat.*, note to line 185.

422 **wafte.** This form occurs again in line 453, and *waft* in line 857; cf. *vpwafte* in line 949. *OED* includes the instances in line 422 and line 453 under Waive, *v.²* (ON *veifa*), but Menner more reasonably takes the infinitive as *OED* Weve, *v.¹* (OE **wǣfan*); cf., in this MS, *leue* (OE *lǣfan*), past tense *laft(e)*. As *OED* notes, *waive* and *weve* may have been identified to some extent; cf. line 453: *wafte he vpon his wyndowe*, beside *GGK* 1743: 'wayueȝ vp a wyndow'.

423 Cf. *Pat.* 147: 'hit reled on roun' (of Jonah's ship in the storm).

425–7 'To assign an exact date [for the beginning of the Flood] in terms of Noah's age: (in) the six hundredth year of his age, with none left over, (on) precisely the seventeenth day of the second month'.

427 **seuenteþe** (Gollancz); MS *seuēþe*, but Gen. VII. 11 has *septimo-decimo*.

429 The line is evidently dependent on *flowed* 428: 'And the flood (flowed) for the next one hundred and fifty days'.

431–2 Gollancz does away with *þer* 431 and emends *þer* 432 to *þat*, but it is possible to make sense of the MS as it stands by taking *þer euer flote*, etc., as dependent on *þat* 431 in the same way as *þer wonyed*, etc.: 'Everything was destroyed that lived there in the world, (that) ever swam there, or flew, or went on foot'.

433–4 'All that remained was that troubled vessel that the storm drives, in which all species were so tightly packed [lit. were brought so close together]'.

433 **roȝly.** There have been many suggestions, but elsewhere in the MS the form *roȝ* always represents 'rough', OE *rūh*. OE *hrēoh*, which largely fell in with *rūh* in ME, has an appropriate sense, 'troubled' (of the sea, the mind); see BT s. hrēoh, *adj.*, and for examples of the differentiated form in early ME see *OED* s. Reh, reȝ, rei, *a*. BT Suppl. gives one example, from Wulfstan, of an OE *hrēohlic*: 'hū hrēohlic ['troubled'] þēos woruld ys'. In *Cl.* the word may be meant to imply both the troubled movement of the Ark, and the troubled situation and thoughts of those inside it. It is used substantivally: 'troubled thing, troubled vessel'. The adjectival form *roghlych* occurs in *Pat.* 64, in the sense 'harsh'.

434 joyst. Emerson (*PMLA* XXXIV. 502), followed by *MED* (s. joissen v., sense (a)) regards this as a participial adjective meaning 'glad'. The form is right, and the participial adjective is used in this way in OF, but the sense is inappropriate; as the Ark is here described, its inmates have little to be cheerful about. Line 491 appears to contrast their misery with the joy which greets the return of the dove with the olive branch. The word is more likely to be a form of *juste* adv. in the sense 'close(ly), tight(ly)'; cf. *MED.* s. just(e adv., sense (b), and justlī adv., senses 2.(b) and (c). The *oy* spelling is unusual, and is perhaps due to the proximity of *joyned*, but it does occur, rarely, in AN, and cf. *joistise* sb. beside *justise, jostise*, etc., in Godef. s. justise.

joyned. Probably 'brought together in one place' (*MED* s. joinen v.(1), sense 7.(a)). But Gollancz's 'enjoined' (by God) is possible.

439 The line reflects Gen. VIII. 2: 'Et clausi sunt fontes abyssi, et cataractae coeli'. But the biblical order is reversed; *stangeʒ* must have *OED*'s sense 3 (s. Stank, *sb.*): 'A dam to hold back water, a weir or floodgate' (although the first instance of this sense in *OED* is dated 1604), here applied to the 'cataractae coeli' (cf. note on *rayn ryfte* 368). Wyclif translates 'fontes abyssi' as 'wellys of the see'.

440 blynne of. The *of* goes with *blynne*, not *bed*, and the sense is 'leave off, cease', as in *Ormulum* 10047-8 (ed. White): 'ʒiff þatt teʒʒ nohht ne blinnen off / To follʒhenn Godess wille'. Cf. *bed tyrue of þe hyde*, line 630. The construction *beden (bidden) of* 'ask, entreat (of)' does not appear to be employed anywhere in the poems of this MS.

441 lowkande togeder 'contracting (itself)'; cf. OE *lūcan tōgædre* in *Phoenix* 225 (ed. Blake), used of ashes contracting into a ball.

446 rasse. The word occurs again in *GGK* 1570, where the boar 'to a hole wynneʒ / Of a rasse bi a rokk þer renneʒ þe boerne'. For *Cl.*, edd. gloss 'peak, top', but give no etymology. For *GGK*, Tolkien–Gordon–Davis gloss '? ledge of rock', referring the word to OF *ras* 'level (ground)'. But OF *ras(s)e*, primarily 'ditch', is a more likely etymology; see the instances in TL s. raisse, rase *s.f.*, e.g. *Le Couronnement de Renart* 761, where Renart, during a chase, 'S'est enbatus en une rasse'. In *GGK*, the 'rasse bi a rokk' is probably where the stream flows (the OF word often means 'watercourse'), and the boar finds a hole in the bank, so that the hunters have to come at him over the water; when Bertilak advances and the boar rushes out at him, they meet in midstream (lines 1590-1). In *Cl.* the appropriate sense is 'cleft, crevice'; cf. line 449, where the Ark seems to be imagined as wedged in the crags rather than simply resting on top of them.

447-8 Cf. *Mand. T*, p. 109: 'another hille that men clepen Ararath (but the Iewes clepen it Taneez) where Noes schipp rested'. The Insular version has *Ararach, Thanez*. The MS form *Mararach* in

Cl. is unparalleled and destroys the linking alliteration with *Armene*.

449 'But though the Ark was lodged [lit. confined to remain] in the crags'. MS *wern*, emended by edd. to *were*, is no doubt due to the fact that the scribe was led astray by the plural *crageȝ* immediately preceding; cf. a similar error in line 385.

457 **fanneȝ** is usually explained as 'flaps, flutters' (wings), but the only other examples of this sense from ME and early MnE in the dictionaries are of the phrase 'fan with wings', where the sense is 'to use the wings as a fan' (to kindle a fire); see *OED* s. Fan, *v*., sense 2. Perhaps 'glides' (with wings outspread like a fan) is better in the present context, the poet imagining the raven as a bird of prey soaring with near-motionless wings as it looks for carrion; cf. the MnE sense 'to be wafted gently along' (*OED* sense 2.b.). In *GGK* 181, *fannand* is used of hair spread out like a fan.

459 The detail that the raven is distracted from his task by finding carrion is not in the Bible, but it had become a widely-accepted part of the Noah story by the later Middle Ages, occurring also in e.g. *Cursor M* 1885–92, Mirk's Festial, and the English miracle plays. It goes back ultimately to early Jewish and Arabic versions of the Noah story, and was apparently first given currency in the West by Isidore of Seville (*PL* 83, col. 233).

461 'He had the smell of the stench, and goes there at once'.

smoltes. This verb is unknown apart from its occurrence here and in line 732. It is used evidently as an alliterative synonym for 'go'. Possibly it is related to *smolt* adj. 'gentle' (used in *GGK* 1763), OE *smolt*, which would give the verb some such primary meaning as 'move gently', a trace of which may remain in line 732.

469 The MS forms *doūe* here and *doveue* 481 are unlikely. It seems simplest to emend to *doue*, *dove* respectively, taking it that the scribe has introduced an abbreviation sign in line 469 and has copied a sequence of letters (*ve*) twice in line 481—both common types of scribal error in this MS.

470 **blessed.** Menner takes this as a participial adjective with *bryȝt*, but Gollancz is more convincing in taking it as a past tense used absolutely, 'pronounced a blessing (on it)', which gives less awkward syntax.

473 **bot** 'boat, the Ark' (so Thomas, *MLR* XVII. 65)—*bot* is used for Jonah's ship in *Pat*. Morris and Gollancz gloss 'help' (OE *bōt*), while Menner takes the form to be a variant of the infinitive *bod(e)* 'announce', with unvoiced final consonant.

484 Cf. *GGK* 929: 'Hit watȝ neȝ at þe niyȝt'.

486 **hym** refers back to *Noe* in line 484.

491 **where jumpred er dryȝed** 'where the motley company had suffered before'. Morris and Menner take *jumpred* as a unique instance of a noun of uncertain formation meaning 'confusion, trouble', with *dryȝed* understood in the unique sense of 'existed'. But perhaps *jumpred* is a participial adjective from ME *jumperen*,

a verb found in Chaucer and Thomas Usk in a sense close to that of the obviously related MnE *jumble*, i.e. 'mix together inappropriately' (see *MED* s. jumperen). In *Cl.* the participial adjective is used as a noun, lit. 'the jumbled ones' (men and beasts together). *Dry3ed* will then mean 'experienced hardship, suffered', a usual sense (*MED* s. drīen v.(2), sense 3.(c)).

493–4 Cf. Gen. VIII. 13: 'sexcentesimo primo anno [sc. of Noah's life], primo mense, primo die mensis'.

496 **dryed.** Probably a past participle, with *wat3* understood; Gen. VIII. 13 has 'exsiccata esset superficies terrae'.

499 Cf. *Pat.* 63: 'Goddes glam to hym glod þat hym vnglad made'.

504 **þrublande.** This and *þrobled* 879, which again has to do with the movement of a crowd, are the only recorded instances of the word, which is of unknown origin. Edd. compare *thrumble* 'crowd together' (recorded in early MnE), which must be related to OE *þrymm* sb. 'crowd', and ME (La3amon) *þrum* v. 'compress'. Cf. also the verb *throb* 'palpitate', found once in ME, in *Piers P.*

510 **his sacrafyse.** The *his* probably refers to God: 'the sacrifice to Him'. Cf. line 1497.

512 'Full of seemly cheer and courteous words'.

514 **mayny-molde** 'main earth, world'; so Gollancz, who regards *mayny* as a variant of *mayne*. There are many OE compounds in *mægen* and ON compounds in *megin*, though the dictionaries do not record any with 'earth' as the second element. Cf. ON *jarðar-megin* 'the earth's main, the wide earth' (CVC s. megin, n., sense II). Morris and Menner emend to *mayny* ['company'] *on molde*.

515 **segge3.** MS *māne3* is obviously miscopied from the previous line.

516 **þo3t of her hertte3** translates Gen. VIII. 21: 'cogitatio humani cordis'.

520 **daye3 of þis erþe.** I.e. 'for as long as the earth shall last', translating Gen. VIII. 22: 'Cunctis diebus terrae'.

521 Cf. *Death and Liffe* 248 (ed. Gollancz): 'Waxe fforth in the word & worth vnto manye'. *Worþe3 to monye* translates Gen. VIII. 17: 'multiplicamini'.

523 **sede** is found also in the OE Bible and in Wyclif as a translation of Vulgate *sementis* in Gen. VIII. 22; the Authorised Version has 'seed-time'.

527 'But they shall run ever-changing—hold sway therein', i.e. on earth, referring back to line 522. *Rengne3 3e þerinne* conveys the import of Gen. IX. 2.

529 **þen wat3 a skylly skyualde** 'then there was a clear splitting-up'. The translation follows that of Luttrell (*Neophil.* XXXIX. 214–15), who derives *skyualde* from an ON **skífald*, a noun formed on the verb *skífa* 'cut into slices' by the addition of the nominal suffix *-ald*; Luttrell compares ON *farald*, primarily 'journey', from the verb *fara*. The sense 'splitting-up, separation' would be appropriate in context. The English verb *skive* 'cut (leather, etc.) into slices or strips' is not recorded until the nineteenth century, but there is

a related ME noun *shive* (? OE **scīfe*) 'slice' (of bread). *Skylly* is then an adjective, probably from ON -*skilligr* (found in the derivatives *fráskilligr* 'separated', *sundrskilligr* 'separable', as pointed out by Luttrell), with the sense 'distinct, clear'; cf. ON *skilinn* and *skiljanligr* 'distinct, clear'. Gollancz reads *skynalde* and emends to *skylnade* 'separation', on the basis of ON *skilnaðr* in this sense—this is a good suggestion, although there is no other trace of this word in English. Luttrell later (*Neophil.* XL. 297) apparently comes to prefer Menner's explanation (following Morris) of *skylly* as a noun (cf. *skyly* 62) and *skyualde* as a past participle: 'Then was a design [*or possibly* separation] manifested'. But Menner has to leave *skyualde* unexplained, apart from a suggested connection with ME *skiften* 'ordain, devise'.

544 **þeweȝ.** Morris, Menner, and *OED* (s. Thew, *sb.*¹, sense 1.b.) gloss 'ordinances', Gollancz glosses 'noble qualities', but the sense here and again in line 755 and line 1436 is clearly 'good disposition, good nature' (a development of the usual sense 'disposition, conduct' which is discernible already in OE), hence 'goodwill, grace, favour'. Cf. *þewed* 733 'gracious'.

549–52 'For there is no man under the sun so seemly in his manners, (but that) if he is polluted by sin that remains uncleansed, one speck of a spot may be enough to (make him) forfeit the sight of the Sovereign who sits so high'. There are several uncertainties, but the poet appears to be thinking of the contrast between superficial cleanness and inner sinfulness, as with the false priests who *conterfete crafte* (13), and the descendants of Adam (lines 253 ff.). Line 550 follows the thought of line 548.

553 **For þat schewe me schale** 'For he who will make an appearance'; cf. Thomas, *MLR* XVII. 65. For *þat* meaning 'he who' cf. line 580, and for the sense of *schewe* see *OED* s. Show, *v.*, sense 28; *me* is ethic dative. Other interpretations are Menner's 'In order that I may appear' (though Menner notes the omission of the subject as peculiar), Gollancz's 'Because it, *i.e.* a speck or spot, is shunned', taking *me* as indefinite pronoun and *schewe* as aphetic of *eschewe* 'avoid', and Bateson's 'For that (spot) shall expose me' (*MLR* XIII. 381).

554–6 The beryl was thought of as a stone like crystal; it is called 'cler and quyt' in *Pearl* 1011. 'Berill shulde not be shape, but hit behoueth to be plain & polisshed' (The London Lapidary, EETS OS 190, p. 28).

556 Cf. *Pearl* 726, where Jesus says that, to enter His kingdom, a man must be 'Wythouten mote oþer mascle of sulpande synne', and also *Pearl* 843: 'mot ne masklle'.

567–8 'So as to kill all living things, whatever mischief occurred, for as long as the world lasted', lit. '. . . because of mischief that might occur, while the period of the duration of the world lasts'.

574 The phrase 'vilanye and venym' is used in *Pat.* 71 (of the people of Nineveh).

577 **þus.** MS *þat* may be picked up from either of the two preceding lines.

579 **heþyng of seluen** 'contempt for one's person' (through perverted sexual practices); the use of *seluen* as a noun in this way is unusual at this early date, perhaps arising from constructions of the kind 'Þe hyȝe Godeȝ self' (*Pearl* 1054), which are common enough.

581–6 Based on Ps. XCIII. (*nova versio* XCIV.) 8–9: 'Intelligite insipientes in populo, et stulti aliquando sapite. Qui plantavit aurem non audiet? aut qui finxit oculum non considerat?' The same verses are quoted, in closer translation, in *Pat.* 121–4.

581 **sauour** translates 'Intelligite'; in *Pat.* 121; the same word in the Vulgate is translated by 'feleȝ'. The appropriate sense, 'consider', is paralleled in OF (Godef. Compl. s. savourer, v.a.). Gollancz retains MS *sauyour* as a genuine variant of *sauour*, but there is no other evidence of such a form. It would obviously be easy for a scribe to confuse *savour* with *saviour*, and the latter word occurs in line 576, five lines earlier.

586 **hit lyfteȝ meruayle** 'that would be a marvellous thing', lit. 'it excites wonder'. The sense of the verb is found in ON *lyptask* 'stir up' (anger, etc.).

588–90 'There is no deed so hidden that He is prevented from seeing it [lit. that closes His eyes]; there is no man so careful or secretive in what he does but that it flies to Him swiftly before he has so much as thought of it'.

592 'Deus scrutans renes et corda' is a biblical formula, occurring in e.g. Ps. VII. 9, Ps. XXV. (*nova versio* XXVI.) 2, Jer. XI. 20, Jer. XVII. 10, Rev. II. 23. Both Wyclif and the Authorised Version translate 'renes et corda' by the phrase 'reins and hearts', which amounts to 'innermost being'.

599 **allyt.** Clearly a variant of *on lite, olite* (*MED* s. alite adv.), from *lite* sb. 'delay'. Cf. *GGK* 1463: 'And mony arȝed þerat, and on lyte droȝen' ('hung back' during the boar chase), and *onlyte lette* 'delay, hold up', *GGK* 2303.

601 **in erde** 'in his own country, at home'. *MED* (s. ĕrd n.(1), sense 3.(b)) quotes this instance of the phrase as an example of the meaning 'on earth', often used merely intensively, especially in the poems of the *Gawain*-group; but Gen. XVIII. 1 has 'in convalle Mambre', Mamre being Abraham's home (cf. Gen. XIII. 18).

608 **last ende** 'conclusion, sequel'; cf. *The Nun's Priest's Tale* (*Cant. Tales*, VII. 3205): 'For evere the latter ende of joye is wo'.

611–88 God here, and later the angels in Sodom, are referred to sometimes in the singular, sometimes in the plural, reflecting the variable biblical usage, as e.g. in Gen. XVIII. 9–10: 'dixerunt . . . dixit'.

611–12 Cf. *Cursor M* 2707–10: 'Toward him com childer thre, / Liknes o god in trinite; / Bot an allan he honired o þaa, / Als anfald godd and in na ma'.

615 **þi pouere** translates 'servum tuum' in Gen. XVIII. 3.

618 'And I shall busy myself to wash your feet'.

fast aboute schal I fare. Cf. *William of Palerne* 30: 'Þat litel child . . . ferde fast a-boute floures to gadere' (quoted by *MED* s. fāren v., sense 6.(a)).

your fette wer waschene. Lit. '(so that) your feet were washed', a close translation of 'et laventur pedes vestri', which was a widely-adopted variant of the standard Vulgate text of Gen. XVIII. 4: 'et lavate pedes vestros'. Wyclif also follows the variant reading, translating even more literally: 'and зoure fete be wayshid'.

619 **rachche.** Menner takes this form with *reche*, OE *rǣcan*; Gollancz, following *OED* (s. Ratch, *v.*¹) suggests a back formation from OE *rāhte*, past tense of *rǣcan*. But the double consonant points to OE *reccan*, which is occasionally spelt with *æ* instead of *e* in OE and early ME. *OED* (s. Recche, reche, *v.*, sense 2) notes the form *rachen* beside *reche* in *Wars Alex.* 1354. The sense 'go' (*OED* sense 3) is appropriate, with *rachche after* equivalent to *fare after* 'go to get'.

620 **baume** 'cheer'. Morris, Menner, and *MED* (s. bannen v., sense 5.(b)) read MS *ba* + four minims + *e* as *banne*, but the senses they give are forced (Morris and Menner 'strengthen', *MED* evidently 'banish care from'). In the light of Gen. XVIII. 5: 'confortate cor vestrum', Gollancz's emendation to *baume* (noted by *MED*), which assumes merely that the scribe has left out a minim, is convincing. *MED* gives no figurative usages of the verb *baumen* 'apply soothing ointment to', but the noun *baume* does occur in the figurative sense 'sweetness'; see the examples in *MED* s. baume n., senses 4.(c) and 4.(d).

627 **sumquat fat** 'an animal which has been fattened for the table', lit. 'something fattened', i.e. the fatted calf which Abraham fetches in line 629. Morris and Gollancz translate 'some kind of vessel', but such a use of *sumquat* would be irregular, and there is no mention of a vessel elsewhere in the passage or in the biblical original. According to his Glossary, Menner would apparently translate 'a little fat' (for baking the loaves?), but this would require 'sumquat of fat'.

630 **tyrue.** *OED* (s. Tirve, *v.*¹, Tirve, terve, *v.*²) takes *tirve* 'strip' (animal skin, etc.) and *tirve* 'turn, overturn, overthrow', used in line 1234 (MS *tuyred*), as separate verbs, but there is no etymological justification for this, and it is possible to see the sense 'strip' as a specialised development from 'turn, overturn' through the idea that an animal's skin is turned inside out as it is stripped. The etymology is obscure; OE *getyrfan* is recorded only in the sense 'assail, attack'. *OED* suggests a connection with OE *tearflian* 'roll over and over'.

643 **vpfolden.** Evidently 'uplifted' (in prayer); cf. *Pearl* 434: *folde vp hyr face* 'with her face upturned' (in prayer). *OED* (s. Upfold, *v.*) records one ME instance of the verb in the transitive sense 'raise up' (a stone). After their escape from Sodom, Lot and his daughters worship God *Wyth lyзt loueз* [hands] *vplyfte* (line 987).

646 **þay of mensk speken.** Probably 'they [Abraham and his guests] made polite conversation', lit. 'they spoke of polite matters'. For the sense of *mensk*, cf. *GGK* 2052: 'Here is a meyny in þis mote þat on menske þenkkeȝ'.

650 **wynne.** Menner in his Glossary gives the common meaning 'obtain', but Isaac can hardly be said to 'obtain' his people. The verb has the rare sense 'beget' in line 112, and Gollancz is probably right to see another instance of this sense here. In the Genesis story, an important, often-reiterated part of God's covenant with Abraham (and with Isaac, Gen. XXVI. 3–5) is that He will multiply Abraham's descendants and make them a great nation, the chosen people (cf. line 652).

652 **þat schal halde in heritage** goes naturally with *þe worþely peple* in the preceding line, though *MED* (s. heritage n., sense 3a.(b)) takes it with *sun* in line 649.

þat I haf men ȝarked. Sc. in the covenant which God has established between Himself and Abraham and his descendants that He will be their God and will give them all the land of Canaan (Gen XVII. 2–8, etc.).

654 **sotyly** 'subtly, slyly', for *occulte* in Gen. XVIII. 12. The emendation, by Gollancz, gives a close equivalent of the Latin word; cf. Wyclif's 'priuely'. The scribe has evidently misread *sotyly* as the common *sothly* 'truly'. The form *sotyle* adj. occurs in *Pearl* 1050.

655 **tykle.** Morris, Menner, and *OED* (s. Tickle, *a.*, sense 5) gloss 'uncertain', thereby turning Sarah's rhetorical question in Gen. XVIII. 12 (and 13) into a statement: 'You may regard it as uncertain that . . .'. Gollancz is more convincing in translating *for tykle* as 'through being wanton', which keeps the question form and gives a lively equivalent of Sarah's words 'voluptati operam dabo?' The noun *tickle* 'wantonness' is not elsewhere attested in ME, but the ME adjective has the sense 'sexually incontinent, wanton' (*OED* sense 3.b.), as in *Piers P*, B-text, III. 130: 'she is tikil of hir taile' (of Lady Meed); cf. *tickle-tail* 'a wanton woman' (Lydgate). See also Emerson, *PMLA* XXXIV. 505, and Fowler, *MP* LXX. 332–3.

teme. MS *tōne* is retained (as *tonne*) by Morris and Gollancz, the latter explaining it as 'to be big [i.e. like a tun or barrel] with child'; but no parallels are given. The obvious word is *teme* (Emerson, *PMLA* XXXIV. 505–6, and Menner), which a scribe might misread as *tonne* easily enough.

657 **hit.** MS *he* would be quite exceptional as a plural form in this MS. Gollancz suggests scribal misunderstanding and alteration of the idiomatic *hit wern*.

659 **had bene.** MS *byene* must be corrupt. Possibly the scribe, having written the word *ay*, then went back in error to the *ay* of *day* earlier in the line and followed with the *by* of *byfore*; then, returning to the end of the line and with a *b-* word in mind, he picked up the last three letters of *bene*.

683 **þat I ne dyscouered to his corse** 'and not reveal to him'. For the

idiom *his corse*, cf. the ambiguous line in *GGK* where the Lady tells
Gawain '3e ar welcum to my cors' (*GGK* 1237), and see *MED* s.
cors n., sense 3.(a).

685 'From whom people shall spring so as to fill all the world'.

689 **synkke3 in my ere3.** Menner compares Dunbar, *Twa Mariit
Wemen and the Wedo* 115 (ed. Small): 'Quhen that the sound of his
saw sinkis in my eris'.

691 **ly3t.** Gen. XVIII. 21: 'descendam'.

692 'To see if they have behaved as the noise is raised on high', i.e. to
see if their behaviour is as bad as is suggested by the noise they
make, which reaches to Heaven. Cf. Gen. XVIII. 21: 'utrum
clamorem qui venit ad me opere compleverint', which Wyclif
translates: 'I shall go down, and see whether the cry that is comen
to me thei han fulfillid in dede'.

695–701 'Each male takes as his mate a man like himself, and they join
together wantonly in female fashion. I devised for them a natural
skill and taught it to them privately, and valued it exceptionally
highly in my plan of creation, and established love, the sweetest of
all gifts, in that skill; and I devised the dalliance of lovers, and contrived in that regard the most pleasant practice of all'.

700 **paramore3** 'lovers', or possibly 'love' (Menner); for the development of the OF phrase *par amurs* 'through love' into an English
noun, 'love', see *OED* s. Paramour, *adv. phr.* and *sb.*

   portrayed 'formed, devised', an OF sense; cf. the quotation from
Caxton's *Mirror of the World* in *OED* (s. Portray, *v.*, sense 5): 'how
it [the world] is by nature made and pourtrayed of God'.

706 **stylle stollen steuen.** Cf. *GGK* 1659: 'Wyth stille stollen countenaunce'.

719 **and weye vpon þe worre half** 'and to weigh on the wrong side (of
the balance)'. The infinitive follows on from *lyke* 717.

726–7 'And be included in your judgement of them, to share their doom?
That was never your way, may it [i.e. the judgement] be retracted'.

727 **vnneuened.** The sole occurrence of this verb. Gollancz and *OED*
define 'unnamed', Menner defines 'unmentioned, i.e. unthought of,
impossible'; but 'unsaid, retracted' is simpler and fits the context
well.

735 **tat3 to non ille.** Cf. *GGK* 1811: 'Tas to non ille'.

736 **þat mul am and aske3.** I.e. 'who am but mortal flesh'; cf. *Pearl*
905 (the Dreamer addressing the Maiden): 'I am bot mokke and mul
among'.

740 **for hortyng on lede** 'so as not to hurt a single person'.

743 **þa3 faurty forfete** 'if forty are to be lost'. *MED* (s. forfĕten v.,
sense 4) gives one other example of this sense.

744 **voyde away my vengaunce.** Cf. *Pat.* 284: 'Dewoyde now þy
vengaunce'.

745 **lo3ly.** Menner, following Fischer, emends to *hy3ly* for the alliteration; cf. *GGK* 773: 'and he3ly he þonke3'. But the alliteration could
be carried by *him* (see p. 113). Gollancz is also unhappy with the

line as it stands, emending extensively to *Þen Þe burne obeched hym*
& boȝsomly him Þonkkeȝ.

746 **symple.** Perhaps 'gentle, mild', a common 'courtly' sense in OF,
rather than 'open, straightforward' (edd.); cf. *Pearl* 1134.

755 **space.** Primarily 'extent', hence 'wide extent' (a sense found more
in OF than ME), or, in context, 'generosity'.

769–76 A non-biblical addition, developed from the hint in Gen. XIX.
29. Cf. *Gen. and Ex.* 1039–40, where Abraham's first thought, on
learning that God is about to destroy Sodom, is for Lot: 'Ðo adde
abram is herte sor, / For loth, his newe, wunede ðor'. Cf. also the
ME metrical paraphrase of the Old Testament, line 577 (ed. H.
Kalen, *Göteborgs Hogskolas Årsskrift*, XXVIII. 1922): 'Abraham had
care then for hys kyne'.

772 **broÞer** is for the biblical *frater* 'kinsman', used of Abraham and
Lot in Gen. XIII. 8, 11, and XIV. 14, 16.

776 **As Þy mersy may malte.** Probably 'as much as your mercy is
able to soften it', with the object (*yre*) understood; for a similar
sense of the verb cf. the quotation from *Piers P* in *OED* (s. Melt,
v.[1], sense 11): 'And melteth her myȝte in-to mercy'.

778 **mornande for sorewe.** MS *wepande for sorewe*, with *sorewe*
written in the second hand over another word. The original word
cannot be distinguished, but it is likely that the first scribe copied
the whole phrase *wepande for care* in error from the previous line,
and that the correcter tried to improve matters by changing the last
word (so Menner).

783 **mekely.** Possibly 'quietly', but the regular ON sense 'nimbly,
briskly' has more point, given the characterisation of the angels as
myry men ȝonge, though it does not appear to be attested elsewhere in
English.

784–5 Gen. XIX. 1: 'et sedente Lot in foribus civitatis'.

786 **so watȝ Þe renkes seluen.** Lot's wealth is mentioned again in line
812 and line 878. Lot is said to be a wealthy man in Gen. XIII. 5–6,
before he parts from Abraham and goes to live in Sodom, and Menner notes that there was also a rabbinical tradition that Lot increased
his wealth in Sodom through usury.

795 **aucly.** So Gollancz (*MLR* XIV. 156), who takes this as the MS
reading; but the MS clearly has *autly*. However *aucly*, which gives
good sense, is accepted as an emendation by Menner and *MED*;
Menner suggests that the scribe may easily have miswritten *t* for *c*
(cf. *plate* 72 for *place*), especially as he had just written *autl* in *fautleȝ*
in the preceding line.

799 The poet of *Cl.* has a habit of beginning a speech in mid-line and
omitting the introductory verb of saying; cf. lines 1059, 1507.

805 Cf. *GGK* 1836: 'And he nay Þat he nolde neghe in no wyse'. These
two lines contain the only instances in English of *nay* as a past tense
form, probably by analogy with *lie, lay*.

813 **welcom as Þe wyf couÞe** 'made welcome by his wife to the best
of her ability'.

821 **hit wroth to dyspyt** 'took it amiss', lit. 'twisted it into a wrong'. Morris suggests *wroʒt* for MS *wroth*, while Menner (followed by *MED* s. děspīt n., sense 2.(a)) thinks that *wroth* can be retained as a variant of *wroʒt*; but such a form, though attested, is very unusual, and *wroʒt* is invariably the form in the poems of the *Gawain*-group. Gollancz is probably right to take *wroth* as a past tense form of *writhe* 'twist', as it is in *GGK* 1200. The figurative sense required by the context here cannot be exactly paralleled so early, but *OED* (s. Writhe, *v.*¹, sense 7) gives similar usages from the sixteenth century, and cf. *Pearl* 488: 'Þat God wolde wryÞe so wrange away', of which a likely translation is: 'that God would twist (matters) so unfairly' (Gordon: '. . . turn so unjustly from the true path'). Cf. the verb *wring*, which is parallel to *writhe* in some of its senses, in *Piers P*, C-text, v. 31: 'Wily-man and wittiman and waryn wrynge-lawe' (quoted by *OED* s. Wring, *v.*, sense 9.b.).

Gollancz and *MED* translate *to dyspyt* here as 'out of spite', but her words suggest that Lot's wife acts not out of simple malice but out of resentment at what she sees as her guests' unreasonable demands. Note the phrase *nimen to despit* 'take amiss' (*MED* s. děspīt n., sense 4.(a)).

822–4 Lot's wife apparently thinks that to take food without salt is a sign of bad breeding. There are Jewish legends of the bad behaviour of Lot's wife concerning salt for her guests, apparently invented to explain the biblical detail that she was turned into a pillar of salt when she looked back at Sodom and Gomorrah (cf. lines 979–84). But her behaviour in *Cl.* is not paralleled in any of the legends; cf. Emerson, *MLR* x. 373–5.

824 **burne** appears to be plural after *oþer*; plural forms without -*s* occur occasionally elsewhere (cf. 'treowest . . . of alle berne' in *A Mayde Cristes*, quoted by *MED* s. běrn n.(1), sense 1.(a)).

827 **scelt.** Cf. *skelt* 1186, 1206, and *skelten* 1554. The only other instances of the word in *OED* (s. Skelt, *v.*) are the present plural *skelton* '?hasten' in *St Erkenwald* 278, and two occurrences of the phrase *skeltyng of harme* '?outbreak of trouble' in *Dest. Troy* 1089, 6042. The origin of the word is obscure, but the range of meaning implied by the contexts suggests a connection with ON *skella* 'make to slam, clash', *skella á* 'burst out (on)' (of a gale, storm), also 'scold'; cf. ON *skjalla* 'clash' and *skelkja* 'mock'. Possibly the ME word is formed on ON *skellt*, past participle of *skella*.

831 **tyl þay waschen hade,** i.e. at the end of the meal.

832 Cf. *GGK* 1648: 'Þenne þay teldet tableʒ trestes alofte'.

tylt. The transitive verb is usually given the sense 'cause to fall' in ME (*OED* s. Tilt, *v.*¹, sense 1), and some variation of this, perhaps 'overturn', is possible here. But Gollancz glosses 'made to lean', which fits the context better, and although the first instance of any such sense in *OED* (sense 4) is dated 1594, the three examples given for sense 1, apart from the present instance, seem to contain the idea of tipping or tilting as well as falling, as in line 1213. The verb is probably from an OE *tyltan, the basic meaning of which, to judge from the extant *tealtian* and *tealtrian*, would be 'shake (*intr.*), be unsteady'.

838 'Clamour rose up as from a startled sentry-patrol'. Edd. and *OED* (s. Scout-watch, sense 1) gloss *scowte-wach* as 'a guard, sentinel', but Menner suggests a collective sense, and it would seem from the context that *OED*'s sense 3, 'a body of men told off for the purposes of watching and keeping guard' (first quotation 1523) is the appropriate one.

839 **clater.** MS *clatȝ*, which *OED*, followed by Menner, regards as the same word as modern dialect *clat* 'chatter', connected with *clatter* (see *OED* s. Clat, *v.*). *MED* also sees the form as a unique instance of a ME verb *claten*, connected with *clateren*. But this is to ignore the fact that the spelling *tȝ* in this MS is equivalent to *s* (p. 110), and as it is not possible to make sense of a form *clas* here, it seems simplest to emend to *clater*, taking it that the scribe has written *ȝ* with the common ending *tȝ* erroneously in mind (cf. *bryȝt* 1506, MS *bryȝtȝ*), instead of writing the *er* abbreviation; possibly, he mistook the abbreviation in his exemplar for *ȝ*. Gollancz emends to *claterȝ*.

840 **þys worde.** MS *þyse worde* is retained by Morris and Menner, the latter glossing *worde* as a plural; but there is no evidence that the OE plural without inflexion survived into the fourteenth century in this word, and the form *þyse* is singular only in genitive collocations elsewhere in the MS, as in line 1802. Gollancz emends to *wordeȝ*, but it is more likely that the scribe was misled into writing *þyse* instead of *þys* by the occurrence of *þyse wones* at the end of the next line.

846 **ȝestande sorȝe** 'festering filth', lit. 'frothing filth'; cf. *froþande fylþe* 1721. *Sorȝe* 'muck, filth' occurs again in *Pat.* 275.

852 'Never for any distressing event was he in such great confusion (of mind)'.

856 'That would stop him passing through the gate to face the danger'. **peril.** MS *pil*; the scribe has omitted to cross the tail of the *p* to make it into the abbreviation for *per*, as again with this word in *Pat.* 114 and *GGK* 1768.

857 **waft.** Menner translates 'shut', apparently going on context alone— there is no other evidence of such a meaning for this form. But 'swing' is a sense attested in the phrase *weve up, waive up* 'throw open, swing open', used regularly of windows (cf. line 453), also of gates (see *OED* s. Weve, *v.*¹, sense 3.a., and Waive, *v.*², sense 2). It seems likely that the sense 'swing (something)' existed as a development of the sense 'move (something) to and fro'. See note to line 422.

863 'For shame! it [the men's *fare* or *dyn*] is to your disgrace, you degrade yourselves'. *Vylaynye* is taken in *OED*'s sense 3.c. (s. Villainy, *sb.*): 'A person or thing that is the source of discredit or disgrace'.

869 **manne.** Probably a verb, OE *mannian* (Menner); there is no parallel in the MS for *manne* as a variant spelling of the noun *man* 'man'.

874 **hurled.** This is usually glossed 'rushed', but 'rang' is better. The dictionaries do not give such a sense for *hurlen*, but there are other contexts in which noise as well as violent motion seems to be implied by the word, as in the quotation from Malory in *MED* s. hurlen v., sense 1a.(a): 'He rorde hurlynge into the castell'. Cf. *MED* s. hurling(e ger., sense 2: 'a loud rumbling noise', once translating L *strepitus*.

879 **vmbe his ere3** 'close about him', as in MnE 'the house fell about his ears'. The idiom is used today only with verbs of falling, but this was not always the case; cf. the mid seventeenth-century example in *OED* (s. Ear, *sb.*¹, sense 1.c.): 'All Sodome was . . . flaming about the ears of the Inhabitants'.

882 **hem** refers to Lot and the men who are harassing him. Gollancz suggests that *hem* is an error for *hym*.

885 **boffet.** Usually 'blow', but Morris's 'blast' seems acceptable— a baleful blast which has the effect of a blow. OF *buffet* means 'bellows' as well as 'blow', and cf. OF *bouffis* and *bouffee* 'blast of wind', and the verb *bouffeter* 'blow' (of wind). *MED* suggests 'a blast of trumpets' (s. buffet n.(2), sense 2), but this sense is unparalleled and unlikely in context.

    in bland. Not adverbial 'together' (edd.), but prepositional 'amongst'. Both usages are attested in the Scandinavian languages; for the prepositional use, cf. the Icelandic version of Matt. XIII. 25: *saaðe illgresi ibland hveitesins* 'sowed tares among the wheat' (quoted from the 1747 edition of the Icelandic Bible, which is a reprint of the edition published at Hólum in 1644). See further A. Jóhannesson, *Isländisches Etymologisches Wörterbuch* (Bern, 1956), p. 953, s. bland, í bland. The adverbial use occurs in *GGK* 1205: 'Boþe quit and red in blande'.

886 **as blynde as Bayard** is proverbial; Bayard was the horse given to Renaud by Charlemagne, and a type of blindness or blind self-confidence. Cf. the quotation from Audelay in *MED* s. blusteren v., sense 2: 'al blustyrne furþ vnblest as bayard þe blynd'.

887 **lysoun.** Obscure; it looks as though line 887 is meant to correspond to Gen. XIX. 11: 'ostium invenire non possent'. OF *luision* is recorded only in the sense 'light', but it may also have meant 'opening', like OF *lumiere*.

888 **nyteled.** A unique and obscure form which has not been satisfactorily explained. Cf. however the noun *nutelnesse*, found uniquely in *Trinity College Homilies* (EETS OS 53, p. 73): 'Nutelnesse leteð þe mannes shrifte þe ne wot neure hwanne he sinegeð'. The context makes plain that the meaning of the noun is 'ignorance', and *OED* (s. Nuteleness, *sb.*) posits an OE **nytolnesse*, from *ne + -witol* 'knowing'; cf. also OE *witolnes* 'wisdom'. If *nyteled* is likewise from OE *ne + -witol*, an acceptable meaning would be 'blundered (in ignorance)'.

889 **ty3t hem.** OE *tyhtan*, which commonly means 'go' in ME, is here used reflexively and absolutely in some such sense as 'took themselves off, went away'; cf. the reflexive use of the cognate *teen* (OE *tēon*), *OED* s. Tee, *v.*[1], sense 6.a.: 'betake oneself, withdraw'.

892 The scribe has probably caught his *þat* from the middle of one of the three preceding lines.

893 **Ruddon.** An obscure form, not found elsewhere. An appropriate meaning would be 'redness, 'red light', which would connect the form with a number of words in OE and ON which have the idea of redness, e.g. OE *rudu* sb., *rudian* v., ON *roðmi* sb., *roðna* v. Cf. *roþum* 1009 (note), and *rudnyng*, *Pat*. 139, in the same sense.

895 **ruþen.** This verb occurs only here, in line 1208, and, reflexively, in *GGK* 1558: 'Then ruþes hym þe renk'. In all three contexts the sense seems to be 'rouse from bed'. The origin of the word is obscure, but Tolkien–Gordon–Davis, *GGK*, note to line 1558, refers to ON *(h)ryðja* as a possibly related word. This verb has the meanings 'clear (out), drive out' in ON, perhaps developed in ME, at least in the usage of the *Gawain*-poet, to 'drive out of bed, rouse'.

907 **trayþely.** Of obscure origin and meaning; this and line 1137 are the only two instances in English. Gollancz, in his note to line 907, refers to ON *tregða* sb. 'reluctance, difficulty', which would correspond formally to ME *trayþe* (ON *tregðalaust* 'willingly' is an example of a derived adverb); but the senses 'reluctantly, with difficulty' are not appropriate for the two English instances. Alongside ON *tregða*, however, is the more common *tregi*, which has the sense, 'grief, pain' as well as the primary senses 'reluctance, difficulty'; cf. the semantic range of the adverb *tregliga* 'with difficulty, reluctantly, woefully'. ON *tregi* corresponds to OE *trega*, ME *tray* 'grief, pain', found especially in the phrase *tray and teen* (*OED* s. Tray, *sb.*[1]); there are also verbs, ON *trega* and OE *tregian* 'grieve, afflict'. It is possible that ON *tregða* came to be regarded as more or less synonymous with *tregi* (although the sense 'grief, pain' is not recorded for it), and this in turn raises the possibility of an adverb based on *tregða* with the sense 'so as to cause pain, pitilessly, violently', a sense which would be appropriate to the contexts in *Cl*. See further Sunden, *SN* II. 41–7.

914–18 'If I should go forward on foot in order to escape, how should I hide myself from Him who has kindled His anger, who consumes all things in the violence of His fury? To steal away from my Creator and not know where to go, nor whether His enmity will seek me out from in front or behind!'

914 **fele** 'advance, go forward', OE *fēolan* (*MED* s. fēlen v. (3)). Morris and Menner translate 'hide' (ON *fela*), which gives weak sense, and Gollancz's 'if I trust myself to my feet' cannot be supported by any known usage of *felen*.

915 **hym.** Menner regards MS *hem* here as a singular (as again in line 889), but elsewhere in the MS *hem* is always plural. To retain it

here as a plural would involve a forced interpretation, and in Gen.
XIX. 19 it is only God's vengeance that Lot fears (cf. line 917).

917–18 An extended exclamation, the implication being 'how absurd for
me to try to steal away from my Creator', etc.

924 Cf. Gen. XIX. 29.

þyn eme appears to be the original reading, though the second
hand has converted it to *þy broþ + er* abbrev., thereby losing the
alliteration. *Broþer* is used of Abraham and Lot in line 772 (note).

hit at himself asked 'asked it of Him'.

927 The Cotton version of *Mand. T* also puts Zoar on a hill, though
most manuscripts of the Insular version have 'a dessouz vne
montaigne' (ed. Warner, p. 51).

930 'With those whom you want (with you), who owe allegiance to you',
i.e. Lot's family. Cf. Gen. XIX. 12: 'Habes hic quempiam tuorum?
generum, aut filios, aut filias? Omnes, qui tui sunt, educ de urbe
hac.' Gollancz however takes *prenge* as subjunctive, 'may follow'.

934 'And two other worthy men (whom) those maidens were to wed',
i.e. two other men besides himself.

935 **as tayt** 'as a game, as a joke', rendering 'quasi ludens' in Gen. XIX.
14. *Tayt* for MS *tyt* was first proposed by Menner, who suggests
that the scribe made an error because he had in mind the common
phrase *as tyt* 'quickly'. For the sense of *tayt*, Menner refers to *Wars
Alex.* 3979 (one knight challenging another): 'Lat vs twa termyn þe
taite be-twene vs alane'. Cf. also *GGK* 988: *þe lorde hit tayt makeʒ*
'the lord makes merry'.

945 **kayre** 'dither, hesitate'. The meaning is conjectural, based on
MnE dialect (especially Scottish) senses such as 'push backwards
and forwards, rake, stir about'; see *OED* s. Cair, *v.*, sense 3. There
is even less warrant for Emerson's sense 'return' (*PMLA* XXXIV.
508), which is accepted by Menner.

948–9 The language recalls that of God's raising of the winds in *Pat.*
131 ff.

951 **torres.** Cf. *Pearl* 875: 'And as þunder þroweʒ in torreʒ blo'. The
word is probably MnE *tor* 'hill, crag' rather than *tower*, although
Morris and Menner take it as the latter (spelt *tour*, *towre*, once *tor*,
elsewhere in the MS). In the contexts in *Cl.* and *Pearl*, it seems
likely that the word is used for the piled-up thunderheads, like
crags in the sky, which are characteristic of thunder-clouds; so
(tentatively) *OED* s. Tor, *sb.*, sense 2. As another instance of
a secondary sense for *torres*, Gollancz, in his note on *Cl.* 951, ob-
serves the meaning 'waves' in *Dest. Troy* 1983: 'There a tempest
hom toke on þe torres hegh'. Gordon (note to *Pearl* 875) allows that
the sense in *Cl.* is probably 'tor-like masses of cloud', but suggests
that in *Pearl* the meaning is literally 'hills': 'as thunder rolls among
dark hills'. But it is unlikely, given the association with thunder in
both contexts, that the word should have the specialised meaning in
the one instance and not in the other.

952 **þunder-þrast** '(bolt of) lightning'. The compound occurs again in

Wars Alex. 554: 'Þe liȝt lemand late laschis fra þe heuyn, / Thonere thrastis ware thra thristid þe welkyn' (quoted by *OED* s. Threst, thrast, *sb.*). *Þrast* 'thrust, stroke' occurs in *GGK* 1443.

953 **rueled.** *OED* (s. Ruel, *v.*) and Menner are hesitant about deriving this word from OF *rueler, roeler* 'roll'; but the OF verb frequently has the necessary sense 'fall down (violently), tumble'. See TL s. röeler, rëoler *vb.*

959–60 The construction is absolute: '(were) all enveloped by the rain, (were) roasted and burned, and the people who dwelt in those towns (were) utterly terrified'.

959 **birolled.** A unique form, presumably from *roll* in the sense 'envelop' (*OED* s. Roll, *v.*², sense 9).

961 **þe houndeȝ of heuen.** Evidently the poet's own metaphor for the elements as instruments of God's vengeance.

967–8 'By the time the stench of the brimstone had spread, all those cities and their environs were sinking to Hell'.

975 **flesch.** Here 'physical being', but the word is best left out in translation: 'they were thoroughly frightened'.

978 'Went ever forward, both eyes before them'. Cf. line 903.

979–84 See note to lines 822–4.

980 It is simplest to take *herkken* in the sense of 'observe, see'; this verb has lost the primary idea of hearing also in lines 458 and 1369, and cf. *herde* 197 'found, learned'. Luttrell (*Neophil.* xxxix. 207) suggests that the *bale* is the *ȝomerly ȝarm of ȝellyng* (971) which Lot's wife turns to listen to, but *blusched* at the beginning of line 980 means 'looked', not 'turned'.

981–3 'That was worthy Lot's wife, who looked once at the town over her left shoulder; but the moment she did so she was turned into a hard stone, a solid image', lit. '. . . but she remained no longer without being transfixed as a hard stone . . .'. The construction, with pleonastic negative in *nas*, is from OF; cf. *Pat.* 231: 'He watȝ no tytter outtulde þat tempest ne sessed'. Looking over the left shoulder is a sign of bad omen; see Bateson, *Folk-Lore* xxxiv. 241–2.

1000 Cf. *Cursor M* 2855–60: 'In a salt stan men seis hir stand / Þat bestes likes o þat land, / Þat anes o þe wok day, / Þan es sco liked al a-way, / And þan þai find hir on þe morn / Hale als sco was ar be-forn.' The detail goes back to rabbinical legend (Emerson, *PMLA* xxxiv. 509).

1002 **nomen.** So Menner and Gollancz, following Emerson (*PMLA* xxiv. 509). The emendation gives better alliteration than MS *no mon*, and makes *leyen* 1003 explicable as another past participle following auxiliary *hade*. The appropriate meaning is 'undergone, endured', a sense not attested for *nimen* in ME; but it is attested in OE (BT Suppl. s. niman, sense v(1b)), and for *taken* in ME (*OED* s. Take, *v.*, sense 34.b.).

1004 'He went up to (the place) where he had left our Lord', based on Gen. xix. 27: 'Abraham autem consurgens mane, ubi steterat prius eum Domino'.

1007 'In that it was like paradise which the Lord created', based on Gen.

XIII. 10: 'subverteret Dominus Sodomam et Gomorrham, sicut paradisus Domini'. Cf. *Cursor M* 2471: '[Gomor] lik to paradis'. The use of *aparaunt to*, which has been misunderstood, is from OF; cf. OF *s'aparer* (*a*) 'be comparable (to)', and *aparier* (trans.) 'compare'. The same usage is found in the quotation from *Knight of La Tour Landry* in *MED* s. ap(p)araunt adj. (though *MED* glosses *apparent* here as 'genuine, true'): 'They be right not apparent nor like vnto the precious margarite'.

1009   **a roþum of a reche** 'a pall of red smoke', lit. 'a redness belonging to a pall of smoke'.

    roþum. Edd. expand MS *roþū* as *roþun*, which Gollancz glosses as 'redness', comparing ON *roðna* 'become red'. Gollancz is probably on the right lines—the poet is elaborating Gen. XIX. 28: 'viditque ascendentem favillam [*Wyclif* multitude of sparkis, *later version* deed sparcle] de terra quasi fornacis fumum'. The MS is here expanded as *roþum*, ON *roðmi* 'redness' (but cf. *ruddon* 'redness', line 893, note).

1013–51   A description of the properties of the Dead Sea became a traditional part of the story of the destruction of Sodom and Gomorrah. The most relevant parallels for *Cl.* are *Mand. T*, pp. 73–4, and *Cursor M* 2861 ff.; cf. also *Gen. and Ex.* 1123–32. The traditional descriptions go back to Josephus, *De Bello Judaico*, IV. 8.4, but the poet of *Cl.* is clearly influenced particularly by the description in *Mand. T* (pp. 73–4): 'And fro Ierico a iii myle is the Dede See. Aboute that see groweth moche alom and of alkatran . . . The water of that see is fulle bytter and salt, and yiff the erthe were made moyst and weet with that water, it wolde neuere bere fruyt. And the erthe and the lond chaungeth often his colour. And it casteth out of the water a thing that men clepen *aspalt* also gret peces as the gretnes of an hors euery day and on alle sydes. And fro Ierusalem to that see is cc. furlonges. That see is in lengthe fyue hundred and foure skore furlonges and in brede an hundred and fifty furlonges. And it is clept the Dede See for it renneth nought but is euere vnmeuable.

'And nouther man ne best ne nothing that bereth lif in him ne may not dyen in that see. And that hath ben preued many tymes be men that han disserued to ben dede that han ben cast therinne and left thereinne iii. dayes or iiii., and thei ne myghte neuer dye therinne for it resceyueth nothing withinne him that bereth lif. And no man may drynken of the water for bytternesse. And yif a man caste iren therein, it wole flete abouen. And yif men caste a fedre therein, it wole synke to the botme. And theise ben thinges ayenst kynde.

'And also the cytees there weren lost because of synne [ayen kynde]. And there besyden growen trees that beren fulle faire apples and faire of colour to beholde, but whoso breketh hem or cutteth hem in two, he schalle fynde within hem coles and cyndres in tokene that be wratthe of God the cytees and the lond weren brente and sonken into Helle. Sum men clepen that see the lake

Dalfetidee, summe the flom of deueles, and summe the flom that is euer stynkynge. And into that see sonken the v. cytees be wratthe of God, that is to seyne, Sodom, Gomorre, Aldama, Seboym, and Segor, for the abhomynable synne of sodomye that regned in hem. But Segor be the preyere of Loth was saued and kept a gret while, for it was sett vpon an hille, and yit scheweth therof sum party aboue the water and men may see the walles whan it is fayr weder and cleer.'

1013 Cf. *Pat.* 370: 'Þe verray vengaunce of God schal voyde þis place'.

1014 **foundered.** Cf. *Mand. T*, Insular version (ed. Warner, p. 51): 'En cel mer fondirent [*Cotton MS* sonken] les v. cites par irour de Dieu'.

1015 **þere fyue** appears to be the original reading, though the second hand has converted it to *þer faur* + curved stroke, probably mindful of the fact that, of the five cities of the plain (line 940), only four were destroyed (lines 956–8). But five is the number of submerged cities in *Mand. T*, *Cursor M* (line 2861), and other medieval accounts of the Dead Sea.

1019 'Which in its sin and its savour is always bitter to taste'.

   synne. Menner and Gollancz emend to *smelle* (cf. *smelle of þe smach* 461), but it may be thought that the MS gives better sense, in particular a better sense-link with line 1018 and lines 1020–1. In the preceding line, as elsewhere in the passage, the poet makes the point that the Dead Sea is unpleasant not only physically (*a styn-kande stanc*) but because it *stryed synne*, and the present line carries on this idea. The sin of the cities is transferred to the sea which engulfs them, and it is for this reason that the sea is *ded in hit kynde* 'dead in its (very) nature' (line 1016, cf. line 1033). Thus, because of its origin in sin, the sea is unnatural and unpleasant both physically (*of smach*) and morally (*of synne*).

1023 Cf. *Cursor M* 2861–4: 'Þar þaa fiue cities war won to be / Es noght now bot a stinkand see, / Þat semes als a lake of hell; / Na liuand thing mai þar-in duell.'

1026 **hit to founs synkkeȝ.** Cf. *Mand. T*, Insular version (ed. Warner, p. 50): 'elle irroit au founz [*Cotton MS* botme]'.

1034 'The clay that clings there consists of strong corrosives'.

1037 **waxlokes.** A descriptive term: 'curls of wax', or 'wax-like curls' (OE *locc* 'lock of hair, curl'). The asphalt is described as *spumande* in the next line. In Guy de Chauliac, asphalt is 'fome indured' (*MED* s. asp(h)alt n.) or 'hardened scume'.

1039 **se halues** 'sea's shores'. The form *se* perhaps owes something to the OE inflexionless genitive *sæ*, but there are several examples of unhistorical inflexionless genitives in this MS; cf. 'þe segge foteȝ', *GGK* 574.

1048 **wyndowande askes.** Menner compares a phrase from *Mand. T* which occurs later on in the same section as the description of the Dead Sea (p. 78): 'And there let Iulianus Apostata dyggen hym [John the Baptist] vp and let brennen his bones . . . and let wyndwe the askes in the wynd'.

1049–51 The Dead Sea is made much of as an example and a warning against unnatural sin in *Cursor M* 2881 ff. Cf. Wisdom x. 7.

1051 **forþered.** The meaning of MS *forferde* 'destroyed' does not suit the context. Gollancz emends to *forþerde*, for *forþered*.

1057–64 These lines are based on *Rom. Rose* 7719 ff., a passage which comes from the portion of the poem written by Jean de Meun (Jean Clopinel). In this passage the Friend advises the Lover to conform to the mood and manner of his mistress if he wishes to win her favour, e.g.: 'De Bel Acueil reprenez garde / Par quel semblant il vous regarde, / Coment qu'il seit ne de quel chiere; / Confourmez vous a sa maniere./ . . . S'il est liez, faites chiere liee; / S'il est courrouciez, courrouciee; / S'il rit, riez; plourez s'il pleure; / Ainsinc vous tenez chascune eure' (lines 7719–22, 7729–32). There is an allusion to this same passage of *Rom. Rose* in *Pat.* 30: 'If we þyse ladyes [the virtues of the Beatitudes] wolde lof in lyknyng of þewes'.

1057 **clene.** The general sense 'excellent' is obviously applicable, but the poet may mean something more specific; *Rom. Rose* was of course regarded as a classic exposition of 'courtesy', which the poet associates with 'cleanness' (cf. line 1089, etc., also *GGK* 653, 1013, *Pearl* 754, etc.).

1061 **in vch a borȝe** probably renders 'en quelque place', var. 'en toute place', in *Rom. Rose* 7789: 'Briement faites en quelque place / Quanque vous pensez, qui li place.'

1063 **wyk.** The usual sense 'wicked, evil' here shades into 'hostile', as in some of the examples in *OED* s. Wick, *a.*, sense 2.a., e.g. that from *The Knight's Tale*: 'Som wikke aspect or disposicioun Of Saturne'.

1065–8 This 'moral' is of course the poet's own, though it preserves the language and flavour of *Rom. Rose*; note line 1067: *confourme þe to Kryst*, recalling *Rom. Rose* 7722: 'Confourmez vous a sa maniere'.

1068 Menner refers to the traditional patristic interpretation of the pearl of great price (Matt. XIII. 45–6) as a symbol of Christ, though here, as also in *Pearl*, the identification of the pearl with Christ is developed obliquely rather than directly.

1069–88 The Virgin is also celebrated, as 'Quen of cortaysye', in *Pearl* 425–55. In *GGK* 645–50, she is the object of Gawain's devotion. Traditionally, she is an example of perfect cleanness, as in the Blickling homily on the Annunciation: 'þæt templ þære geþungennesse & ealre clænnesse' (EETS OS 73, p. 5).

1070 **clos.** The verb *clos* is used of the pearl in *Pearl* in the sense 'place (a jewel) in a setting': 'To clanly clos in golde so clere' (*Pearl* 2).

1072 'But much cleaner was her body in that God was conceived in it'.

1073–80 As Menner notes, the Virgin's painless delivery is traditional. It is reflected for instance in many of the hymns on the Five Joys of the Virgin, the Nativity usually being counted as one of the Five Joys.

1081–8 The singing of the angels around the crib, and the adoration of the ox and ass, are traditional, originating in the apocryphal gospels, e.g. *Pseudo-Matthew* XIV.

1083 **alle hende.** In the light of the *wat3* in the next line, the right translation is 'everything pleasant', not, as edd., 'all pleasant things'.

1096 **drye folk and ydropike** means people suffering from diseases produced by excessive dry humour, and people suffering from dropsy, produced by excessive moist humour.

1101–2 'So clean was His handling that every filthy thing fled from before it, and so good was the touching of Him who was both God and man'.

1105–8 Menner and Gollancz refer to a traditional explanation of Luke XXIV. 35: 'et quomodo cognoverunt eum in fractione panis'. The explanation was that the disciples at Emmaus recognised Christ because He broke the bread more cleanly than would be possible for any ordinary man, as if he had cut it with a knife. The tradition is reflected in the cycle plays, e.g. in the Towneley *Thomas of Inde* 265 (EETS ES 71), where Peter says of Christ at Emmaus: 'Ther bred he brake as euen as it cutt had beyn'. Gollancz also points out that, according to medieval rules of good breeding, bread was always to be cut with a knife, not broken.

1107 **displayed.** Probably not 'displayed, revealed' (edd.), but 'fell apart, was broken'. The verb has the technical sense 'carve' (a crane) (*MED* s. displaien v., sense 2(c)), and cf. the eighteenth-century instance in *OED* (s. Display, *v.*, sense 2.b.): 'He carves, displays, and cuts up to a wonder'. The verb is used intransitively, in the sense 'spread' and related senses, in both ME and OF.

   pryuyly must be used in a developed sense such as 'delicately, cleanly'; cf. *preue poynte3* 'delicate, discreet questions', *GGK* 902.

1108 Toulouse was not noted for its cutlery; Gollancz suggests confusion with Toledo, whose blades were famous.

1111 **sore.** Probably 'vile' (Gollancz), as again in line 1136, with *sore* equivalent to *sorry*. *OED* (s. Sore, *a.*[1], sense 8) gives several modern dialect instances of such use, and refers to *Dest. Troy* 10445: 'Þerfore ses of þi saghis, þou sore homer' (although *OED* suggests that *sore* in *Cl.* may be an error for *sori*).

1114 **tomarred in myre** carries on the idea of *fenny* 'muddy, foul' in the previous line. *Marred* can mean 'astray' in both physical and moral senses; see *OED* s. Mar, *v.*, senses 3.c., 4, 5, and s. Marred, *ppl. a.*, in the quotation from Cotgrave (1611): '*Mauvais* . . . depraued, corrupt, mard'.

1117–28 The poet's remarks about the pearl owe very little to the main medieval lapidary traditions (Pliny, Isidore, Marbod).

1117 **Perle praysed is prys** 'the pearl is deemed precious'. *Prys* is taken as an adjective (equivalent to *of prys*, OF *de pris*), as in *GGK* 1945: 'suche prys þinges', and *Pearl* 730: 'perre pres'. For the use of *praysed* with an adjective, cf. line 146 (note).

1118 I.e. 'though it is not considered to have the highest money-value'.

   ho. Gollancz emends MS *hȳ* to *hyt*, but this would be anomalous in this passage, where the other pronouns are all feminine (though in *Pearl* the jewel is always referred to in the nominative as *hit*).

1123–4 'And, however long it may be worn (in the world), yet the pearl does not deteriorate during its lifetime'.

1124 **whyle ho in pyese lasttes.** Lit. 'while she still endures'; *in pyese* is from OF *en piece* 'for a long time' (in negative constructions), here reduced to a mere intensive. Cf. examples of ME *a pece, o pece* in *OED* (s. Piece, *sb.*, senses 14.a., b.), again used as intensives, from OF *a piece* 'for a long time'.

1129 **folk.** Probably an instance of the indefinite pronoun thought of as singular (so Mustanoja, p. 223), paralleling the frequent use of *men* as singular indefinite pronoun in ME (Mustanoja, p. 221).

1130 **seche to schryfte** 'let him resort to confession'. 'The pronoun of the indefinite person is sometimes not expressed when it is understood from a previous, different, expression of indefinite agency' (Mustanoja, p. 143).

1131 Cf. the Green Knight's words to Gawain, *GGK* 2391–3: 'Þou art confessed so clene, beknowen of þy mysses, / And hadʒ þe penaunce apert of þe poynt of myn egge. / I halde þe polysed of þat plyʒt . . .'.

1137 **tene** 'be angry' (*OED* s. Teen, *v.*[1], sense 2.d.). Edd. take *tene* here and *hate* in the next line as nouns, but to do this leaves the adverbs *trayþly* 'pitilessly, violently' (see note to line 907) and *hatter* 'more hotly' modifying *entyses*, when their sense goes better with *tene* and *hate*, understood as verbs used absolutely.

1141 **likkes** 'tastes'. Menner and Gollancz gloss 'likes', but nowhere else in the MS does *like* have the doubled consonant. The form more probably represents OE *liccian* 'lick'; cf. *likked* 'tasted' in line 1521. *OED* (s. Lick, *v.*, sense 3) refers to 'many specialized uses' of the verb in a figurative sense, as in the example from the Towneley Plays there quoted: 'Ye shal lik on the whyp'. Cf. also the comment on the young woman whom the old lady leads by the hand in *GGK* 968–9: 'More lykkerwys on to lyk / Watʒ þat scho hade on lode'.

1154–5 'How the fate of that man who would not respect them was more grievous than that of his erring father, who carried them off by force'.

1155 **forloyne.** The verb *forloyne*, OF *forloignier* 'set at a distance', etc. (a hunting term), is peculiar to the *Gawain*-group in ME. It occurs in lines 282, 750, 1165, and in *Pearl* 368, always in the figurative sense 'go astray (from)'. Here the form is evidently a participial adjective meaning 'gone astray', hence 'erring' (OF (*de*) *forloignie* 'at a distance'); the final *e* will be syllabic. *Fader* is read as a genitive.

1157 The detail of the bringing to Nebuchadnezzar of Daniel, Hananiah, Mishael, Azariah, and others of the Jewish nobility (lines 1297–1304) is based on Dan. i. 3–6, but apart from this the account of the siege and destruction of Jerusalem comes not from Daniel but from Jer. LII. 1–27 (cf. 2 Kings XXIV. 18 – XXV. 21), conflated with 2 Chron. XXXVI. 11–20.

1157–8 **dialokeʒ, profecies.** The terms refer to a recognised distinction between the first six chapters of the Book of Daniel and the last six. The later Wyclif version has a note, justifying the order of Daniel's visions, at the head of Dan. VII (ed. Forshall and Madden, vol. III, p. 645), part of which reads: 'this visioun is clenly of profecie, and therfor it is set with the visiouns suynge, that ben of the same condicioun; but the visiouns bifor goinge ben ether of pure stori, ether in parti of profesie, and in parti of stori'. *Dialoke3* should therefore be understood in a weakened sense, 'stories, narratives'.

1166 **wrast hit so hy3e** 'worked it up to such a pitch', a figurative use of the verb based on *OED*'s sense 1.b. (s. Wrest, *v.*): 'to tighten the strings of an instrument', etc.

1169 **Zedethyas.** So MS; edd. emend to *Zedechyas*, but *t, th* regularly alternate as spellings with *c, ch* in Latin and French. Cf. *Ararach* 447, for *Ararat(h)*.

1190 See note to lines 1383-4.

1193-4 'In the end, after a long time, the people inside became desperately short of food, (and) many starved'.

1205 **atwappe.** The verb is found elsewhere only in *GGK* 1167: 'What wylde so atwaped wy3es þat schotten, / Wat3 al toraced and rent at þe resayt'. The general sense is clearly 'escape' (so edd., *MED*), but 'dodge, dart past, slip past' would convey more of the idea of rapid erratic movement contained in ME *wappen* 'blow in gusts, flap' and ON *vappa* 'waddle, wobble'.

1226 **Nabugo.** Nebuchadnezzar's name is always written as a French name in the MS (*Nabugo de No3ar*), and here *Nabugo* is evidently thought of as a forename. Menner compares the form *Nabugod* in Gower, *Miroir de l'Omme* 1887, 10338 (ed. Macaulay).

1229-32 'For had the Father whom he once heeded been his friend, and had he never offended against Him in the sin of wrong faith, then all Chaldea and the lands of India would have been too weak (to do him any harm)—take Turkey with them as well, their hostility would have been of little account'.

1231 Menner emends to *To Calde wer alle calde* ('called'), but this gives worse sense than the MS if *colde* can be taken to mean 'sluggish, weak'. Cf. *Pat.* 264: 'colde wat3 his cumfort', and other quotations in *MED* s. cōld adj., sense 5.(a), e.g. that from *Revelations of St Birgitta*: 'My wille was coolde and wolde not . . . flee tho thinges þat delited me'.

1238 'The leader of his [Nebuchadnezzar's] knights in carrying out his attacks'. The *his* in the preceding line will also refer to Nebuchadnezzar.

1253 A relative is omitted after *alle*, as also in e.g. *Pearl* 732 (Mustanoja, pp. 204-5).

1259 **cayre at** 'drive' (Gollancz). Menner and *MED* (s. cairen v., sense (c)) give the meaning as 'pull (at)', but the word does not appear to have this meaning elsewhere. On the other hand, 'drive, urge' is the basic meaning of ON *keyra*, as in *keyra plóg* 'drive the plough'.

1267 **hokyllen.** Gollancz is no doubt right to take this as an early use of MnE dialect *hockle* 'cut up stubble', related to OE *hōc* 'hook, scythe'. The maidens are mown down like grass before the scythe.

1269–80 Cf. Jer. LII. 17–19, but for his list of Temple furniture here and in lines 1441–88 the poet also draws loosely on the biblical descriptions of the Temple, principally 1 Kings VII. 15–50 and 2 Chron. III. 15 – IV. 22. He also uses the descriptions of Moses's Tabernacle, especially for the *condelstik* (principally Ex. XXV. 31–9 and XXXVII. 17 – XXXVIII. 3).

1271 **pourtrayd in** 'painted (over) with, decorated with'; cf. OF *portrait a* in this sense (examples in TL s. portraire *vb.*, col. 1610, e.g. 'un jupel . . . Tot portret a fin or').

1272–3 The lampstand in Ex. XXV. 31–9 and XXXVII. 17–24 has a base and shaft, six branches and seven lamps. In Lev. XXIV. 1–4, God requires Moses to ensure that a light is always kept burning on the lamp-stand.

1274 Cf. lines 1491–2.

1275 The crown on the altar is from Ex. XXXVII. 27: 'Fecitque ei coronam aureolam per gyrum'.

1282 **precious.** Here and in line 1496 the basic sense is 'worthy of respect, worshipful', but extension to 'holy' would seem permissible in context; cf. the use of the adjective in the phrase 'Christ's precious blood'. In OF the sense 'worthy of respect, worshipful' occurs in both religious and non-religious contexts; see quotations in TL s. precïos *adj.* under the definition 'verehrungswürdig'.

1285 **sped** is explained by Gollancz as a participial adjective from *speden* 'speed'; thus *sped whyle* 'time that has passed quickly, short time'. Cf. *OED* s. Speed, *v.*, sense 13.b.: 'Of time: To advance or pass quickly'.

1287 **clene to wyrke** 'in fine workmanship', lit. 'in working excellently'.

1294 **hyrne** 'hinterland', primarily 'corner'. Gollancz emends to *hyrneȝ*, but the singular is possible in a developed sense; cf. ME *cost(e)* 'side', hence 'border region, hinterland'.

1298 'Many a man of noble rank in his time', lit. '. . . while their pros-perity lasted'.

1301 The names are from Dan. I. 6, 11, etc.

1311 **þat vayled so huge** '[that were] of such great value'. The verb is used as in OF; see Godef. Compl. s. valoir, and cf. OF *vaillant* adj. 'of (great) value'. See note to line 146.

1313 **with solemnete** 'with reverence, with respect'. For the sense, cf. OF *solemneement, solemneusement* 'with great care' (Godef.).

1315 **gounes.** MS *gomes*, but a reference to the prisoners is out of place in this line, especially in view of line 1317. Gollancz suggests *gounes*, which the scribe might easily have misread or miswritten as *gomes* by missing out a minim. The *vestures* of the Temple are mentioned in line 1288.

1326 **samples** 'examples, parables', evidently with reference to Daniel's interpretations of Nebuchadnezzar's dreams.

1341–3 'But he addresses as mighty gods false images of devils made by hand, with tools out of hard wood and stocks and stones, and raised upright'.

1346 **And þay reden him ryȝt** 'if they will deal well with him'. Cf.
  GGK 373: 'And if þou redeȝ hym ryȝt', with similar meaning.
1358 **on** is a variant of *an* found also in *Pearl* 9: 'I leste hyr in on erbere'.
1365–6 'The man was determined to prepare a banquet such that the
  kings of all countries should come to it'.
1381 **wruxeled.** Cf. *GGK* 2191: 'þe wyȝe wruxled in grene'. The form,
  found nowhere else, must be a variant of ME *wrixlen*, OE *wrixlan*
  'change, exchange'. Contextually, the meaning in *GGK* is 'wrapped,
  clad', perhaps from a basic sense 'wrapped in alternate folds'. The
  meaning in *Cl.* is less clear, but it may be 'built up' (with alternating
  courses of masonry); cf. J. C. McLaughlin, *A Graphemic–Phonemic
  Study of a Middle English Manuscript* (The Hague, 1963), pp. 65–6.
1383–4 'Pinnacled towers at intervals of twenty spear-lengths, and
  horizontal paling set round about at closer intervals'. The *ouerþwert
  palle* here and the *brutage of borde* on the walls of Jerusalem (line
  1190) must refer to the hoarding or bratticing which was a usual
  feature of castle architecture from the thirteenth century onwards.
  It consisted of a wooden gallery, roofed, floored, and faced, on the
  outside of the parapet. There were slits in the face and floor for
  directing missiles, which allowed the defenders to command the
  foot of the castle wall. The *ouerþwert palle* will be the horizontal
  paling forming the face of the hoarding, as in the drawing (reproduced from R. A. Brown, *English Castles*, 2nd ed., London, 1962,
  p. 71).

1385 'The area that the surrounding wall enclosed'. Bateson, *MLR*
  XIII. 384, has a similar translation.
  plyed. Cf. the OF sense 'enclose, encircle', especially in an
  embrace (TL s. ploiier *vb.* 'umlegen, umschlingen'), and cf. the
  ME verbs *implien, emplien* (OF *emplier*) 'enclose, surround'.
  pursaunt. The word occurs again in the same sense in *Pearl*
  1035 (*poursent*), where it is used for the wall surrounding the
  Heavenly City. The usual sense is 'precinct, compass'; the sense
  'girdle' occurs in AN.
1386–7 In Rev. XXI 16, the Heavenly City is described as square, of
  equal length and breadth, and its measurements are given. Cf.
  Pearl 1023–4, 1029–30.
1390 **of werk** and **of wunder** are best given adjectival force, like *of
  pryde* in the preceding line. Cf. the quotation from *Early English*

Wills in *OED* s. Work, *sb.*, sense 15: 'Too fyne borde-clothes, þe one of werk ['embroidered, ornamental'], þe oþer playn'.

walled. MS *walle* is probably on account of *halle* in the next line.

1391 **to hit med.** There have been several suggestions (Menner emends to *mad* 'made'), but a likely sense is 'appropriate to it [the palace], in keeping with it', with *med* from OE *gemede* (+dat.) 'agreeable, appropriate (to)'. Cf. *mede wordes* in *William of Palerne* 604 (*MED* s. ? mede adj.), which is undoubtedly another ME instance.

1392 'Spaciously built in the shape of a bay, so that horses might run there'. The reference is probably to a curved arena or racetrack like that of the Hippodrome at Constantinople, mentioned in *Mand. T*, p. 12: 'At Costantynoble is the palays of the emperour right fair and wel dyght. And therein is a fair place for iustynges or for other pleyes and desportes, and it is made with stages and hath degrees aboute that euery man may wel se'. *MED* (s. bai n.(2)) refers *baie* here to OF *beee* 'opening', but this word normally means a stall or other small compartment in ME.

1395 'And Belshazzar was made ready for his place at table', perhaps by the noblemen of line 1394, who would then retire (cf. line 1399). Cf. *wenten to sete* 'went to their places at table', *GGK* 72, 493.

1396 Cf. the jewelled thrones of the Great Chan and of Prester John in *Mand. T*, pp. 156 and 199 respectively.

1398 'And everywhere there were (present) barons at the side-tables'.

bounet. Morris, Menner, and *MED* (s. bounen v., sense 4.(a)) take this as a past tense plural meaning 'went'. Gollancz takes it as a past participle paralleling *hiled* 1397, which is probably right, but a better gloss than his 'prepared, in readiness' is 'present, at hand', a usual sense of the adjective *boun* from which the verb is derived. Cf. *MED*'s sense 3 (s. bounen): 'To be in a place'.

1401–16 Cf. the description of King Arthur's feast, with several closely similar details, in *GGK* 116–25; thus lines 1401–4 recall *GGK* 116–17: 'Þen þe first cors come with crakkyng of trumpes, / Wyth mony baner ful bry3t þat þerbi henged'.

1402 '(There was) a loud blast of trumpets, clamour in the hall'. Cf. *Wars Alex.* (Dublin MS) 1386: 'Sterne stevyn vpon stroke straked trompettes'. In *Cl.* however *strake* cannot be a verb unless *trumpen* is a quite exceptional plural form. It is therefore taken as the noun *strake* 'call, blast' (on horn, etc.), which is attested in ME (see *OED* s. Strake, *sb.*²), and *trumpen* is read as a genitive plural used adjectivally; cf. *blonkken bak* 1412, *nakeryn noyse* 1413, etc. The line then has an absolute construction of a kind characteristic of this passage; cf. lines 1404, 1405, 1407, 1409, etc. MS *sturnen* is no doubt by scribal attraction to *trumpen* (Gollancz).

1403 **wrasten.** Edd. (taking *trumpen* as the subject) gloss 'raised, blew, sent forth'. With *krakkes* as subject, the sense required is 'broke forth, burst out' (so *OED* s. Wrest, *v.*, sense 10). This is *OED*'s only instance of the sense 'break forth' (of sound), but cf. *OED*'s sense 9: 'force a way (out), find egress', etc.

1405–12 and 1441–88. In general, the decoration of the serving dishes and the Temple vessels, especially the foliage, birds, animals, and flowers, suggests English decorative art of the first half of the fourteenth century; see Joan Evans, *English Art 1307–1461* (Oxford, 1949), pp. 38–44. Cf. the birds and butterflies embroidered on the clothing of the Green Knight (*GGK* 166) and of Gawain (*GGK* 609–14), and, for the castellated cups especially, the description of the castle towers in *GGK* 795–802. The poet draws to some extent on the elaborate biblical descriptions of the Temple (e.g. the cherubim, palm trees, and flowers on the sanctuary doors, 1 Kings VI. 32, and the pomegranates and lily-work on the tops of the pillars, 1 Kings VII. 18–19), and of the lampstand in the Tabernacle, with its cups, capitals, and flowers (Ex. XXXVII. 17, etc.). Some of the poet's detail of birds and jewels comes from the account of the Great Chan's palace in *Mand. T*, pp. 157–8: 'And [at] grete solempne festes before the emperoures table men bryngen grete tables of gold. And thereon ben pecokes of gold and many other maner of dyuerse foules alle of gold and richely wrought and enameled. And men maken hem dauncen and syngen clappynge here wenges togydere and maken gret noyse . . . Also aboue the emperoures table and the othere tables and abouen a gret partie in the halle is a vyne made of fyn gold, and it spredeth alle aboute the halle. And it hath many clustres of grapes, somme white, somme grene, summe yalowe and somme rede and somme blake, alle of precious stones. The white ben of cristalle and of berylle and of iris. The yalowe ben of topazes. The rede ben of rubies and of grenaz and of alabraundynes. The grene ben of emeraudes, of perydos, and of crisolytes. And the blake ben of onichez and garantez. And thei ben alle so propurlych made that it semeth a verry vyne berynge kyndely grapes . . . And alle the vesselles that men ben serued with in the halle or in chambres ben of precious stones, and specyally at grete tables, outher of iaspre or of cristalle or of amatystez or of fyn gold. And the cuppes ben of emeraudez and of saphires or of topazes, of perydoz, and of many other precyouse stones.'

1408 **Pared out of paper.** Cf. *GGK* 802: 'þat pared out of papure purely hit semed' (Bertilak's castle). Contemporary evidence of elaborate paper decorations for dishes comes from *The Parson's Tale* (*Cant. Tales*, ed. Robinson, 2nd ed., p. 241) in which the Parson castigates, as examples of 'pride of the table': 'bake-metes and dissh-metes, brennynge of wilde fir and peynted and castelled with papir'. See further R. W. Ackerman, *JEGP* LVI. 410–17.

    poynted. Edd. gloss 'pointed, tipped (with)', but OF *peint a, point a* is usual for 'painted over with, decorated with' (gold, etc.); see examples in TL s. peindre, poindre *vb*.

1409 **baboynes.** This is the usual word for the grotesque figures, not necessarily monkeys, which were a distinctive feature of English decoration during the first three or four decades of the fourteenth century (Joan Evans, *English Art*, pp. 38–42).

1410 **foler** 'foliage, ornamentation resembling foliage'. This noun has the forms *felour, feylour, filour* in *Wars Alex*. (see *MED* s. feilŏur n.). The normal OF forms are *fueillier, fueilleur(e)*, but spellings in *o* exist for related words in OF (as *follu* 'with leaves', beside *foillu, fueillu*; see TL s. foillu). Cf. MScots *fulȝery* 'ornamentation resembling foliage' (Douglas).

    flakerande 'fluttering'. The word is used especially of birds' wings (see examples in *MED* s. flakeren v., flakering ger.).

1412 'And all (the servants) carried it in their hands on horseback'. The *hit* presumably refers to *al* 'everything' in the preceding line. Horses were by no means unknown in medieval banqueting-halls on great occasions; thus Holinshed, in an account of the coronation feast of Catherine, queen of Henry V, in 1420, describes how the Earl Marshal 'rode about the hall upon a great courser . . . to make and keep room' (W. E. Mead, *The English Medieval Feast*, London, 1931, p. 187).

1413 Cf. *GGK* 118: 'Nwe nakryn noyse with þe noble pipes', and *GGK* 1016–17: 'Trumpeȝ and nakerys, / Much pypyng þer repayres.' In all three instances the 'nakers' are probably horns of some kind, not drums. See J. F. Huntsman, *MP* XXIII 278, who notes that L *timpanum*, primarily 'drum', is sometimes glossed *taburne* in medieval dictionaries, and was apparently used for both wind and percussion instruments.

1414 **tabornes.** TL gives one instance of a form *taborne* in the sense of 'clamour', beside *tabor* 'drum, clamour'; cf. also the OF verb *taborner* 'beat the drum'. The phrase 'timbres et tabors' is common in OF.

    tulket. Perhaps a genuine variant of *tukken* 'beat, sound' (of musical instruments). Menner calls attention to the form *tulkid* (? 'beat, attack') in both MSS of *Wars Alex*. 2427; thus the Ashmole MS: 'Þe Tebies tulkid vs with tene a-tired þam in armes, / Ȝit rad for all þaire rebelte resayued þai þaire medis'.

1422 **And al waykned his wyt** 'and his reason was all enfeebled'. *Waykned* is a unique verbal form, either from ON *veikr* 'weak' (cf. *wayke* 'weak', *GGK* 282) + verbal -*en*, or from an ON **veikna* (cf. Norw. dialect *veikna*, MSw. and Sw. *vekna* 'become weak'). OE *wācian* 'become weak' survives in ME (*OED* s. Wake, *v.*).

1423 **on wyde** appears to be a unique variation of *on brod(e)*, which can mean 'on every side, around' (*MED* s. brōd n.(3), sense 2.(b)).

1445 Cf. line 1718.

1447–8 **þat goud sauor . . . lorde** 'that smelt sweet to the Lord', i.e. 'that was well received by the Lord'. *Goud sauor bifore þe lorde* translates the biblical formula 'suavem odorem Domino' (Lev. I. 9, etc.). See *OED* s. Savour, savor, *sb.*, sense 2.c.: 'the smell of sacrifices and incense regarded as pleasing to God'.

1456 Cf. *Siege Jerus*. 1261: 'Bassynes of brend gold and oþer bryȝt ger' (referring to the vessels of the Temple).

1459 Probably 'machicolated [i.e. provided with an external gallery] under the battlements, with skilfully-made stepped corbels'. The word *enbaned* is found in English only here and in the description of Bertilak's castle in *GGK*: 'Enbaned vnder þe abataylment in þe best lawe' (*GGK* 790). *Bantels* is found only here and in the description of the Heavenly City in *Pearl*: 'Wyth banteleȝ twelue on basyng boun' (*Pearl* 992), and 'Þe wal abof þe bantels bent' (*Pearl* 1017). *Enbaned* must be from Prov. *ambanar, embanar*, which E. Levy, *Petit Dictionnaire Provençal–Français* (1909, reprinted Heidelberg, 1966) defines as 'munir d'un *amban*'; *amban* is defined as 'partie de la fortification (galerie ou parapet?)'. Examples in Levy's *Provenzalisches Supplement-Wörterbuch* (Leipzig, 1898–1924) show clearly that the sense 'gallery running round a parapet' is usual. A Provençal connection is not unlikely, as several other English and French terms for features of castle architecture are found in Provençal, and certainly or probably originate there, e.g. ME *brutage* (1190), *brutaske*, etc., OF *bretesque*, Prov. *bertresca* 'brattice'; ME *carnel* (1382), OF *crenel*, Prov. *crenel* 'embrasure'; MnE *machicolation*, OF *machicoler*, Prov. *machacol*, from *macar* 'beat, crush' + *col* 'neck'. In *Cl.* and *GGK*, *enbaned* applies to a feature below the battlements, and the obvious one is the machicolation, a stone version of the hoarding discussed in the note to lines 1383–4. Gordon and Onions (*MÆ* II. 184–5) convincingly explain the bantels in *Pearl* as the tiers or coursings, arranged in the form of steps, which serve as the foundations of the Heavenly City, and they suggest that the *bantels* in *Cl.* are projecting horizontal coursings at the top of the wall. But if it is the idea of stepped construction rather than of coursing which is central to *bantel*, then the word would apply naturally to the stepped corbels which normally supported, and were part of, the machicolation. The etymology of *bantel* is obscure, but the idea of steps suggests OF *banchel, banquelet* 'petit banc'. F. Mistral, *Dictionnaire Provençal–Français* (Paris, 1878–86), s. *bancau, bancal*, and *bancèu, bancel*, notes a sense 'terrace' (of cultivated land). The drawing is reproduced from Brown, *English Castles*, p. 71.

1460 **on.** MS *of*, which the scribe has no doubt caught from *of ferlyle* later in the line, or from the next line. Cf. *formed out in* two lines later.

1466 **piked of.** Probably used as a synonym for *eat of*; cf. *Pat.* 393: 'ne pike non erbes', referring to cattle grazing.

1469–72 The list of twelve jewels draws on the descriptions of the vine and the vessels in the Great Chan's palace in *Mand. T* (see note to lines 1405–12); of the fifteen different jewels there mentioned, eight are found in *Cl.* Cf. also the twelve kinds of precious stones, standing for the twelve tribes of Israel, which are set in the high priest's ephod in Ex. XXVIII. 17–21, with which the list in *Cl.* has five stones in common, and the twelve stones in the foundations of the wall of the Heavenly City in Rev. XXI. 19–20, also *Pearl* 999–1016 (seven stones in common, or eight out of thirteen if the pearls of the gates of the Heavenly City are counted).

1469 **sardiners.** OF *sardine*, but the form may be genuine; cf. the ME form *alemandres* beside usual *alabaundine* (and see next note).

1470 **alabaundeirynes.** Morris reads *alabaunderynes*, Menner and Gollancz (followed by *MED* s. alaba(u)ndine n.) *alabaundarynes*, and *OED* (s. Alabandine) *alabaunderrynes*. But the *de* ligature is clear, and the following letter looks more like *i* than anything else, with the curved stroke which the scribe uses as a dot above it. *MED* cites ten instances of the word, in nine different spellings.

    amastised 'amethystine, of amethyst'. The MS appears to read *amaffised*. Menner and Gollancz suggest *amattised* (though they do not emend), but in this script *ff* is closer in form to the *st* ligature than it is to *tt*, and while *MED* (s. amatist(e n.) gives a form *emastice*, it does not record any forms in *tt*.

1472 **penitotes.** In *Siege Jerus.* 1251, *peritotes* (var. *petitotes*) adorn the roof of the Temple. Other ME spellings are *periot, pelidod, pelicocus*.

1473–6 'Thus all (the vessels) had trailing designs and trefoils across them, on each beaker and bowl, all round the edges; the goblets of gold were engraved round the circumference, and the bowls for incense were inlaid with flowers and butterflies of gold'.

1473 **tryfled** 'ornamented with trefoils', i.e. with three-leaved figures— a common ornamental motif. Cf. *Anturs of Arthur* 510: 'Trayfolede [*var.* Trifeled] with trayfoles, and trewluffes by-twene' (quoted by *OED* s Trefoil, *sb.*, sense 3). The noun has many forms in ME and early MnE; usual ME forms are *trayfole, treyfoyle, trefoil* (OF *trefeu(i)l*). But OF *trefle* is common, and Godef. Compl. (s. Trefle s.m.) gives one AN example of a form *triffle*: 'Coiffe de perles assise a maniere de triffle'. The *tryfleʒ* on the old lady's head-dress in *GGK* (line 960) and embroidered on the Green Knight's clothing (*GGK* 165) can hardly be other than trefoils, though Tolkien–Gordon–Davis glosses 'trifle, detail of ornament' (cf. OF *trufle*), a reasonable sense for *trifle* but one not elsewhere attested.

1474 **bekyr ande bolle.** So Emerson (*PMLA* XXXIV. 515), Menner, and Gollancz, for MS *bekyrande þe bolde*. The scribe has probably confused the conjunction *ande* with the ending of the present participle, introduced *þe* from *þe brurdes*, and written *bolde* instead of *bolle* because of *golde* in the next line.

1478 **bi acost** 'alongside', based on OF *par a coste* with the same meaning (Godef. Compl. s. costé). Cf. ME *acost*, OF *a coste*, and OF *coste* prep. 'beside'. Morris's reading *bi a cost* 'by a contrivance' has been accepted by *OED*, *MED*, and edd., but it involves a forced and unsupported sense of *cost* (OE *cost*) 'way, means'.

1483 There may be a word missing in the first half of the line; Bülbring, followed by Menner, conjectures *curious kyndes*.

1485 The MS has *of þe lampes*, but the sense requires another noun after *of þe*, and Bülbring's conjecture *launces* 'branches', adopted by Menner, is plausible; the word is used in *Pearl* 978: 'launce3 so lufly leued'.

1492 **Expouned his speche spiritually** 'made spiritual utterance', lit. 'uttered His speech spiritually'.

    special 'chosen' (by God); for the sense, cf. Wyclif's translation of Deut. VII. 6: 'For an holy puple thou art to the Lord thi God; the Lord thi God hath chosen thee, that thow be to hym a special puple [L *populus peculiaris*]'.

1494 **stronge** is for *stra(u)nge*, as again in *GGK* 1028; cf. *bronch* 487 beside *braunches*.

1506 **and stared ful bry3t** 'and it [the *guere*] shone most brightly'. *OED* (s. Starred, *ppl. a.*, sense 2) and Gollancz take *stared* as 'starred, adorned with star-like figures', which keeps the sequence of past participles; but the sense is contextually unlikely, and one would expect a form with double *r*.

1507 **Bede vus þerof!** Probably 'Serve us (drink) from it!' (the *guere* of line 1505), with *bede* used absolutely in the same way as *serve* (*OED* s. Serve, *v.*¹, sense 32). There are other instances in the poem of an abrupt change into direct speech in the middle of a line; cf. line 799 (note). But edd. do not regard this half-line as part of the direct speech, which they begin with line 1508. Morris and Gollancz take *vus* as an unusual variant form of *use* 'use, drink', although elsewhere in the MS *vus* is always the pronoun. Menner, followed by *MED* s. bŏusen v., emends to *bus* v. 'booze, drink'.

1511 **birlen þise oþer** '(they) offer drink to them', lit. ' . . . to these latter', the kings. For the usage, cf. *GGK* 1590–1: 'þe burne and þe bor were boþe vpon hepe3 / . . . þe worre hade þat oþer'.

1512 Probably 'and each servant strives for his master alone' (so Luttrell, *Neophil.* XL. 297), the idea being that the servants compete with each other in racing to seize the vessels and fill them with drink for their masters (cf. lines 1509, 1514). For the sense of *machches*, cf. *Dest. Troy* 9678: 'Thus macchit þose men till the merke night' (quoted by *MED* s. macchen v., sense 3.(b): 'to fight, contend'). But *MED* gives *machches for* in *Cl.* the unique sense 'to be paired with (sb.), work for, serve' (sense 1.(c)).

1514 **rok.** Gollancz is probably right to take this as another instance of the word which occurs in *Dest. Troy* 7149: 'All the Remnond and Roke radly þai broght, / And brent vp the bodies vnto bare askis'. The sense here appears to be 'common crowd', as opposed to the nobility; in *Cl.* the sense will be the general one, 'crowd'. Cf. *ruck* 'heap' (ME), later 'multitude, crowd', the latter sense being first attested in 1581 (*OED* s. Ruck, *sb.*¹, sense 3.b.); the relation of *rok(e)* to this word is uncertain. Menner derives *rok* in *Cl.* from OF *roque*, *roche* and glosses 'castle', a sense well attested in OF but not found elsewhere in ME.

hit. The vessels are again regarded collectively, as in line 1505.

1518 Most edd. and commentators supply a word beginning with *d* in the first half of the line; thus Gollancz conjectures *And þenne þat derrest arn dressed.*

1520 'As each man was aged, (so) he drank from the cup', translating Dan. v. 1: 'unusquisque secundum suam bibebat aetatem'. Wyclif has: 'eche man dranke after his age'. For other examples of forms of *elde* with initial *h*, see quotations in *MED* s. ēlde n. (e.g. *Havelok* 128, *Gen and Ex.* 1063).

1525 **gauleȝ.** The form is found again in *Pat.* 285 (where the sense is 'wretched one' or 'scum, refuse'), and in *Pearl* 463 ('rancour, bad feeling'), where it rhymes with *sawle.* It may be from OE *gagol* adj. 'wanton', a variant of *gāl* adj. and sb. 'wanton(ness), wicked(ness)'. The usual explanation of it as a variant of *galle* 'gall' or 'sore' would make the form quite exceptional; the *au* spelling occurs in none of the many instances of this latter word in *MED* (s. galle n.(1) and (2)), and *galle* is the established spelling in *Pearl* (once in *Cl.*, line 1022).

1527 **Heyred.** For the form, cf. *heyred* 1786 (OE *hergian*). The form *heyre* instead of *herie* (OE *herian*) occurs in one MS of *Piers P.*, A-text, XI. 247.

1532 **In contrary of þe candelstik.** Dan. v. 5: 'contra candelabrum'.

1541 An inversion of Dan. v. 6: 'et compages renum ejus solvebantur, et genua ejus ad se invicem collidebantur'.

1542 'And he tears his cheeks by beating his fists (against them)', lit. '... by the beating of his fists'.

1544 **til hit hade al grauen** 'till it had finished engraving'.

1556–7 'Nor (to understand) what people's lore or language, what message or meaning, those characters represented'.

1559 'And commanded men to be sought throughout the city', evidently equivalent to Dan. v. 7: 'Exclamavit itaque rex fortiter ut introducerent magos ...'. *Bede* for MS *ede* is Morris's suggestion and Menner's emendation. Gollancz emends to *eþede*, past tense of *eþe* 'entreat', found in *GGK* 379, 2467 in the phrase 'I eþe þe'.

1576 **sathrapas.** Here taken not in the proper sense of 'governor of a province', but 'wise man, sage', a sense which Wyclif, evidently unfamiliar with the term, sometimes gives it; he glosses it as such in Dan. III. 2: 'And so Nabugodonosor sent for to gedre satrapis, *or wijse men*, magistratis, and iugis ...'.

1577 **Wycheȝ and walkyries** is an alliterative phrase in OE (e.g. *wyccan and wælcyrian* in Wulfstan). The phrase in *Cl.* and perhaps already in OE seems to be used for enchanters in general, not necessarily female.

1579 **Sorsers of exorsismus** 'exorcists', lit. 'sorcerers who have to do with exorcisms'. *Of* is Gollancz's emendation; MS *&* is perhaps picked up from *wyche3 & walkyries* two lines earlier. For the plural inflexion *-us*, cf. *auenturus*, *GGK* 95, 491.

1586 **chambre.** Not 'private room' (edd.), but 'officers of the chamber, household', for 'optimatibus' in Dan. v. 10. *OED* (s. Chamber, *sb.*, sense 4.b.) attaches this instance to the sense 'a judicial or deliberative assembly or body', and cf. *MED* (s. chaumbre n.), sense 5.(b): 'body of officers meeting in a chamber', and sense 6: 'the department of a ruler's or noble's household concerned with his private quarters and affairs'.

1608 **godelest.** So MS, retained by Morris, Menner, and *MED*, though Gollancz emends to *godeliest*. *MED* (s. gōdlī adj.(2), sense 1.(b)) notes the positive form *godele* in *Émaré* 503.

   godde3. The plural here, which contrasts with the singular in lines 1598, 1627, is from Dan. v. 11: 'vir . . . qui spiritum deorum sanctorum habet in se', and again 'spiritum deorum' in Dan. v. 14.

1622 **vmbebrayde** 'embraced', lit. 'seized round'. The form is one of many ME derivatives in *umbe-* which occur once only; the poet of the *Gawain*-group readily uses the *umbe-* prefix with a verb of motion to give the general sense 'surround', the precise sense being determined by the context, as in *vmbesweyed* 1380, *vmbewalt* 1181, *vmbegon*, *Pearl* 210, *vmbeclyppe*, *GGK* 616, *vmbefold*, *GGK* 181, *vmbete3e*, *GGK* 770, *vmbeweued*, *GGK* 581. Morris, followed by Menner and Gollancz, glosses 'accosted', but this ignores the prefix, as does Gollancz's comparison with OE *upbregdan* 'reproach'.

1634 **tede** is an obscure word, which can hardly be from the past participle of *tie*, as edd. suggest. It may be a unique survival of OE *getēod(e)*, ppl. adj. from *getēon*, which is common in the sense 'ordained (by God), fated'; such a sense would be appropriate to the context in *Cl*. See BT and BT Suppl. s. ge-tēon.

1635 **mode** 'thought, inner meaning', an unusual but readily understandable figurative application of the basic meaning of OE *mōd*: 'the inner man, the spiritual as opposed to the bodily part of man' (BT s. mōd, sense 1). Belshazzar differentiates between the interpretation of the outer form (*tyxte*) of the mysterious writing, and the inner meaning, as does Daniel when he comes to read the inscription (lines 1725 ff.). The word is also used with an inanimate reference in *Pearl* 738, where the pearl of great price is said to be *blype of mode* '? beautiful by nature, inherently beautiful'.

1638 Cf. *Piers P*, C-text, I. 178: 'Bere by3es of bry3t golde abowte þyn nekke'. The B-text has (Prol. 161): 'Beren bi3es ful bri3te abouten here nekkes'.

1639–40 'And you shall be a lord of the king's council, I promise you no less, and the third most worthy who owes allegiance to me'.

1641–1708 Based on Dan. v. 18–21, conflated with Dan. IV. 25–34.

1646 **welde.** It makes better sense of the present tense *lykes* to take *welde* not as infinitive dependent on *Gart* (edd.), but as subjunctive: 'made him the greatest of all rulers, and (made) all the world (to be) at his command, let him govern as it pleases him'.

1647 'Whoever he wished to be well off, good fortune befell him'. It seems clear that the first words must express the 'quos volebat' formula of the Vulgate, as do the first words of the next three lines. The omission of the subject-pronoun may be due to scribal error, but there are other instances of elliptical expression in this part of the poem (cf. e.g. line 1652). For *don well* 'be well off, prosper', see *MED* s. dōn v.(1), sense 10. The line departs from Dan. v. 19: 'Quos volebat interficiebat', probably because, as Menner suggests, the poet wants to make a contrast with the next line, thereby paralleling the contrast in the two subsequent lines; this second contrast is already present in the Bible.

1655 Perhaps a word is missing after *þat*—Bülbring suggests *counseyl*, Gollancz *coyntise*.

1661 'Then he does not refrain from blasphemy, from uttering impiety against the Lord'. *On*, though displaced, goes with *blame* (Menner compares *on to pyche* 477 and 'on to sene', *Pearl* 45), which is here used in its OF sense 'blaspheme (against), utter impiety against'. There appears to be no comparable use of *blame* elsewhere in ME, but *blasfemen* 'blasfeme' is sometimes found with the prepositions *in*, *(up)on*; there are two Wyclifite examples in *MED* (s. blasfēmen v., sense 1): 'Þei [friars] blasfemen in Crist and seien þat he beggide', and 'ȝif freres by gabbingis blasfeme upon Crist'.

1663–86 These lines reflect Dan. IV. 27–9.

1667 **in strenkþe of myn armes.** The import is 'with my own strength' (Dan. IV. 27: 'in robore fortitudinis meae'). Cf. the biblical use of *arm* sg. in the sense of 'strength' (*MED* s. arm n., sense 4.(a)).

1675 Cf. *Pat.* 392: 'Ne best bite on no brom ne no bent nauþer'.

1684 **ay.** Not 'ever' (Menner and Gollancz), but 'hay' (Morris's suggestion, followed by *MED* s. hei n.), for 'foenum' in Dan. v. 21.

1687 'By then many a thick thigh crowded about his flesh' (Thomas, *MLR* XXII. 66)—something of an exaggeration, but Nebuchadnezzar is now four-legged (line 1683).

1690 **schyre-wykes.** The explanation of this as a compound meaning 'groin, middle of the body', lit. 'corners of the groin', is due to Menner, who notes that *wick* is used regularly in ME of parts of the body—the corner of the eye, or mouth (as in *GGK* 1572). He compares the ON compound *munnvik* 'corners of the mouth'. Menner, followed by Gollancz, emends MS *schyre* to *schere* (OE *scearu* 'groin'), but the MS form may be genuine, from *scyru*, which is recorded as a variant of OE *scearu*. BT has two articles, one for *scearu*, var. *scyru* 'tonsure', another for *scearu* 'groin', but it is reasonable to regard these as one word, with the basic sense 'cutting, division'; cf. *OED* s. Share, sb.2 and sb.3

1691 **twentyfolde** is probably hyperbolical, as *twenty* sometimes is; see *OED* s. Twenty, **numeral a. and sb.**, sense 1.d.: 'Used vaguely or

hyperbolically for a large number' (as in the common ME exclamation 'a (in) twenty devil way').

1692 'Where many a bur stuck it together like a poultice'. Gollancz's
view that *clyuy* represents OE *clife* 'burdock', a plant with burs,
is accepted, though the word is not found elsewhere in ME until
the early fifteenth century, when it appears in the form *cliver*.
From the quotations in *OED* (s. Cleavers, clivers) and *MED* (s.
cliver n.(2)), the plant was well known for its property of adhering
to clothes, etc. Morris and Menner take *clyuy* as a verb, OE
clifian 'adhere', but this poses obvious difficulties of interpretation,
as well as merely repeating previous sense. Menner would evidently
translate: 'where many (hairs) cling together, it stuck together like
plaster'; cf. his note to line 1687.

1694 **bresed** 'bristled'; the word occurs only here and in *GGK* 305:
'bresed bro3e3'. *MED* suggests that the word is akin to ME *bristel*
and OE *byrst*, but cf. also ON *brúsi* 'he-goat', Norw. dial. *brus(e)*
'tuft of hair'.

1695 **campe hores.** The collocation occurs again in *The Knight's Tale*
(*Cant. Tales*, I. 2134): 'With kempe heeris on his browes stoute'.

1696 **clawes.** MS *clawres*, with the *res* probably from *hores* in the
preceding line.

1697 **paume** 'claw, talon' (*OED* s. Palm, sb.², sense 2.b.). MS *pa* + four
minims + *e* can hardly be retained, either as *paune*, an anomalous
plural of *paw* (Menner), or as *pauue* = *paw* (Gollancz, but *uu* is not
used for *w* in this MS).

1698 **ouerbrawden.** Perhaps not merely 'covered (over)', which is the
sense of OE *oferbregdan*, but 'over-braided', i.e. covered with
something of woven texture, with reference to the eagle's plumage;
cf. Dan. IV. 30: 'donec capilli ejus in similitudinem aquilarum
crescerent'. Cf. OE *bregdan* 'weave', ppl. adj. *brogden*, *bregden*
'woven' (of mail, feathers); *brawden bryne* 'woven mail-shirt' occurs
in *GGK* 580, and *browden perles* 'linked pearls' in *Cl.* 1132.

1701 **he** is God, not (as Morris and Menner understand) Nebuchadnezzar. Menner has to take *wayned hym* reflexively, and he glosses
'recovered', an unparalleled use.

1707 'He was properly restored to his own shape', based on Dan. IV. 33:
'et figura mea reversa est ad me'. *Heued* here has the basic sense
'person' (*MED* s hēd n.(1), sense 2a.(a)). *MED* gives several
examples of *his hed, your hed*, etc. in the sense 'his person, your
person', hence 'him, you', in this instance (not in *MED*) 'he'. Cf.
GGK 1523: '3et herde I neuer of your hed helde no worde3 / Þat
euer longed to luf'.

1708 **3arked and 3olden** 're-established' is doubtless formulaic; cf. the
phrase '3euyn and 3olden' in *Wars Alex.* 2107.

1710 **syngnes.** Cf. *OED* s. Sign, *sb.*, sense 10: 'An act of a miraculous
nature, serving to demonstrate divine power or authority . . . after
L *signum*'.

1717 **þede** must have the general collective sense 'vessels', but the usual sense is 'brewer's strainer' (*OED* s. Thead). The only other ME occurrence is in *Promptorium Parvulorum* (EETS ES 102, col. 478): 'Thede, brueris instrument: *Qualus . . .* vel *calus*'; the sense of the Latin is 'vessel for straining'.

1726 'Character by character as I understand them, as our Father permits'.

1735 **fewe.** The context requires the sense 'lacking (in)' (cf. Dan. v. 27), a usage not recorded in *MED*, but which may be explained as analogous to the ON prepositional use of *fátt* (*í*, *á*) with numerals to mean 'short of', as in *lítið fátt í fimm tigi vetra* 'little short of fifty years' (quoted by CVC s. fár, sense III. *γ*.); cf. also the use of *fátt* in compounds such as *svefn-fátt* adj. 'lacking sleep' (so Gollancz).

    fayth dedes. Menner and Gollancz print *fayth-dedes*, and *MED* (s. feith n., sense 7) notes *fayth* here as one of three ME instances of the noun used attributively; but the other instances given by *MED* (especially the phrase 'be fayth and credible personys') suggest full adjectival force (= *faithful*).

1736 **to frayst þe trawþe.** Probably not 'to test, prove, the truth' (edd. and *MED* s. fraisten v.), but rather a conventional expression, 'to seek the truth', equivalent to modern 'to tell the truth'. Cf. *GGK* 355: 'quo laytes [seeks] þe soþe', used similarly.

1748 **pryuyest . . . þe þrydde** 'the third most important', lit. 'the third most intimate' (with Belshazzar).

1752 **þat folȝed hym tylle** 'who owed allegiance to him'. *Follow till* (*to*) is not unusual in MScots; cf. the quotation from *Rauf Coilȝear* in *OED* (s. Follow, *v.*, sense 14): 'He followit to him haistely' (in literal sense).

1761 If the mist is imagined as coming down from high ground, the line refers to the manner in which the people skirt it by going home over low-lying ground.

1762 **Vche haþel.** Not Belshazzar's guests, who would hardly be in need of *soper*, but the ordinary people of the town who hurry home to escape the worsening weather, and whose simple pleasures contrast with the luxury of the palace.

1764 It is probably best to take *fyrre* with *at forþ naȝtes*: 'Then later on in the night each party (of guests) departs'.

    at forþ naȝtes. On the idiom see Mustanoja, pp. 88–9; the usage goes back to OE ('oþ forþ nihtes' in Ælfric; see BT Suppl. s. forþ, sense (4)).

1772 **Porros of Ynde** is associated with Darius in the Alexander romances.

1776 **scaled** (Bateson) gives better sense than MS *scaþed* in view of the next line. For the form, cf. *scale* (OF *escale*), *Pearl* 1005.

1779 For the alliteration, the poet probably intends *an oure* and *an entre* to be read as *a noure* and *a nentre*.

1784 **scarred.** This verb is used in lines 598, 838 in the usual senses 'alarm, take alarm', from ON (*OED* s. Scare, *v.*, senses 1.b., 2). But here the sense appears to be rather that of OF *escarrir* 'abandon' (trans.), 'fly off, bolt' (intrans.), with the idea of very rapid movement; hence *scarred on þe scue* 'flew up to the sky'.

1786 **heyred.** See note to line 1527.

1804 'Looking on our gracious Lord will be long deferred (for him)', lit. '. . . will happen late', i.e. it will never happen.

1805 **vpon þrynne wyses.** See Introduction, p. 2.

1806 **tocleues in.** Edd. translate 'is cleft asunder in, etc., regarding the verb as from OE *tōclēofan*. But a better etymology is OE *clēofian* 'adhere', giving the sense 'sticks in' (like mud or other filth), or, in abstract terms, 'strongly affects'; this verb is regularly used with *on*, also *in*, in ME. The prefix *to-* supplies intensive force. Once having perceived uncleanness, God remains very much aware of it and will not rest until He has dealt with it.

1808 **telled vp his wrake.** The construction is absolute: 'His hostility aroused'. *Telled* is from *telden* (OE *teldian*) 'spread, raise up' (a tent, etc.), here used figuratively; for the form, cf. *Piers P*, A-text, II. 44: 'Tentes I-tilled [*varr.* teled, teldit, etc.]' (quoted by *OED* s. Teld, tild, *v.*, sense 1).

APPENDIX

LANGUAGE AND VERSIFICATION

VOCABULARY AND SYNTAX

The language of *Cleanness*, and of the other poems in MS Cotton Nero A.x., is founded in a North-west Midland dialect, but it is a distinctive literary language. Compared with fourteenth-century English generally, and with the language of other poems of the alliterative revival, the vocabulary of *Cleanness* has a high proportion of words from ON and OF. The poem has a total of some 2,520 different words (excluding proper names, counting elements of compounds formed in ME as separate words, and counting derivatives which are treated under the one heading in the Glossary as one word). Of these, about 240 words (9·5 %) are from ON, the proportion being about the same as in *Pat.* and *GGK*, rather higher than in *Pearl*. About 780 words (31·0 %) are from OF, about the same proportion as in *Pearl*, rather higher than in *Pat.* and *GGK*. The OE element consists of approximately 1,430 words (56·7 %), and about 70 words (2·8 %) are of other or uncertain origin. Most of the poem's words may be regarded as part of the common English stock of the time, but, in the tradition of alliterative poetry, there are also words and phrases which make up a special poetic vocabulary. The most important of these are the synonyms for 'man', which go back to the special vocabulary of OE poetry; they are: *burne, freke, gome, haþel, lede, renk* (*ring*), *schalke, segg*(*e*), *wyȝ*(*e*), together with *tolk*(*e*) added from ON. Apart from this group of synonyms, the special vocabulary of OE poetry is not much used in *Cl.*, but there is a considerable number of words of OE origin which are used in *Cl.* (occasionally in other ME alliterative poems also) in distinctive poetic senses: *borne* 'water', *loȝe* 'sea', *lome* 'vessel, ship'. Originally specialised senses may become generalised, as with the many verbs in *Cl.* meaning 'go' (*bowe, tee*, etc.). Several words from ON appear in the poetic vocabulary (e.g. *balterande, carp, glam, tolk*(*e*)); many have senses developed or altered from the original ON sense. There are one or two such words from OF (notably *forloyne*), but the poet draws on OF most obviously for technical terms, such as architectural terms and names of jewels. There is a striking readiness to use borrowed words in senses and idioms from the original languages which are not attested elsewhere in ME; thus, from ON, *in blande* 'amongst', *mekely* 'briskly', *rape* 'fall'; from OF, *bi acost* 'alongside', *bi bot* 'quickly', *blame* 'blaspheme', *displayes* 'tears'.

The distinctiveness of the poet's language is a matter of syntax as well as of vocabulary. A characteristic syntactical feature is the freedom shown in the use of verb tense, number, and mood; tense will often change from present to past, or vice versa, within the sentence. There is considerable freedom also in the use of pronouns; thus a subject consisting of *vch*(*e*) 'each' + singular noun may have plural agreement (lines 378, 889, 1762-3);

alle is usually plural, occasionally singular, once both in the same line (line 62). Absolute and elliptical constructions are frequent, e.g. pronouns are omitted (line 1652), and participial clauses are used absolutely (line 1808). The poet moves readily, sometimes abruptly, in and out of direct speech (see note to line 799). Unusual constructions which the poet favours are the *þat . . . hit* = 'which' construction (see Glossary s. *þat pron. rel.*), and the *he . . . þat* construction, used where MnE would naturally employ a construction with present participle (e.g. line 85: *Þen þay cayred and com þat þe cost waked* 'then they went to and fro, rousing the countryside'; also lines 110, 465, 476, 499, etc.).

SPELLING

Vowels of stressed syllables
Letters are occasionally doubled to indicate a long vowel: *dool(e)*, *leede*, *niȝt*. Spellings in words of French origin normally reflect Anglo-Norman spelling practice; the sounds and spellings of Old Norse words are usually accommodated to the English spelling system. The following table gives a summary of the main developments, with the spellings in *Cl.* in the right-hand column.

OE *a*	*a*: *asse*
OE *ā*, ON *á*	*o*: *brode, lot.* Exception: *halde* (12 times), beside *holde* (once)
OE *a*/*o* + nasal	*o*: *mon, honde. a*: *man, hande*
OE *æ*	*a*: *bak.* Also *e*: *feste, geder, gresse*
OE *ǣ*	*e*: *clene*
ON *au*	*au*: *lauce*
AN *au*, OF *a*, + nasal	*au*: *graunt.* Also *a*: *lampe*; *o*: *bronch*
OE *e*	*e*: *bed.* Also *i*: *kynned, hynde*
OE *ē*	*e*: *bed, dede*
OE *i*	*i, y*: *him, hym.* Also *e*: *þeder, þretty, wekked*; *u*: *luly, wruxeled*
OE *ī*	*i, y*: *abide, abyde*
OE *o*	*o*: *bodi*
OE *ō*	*o*: *god.* Exceptions: *goud, gvd*
OE *u*	*u, o*: *luf, lof*; *v* initially: *vnder.* Also *ou*: *foul, louflych, soun*
OE *ū*	*ou, ow*: *hous, hows.* Also *o*: *schor, stonde*
OE *y,ȳ*	*i, y*: *hille, hylle, hyde.* Also *u, o, uy*: *blusch, gult, huyde, kuy, luþer, stalworth*; *e*: *euel, mery, schepon*
OE *ea*	*a*: *harme.* Also *e*: *merkkeȝ, sleke*
OE *ēa*	*e*: *deþe, herneȝ*
OE *eo, ēo*	*e*: *hert, deþe.* Also *u, o*: *burne, chorles, ludych*
OE *ag, aw*	*aw, aȝ, au*: *sawe, clawes, saȝe, saueȝ*
OE *āg, āw*	*aw, au*: *knawe, aune. ow, oȝ*: *owne, woȝe*
OE *ah*	*aȝ*: *aȝt*

OE *æg*, ON *ei*	*ay*: *sayde, laykeʒ*. Exception: *sade*
OE *ǣg*	*ay*: *ayþer*. *ey*: *seyed*
OE *ēg* (final and before cons.)	*ay*: *ay*. *ey*: *seyed*
OE *ēg* (before vowel), also *ēog, ēh*	*iʒ, yʒ*: *hiʒe, yʒe, dryʒe, wel-nyʒe*. *eʒ*: *dreʒe, heʒe, wel-neʒe*. Note simplified spellings *fleeʒ, swe, swyed*
OE *eht*	*yʒt*: *bryʒt*
OE *og*	*aw*: *ouerbrawden*. *ow*: *browden*
OE *ōg*	*oʒ, ow*: *droʒen, plow*
OE *oh, ōh*	*oʒ, ogh*: *doʒtereʒ, inogh*
OE *ōw*	*ow, oʒ*: *flowed, stowed, floʒed*. *aw, au*: *stawed, staued*
OE *ug*	*ow, ou*: *fowle, fouleʒ*. Also *u, o*: *duthe, foles*
OE *ūg*	*ow, oʒ*: *bowe, boʒ*
OE *ēaw*	*ew, eu*: *schewe, scheued*. Also *aw*: *schawe*
OE *ēow*	*w(e), u(e), ew*: *trwe, true, bicnv, knew*. Also *aw, au*: *fawre, faure*; *ow, ou, o*: *fowre, foure, forty*

Vowels of unstressed syllables

Unstressed final *-e* is used unsystematically for the most part. Occasionally, *-ee, -y* appear instead of syllabic *-e* (*hardee, swypee, clyuy*). Etymological /i/, when final, is occasionally written *-e* (*prette* beside *pretty*).

A glide vowel appears in *dowelled* (beside *dwelleʒ*).

There is the usual instability in the vowel spellings of words from OF in syllables which may have been pronounced with relatively weak stress (*cite, cete; sacrafyse, sacrefyse, sakerfyse*).

Consonants

Double consonants after a short vowel are sometimes historical (*likkes*), sometimes not (*schalkkeʒ*). Consonants historically double are often simplified (*lache*).

The symbol ʒ is used as both native 'yogh' and continental 'z'. As 'yogh' it represents /j/ initially (*ʒet*), as originally it must have also in the spellings *eʒ, iʒ/yʒ* (*seʒen, wyʒ(e)*), though rhymes in *Pearl* and *GGK* indicate that the sound represented by these spellings in the poems has been simplified to /i:/. Medially ʒ represents /w/ after the vowels *a, o* and the consonants *l, r* (*boʒed, folʒes*), when it reflects OE *g* = /ɣ/. When it is used for original *h*, finally and in the combination *ht*, ʒ represents either the voiceless palatal fricative /ç/ (*bryʒt, hyʒ(e)*), or the voiceless velar fricative /x/ (*poʒt, paʒ*), according to the front or back quality of the preceding vowel. The spelling *gh* is more or less interchangeable with ʒ 'yogh' in all positions except initially, but it occurs much less frequently than ʒ. As 'z', ʒ occurs most commonly in the ending *-eʒ* beside *-es*. The French spelling *tʒ* occurs finally in monosyllables, mainly verbs (*gotʒ, watʒ, metʒ*), where it represents /s/.

The symbol þ is usual for /θ/, /ð/, but *th* is also used (*þat, that*).

The spelling *qu* is normally used for OE *cw*, but it also varies with *wh* (*quen, when*) and *c, k* (*quoynt, coyntyse, koynt*).

The spelling *w* is normally used for OE *w*, but it also varies with *v* (*awayled, vayled*).

The vowel symbol *i*, alongside *j*, is commonly used for initial /dʒ/ (*ioy, joy*).

The vowel symbol *u* is usually used for /v/ in medial position.

There is some variation in the use of initial *h* (*Abraham, Habraham; ayre, hayre; elde, helde; ay* 'hay').

Voiced consonants sometimes vary with their voiceless equivalents when final after a nasal in monosyllables (*þynk, þyng; renk, ring*), and when final in final unstressed syllables (*dresset, dressed*).

ACCIDENCE

Nouns

The most common endings are: sg. nom. acc.: -, -*e*; gen.: -(*e*)*s*, -*eʒ*; dat.: -*e*, -; pl.: -(*e*)*s*, -(*e*)*ʒ*, once -*us* (*exorcismus*). The genitive singular is frequently uninflected in genitive combinations: *ʒisterday steuen, kyte paume, Baltaʒar þewes, Israel dryʒtyn*. A few uninflected plurals occur, mainly from OE: *bonk, course, ʒer, hyne, lyʒt, þink*. There are also plurals which are uninflected after numerals: *lenþe, myle, syþe*. The OE weak plural in -*an* survives in *yʒen, oxen. Half* (beside *halues*) is a variant of *halue* (found in *GGK* 2070, 2165), a survival of the OE feminine plural in -*a*, -*e. Deʒter, fet(t)e, men, teþe* are from OE mutated plurals. *Childer* is from the OE plural in -*ru*. The OE weak genitive plural inflexion -*ena* survives with adjectival force in *besten, blonkken, chyldryn, fenden, folken, Iuyne, kythyn, nakeryn, trumpen*.

Adjectives

The endings are: sg.: -, -*e*; pl.: -*e*, -. Weak forms cannot normally be distinguished from strong. The OE genitive plural inflexion -*ra* survives in *alþer-* (in compounds). Comparative and superlative adjectives normally end in -*er*, -*est* respectively. Adjectives (and adverbs) ending in -*ly(ch)* have comparatives in -*loker* and superlatives in -*lokest*. For forms of the definite article and demonstrative adjectives, see Glossary s. *þat, þe, þis*.

Pronouns

Forms are recorded in the Glossary; for the personal pronouns, see Glossary s. *ʒe, he, hem, hit, ho, I, þay, þou, we*.

Verbs

The strong verbs show a certain amount of vowel levelling within and between conjugations, and transference of verbs from one conjugation to another. Several verbs originally strong have weak past tenses, and strong and weak forms may exist side by side: *ros, rysed*. Verbs borrowed from

French follow the weak pattern, with the exception of the past tense forms *fon* and *nay*. The following endings occur:

Infin.: *-e*: *cache*; *-*: *cach*; *-en*: *gremen*; *-y*: *lyuy*; *-an*: *wakan*

1 sg. pres.: *-e*: *tene*; *-*: *graunt*

2 sg. pres.: *-es, -eʒ, -tʒ*: *redes, hatʒ*

3 sg. pres.: *-(e)s, -(e)ʒ, -tʒ, -us*: *calles, callʒ, dos, gotʒ, flemus*

Pl. pres.: *-(e)n*: *cachen, schin*; *-es, -eʒ*: *borgouneʒ*; *-e*: *reche*; *-*: *hondel*

Sg. pres. subj.: *-e*: *conterfete*; *-*: *aproch*. Pl. as for indic.

Sg. pa.t. strong: *-*: *bed*; *-e*: *bede*

1, 3 sg. pa.t. weak: *-ed(e), -de, -t(e)*: *cached, batede, calde, spylt, mette*

2 sg. pa.t. weak: *-teʒ*: *wroʒteʒ*

Pl. pa.t. strong: *-en*: *token*; *-*: *tok*; *-e*: *fonde*

Pl. pa.t. weak: *-(e)d, -t(e)*: *rer(e)d, profert, flette*; *-den, -ten*: *pulden, metten*

Pa.t. subj.: As for indic.

Sg. imper.: *-*: *enter*; *-e*: *make*

Pl. imper.: *-(e)s, -eʒ, -tʒ*: *fecheʒ, bes, gotʒ*; *-*: *rest*; *-e*: *bede*

Pres. p.: *-and(e)*: *glydande, biholdand*

Pp. strong: *-en, -(e)ne, -n*: *founden, don(e), waschene*; *-e*: *founde*

Pp. weak: *-ed, -de, -t(e)*: *losed, sende, lost, rafte*

VERSIFICATION

Cleanness, like *Patience*, *Sir Gawain*, and other ME alliterative poems, is composed in alliterative long lines which are based on the metrical principles of OE verse, i.e. the alliterative long line is divided into two half-lines each containing two stressed syllables and a varying number of unstressed syllables, the two halves of the line being linked by alliteration on at least two, usually three, of the stressed syllables. The length of the line in *Cleanness* varies between four and nine syllables for the first half-line, between four and seven syllables for the second half-line. 'Extended' first half-lines, containing three stressed syllables instead of two, are common. The usual rhythmic pattern of the half-line is a rising one:

And in þe cóntrare kárk (4)

The common rising-falling pattern may be considered a variant of the rising pattern:

Þe góme watʒ vngárnyst (137)

Falling patterns are less common:

Clánnesse who-so kýndly (1)

Clashing patterns are also less common:

in þat goún fébele (145)

A second half-line may contain a single dip between the two stressed syllables:

fátted with sclá3t (56)

Or the dip may come before the two stressed syllables:

and his séte rýche (176)

Rhythmic patterns for extended first half-lines are very varied. Most are based on one of the first four patterns above, sometimes on two of these patterns in combination. But another usual extended type stresses both the first and last syllables of the half-line:

Fýlter fénden fólk (224)
Wáter wýlger ay wáx (375)
Brýng bódworde to bót (473)

The normal alliterative pattern for the long line is aa/ax (or aaa/ax), which is found in at least 1770 of the poem's 1812 lines. Sometimes this pattern is extended to aa/aa (1, 50, 150, etc.). Other patterns are ax/ax (427, 770, 779, etc.), and xa/ax (67, 1073, etc.). Patterns of cross alliteration (ab/ab, ab/ba, etc.) can be found (608, etc.), but most instances, if not all, are probably accidental. The poet is prepared to alliterate unstressed as well as stressed syllables to give an effect of particularly dense alliteration (113, 661, 1681, etc.), though he is more sparing in the use of this device than some of his contemporaries. He is also prepared to alliterate structurally on what would normally be a syllable with weak word-stress or sentence-stress, e.g. a prefix or other weakly stressed first syllable (thus *defence* 243 alliterates on *d*; *defence* 245 alliterates on *f*), or a 'grammatical' word such as a preposition, pronoun, or auxiliary verb (*by* 63, *my* 309, *haf* 652, etc.). Several lines in which the alliteration apparently fails to link the two halves of the line may possibly be explained by vowel alliteration involving unstressed syllables (1573, 1622, etc.).

The poet alliterates a vowel with any other vowel. *H* alliterates with vowels rather more often than with itself alone (63 times as opposed to 54). There are occasional instances of other sounds which alliterate at times not with themselves but with similar sounds, as *ch* with *k* (464), probably *m* with *n* (1304), *s* with *ȝ* (1169), *sch* with *sc* (600) and *sw* (58). In *excused* 62, the *xc* alliterates with *sc*, but cf. *excuse* 70, alliterating on *c*. In the word *expowne* (1729, etc.), the *xp* always alliterates with *sp*. There is a considerable number of consonant groups which may be regarded by the poet as single consonants for purposes of alliteration. Some groups are almost always so regarded (notably *sc* (*sk*), *sm*, *sp*, *st*), others only rarely (e.g. *cr*, *gl*).

GLOSSARY

The Glossary is intended to record every occurrence of every form and meaning in *Cleanness*, with the following exceptions: frequently recurring forms and meanings have one or two line-references followed by the sign 'etc.'; the common spelling variations between *i, y*, and between *s, ʒ* in inflexions, are usually disregarded; common inflexions, in particular -(*e*)*s*, -(*e*)*ʒ* in the plural of nouns and in the third person singular of verbs, -(*e*)*n* in the third person plural of verbs, and -(*e*)*d* in the past tense and past participle of verbs, are usually not noticed separately. Line-references to emended or doubtful readings are italicised, and the sign 'n.' following a line-reference indicates that the Notes should be consulted.

In etymologies, Old English forms are normally those of Anglian Old English, and Old Norse forms are those of Old Icelandic, unless otherwise indicated. In Old English forms, the sign ´ indicates a vowel which was certainly or probably lengthened during the Old English period, and the sign ⌣ indicates either a vowel which was shortened, or a vowel of uncertain quantity. A hyphen beginning an etymon indicates that the etymon is recorded only in prefixed forms. An asterisk denotes a hypothetical form. The sign + shows that a compound or derivative is first recorded in Middle English; 'from' is used when the word glossed is a different part of speech from its etymon, or has a suffix not present in the etymon; 'cf.' indicates indirect or uncertain relationship.

In the alphabetical arrangement, *ʒ* = *z* is treated as *z*, otherwise *ʒ* has a place after *g*. Vocalic *y* is treated as *i*, consonantal *i* is treated as *j*, and *th* is treated as *þ*, which has a place after *t*. Vocalic *v* is treated as *u*, and consonantal *u* is treated as *v*.

a *indef. art.* a, any 23, 36, etc., (before vowel or *h*) **an** 65, 442, etc., **on** 1358n. [OE *ān*].

aa *interj.* ah 733.

abayst *pp.* abashed (*of* at) 149 [AN *abaiss-*, OF *e(s)baiss-, e(s)bair*].

abate *v.* put an end to 1356 [OF *abatre*].

abide *v.* 764, etc.; *sg. pa. t.* **abod** 365. wait for 486, 764, hope for 436, face, meet 856, remain 365, live 1673 [OE *abīdan*].

abyme *sb.* abyss, depths of the earth 363n., 963, pit (of Hell) 214 [OF *abi(s)me*].

abyt *sb.* garment, apparel 141 [OF *(h)abit*].

abof, aboue (1382) *adv.* above, on top 1382, 1409, on the surface 1464; *prep.* above 38, 1120 [OE *abufan*].

abominaciones *sb. pl.* abominations, abominable customs 1173 [OF *abomination*].

aboute, aboutte (1084), **abowte** (30,

1638) *adv.* (round) about 83, 346 etc., round the circumference 1475; *prep.* (round) about, round 78, 817, etc. [OE *abūtan*].

achaped *sg. pa. t. subj.* might escape 970 [OF *achaper*].

achaufed *pp.* kindled 1143 [OF *eschaufer*].

acost *adv.* alongside; *bi. a.* alongside 1478n. [OF (*par*) *a coste*].

adoun *adv.* down 953 [OE *adūn(e)*].

adreʒ *adv.* away, back 71n. [*a-*+ON **dréug-*, cf. OI *drjúgr*].

afrayed *pl. pa. t.* alarmed 1780 [OF *esfraer*].

after *adv.* afterwards, then 261, 570, etc., behind 503; *cj.* after 442; *prep.* after 6, 681, etc., (temporal) 650, 1755, for 420, 619, 1345, about 1098 [OE *æfter*].

agayn *adv.* back 1705, **aʒayn** 665; *prep.* **agayn(e), agaynes** against 266, etc., towards 611 [(from) OE *on gegn*, ON *í gegn*].

agayn-tote *sb.* backward glance 931 [from prec. + OE *tōtian*].

age *sb.* age 426, 656 [OF *age*].

aȝly *adv.* fearsomely 874, 937 [from ON *agi*, cf. OE *egeslīce*].

aȝt *sg. pa. t.* ought 122 [OE *ǎhte*, pa. t. of *āgan*].

aȝt(e) *adj.* eight 24, 331, 357 [OE *æhta, eahta*].

aȝtsum *pron.* one of eight 411n. [OE *eahta sum*].

ay *adv.* always, ever 114, 132, etc.; *ay a* each 117n. [ON *ei*].

ay *sb.* hay 1684n. [OE *hēg*].

ayre *sb.* air 1010 [OF *air*].

ayre *sb.* heir 650, 1709, **hayre** 666, **here** son 52 [OF (*h*)*eir*].

ayþer *adj.* each; *a. oþer* each other 338, 705 [OE *ǣgþer*].

aywhere *adv.* everywhere 228, etc. [OE *ǣghwǣr*].

al(le) *adj.* all 2, 779, etc.; *pron.* all, everything 17, 19, 1083n., etc., everyone 1211; *adv.* (intensive) all, utterly 14, 247, 1544n., etc. [OE *al(l)*].

alabaundeirynes *sb. pl.* almandines, red gems 1470n. [OF *alabaundine*, etc.].

alarom *sb.* alarm 1207 [OF *alarme*].

alce, aldest, aled. See **als, olde, haleȝ.**

aliche *adv.* alike, without distinction 1477 [OE *on līce*].

alkaran *sb.* bitumen 1035 [OF *alkoran* (once), *alketran*, ML *alchitrum*].

allas *interj.* alas 853 [OF (*h*)*alas*].

allyt *adv.* back 599n. [from *a-* + ON *hlíta*].

alofte *adv.* above 1183 [ON *á lopt(i)*].

aloȝ *adv.* quietly 670 [from *a-* + ON *lágr*].

alone *adv.*. alone 1512; *hym a.* on his own 784 [OE *al(l) āna*].

along(e) *adj.* entire; *alle a. day* all through the day 476; *prep.* towards, to 769 [OE *andláng, andlángne dæg*].

alosed *pp.* renowned 274 [OF *aloser*].

als(o). See **as.**

als(o), alce (1377) *adv.* also, besides 65, 194, etc., thus, in this way 827 [OE *alswā*].

altogeder *adv.* utterly 15 [OE *al(l)* + *tōgædere*].

alþer- *prefix intensifying superl.* in **alþer-fayrest** very best 1379; **alþer-fynest** finest of all 1637; **alþer-rychest** mightiest of all 1666; **alþer-swettest** sweetest of all 699 [OE *alra*, gen. pl.].

alum *sb.* alum 1035 [OF *alum*].

am 1 *sg. pres.* am 736, 747, 1663 [OE *am*].

amaraunȝ *sb. pl.* emeralds 1470 [OF *emeraude*].

amastised *adj.* of amethyst 1470n. [from OF *amatiste*].

amed *sg. pa. t.* valued 698 [OF *aesmer*].

amended *pp.* mitigated 248 [OF *amender*].

amonestes 3 *sg. pres.* urges, charges 818 [OF *amonester*].

amen *interj.* amen 1812 [L *amen*].

among(e) *adv.* constantly 1414; *prep.* among 25, 774 [OE *onmáng*].

amounted *sg. pa. t.* amounted to 395 [OF *amunter*].

and(e) *cj.* and 2, 1469, etc., (pleonastic, correl. with *and*) 1469 (1st), but 265, 386, 562, 664, 805, 935, 945 (2nd), 1165, 1347, 1809, if 730, 739, 749, 864, 1346, (correl. with *why*) when, seeing that 1597 [OE *and*].

angeleȝ. See **aunge(l)l(e)s.**

anger *sb.* fury 572, fit of anger 1602 [ON *angr*].

angre *adj.* caustic 1035 [from prec.].

ani *adj.* any 30, 42, etc. [OE *ǣnig*].

ankreȝ *sb. pl.* anchors 418 [OF *ancre*, OE *ancor*].

anoynted *pp.* consecrated (by anointing) 1446, 1497 [OF *anoint*, pp. of *enoindre*].

anon *adv.* at once 480, 1741 [OE *on ān*].

anoþer *adj.* another 469, 481, 1755; *pron.* 65, 1668 [OE *ān oþer*].

anournements *sb. pl.* furnishings 1290 [cf. OF *ao(u)rnement*].

anvnder *adv.* below, underneath 1409; *prep.* under 609, 1206, 1378 [*an-* + OE *under*].

aparaunt *adj.* comparable; *a. to* like 1007n. [from OF *aparier, s'aparer* (*a*)].

apered *sg. pa. t.* appeared 1533 [OF *aper-, apareir*].

apert *adv.* elegantly, skilfully 1463 [from OF *apert*].

apyke *v.* array 1637, display, set 1479 [*a-* + OE **pīcan*, cf. *pīcung*].

apparement *sb.* furniture 1270 [OF *aparement*].

apple *sb.* apple 241 [OE *æppel*].

apple-garnade *sb.* pomegranate 1044 [prec. + OF *garnate, grenade*].

aproche *v.* approach 68, etc.; *sg. pres. subj.* **aproch** 167 [OF *aproch(i)er*].

ar(n) *pl. pres.* are 8, 15, 1034n., etc. [OE *aron*].

arayed *pp.* dressed 134, 816, adorned 812, set out 1442, shaped 1458 [AN *araier*].

are *adv.* before 438, 1128 [ON *ár*, OE. *ǣr*].

arest *sg. pa. t.* stopped 766 [OF *arester*].

arȝed *sg. pa. t.* terrified 572, was afraid 713 [OE *eargian*].

ark *sb.* Ark 335, etc., **arc** 413 [OE *ærc*].

armes *sb.*[1] *pl.* arms 643, 1667n. [OE *earm*].

armes *sb.*[2] *pl.* arms, military arts 1306, 1773 [OF *armes*].

art 2 *sg. pres.* are 142, etc. [OE *eart*].

as, als(o) *adv.* (such) as 7, 14, etc., (intensive) 64, 1099, etc., (correl. with *as* cj.) 1134, etc.; *also as* just as 1618; *as to* so as to 567; *cj.* **as** as, like 222, etc., (according) as 92, 1520, 1726, while 133, 433, etc., as if, as though 1142, etc., as being, in that it was 1007, 1018, as one who 748, to the extent that, as much as 776, 813 [(shortened from) OE *alswā*].

asayled *sg. pa. t.* assailed 1188 [OF *asaill-, asalir*].

as(s)caped *pa. t.* left 569, slipped 1776 [AN *ascaper*].

as(s)cry *sb.* clamour, alarm 838, 1784, **askry** 1206 [OF *escri*].

asent *sb.* accord; *in a.* together 788 [OF *asent*].

as(s)yse *sb.* custom 844; *in a gvd a.* in a fitting manner 639 [OF *as(s)ise*].

askes *sb. pl.* ashes 626, etc. [ON *aska*, OE *ascan*, pl.].

askes *v.* ask (*at* of) 924n., (*after* about) 1098, require 1127, 1742, seek 1109; *þat ho . . . a.* that are hers 2 [OE *ǣcsian, ǎxian*].

aspaltoun *sb.* asphalt 1038 [OF *asphaltoun*].

asse *sb.* ass 1086; *wylde a.* wild asses, onagers 1676 [OE *assa*].

assemble *v.* assemble 1364, 1769 [OF *asembler*].

astel *sg. pa. t.* escaped 1524 [*a-* + OE *stelan*].

asure *sb.* azure 1411, **aȝer** 1457 [OF *asur*].

at *prep.* at, by, in, on 40, 70, etc., (in expressions of time and manner) 1163, etc., of, from 924, 1619, at the hands of 1131 [OE *æt*].

at(t)yred *pp.* attired 36, 114 [OF *atirer*].

atlyng *sb.* intention 688 [from ON *ætla*].

a-trauerce *adv.* across (them) 1473 [OF *a travers*].

attled *pp.* created 207 [ON *ætla*].

atwappe *v.* slip past 1205n. [*at-* + ON *vappa*].

aþel *adj.* noble, fine, proud, excellent, glorious 207, 1276, etc. [OE *æþele*].

aucly *adj.* amiss; (as *sb.*) blemish 795n. [ON, cf. OI *ǫfugr*, OE *afulic*].

auncetereȝ *gen.* forefather's 258 [OF *ancestre*]

aune *adj.* own 11, 1659, 1707, **auen** 595, 1222, **owne** 75 [OE *āgen*].

aunge(l)l(e)s, a(u)ngeleȝ *sb. pl.* angels 19, etc. [OF *angele*].

aunteres *sb. pl.* happenings 1600 [OF *aventure*].

auter *sb.* altar 10, 506, etc., **avter** 1477 [OF *auter*].

auwhere *adv.* anywhere 30 [OE *āhwǣr*].

auayed *pp.* informed; *a. of* made aware of, shown 1311 [OF *avei-, avier*].

avayment *sb.* display 1358 [OF *aveiement*].

avaunt *sb.* vow 664 [from OF *avanter*].

avyled *sg. pa. t.* defiled 1151; *pp.* 1713 [OF *aviler*].

auised *pp.* determined 1365 [OF *aviser*].

avoy *interj.* for shame 863 [OF *avoi*].

avow v. affirm 664 [OF *avouer*].
away adv. away 286, etc., gone, absent 1241 [OE *on weg*].
awayled sg. pa. t. availed 408 [a- + OF *vail-, valoir*].
awrank adv. awry, wretchedly *891* [a- + OE *wráng*].
aзer. See **asure**.

babel adv. as a fool, foolishly 582 [cf. AN *bable* 'babble (of fools)', L *babulus* 'fool'].
baboynes sb. pl. baboons, grotesques 1409n. [OF *babuin*].
bachlereз sb. pl. young knights 86 [OF *bacheler*].
badde adj. bad, vile 1228 [? from OE *bǽddel*].
bay sb. bay 1392n. [OF *baie*].
bayn adv. eagerly 1511 [from ON *beinn*].
baytayled pp. battlemented 1183 [OF *bataill(i)er*].
bayted pp. baited (by dogs) 55n. [ON *beita*].
bak sb. back 155, 980, 1412 [OE *bæc*].
bale sb. evil-doing 276, disaster 980n., misery 1256; adj. terrible 1243; **balleful** wretched 979 [OE *balu(ful)*].
balterande ppl. adj. hobbling 103 [? ON, cf. ODa. *bolte*].
baneres sb. pl. banners (hung on trumpets) 1404 [AN *banere*].
banne sb. edict 95, 1361 [OE *gebann*, OF *ban*].
banned sg. pa. t. cursed 468; ppl. adj. accursed 885 [OE *bannan*].
bantelles sb. pl. stepped corbels 1459n. [see note].
barayn adj. barren, infertile 659 [AN *baraine*, f.].
bare adj. bare, naked 452, etc., (as sb.) bare skin 791; adv. only 1573 [OE *bær*].
bared pp. shown 1149 [OE *barian*].
bare-heued adj. bare-headed 633 [OE *bær* + *héafod*].
barer(e)s sb. pl. barriers (in front of gates) 1263, outworks 1239 [AN *barrere*].
barn(e) sb. child, son 329, 378, etc.; **barnage** childhood 517 [(from) OE *bárn*].

baronage sb. (company of) barons 1424 [OF *baronage*].
baroun sb. baron, lord 1372, etc. [AN *barun*].
barreз sb. pl. bars 884, 963 [OF *barre*].
barst. See **brestes**.
bases sb. pl. bases 1278, 1480 [OF *base*].
bassyn sb. basin 1145, 1278, 1456 [OF *bacin*].
basteles gen. of a bastille (turret on wheels) 1187 [OF *bastille*].
batede sg. pa. t. abated, stopped 440 [OF *abatre*].
batelment sb. battlements 1459 [from OF *bataill(i)er*].
batered sg. pa. t. reverberated 1416 [AN *baterer*].
baþed pl. pa. t. bathed 1248 [OE *baþian*].
baume v. cheer 620n. [from OF *ba(u)me*].
bauseneз sb. pl. badgers 392 [OF *bausen*].
bawelyne sb. bowline 417 [OE *boga* + *line*, cf. AN *boeline*, MLG *bōlīne*].
be v. be 42, 45, etc., **by** 104, 212, 356, 1610; sg. subj. **be** 83, 148, etc., **bi** 1330; pl. subj. **be(n)** 12, 103, etc.; sg. imper. **be** 1061; pl. imper. **bes** 904; pp. **ben** 328, 424, etc., **bene** 659n. [OE *bēon*].
becom v. become 1128 [OE *bicuman*].
bed(d), bedde sb. bed 834, 1765, 1787 [OE *bed(d)*].
bede v. 1640; sg. pa. t. **bed(e)** 440, *1559*n., etc.; pl. **beden** 942; pl. imper. **bede** 1507; pp. **beden(e)** 95, 351. bid, command, ask 95, etc., offer, serve 1507n., promise 1640 [OE *bēodan*].
beholde. See **byholde**.
beke sb. beak 487 [OF *bec*].
bekyr sb. beaker, (large) cup *1474* [ON *bikarr*].
bem sb. sun's rays 603 [OE *bēam*].
bench(e) sb. bench, seat 854; (vp)on (þe) b. at the table 130, 1395, 1499; baroun vpon b. lord of the king's council 1640 [OE *benc*].
bent sb. pasture 1675 (OE *benet*].
berde sb. beard 1693; adj. **berdles** beardless 789 [OE *béard(lēas)*].

bere *v.* 649, etc.; *sg. subj.* 582; *pa. t.* **ber(e)** 1273, 1412, 1480; *pres. p.* **berande** 1405; *pp.* **bor(n)e** 584, 1073. bear, carry 1405, have 333, 1023, give birth to 649, (be) born 584, 1073, produce 1042, (refl.) behave 582; *b. vp(on lofte)* held up, supported 1273, 1480; *b. hit on honde* carried it in their hands 1412n.; *sb.* **beryng** disposition, behaviour 1060, 1228 [(from) OE *beran*].

berfray *sb.* siege-tower 1187 [OF *berfrei*].

beryl *sb.* beryl 554n., 1132 [OF *beril*].

best(e) *adj. superl.* best, noblest 114, 913, etc.; *of þe b.* the best of 170; *adv.* best 275, 539, 1060 [OE *betst*].

best(e) *sb.* beast, animal 288, 532, etc., *pl.* **best(t)es** 351, etc.; *pl. gen.* (as adj.) **besten** of animals 1446 [OF *beste*].

bete *sg. imper.* kindle 627; *pp.* **bet** 1012 [OE *bētan*].

betes *pl. pres.* 1263; *pp.* **bet(en)** 1292, 1787. beat 1263, 1787; *b. doun* razed, destroyed 1292 [OE *bēatan*].

better *adj. compar.* better 80, 704, etc. [OE *betera*].

beuerage *sb.* drink 1433, 1717 [OF *bevrage*].

bi. See **be.**

bi, by *prep.* by, beside 86, 622, etc., along 974, around, on 1474, by (means of), through 62, 104, etc., with the help of 1652, in accordance with 865, concerning 1174, (distributive) 338, (as cj.) by the time that 403; *b. þat* by the time that, when 397, 967, by then 1211, 1687; *b. þenne* by then 989; *adv.* by, past 985 [OE *bī*].

bibbes 3 *sg. pres.* drinks 1499 [? L *bibere*, or imit.].

bicnv *sg. pa. t.* accepted 1327 [OE *bicnāwan*].

biddeȝ 3 *sg. pres.* commands 154, 482, 843 [OE *biddan*].

byde *v.* 32, etc.; *sg. pa. t.* **bod** 467, 982; *pl.* **byden** 1243; *sg. pa. t. subj.* **bode** 1030; *pp.* **biden** 616. endure 32, stay, remain 449n., 982n., 1030, remain behind 1243, pass the time, sit 604, 616, wait for (fut. sense) 622; *b. to* awaited 467 [OE *bīdan*].

bifel *sg. pa. t.* took place 1529; *pp.* **bifallen** 1563, 1629 [OE *bifallan*].

bifore *adv.* before, previously, once 659, etc., at the front 114, (from) in front 918; *prep.* before, in front of 602, etc. [OE *biforan*].

bigge, byg(g)e *adj.* great, strong, mighty 229, etc., sharp 43; *superl.* **big(g)est** mightiest (of men) 1335, most prominent 276 [uncertain].

bigged *pp.* built 1666; *sb.* **byggyng** house, home 378, 811 [(from) ON *byggja*].

bygynnes 3 *sg. pres.* 280, etc.; *sg. pa. t.* **bigan** 1337; *pl.* **bigonne** 123; *pp.* **bygonnen** 749. begin 123, 947, 1401, (absol.) 359, 749, 1337, begin to speak 280 [OE *biginnan*].

byȝe *sb.* collar 1638 [OE *bēah*].

bihynde, byhynde(n) *adv.* behind 155, 918; *prep.* 653, etc. [OE *bihindan*].

byholde *v.* behold, look at, see 64, 150, 1423, **beholde** 607; *sg. pa. t.* **byhelde** 452; *pres. p.* **biholdand** 1544 [OE *biháldan*].

byhoueȝ, bos (687) *v.* is required to, must 554; *impers.* as in *me b.* I must 68, 398, 687 [OE *bihōfian*].

bikennes 3 *sg. pres.* delivers 1296 [*bi-* + OE *cennan*, ON *kenna*].

bilde *pp.* built 1392, **bulde** 1190 [OE *býldan*].

bileued *pl. pa. t.* remained 1549 [OE *bilǣfan*].

bilyue *adv.* quickly, at once 156, 688, 626, etc., after a short time, soon 365; *as b.* at once 1239 [OE **bi līfe*].

biloogh *adv.* below 116n. [*bi-* + ON *lágr*].

byndeȝ *pl. imper.* bind 155; *ppl. adj.* **bounden** enclosed, secured 322 [OE *bindan*].

bynne *prep.* within, on 452, 467 [OE *binnan*].

birlen *v.* offer drink to, serve 1511, 1715 [OE *byr(e)lian*].

birolled *pp.* enveloped 959n. [*bi-* + OF *ro(u)ler*].

bischopes *pl. gen.* bishops' 1445 [OE *biscop*].

biseche *v.* beseech 614 [*bi-*+OE *sēcan*].

biseged *sg. pa. t.* besieged 1180 [*bi-*+ OF *asegier*].

bysulpe3 3 *sg. pres.* defiles 575 [cf. Norw. dial. *sulpa* 'splash'].

byte *v.* 532, 1675; *pp.* **biten** 1047, 1243. bite 1047, feed (*on* on) 532, 1675, afflict, waste (*with* by) 1243 [OE *bītan*].

biteche *v.* deliver, give 871; *sg. pa. t.* **byta3t** 528 [OE *bitǣcan*].

bitydes 3 *sg. pres.* 1804; *sg. subj.* **bytyde** 522; *sg. pa. t.* **bitide** 1647, 1657. befall, happen 522, etc., (fut. sense) 1804n. [*bi-*+OE *tīdan*].

bitter *adj.* bitter 1022; *adv.* **bytterly** bitterly 468 [OE *biter(līce)*].

bitwene *adv.* at intervals, here and there 637, etc.; *prep.* between 703, 707 [OE *bitwēonum*].

biþenkkes *v. refl.*, 3 *sg. pres.* takes thought, considers, decides 1357; *sg. pa. t.* **biþo3t** 125; *sg. imper.* **byþenk** 582 [OE *biþencan*].

blades *sb. pl.* blades 1105 [OE *blæd*].

blak(e) *adj.* black 221, etc.; *sb.* blackness 1009 [OE *blæc*].

blame *sb.* rebuke 43; *boute b.* blameless 260 [OF *blame*].

blame *v.* find fault with 877, utter impiety (*on* against) 1661n. [OF *blamer*].

blande *sb.* mingling; *in b.* amongst 885n. [ON *í bland*].

blasfemy *sb.* blasphemy 1661, **blasfamye** 1712 [OF *blasfemie*].

blastes *sb. pl.* blasts 1783 [OE *blǣst*].

ble *sb.* complexion 791, colour 1126, 1759 [OE *blēo*].

blemyst *sg. pa. t.* dulled, befuddled 1421 [OF *blemiss-*, *blemir*].

blench *sb.* trick 1202 [from OE *blencan*].

blende *pl. pa. t.* mingled 1788; *pp.* spread 967n. [ON *blend-*, *blanda*].

blesse3 *v.* bless 470n., etc.; *pp.* **blest** 1718 [OE *blētsian*].

blykked *sg. pa. t.* shone 603 [OE *blician*].

blykned *sg. pa. t.* faded 1759; *ppl.*

adj. **blyknande** shining 1467 [ON *blikna*].

blynde *adj.* blind 103, etc. [OE *blínd*].

blyndes 3 *sg. pres.* grows dull; *b. of ble* loses colour 1126 [from prec.].

blynne *v.* end 1812, refrain (*of* from) 1661; *b. of* cease 440n. [OE *blinnan*].

blysse *sb.* joy 260, 473, eternal bliss 177, 237, 546, ceremony 1765; *adj.* **blysful** joyful 1075 [(from) OE *bliss*].

blyþe *adj.* fair 1085, gracious 1228, glad (*of* of) 1706; *adv.* **blyþ(e)ly** graciously 82, zealously 1718 [OE *blīþe; blīþlīce*].

blo *adj.* livid 1017 [ON *blár*].

blod *sb.* blood 1248, 1446, 1788, race, nation 686 [OE *blōd*].

blomes *sb. pl.* blooms 1042, 1467 [ON *blóm*].

blonke3 *sb. pl.* horses 87, **blonkkes** 1392; *pl. gen.* (as adj.) **blonkken** in *b. bak* horseback 1412 [OE *blanca*].

blowe *v.* blow 437; *pl. pa. t.* **blwe** 885 [OE *blāwan*].

blubrande *ppl. adj.* bubbling 1017 [imit.].

blusch *v.* glance, look 904, etc.; *sg. pa. t.* **bluschet** 982 [OE *blyscan*].

blusnande *pres. p.* gleaming 1404 [cf. OE *blysian*].

blustered *pl. pa. t.* stumbled about 886 [? LG *blustern* 'flutter'].

bobaunce *sb.* arrogance 179, 1712 [OF *bobance*].

bod(e). See **byde.**

bode *sb.* command 979 [OE *bod*].

bodi *sb.* body 11, person 32, appearance 1061, (as indef. pron.) one, a man 260 [OE *bodig*].

bodworde *sb.* message 473 [ON, cf. OI *boð-ord*].

boffet *sb.* blow 43, blast 885n. [OF *buffet*].

bo3(ed). See **bowe.**

bo3e *sb.* bough(s), branch(es) 616, 1467, 1481 [OE *bōg, bōh*].

bo3t *pl. pa. t.* bought 67; *pp.* (refl.) 63 [OE *bōhte*, pa. t. of *bycgan*].

boy *sb.* churl, man of no account 878 [uncertain].

boyles 3 *sg. pres.* boils 1011 [AN *boiller*].

boke *sb.* book 197, 966 [OE *bōc*].
bok-lered *adj.* learned (in books) 1551 [prec.+OE *lǣred*].
bol *sb.* bull 1682; *pl.* **boles** 55, **bule3** 392 [OE *bula*, ON *boli*].
bolde *adj.* bold, worthy, fine 789, etc., (as *sb.*) bold man 811; *bes so b.* dare 904 [OE *báld*].
bole *sb.* trunk (of tree) 622 [ON *bolr*].
bolle *sb.* bowl 1145, *1474*n., 1511 [OE *bolla*].
bolled *pp.* decorated in relief, embossed 1464 [? ON, cf. OI *bolgna*].
bolned *sg. pa. t.* swelled 363; *ppl. adj.* **bolnande** overweening 179 [ON *bólgna*].
bonde *adj.* (as *sb.*) bondmen, serfs 88 [from OE *bónda*].
bone *sb.* command 826 [ON *bón*].
boner *adj.* kind 733 (OF in *de bon aire*).
bones *sb. pl.* bones 1040 [OE *bān*].
bonk(k)e3, bonk (379n.) *sb. pl.* slopes 379, 383, 392, land (sg. sense) 363n., 482; *by b.* by the way 86 [ON **banke*, cf. OI *bakki*].
borde *sb.* table 1433, 1717; *bynne b.* on board (ship) 452, 467; *vpon b.* on deck 470; *of b.* wooden 1190 [OE *bórd*].
bore. See **bere.**
bore3 *sb. pl.* boars 55 [OE *bār*].
borgoune3 *pl. pres.* flourish 1042 [OF *bourgeonner*].
bor3(e), bur3(e), bour3 (1377) *sb.* town, city 982, 1239, etc., great house, mansion 45, 82, property, estate 63n.; *in vch a b.* in every place 1061n.; *in b. and in felde* in town and country 1750 [OE *burh*].
borlych *adj.* noble 1488 [cf. OE *borlīce*, adv.].
borne. See **bere.**
borne *sb.* water 482 [OE *búrne*].
bornyst. See **burnyst.**
bos *sb.* cow-house, manger 1075 [cf. OE *bōsig*, MLG *bōs*].
bos, bosk(ed). See **byhoue3, buske3.**
boske3 *sb. pl.* cow-houses 322n. [see note].
bost *sb.* boasting 179, defiance 1712; *wyth b. and wyth pryde* with pomp and ceremony 1450; **boster** boaster 1499 [(from) AN *bost*].
bot *adv.* only, merely 216n., 335, etc.;

cj. but 13, 133, etc., unless 1119; *b. if* unless 1110, 1360; *b. þat* were it not for the fact that 881; *prep.* but, except 209, 374, etc. [OE *būtan*].
bot *sb.*[1] boat, Ark 473n. [OE *bāt*].
bot *sb.*[2] end; *bi b.* quickly 944 [OF *a (de) bot*, *(tot) de bot* 'quickly' (AN sense)].
bote *sb.*[1] assistance 1616 [OE *bōt*].
bote *sb.*[2] boot, shoe 1581 [OF *bote*, ON *bóti*].
boþe *adj. and pron.* both 242, 824, etc.; *b.* two both 155; *adv.* both 20, 80, 1102n., etc., as well 11, 57, 187, 794, 832 [ON *bǽðir*].
boþem, boþom *sb.* pit 1030, valley (-bottom) 383, 450; *adj.* **boþemle3** bottomless 1022 [(from) OE **boþm*, *botm*].
bougoun3 *pl. gen.* of drumsticks 1416 [OF *bougon*, *boujon* 'bolt'].
bounden. See **bynde3.**
bounet *pp.* present 1398n. [ON *bún-*, *búinn*].
bounte *sb.* bounty 1436 [OF *bo(u)nte*].
bour *sb.* bower, chamber, (private) room 129, 1075, 1126, compartment (for animals) 322 [OE *būr*].
bour3. See **bor3(e).**
boute *prep.* without 260; *be b.* be without, go without 824 [OE *būtan*].
bowe *v.* 45, etc., **bo3** 1551, etc. *pl. subj.* **bowe** 944; *pl. imper.* **bowe3** 944. go 45, 1242, etc., owe allegiance to 1746; *b. after* follow, pay homage to 1750, 1796; *b. to* (absol.) approach 1551 [OE *būgan*].
boweles *sb. pl.* entrails 1251 [OF *bo(u)el*].
brayd(e) *sb.* sudden movement; *in (at) a b.* forthwith 539, 1507 [OE *brǣgd*, *gebregd*, ON *bragð*].
brayden *pp.* embellished (*of* with) 1481; *ppl. adj.* **browden** linked (in jewellery) 1132 [OE *bregdan*].
brayn *sb.* brain(s) 1248, 1421, 1788 [OE *brǽgen*].
braken *sb.* bracken 1675 [ON **brakni*, cf. Sw. *bräken*].
bras(se) *sb.* brass, bronze 1271, 1443, 1480, brass trumpets 1783 [OE *brǽs*].
brath *sb.* violence 916 [ON, cf. OI *bráþr*].
braunches. See **bronch.**

bred *sb.* bread 620, 636, 1105 [OE *brēad*].

bred *sg. pa. t.* bred 257, grew, became 1558 [OE *brēdan*].

bredande *pres. p.* spreading (out) 1482 [OE *brǣdan*].

brede *sb.* width 316 [OE *brǣdu*].

bredes *sb. pl.* roast meats 1405 [OE *brēde*].

breyþed *sg. pa. t.* rushed 1421 [ON *bregða*].

brek *sg. pa. t.* 1105, 1239; *pp.* **broken** 1047. break 1047, 1105, breach 1239 [OE *brecan*].

brem *adj.* fearful 229; *adv.* **bremly** vigorously 509 [(from) OE *brēme*].

brenneʒ 3 *sg. pres.* burns 916; *pl.pa. t.* **brened** 509; *pp.* **bren(ne)d** 959, (*in* to) 1292; *ppl. adj.* **brennande** 1012; **brende** in *b. golde* gold refined by fire, pure gold 1456, 1488 [ON *brenna*].

brentest *adj. superl.* steepest 379 [ON **brent*-, cf. OI *bretta*, OE *brant*].

brere-flour *sb.* briar-rose 791 [next + OF *flo(u)r*].

breres *sb. pl.* briars 1694 [OE *brēr*].

bresed *pl. pa. t.* bristled 1694n. [see note].

brest *sb.*[1] breast 1693 [OE *brēost*].

brest *sb.*[2] calamity 229 [ON *brestr*].

brestes *pl. pres.* 1263, 1783; *sg. pa. t.* **barst** 963. burst (*out of* out from) 1783; *b. vp* burst, smash 963, 1263 [OE *berstan*, ON *bresta*].

breþe, breth(e) *sb.* smoke 509, fumes, stench 967, fury 916 [OE *brǣþ*, cf. ON *brǣði*].

breued *pp.* written (down) 197 [ON *bréfa*].

brych *sb.* sin 848 [OE *bryce*].

brydale *sb.* wedding feast 142 [OE *brȳdealu*].

bryddes *sb. pl.* birds 288, 1482 [OE *brid*].

bryʒt *adj.* bright, shining, beautiful 1278, etc., fine, clean 20, (as *sb.*) fair one 470; *compar.* **bryʒter** brighter 1132; *adv.* **bryʒt** brightly 218, 603, *1506; adv. superl.* **bryʒtest** most finely, most cleanly 114 [OE *breht, beorht(e)*].

brymme *sb.* bank 365 [cf. MHG *brem*].

brynge *v.* bring 620, etc.; *sg. pa. t. and pp.* **broʒt** 95, 487, etc.; *pl.* **broʒten** 86, 1375; *pl. imper.* **bryngeʒ** 82 [OE *bringan*].

brynkeʒ *sb. pl.* edges, brink 384 [cf. OI *brekka*, MLG *brink*].

brynston *sb.* brimstone 967 [?OE *bryne + stān*, cf. ON *brennistein*].

brod(e) *adj.* broad, large, great 584, 603, etc., long 659; *b. ʒates* main gateway 854; *b. halle* great hall 129; *adv.* spaciously 1392 [OE *brād(e)*].

broken. See **brek.**

bronch *sb.* (small) branch 487; *pl.* **braunches** 1464, 1482 [OF *bra(u)nche*].

bronde *sb.* sword 1246, brand, piece of firewood 1012 [OE *bránd*].

broþe *adj.* angry 149, fearsome 1409; **broþelych** wild *or* vile 848; *adv.* **broþely** wretchedly 1030, 1256 [(from) ON *brāðr*].

broþer *sb.* kinsman 772n. [OE *brōþor*].

browden. See **brayden.**

browes *sb. pl.* eyebrows 1694 [OE *brū*].

brugge *sb.* drawbridge 1187 [OE *brycg*].

brurdes *sb. pl.* edges 1474; *adj.* **brurdful** brimful 383 [OE *bré(o)rd-(ful)*].

brused *pp.* bruised 1047 [OE *brȳsan*, AN *bruser*].

brutage *sb.* bratticing, hoarding 1190 (see note to lines 1383–4) [OF *bretesche, bretesque*].

bukkeʒ *sb. pl.* bucks 392 [OE *bucca*].

bulde, buleʒ. See **bilde, bol.**

burde *sb.* woman, lady 80, 378, etc. [OE **byrde*, cf. *byrdicge*].

burʒ(e). See **borʒ(e).**

burne *sb.* 142, 149, etc.; *pl.* **burne** 824n. man 80, etc., servant 616, (in address) sir 142 [OE *béorn*].

burnyst *pp.* burnished, polished 1085; *ppl. adj.* **bornyst** 554 [OF *burniss-, burnir*].

burre *sb.* blow, shock 32 [ON *byrr*].

burþen *sb.* burden 1439 [OE *býrþen*].

busch *sb.* beating, rattle 1416 [from OF *buschier*].

busily *adv.* zealously 1446 [from OE *bysig*].

buske3 v. 633, etc.; *pl. pa. t.* **bosked** 834; *sg. imper.* **busk** 333, **bosk** 351. go 834, drive 351, make ready 1395, (refl.) hasten 633, (refl.) take 333; *b. in wede3* dressed 142 [ON *búask*].

busmar *sb.* scorn 653 [OE *bysmer*, *bysmor*].

butter *sb.* butter 636 [OE *butere*].

cach(e) v. 898, etc.; *pl. pres.* **cach-ches** 1541; *sg. pa. t.* **ca3t** 1426; *pl.* **ca3t** 1275; *pp.* **ca3t** 1296, 1612, **ka3t** 1215, 1254, 1789. catch, sieze, capture 1215, etc., take 898, 1275, accept 1619, overtake 1800, conceive 1426, drive 16, fix, tie 1254, hasten, go 629; *c. to close* hasten to come together, knock together 1541 [AN *cachier*].

cagged *pp.* bound 1254 [uncertain].

cayre, kayre v. go 901, bring 1478, ? dither, hesitate 945n.; *c. at* drive 1259n.; *c. and com* went to and fro 85n. [ON *keyra*, partially confused with AN *carier*].

cayser *sb.* emperor, ruler, master 1322, 1374, **kayser** 1593 [ON *keisari*].

caytif *adj.* evil, wretched 1426, 1605 [AN *caitif*].

cal *sb.* summons 61 [ON *kall*].

calf *sb.* calf 629 [OE *cælf*].

calle v. 1370, etc.; *pl. pres.* **calles** 1522; *sg. pa. t.* **calde** 1583. call, name, address as 8, etc., adduce 1119, summon 162, 948, 1562, call out 1345, 1564, ask for 1522; *c. vpon* calls for 1427; *c. on* appealed to 1097; *be (is) c.* be known as, be 1015, 1119; *sb.* **callyng** summons 1362 [(from) ON *kalla*].

campe *adj.* rough 1695n. [from ON *kampr* 'beard'].

candelstik *sb.* lamp-stand 1478, 1532, **condelstik** 1275 [OE *candelsticca*].

capeles *sb. pl.* horses 1254 [cf. ON *kapall*].

capstan *sb.* capstan 418 [Prov. *cabestan*].

captyuide *sb.* (Jewish) captivity 1612 [cf. L *captivitas*].

carayne *sb.* carrion 459 [AN *caroine*].

care, kare (234) *sb.* distress 393, 777, 1550, misfortune 234; *adj.* **careful** anxious 770; *adv.* **carfully** ignominiously 1252, 1679 [OE *caru*; *carful(līce)*].

caryed *pp.* brought 1765 [AN *carier*].

carle *sb.* churl 876, **karle** 208 [ON *karl*].

carneles *sb. pl.* (embrasures in) battlements 1382 [OF *carnel, crenel*].

carp *sb.* speech 23, words 1327 [ON *karp*].

carpes 3 *sg. pres.* speaks 74, 1591; *sb.* **carping** speech, words 1550 [(from) ON *karpa*].

casydoynes *sb. pl.* chalcedonies 1471 [OF *cassidoine*].

cast. See **kest** *sb.*

casteles *sb. pl.* castles 1458 [AN *castel*].

catel *sb.* treasure 1296 [AN *catel*].

cause *sb.* cause, reason 1119, 1587, **cawse** 65; *bi c. of* for the sake of 1519 [OF *cause*].

certe3 *adv.* certainly 105 [OF *certes*].

cerues. See **kerue.**

cete *sb.* city 78, etc., **cety** 679, 722, **cite** 673, 926; *pl.* **ceteis** 958, **citees** 968, 1015, **cities** 940 [OF *cite*].

chayer *sb.* throne 1218 [AN *chaere*].

chambre *sb.* officers of the chamber, household 1586n. [OF *chambre*].

charged *sg. pa. t. and pp.* burdened 1258, enjoined 464, entrusted 1272; *ppl. adj.* laden 1295, heavy, grievous 1154 [OF *charger*].

chariotes *sb. pl.* chariots, wagons 1295 [OF *chariot*].

chast v. chasten 860 [OF *chastiier*].

chastysed *sg. pa. t.* punished 543 [? from prec.].

chaufen v. encourage 128 [OF *chaufer*].

chaunce *sb.* fortune, circumstance 1125, 1129, 1588, fate 1154 [AN *ch(e)aunce*].

chaundeler *sb.* lamp-stand 1272 [AN *cha(u)ndeler*].

chaunged *sg. pa. t.* changed 713; *pp.* (*to* into) 1258; *ppl. adj.* **chaun-gande** 1588 [AN *cha(u)nger*].

chef *adj.* chief, main, great 1272, 1586, first 684; *c. halle* great hall 1588 [OF *chef*].

chef *sb.* leader 1238 [as prec.].

cheftayn *sb.* chieftain, lord 1295, **cheuetayn** 464 [OF *chevetaine*].

chekes *sb. pl.* cheeks 1694 [OE *cēce*].

chekkes *sb. pl.* attacks 1238 [OF *eschec*].

cher(e) *sb.* countenance, bearing 28, 139, composure 1539, hospitality 128; *mad god c.* behaved pleasantly 641 [OF *ch(i)ere*].

cherisch, cherych *v.* cherish, look after 543, 1644, respect 1154; *c. with cher* treat hospitably 128 [OF *cheriss-, cherir*].

cheualrye *sb.* (body of) knights 1238 [OF *chevalerie*].

cheue *sg. pres. subj.* should happen; *if hit c. þe chaunce* if it should happen 1125 [OF *chever*].

chyde *v.* rail (*to* at) 1586 [OE *cīdan*].

chylde *sb.* son 1303; *pl.* **childer** children 1300; *pl. gen.* (as adj.) **chyldryn** of the children of Israel 684 [OE *cild*, pl. *cildru*].

chynneȝ *sb. pl.* chins 789 [OE *cinn*].

chysly *adv.* solicitously, lovingly 543 [from OE *cīs*].

chorles *sb. pl.* churls, peasants, slaves 1258, 1583 [OE *céorl*].

chosen *pp.* chosen 684 [OE *cēosan*].

ciences, cite(es), cities. See **syence, cete.**

clay *sb.* clay 312, etc., plaster 1618 [OE *clæg*].

clay-daubed *adj.* daubed with clay 492 [from prec. + OF *dauber*].

claymed *pl. pa. t.* claimed 1097 [OF *claim-, clamer*].

clam *sg. pa. t.* climbed up 405 [OE *clímban*].

clanly(ch) *adv.* in a clean manner 1089, (*and* duly) 264, smoothly 310, politely 1621, completely 1327 [OE *clænlīce*].

clanner. See **clene.**

clannes(se) *sb.* cleanness 1, 12, 26, 1087, 1809 [OE *clǽnness*].

claryoun *sb.* (appos.) clarion 1210 [ML *clario(n-)*, cf. OF *claron*].

clater *v.* clatter, beat *839*n., crash down 912, resound 972; *sb.* **clatering** clattering *1515* [OE **clatrian; clatrung*].

clawes *sb. pl.* claws *1696*n. [OE *clawu*].

cleches 3 *sg. pres.* 634, 1348; *pl.* **cleche** 12; *sg. pa. t. and pp.* **cleȝt** 858, 1655. obtain 12, fasten 858, fix 1655; *c. to* seizes, takes up 634, 1348 [OE **clæcan*].

clef *sg. pa. t.* split, shattered 367; *pl.* **clouen** 965 [OE *clēofan*].

cleme *sg. imper.* seal, caulk 312 [OE *clǽman*].

clene *adj.* clean, bright, pure, elegant, well-bred, fair, splendid, excellent 17n., 119n., 1057n., 1072, etc., (in technical religious sense) 334, 508; *c. of* free from 730; *bi a c. noumbre* in a full reckoning 1731; *compar.* **clener** cleaner 1072; *adv.* **clene** brightly 175, fully 1606, excellently 1287n., 1382, 1455; *adv. compar.* **clanner** more cleanly *and* more fully 1100 [OE *clǽne*].

clenges 3 *sg. pres.* clings 1034 [OE *clingan*].

clepes 3 *sg. pres.* asks 1345 [OE *cleopian*].

cler(e) *adj.* clear, bright, beautiful 792, 1400, etc., shrill 1210, plain 26; *compar.* **cler(r)er** brighter 1128, better 1056; *adv. superl.* **clerest** most brightly 1532; *sb.* **clernes** beauty 1353 [(from) OF *cler*].

clergye *sb.* learning; *pure c.* religion 1570 [OF *clergie*].

clerk(k)es *sb. pl.* scholars, learned men 193, etc., (minor) clerics 1266 [OE *clerc*, OF *clerc*].

cleþe *v.* clothe, be clothed 1741 [OE *clǽþan*].

clyde *sb.* plaster, poultice 1692 [OE *cliþa*].

clyffe *sb.* cliff 405, 460, 965 [OE *clif*].

cleȝt. See **cluchches.**

clyket *sb.* catch 858 [OF *cliquet*].

clyppe *v.* attach 418 [OE *clyppan*].

clyues 3 *sg. pres.* is fixed 1630 [OE *clīfan, clifian*].

clyuy *sb.* burdock, bur 1692n. [OE *clīfe*].

clobbeȝ. See **klubbe.**

clos *adv.* firmly 858, 1655 [OF *clos*].

clos *sb.* dwelling 839, 1088 [as prec.].

close *v.* 1541; *pp.* **clos(ed)** 12, 346, etc. enclose, lodge 449n., 1070n., caulk 346, fasten 1569, come together 1541; *c. in* steeped in, full of

12, 512; *ppl. adj.* **closed** closed-in 310 [OF *clos-*, *clore*].

cloþ(e) *sb.* cloth 634, etc.; *pl.* clothes 1400, bedclothes 1788 [OE *clāþ*].

cloþed *pp.* clothed 135 [OE **clāþian*, from prec.].

cloutes *sb. pl.* pieces, shreds 965, **clowteӡ** 367 [OE *clūt*].

clouen. See **clef.**

clowde *sb.* cloud 367; *pl.* **cloudes** 972, **clowdeӡ** 414, 951 [OE *clūd*].

cluchches *pl. pres.* double up 1541; *pl. pa. t.* **clyӡt** stuck 1692 [OE *clyccan*].

clustered *pl. pa. t.* clustered, massed 951; *ppl. adj.* massed 367 [from OE *cluster*, *clyster*].

clutte *ppl. adj.* patched 40n. [OE *geclūtod*].

cnes, cnowen. See **kne, knawe.**

cof *adj.* prompt 624; *adv.* quickly 60, 898; **cofly** quickly 1428 [OE *cāf(e); cāflīce*].

cofer *sb.* coffer 1428, Ark 310n., 339, 492 [OF *coffre*].

coyntyse. See **quoyntis.**

cokreӡ *sb. pl.* leggings 40 [OE *cocer*].

colde *adj.* cold 60, 1591, sluggish, weak 1231n. [OE *cáld*].

cole *sb.* coal 456 [OE *col*].

coler *sb.* collar 1569, *1744* [AN *coler*].

colored *pp.* coloured 456 [OF *coulourer*].

coltour *sb.* (blade of) ploughshare 1547 [OE *culter*].

colwarde *sb.* villainy 181 [OF *culvert*].

com(e) *v.* come 54, 61n., *703*, etc.; *pl. pres.* **com(en)** 1326, 1680; *sg. pa. t.* **com** 361, 878, etc.; *pl.* **com(en)** 85n., 946, etc.; *sg. pa. t. subj.* **com** 36; *pl. imper.* **comeӡ** 60, 801 [OE *cuman*].

comaundes *v.* command 1428, etc. [AN *comaunder*].

combraunce *sb.* difficulty 4 [OF *encombrance*].

combreӡ *v.* overwhelm, overturn 901, 920, 1024 [OF *encombrer*, *acombrer*].

come *sb.* coming 467 [OE *cyme*, vowel from *cuman*].

comende *v.* praise 1 [ML *commendare*].

comfort *sb.* pleasure, delight 459, 492, 1809, cheer 512 [OF *confort*].

comynes *sb. pl.* commons, people 1747 [OF *comune*].

comly(ch) *adj.* seemly 54, etc.; *adv.* **comly** well 312 [OE *cymlic; cymlīce;* vowel from *cuman*].

compaynye *sb.* company (of diners) 119 [AN *compainie*].

comparisuneӡ 3 *sg. pres.* compares 161 [OF *compar(a)isoner*].

compas *sb.* compass; *in þe c. of* in the dimensions of, measuring 319, in (the course of) 1057 [OF *compas*].

compas *v.* 1455; *sg. pa. t.* **compast** 697. devise 697; *c. and kest* set his wits to work 1455 [OF *compasser*].

con *v.*[1] 1056; *pa. t.* **couþe, cowþe** 1, 531, etc. can, may, be able, know how to 1, 813n., 1700, etc.; know, possess 1056, 1287, 1576 [OE *can(n)*, *cūþe*].

con *v.*[2] *pa. t.* (with infin., as equivalent of simple pa. t.) 301, 344, 363, 768, 945, 1362, 1561 [prec. confused with ME *gan* 'did'].

concubines *sb. pl.* concubines 1353, 1400, 1519 [OF *concubine*].

condelstik. See **candelstik.**

confourme *sg. imper. refl.* in *c. þe to* be like 1067n. [OF *conformer*].

connyng *sb.* understanding 1625; *pl.* **coninges** arts 1611 [? ON *kunnandi*].

conquere *sg. pres. subj.* succeed in deciphering 1632; *sg. pa. t.* **conquerd** captured 1431 [OF *conquerre*].

conquerour *sb.* conqueror 1322 [AN *conquerour*].

conquest *pp.* conquered 1305 [OF *conquester*].

consayue *v.* conceive 649 [OF *conceiv-*, *concevoir*].

conterfete *pl. pres. subj.* feign 13 [AN *countrefeter*].

contrare *adj.* perverted, immoral 266 [AN *contrarie*].

contrare *sb.* opposite 4n.; *in contrary of* opposite 1532 [from prec.].

contre *sb.* country, land 281, 1679, **cuntre** 1362, 1612 [OF *cuntree*].

controeued *pl. pa. t.* contrived 266 [OF *contreuve*, *controver*].

conueye(n) v. escort 678, follow (with the eyes) 768 (OF *conveier*].
cooste3. See **cost(e).**
coperounes sb. pl. ornamental tops 1461 [OF *coperoun*].
corage sb. heart 1806 [OF *corage*].
corbyal sb. raven 456 [OF *corb(i)el, corbiaus*].
coroun sb. crown 1444, **crowne** 1275 [AN *corune*].
cors sb. course, way(s), function(s) 264n.; pl. **course** courses (of a meal) 1418 [OF *cours*].
corse sb. body 1072; *his c.* him 683n. [OF *cors*].
corsed sg. pa. t. cursed 1583; pp. 1033, 1800 [OE *cursian*].
corsyes sb. pl. corrosives 1034 [from OF *corosif*].
cort(e), court(e) sb. court 191, etc. [OF *co(u)rt*].
cortays(e) adj. courteous, well-bred 512, 1089, (as sb.) courteous one, gracious one 1097; adv. **cortaysly** graciously 564, 1435 [(from) OF *co(u)rteis*].
cortaysye sb. courtesy, virtue 13 [OF *co(u)rteisie*].
cortyn sb. bedcurtain 1789 [OF *cortine*].
coruppte adj. corrupt 281 [OF *corrupt*].
coruen. See **kerue.**
cost(e) sb. 85, 478, 1322, **koste** 912; pl. **cooste3** 1033, **costes** 460. land 1322, (sg. sense) 460, region, countryside 85, 478, part 912, shore 1033 [OF *coste*].
coste3 sb. pl. ways; *c. of kynde* laws of nature 1024 [OE *cost*].
costoum sb. custom 851 [OF *co(u)stume*].
cov-hous sb. cow-house 629 [OE *cū + hūs*].
counsayl, counseyl (1619) sb. counsel 1056, 1605, 1619, purpose, plan 683, 1426, decision 1201 [OF *c(o)unseil*].
countenaunce sb. expression, glance 792 [AN *c(o)untenaunce*].
countes 3 sg. pres. (refl.) counts himself 1685; pp. assessed 1731 [OF *c(o)unter*].
course, court(e). See **cors, cort(e).**

cout v. cut 1104 [cf. OI *kuti*, sb.].
couþe. See **con** v.[1]
couþe adj. known 1054 [OE *cūþ*].
couacles sb. pl. lids (of vessels) 1461, 1515 [OF *cove(r)cle*].
coueytes 2 sg. pres. desire 1054 [OF *coveitier*].
couenaunde sb. covenant 564 [OF *covenant*].
couered. See **keuer.**
couered pp. covered 1440; ppl. adj. lidded 1458 [OF *covrir*].
couetyse sb. covetousness 181 [OF *coveitise*].
cowpes, cowþe. See **cuppe, con,** v.[1]
cowwardely adv. miserably 1631 [from OF *cuard*].
crafte sb. skill, art 697, etc., virtue 13; pl. manners, conduct 549 [OE *cræft*].
crage3 sb. pl. crags 449 [? Old British **crag*].
crak sb. blast, flourish (of trumpet, etc.) 1210; pl. **krakkes** 1403 [from OE *cracian*].
craue v. beg 801 [OE *crafian*].
creato(u)r sb. creator 394, 917; gen. **creatores** 191 [OF *creator*].
crepe v. creep, steal (away) 917 [OE *crēopan*].
cry sb. cry, proclamation 1564, 1574 [OF *cri*].
crye v. cry (out) 153, 1080, etc., cry out for 394, sound 1210, proclaim 1751, (as pass. infin.) 1361 [OF *crier*].
crysolytes sb. pl. chrysolites 1471 [OF *crisolite*].
croked adj. curved 1697, unjust 181 [from ON *krókr*].
crone3 sb. pl. cranes 58 [OE *cran*].
crouke3 3 sg. pres. croaks 459 [imit.].
crowne. See **coroun.**
cruppele3 sb. pl. cripples 103 [OE *crypel*].
cubit sb. cubit 319; pl. **cubites** 405, **cupyde3** 315 (L *cubitum*].
cuntre. See **contre.**
cupborde sb. sideboard 1440 (OE *cuppe,* OF *cupe* + OE *bórd*].
cuppe sb. 1461, 1520; pl. **cowpes** 1458, **kowpes** 1510. cup 1458, etc., (coll. sense) cups 1461 [OE *cuppe,* OF *cupe*].

cupple *sb.* couple 332 [OF *cuple*].

curious *adj.* elegant 1353, subtle 1452, **kyryous** skilful *and* fastidious 1109 [OF *curios*].

daȝed *sg. pa. t.* dawned 1755 [OE *dagian*].

day *sb.* day 361, 427, etc.; *gen.* **dayeȝ** in *vpon d.* by day 578; *pl. gen.* **dayeȝ** 224 [OE *dæg*].

dayntys *sb. pl.* dainties 38; *of dayntyeȝ* attractive 1046 [OF *daint(i)e*].

day-rawe *sb.* dawn(-ray), first light 893 [OE *dæg + rāw, ræw*].

dale *sb.* dale 384 [OE *dæl*].

dalt. See **dele.**

dam *sb.* sea 416 [ON *dammr*, MLG, MDu *dam*].

dampped *pp.* damned 989 [OF *dam(p)ner*].

dasande *ppl. adj.* numbing 1538 [ON, cf. OI *dasask*].

date *sb.* date 425 [OF *date*].

daube *sg. imper.* daub, cover (with clay) 313 [OF *dauber*].

daunger *sb.* danger 416, awe (of God) 342; *with d.* disdainfully 71 [AN *daunger*].

debonere *adj.* courteous 830 [OF *de bon aire*].

dece *sb.* dais, platform for high table 38, 1399, 1517, **des(e)** 115, 1394 [OF *deis*].

declar *v.* explain 1618 [L *declarare*].

decre *sb.* decree 1745 [OF *decre*].

ded(e) *adj.* dead 289, etc. [OE *dēad*].

dedayn *sb.* disdain; *hade d. of* took offence at 74 [AN *dedeigne*].

dede *sb.* deed, act, action 181, 588, etc., behaviour 74, task 110, work 1021 [OE *dēd*].

defence *sb.* prohibition 243, prohibited thing 245n. [OF *defens*].

defowle *v.* defile 1129, 1147, 1798 [from OE *fūlian*, infl. by OF *defoler*].

degre *sb.* rank 92 [OF *degre*].

deȝter *sb. pl.* daughters 270, 866, etc., **deȝteres** 933, **deȝtters** 899, **doȝtereȝ** 814 [OE *dohtor*, dat. *dehter*].

deystyne *sb.* destiny, fate 400 [OF *destinee*].

dekenes *sb. pl.* deacons 1266 [OE *deacon, diacon*].

dele *v.* 137, etc.; *pp.* **dalt** 1756. deal out, fulfil 1756, sell 1118, speak 344, 1641; *d. with* have to do with 137, deal in, practise 1561; *d. drwrye* have love-dealings 1065 [OE *dǣlan*].

delful *adj.* wretched 400 [from OF *doel, duel*].

delyuer *adj.* delivered (of a child) 1084 [OF *delivre*].

delyuer *v.* deliver, save 500, purge, destroy 286 [OF *delivrer*].

demed *pl. pa. t. and pp.* considered 1118, called, named 1020, 1611, proclaimed 1745, made proclamation 110n. [OE *dēman*].

demerlayk *sb.* magic arts 1561; *pl.* **demorlaykes** 1578 [OE *(ge)dwimor + ON -leikr*].

demmed *sg. pa. t.* was filled up, overflowed 384 [OE in *fordemman*].

denounced *pp.* borne witness to, honoured 106n. [OF *denoncier*].

departed *pa. t. and pp.* departed, went 396, 1677, parted (from each other) 1074, divided 1738 [OF *departir*].

depe *adj.* deep 374, 384, 416, profound 1609, grievous 1425; *adv.* deeply, gravely 852, deep, far down 158 [OE *dēop(e)*].

depryue *v.* take away, steal 185n., strip 1227, depose 1738 [OF *depriver*].

dere *adj.*[1] stern 214, 683; *superl.* **derrest** bravest 1306 [OE *dēor*].

dere *adj.*[2] noble, worthy, excellent 1302, etc., precious, valuable, costly 1279, 1743, 1792, dear, beloved 52, 814, high (in rank) 92n., innermost 1604, (as *sb.*) great one 1399, noblemen 1394; *superl.* **derrest** noblest 115, bravest 1306, most valuable 1118; *adv.* **dere** highly 698; **derelych** exceedingly 270 [OE *dēore; dēorlīce*].

dereȝ *pl. imper.* harm 862 [OE *derian*].

derf *adj.* great 862; *adv.* **derfly** boldly 1641, **deruely** without hesitation 632 [(from) OE (Nhb.) *dearf*].

derk *adj.* dark 1020; *sb.* night 1755 [OE *de(o)rc*].

derne *adj.* hidden, secret 588, 1611; *adv.* privately 697 [(from) OE *dérne*].

des(e). See dece.

desyres 2 *sg. pres.* desire 545; *sg. subj.* **de3yre** 1648 [OF *desirer*].

depe, deth(e) *sb.* death 1032, etc. [OE *dēap*].

deuel *sb.* Devil 1500; *gen.* **deuele3** 180 [OE *dēofol*].

deuine *sb.* prophet 1302 [OF *devin*].

deuine *v.* interpret 1561 [OF *deviner*].

deuinores *sb. pl.* diviners; *d. of demor-laykes* practitioners of magic arts 1578 [OF *devineor*].

devyse, deuice (1046) *v.* ordain 110, 238, fashion 1288, conceive 1046, (absol.) contrive, make it 1100, explain, expound, describe 1157, etc. [OF *deviser*].

devoyde *v.* (absol.) do away with (it) 908; *sb.* **devoydynge** purging 544 [(from) OF *devoidier*].

deuoutly *adv.* respectfully 814 [from OF *devot*].

dew *sb.* dew 1688 [OE *dēaw*].

dialoke3 *sb. pl.* stories, narratives 1157n. [OF *dialoge*].

dych *sb.* ditch 1251, 1792 [OE *dīc*].

diden. See do.

dy3e(n) *v.* die 400, 1329 [ON *deyja*].

dy3t *v.* 818; *sg. pa. t. and pp.* **dy3t** 632, etc.; *pl.* **di3ten** 1266. ordain, establish 699, (*of* by) 243, prepare 632, 818, place 1794, array, adorn 1688, deal with 1753; *d. to depe* put to death 1266 [OE *dihtan*].

dym(me) *adj.* dark 472, 1016 [OE *dim(m)*].

dyn(e) *sb.* din, noise, clamour 692, 862 [OE *dyne*].

dyngnete *sb.* dignity, high estate 1801 [OF *dignete*].

dysche *sb.* dish, plate 1146, 1279 [OE *disc*].

dyscouered *sg. pa. t. subj.* should reveal 683n. [OF *descovrir*].

dysheriete *v.* misappropriate 185n. [OF *desheriter*].

dispysed *pp.* maltreated 1790 [OF *despis-, despire*].

dyspyt *sb.* wrong 821n. [OF *despit*].

displayes 3 *sg. pres.* tears (open)

1542; *sg. pa. t.* ? fell apart, was broken 1107n. [OF *despleier* ('tear to pieces' in AN)].

dyspleses *v.* displease 196, 1136, be displeased 1494 [OF *desplaisir*].

disserued *sg. pa. t.* deserved 613 [OF *deservir*].

disstrye *v.* destroy, overthrow 520, 1160, (absol.) 907 [OF *destruire*].

distres(se) *sb.* power 307n.; *wyth d.* forcibly 1160 [OF *destresse*].

distresed *sg. pa. t. subj.* would have hurt 880 [AN *destresser*].

ditte3 3 *sg. pres.* closes, shuts 588n.; *sg. pa. t.* **dutte** 1182; *ppl. adj.* **dutande** closing, fastening 320 [OE *dyttan*].

diuinite *sb.* divinity, spiritual knowledge 1609 [OF *devinite*].

do *v.* 286, 342, 1647; 3 *sg. pres.* **dos** 341; *pl. pa. t.* **diden** 110; *pl. imper.* **dot3** 862; *pp.* **don(e)** 320, 1801, etc., do, perform 110, 341, 342, behave 692, make 320, put 1224, destroy 989; *d. away* do away with 286, cease 862; *d. doun* of struck down from 1801; *wel d.* be well off 1647n. [OE *dōn*].

dobler *sb.* (large) plate, platter 1146; *pl.* **dubleres** 1279 [AN *dobler, dubler*].

doel *sb.* misery 158, distressing event 852; *with d.* pitifully 1329 [OF *doel, duel*].

dogge *sb.* dog 1792 [OE *docga*].

do3tere3. See de3ter.

do3ty *adj.* bold 1182, 1791; *superl.* **do3tyest** 1306 [OE *dohtig*].

dom(e) *sb.* doom, judgement, punishment, penalty 717, etc., bidding 632, advice 1325, wit 1046 [OE *dōm*].

do(u)ngoun *sb.* dungeon 158, 1224 [OF *donjon*].

dool(e) *sb.* part 216, gift (of grace) 699 [OE *dāl*].

dor(e) *sb.* door 44, 320, etc., doorway 784, gate 1182 [OE *dor, duru*].

dorst *sg. pa. t.* dared 476, **durst** 342; *pl.* **dorsten** 976; *sg. pa. t. subj.* **durst** 615 [OE *dorste*, pa. t. of *dearr*].

dotage *sb.* folly 1425 [cf. MDu. *doten*, OF *radotage*].

dotel *sb.* fool 1517 [? from next].

dotes *v.* act senselessly, drivel 286, 1500, be in confusion 852n. [cf. MDu *doten*].

dot3. See **do.**

doun *adv.* down 150, 289, etc. [OE *dūne*].

doungoun. See **do(u)ngoun.**

douþe, d(o)uthe *sb.* (race of) men 270, 597, retinue 1367, army 1196 [OE *duguþ*].

doue *sb.* dove *469*n., **dove** *481*, **dowue** 485 [ON *dúfa*].

dowed *sg. pa. t.* availed 374 [OE *dugan*].

dowelle *v.* dwell, be, wait 1674 etc.; 3 *sg. pres.* **dwelle3** 158 [OE *dwellan*].

dowrie *sb.* dower(s), property 185 [AN *dowarie*].

dra3tes *sb. pl.* characters (in writing) 1557 [? OE **dræht*, cf. *dragan*, v.].

drank *sg. pa. t.* drank 1517, 1791; *ppl. adj.* **dronkken** drunk 1500 [OE *drincan, druncen*].

draw(e) *v.* 500, 599; *pl. pa. t.* **drawes** 1329; *pl. pa. t.* **dro3(en)** 71, 1394; *pp.* **drawen** 1160. go, come 500, etc.; *d. allyt* hold back, delay 599n.; *d. adre3* (refl.) draw back 71n.; *d. to þe erþe* laid low 1160 [OE *dragan*].

dred(e) *sb.* fear 390, etc., (of God) 295, 342 [from OE *-drǣdan*].

dre3e, dre3ly. See **dry3(e)** *v.* and *adj.*

dremes *sb. pl.* dreams 1578, 1604 [OE *drēam* 'joy', cf. ON *draumr* 'dream'].

drepe3 *v.* strike (down), kill 246, etc. [OE *drepan*].

dressed *pp.* assigned 92, seated 1399, served 1518, **dresset** placed 1477 [OF *dresser*].

dr(u)ye *adj.* dry 412, 460, (physiological) 1096n., (as sb.) dry land 472 [OE *drýge*].

dryed *pp.* made dry 496n. [OE *drýgan*].

dry3(e) *adj.* great 342, enduring, secure 385n.; *adv.* **dry3ly** gravely 74, 344, **dre3ly** continuously, on and on 476 [ON, cf. OI *drjúgr*].

dry3(e), dre3e (1224) *v.* bear, suffer, endure, meet 372n., etc., (absol.) 491 [OE *drēogan*].

dry3tyn *sb.* the Lord, God 214, 243, *1711*, etc., **dry3ttyn** 344; *gen.* **dry3tyne3** 219 [OE *dryhten*].

drink *sb.* drink 123, 182 [OE *drinc*].

dryues 3 *sg. pres.* 433, etc.; *sg. pa. t.* **drof** 214, etc.; *sg. imper.* **dryf** 472; *pp.* **dryuen** 289. drive 214, 289, 433, (*vpon* over) 416, be raised 692, drive in 1760, press on 472; *d. to* reached 219, entered 1425; *ppl. adj.* **dryuen** studded (with nails), riveted 313 [OE *drīfan*].

dro3(en). See **draw(e).**

dro3þe *sb.* drought, dry weather 524 [OE *drūgaþ*].

dronkken. See **drank.**

drouy *adj.* murky 1016 [OE *drōfig*].

drowned *pl. pa. t.* (were) drowned 372; *pp.* 989 [? OE **drūnian*, cf. ON *drukna*].

druye. See **dr(u)ye.**

drwry(e) *sb.* love 699, 1065 [OF *druerie*].

dubbed *pp.* dressed, arrayed 115, 1688, 1743 [OE **dubbian*].

dubleres. See **dobler.**

duk, duc (1235) *sb.* duke, chieftain 38, 1182, etc. [OF *duc*].

dungen *pl. pa. t.* struck 1266 [cf. ON *dengja*].

dunt *sb.* blow 1196 [OE *dynt*].

duren *v.* continue 1021, 1757 [OF *durer*].

durst. See **dorst.**

dusched *sg. pa. t.* struck; *d. to* struck, came over 1538 [imit.].

dutande, dutte, duthe, dwelle3. See **ditte3, douþe, dowelle.**

efte *adv.* again, afterwards 248, 481, etc. [OE *eft*].

egge *sb.* blade 1104, 1246, (valley-) edge, top 383, 451 [OE *ecg*].

eggyng *sb.* urging 241 [from ON *eggja*].

elde *sb.* age 657; *hade hym in helde* was aged 1520n. [OE *éldu*].

elle3 *cj.* as long as 466, 705 [OE *elles*].

eme *sb.* uncle *924*n. [OE *ēam*].

emperour *sb.* emperor 1323 [OF *emperour*].

empire *sb.* (imperial) power, rule 540, 1332, 1349 [OF *empire*].

enaumayld(e) *pp.* enamelled 1411, 1457 [AN *enamailler*].

enbaned *pp.* machicolated 1459n. [Prov. *am-*, *embanar*].

enclyned *pp.* inclined 518 [OF *encliner*].

enclose *sg. imper.* enclose, take in 334 [OF *enclos(e)*, pp. of *enclore*].

ende *sb.* end 303, 1732; *last e.* conclusion, sequel 608n.; *dayes of e.* last days, end of the world 1032; *worlde withouten e.* for all time 712; *on e.* on its end, upright 423; *vpon e.* in the end 1329 [OE *énde*].

ende *v.* end 402 [OE *éndian*].

endentur *sb.* (notched) jointing 313n. [OF *endenture*].

enfaminied *pl. pa. t.* starved 1194 [OF *enfaminer*].

enforsed *pl. pa. t.* drove 938 [OF *enforcier*].

engendered *pl. pa. t.* engendered 272 [OF *engendrer*].

enherite *v.* inherit, come into 240 [OF *enheriter*].

enmies *sb. pl.* enemies 1204 [OF *enemi*].

enourled *pp.* enclosed, steeped (*in* in) 19 [OF **eno(u)rler*, cf. *o(u)rler*, *enorleure*].

enpoysened *sg. pa. t.* poisoned 242 [OF *empoisonner*].

enprysonment *sb.* imprisonment 46 [OF *emprisonnement*].

enteres *v.* enter 349, 1240; *pl. pa. t.* **entred** 842 [OF *entrer*].

entyses *sg. pres.* incite 1137, 1808 [OF *enticier*].

entre *sb.* entry 1779 [OF *entree*].

er *adv.* before, formerly 491; *cj.* before, (after neg.) until 60, 360, etc.; *prep.* in *er þenne* before that time, until that time 1088, 1312, 1339, (as cj.) before 1670 [OE *ǣr*].

erbes *sb. pl.* plants, grass 532, 1675, 1684 [OF *erbe*].

erd(e) *sb.* region, place 1006, dwelling 596; *in e.* in his own country, at home 601n.; *on e.* on earth 892 [OE *éard*].

eres *sb. pl.* ears 879n., etc. [OE *éare*].

erigaut *sb.* (outer) garment, cloak 148 [OF *herigaut*].

erly *adv.* early 895, 946, 1001 [OE (Nhb.) *ǣrlīce*].

erne-hwed *adj.* coloured like an eagle 1698 [from OE *éarn* + *hēow*].

ernestly *adv.* in earnest 277, wrathfully 1240 [OE *éornostlīce*].

erþe, vrþe *sb.* earth, ground 150, 277, 520n., etc., piece of ground 1027 [OE *éorþe*].

ese *sb.* ease 124 [AN *ese*].

ete *sg. pa. t.* ate 1684; *e. of* ate 241 [OE *etan*].

eþe *adj.* easy 608 [OE *ēaþe*].

euel *adj.* vile, sinful 747; *sb.* evil (practice) 277, 573 [OE *yfel*].

euen *adv.* directly, right 510, 602, 1654, exactly 317 [OE *efne*].

euentyde *sb.* evening 479, 485, 782 [OE *ǣfentīd*].

euer *adv.* (for) ever, always 158, 328, etc., at any time 164, 198, etc., (intensive) 834, exceedingly 812; *for e.* for ever 402, 1802 [OE *ǣfre*].

euermore *adv.* (for) evermore 1020, 1031, ever, always 1273, 1523 [prec. + OE *māre*, neut.].

euervchone *pron.* every one (of them) 1221 [OE *ǣfre* + *ylc* + *ān*].

eweres *sb. pl.* ewers, pitchers (accompanying basins) 1457 [AN *ewer*].

excused *v.* excuse, make excuses for 70, (refl.) 62 [OF *excuser*, *escuser*].

exorsismus *sb. pl.* exorcisms; *sorsers of e.* exorcists 1579n. [OF *exorcisme*, ML *exorcismus*].

expowne *v.* expound, explain, set forth 1729; 3 *sg. pres.* **expouneȝ** 1058; *sg. pa. t.* **expouned** 1492n., **expowned** 1606; *sb.* **expouning** explaining, interpretation 1565 [(from) OF *expondre*, *espondre*].

expresse *adv.* plainly 1158 [L *expresse*, cf. OF *expres*, adj.].

face *sb.* face 304n., 903, 978n., etc. [OF *face*].

fader *sb.* father 112, 684, etc., (of God) 542, 680, etc.; *gen.* 1155n. [OE *fæder*].

fayly *sg. pres. subj.* 548; *pl. subj.* **faylen** 737; *sg. pa. t. and pp.* **fayled** 236, 658, etc.; *pres. p.* **faylande** 1535. fail 236, 548, 1631, break down 1539, set 1758, be wanting 737, become short of 1194, come to an end 658, (as prep.) lacking, without 1535; *f. of* failed to find 889 [OF *faillir*].

fayn *adj.* glad 962, 1752, pleased (*of* with) 642; *superl.* **faynest** happiest 1219; *adv.* **fayn** fain, gladly 1629 [(from) OE *fægen*].

fayned *ppl. adj.* spurious 188 [OF *feindre*].

fayr(e) *adj.* fair, excellent, attractive, beautiful 3, 174, etc.; *superl.* **fayrest** 207, etc.; *adv.* **fayre** well, excellently 27, 1486, properly, duly 89, 294, 506, fully 639, exactly 316; *adv. superl.* **fayrest** fairest, best 115 [OE *fæger; fægre*].

fayth(e) *sb.* faith 1161, 1165, 1168; *in f.* indeed 1732; *adj.* honest 1735n.; **faythful** faithful 1167 [from OF *feid, feit*].

falce, fals(e) *adj.* false 1168, etc., [OF *fals*].

falewed *sg. pa. t.* blanched, grew pale 1539 [OE *feal(u)wian*].

falle *v.* 22, etc.; *sg. pa. t.* **fel** 450; *pl.* **fellen** 221, 399; *pp.* **fallen** 304, 559, 1684. fall, go down 221, 450, sink 559, befall, come, be 22, 304, 494n., 567, perish 725, wither 1684; *f. fro* spring from 685; *f. in* fall into, take to 271; *f. in fere* came together 399; *f. on* falls on, attacks 462; *f. to* rush at 837 [OE *fallan*].

famacions *sb. pl.* rumours 188 [OF *diffamation*].

famed *pp.* famed; *f. for* reputed (to be) 275 [OF *famer*].

fande. See **fynde**.

fanne3 3 *sg. pres.* glides (with outspread wings) 457n. [OE *fannian*].

fantummes *sb. pl.* (empty) images 1341 [OF *fantosme*].

farand(e) *adj.* handsome 607, pleasant 1758 [ON *farandi*].

fare *sb.* behaviour 861 [OE *faru*].

fare *v.* 618, etc.; *pl. pres. subj.* 100, 466; *sg. pa. t.* **ferde** 1106; *pp.* **faren** 403. go, be 100, pass 403, fare, get on 466, 1106; *f. fast aboute* busy myself 618n.; *f. forth* goes about 1683, go on your way 621, 929 [OE *faran*; pa. t. from *fēran*].

fast(e) *adv.* fast, quickly 380, 631, etc., freely 1420, earnestly, sternly

936, 1147, greatly, desperately 1194; *a(l)s f.* immediately 440, 1648, 1751 [OE *fæste*].

fat *adj.* fattened (for the table) 627n. [OE *fǣt(t)*].

fatte *sb.* tub 802 [OE *fæt*].

fatted *pp.* fattened (for the table) 56n. [OE *fǣttian*].

faþmed *pl. pa. t.* embraced 399 [OE *fæþmian*].

faure *adj.* 958, 1683, **fawre** 938, 950, **fourre** 1244, **fowre** 540. four 938, etc.; *on alle f.* on all fours 1683 [OE *fēower*].

faurty *adj.* forty 741, 743, **forty** 224, 369, 403 [OE *fēowertig*].

faut(e) *sb.* 236, etc.; *pl.* **fawtes** 1736. fault, offence, sin 177, etc., blemish 1122; *adj.* **fauty** sinful 741; **fautle3** faultless 794 [(from) OF *faute*].

fax(e) *sb.* hair 790, 1689 [OE *feax*].

feb(e)le *adj.* poor 47, 145, timid 101 [OF *feble*].

fech *v.* fetch 98, etc., carry off 1155 [OE *fecc(e)an*].

fedde *ppl. adj.* well-fed (for the table) 56 [OE *fēd(d)*, pp. of *fēdan*].

fees *sb. pl.* feudal estates; towns 960 [AN *fee*].

fe3t *sb.* fighting, strife 275n. [OE *feoht*].

fe3t *pl. pres.* attack 1191; *ppl. adj.* **fe3tande** turbulent 404n. [OE *fe(o)htan*].

fel. See **falle, felle**.

fela3schyp *sb.* party (of guests) 1764; *fallen in f.* couple 271 [OE *fēolagscipe*].

felde *sb.* field 370, country(side) 98, 1750; *in þe f.* in battle 1767 [OE *fēld*].

fele *adj.* many 177, etc., (as sb.) 88, 162 [OE *fela*].

fele *v.*[1] taste 107, 1019 [OE *fēlan*].

fele *v.*[2] *sg. pres. subj.* should go forward 914n. [OE *fēolan*].

felle *adj.* fierce, grim, terrible, cruel 139, etc.; *adv.* **fel** cruelly 1040; **felly** fiercely 559, 571 [(from) OF *fel*].

fellen. See **falle**.

felonye *sb.* felony 205 [OF *felonie*].

feloun *sb.* felon, wretch 217 [OF *felon*].

felt *ppl. adj.* matted 1689 [from OE *felt*].

femmale3 *sb. pl. gen.* of females, female 696 [OF *femelle*].

fende *sb.* devil 205, 221, 1341; *pl.* **fende** 269; *pl. gen.* (as adj.) **fenden** fiendish 224 [OE *fĕond*].

fende *pl. pres.* fend; *f. of* make defence, defend 1191 [OF *defendre*].

feng. See **fonge3**.

fenny *adj.* muddy, foul 1113 [OE *fennig*].

fer(re) *adv.* far 31, 98n., 1680; *compar.* **fyrre** further 131, 766, 1780, later (on) 1764n., **ferre** further afield 97 [OE *feor(ran)*, compar. *firr*].

ferd(e) *ppl. adj.* frightened 897, 975 [OE *fǣran*].

ferde. See **fare** *v.*

ferde *sb.* fear 386 [from OE *fǣran*].

fere *sb.*[1] mistress 1062 [OE *gefĕra*].

fere *sb.*[2] company; *in f.* together 399, 696 [OE *gefĕr*].

feryed *pp.* brought 1790 [OE *ferian*].

ferke3 3 *sg. pres.* moves quickly; *sg. pa. t.* moved 133; *f. vp* starts up 897 [OE *fercian*].

ferly *sb.* marvel 1529, 1563, 1629; *adj.* **ferlyle** marvellous 1460; *adv.* **ferly** exceedingly, thoroughly 269, 960, 975; **ferlyly** thoroughly 962 [from OE *fǣrlic; fǣrlīce*].

fers *adj.* proud, bold 101, 217 [OF *fers*].

fest(e) *sb.* feast 164, etc. [OF *feste*].

festen *v.* 327; *pl. imper.* **festene3** 156; *pp.* **festned** 1255. fasten 156, 1255, establish, make 327 [OE *fæstnian*].

festiual *adj.* appropriate to a festival, festive 136 [OF *festival*, ML *festivalis*].

festres 3 *sg. pres.* rots *1040* [OF *festrir*].

fet(e). See **fote**.

fete *sb.* fact; *in f.* in fact, indeed 1106 [AN *fet*].

fet(t)e *v.* fetch 627, 802 [OE *fetian*].

fetys(e) *adj.* neat 174, (as sb.) skill 1103; *adv.* **fetysely** elegantly, skilfully 1462 [(from) AN *fetis*].

fetly *adv.* skilfully 585 [from prec.].

fette. See **fet(t)e**, **fote**.

fettere3 *sb. pl.* fetters 156, **fettres** 1255 [OE *feter*].

fettled *sg. pa. t.* fixed 585; *pp.* prepared 343 [? from OE *fetel*].

feture3 *sb. pl.* features 794 [OF *feture*].

fewe *adj.* lacking (*of* in) 1735n. [OE *fēawe*].

fyftene *adj.* fifteen 405 [OE *fíftēne*].

fyfty, fyfte (422) *adj.* fifty 316, 429, etc. [OE *fíftig*].

fygure *sb.* figure 1460, character (in writing) 1726n. [OF *figure*].

fyled *pp.*[1] filed; *f. out* fashioned 1460 [OE *filian*].

fyled *pp.*[2] stained 136 [OE *fŷlan*].

fylyoles *sb. pl.* turrets 1462 [OF *filloele*].

fylle3 *v.* fill 462, etc.; *sg. imper.* **fylles** 1433 [OE *fyllan*].

fylsened *sg. pa. t.* helped 1167, 1644 [cf. OE *fylstan*].

fylter *pl. pres.* mingle (in falling), tumble 224, join, copulate 696; *f. togeder* struggle together, join battle 1191; *ppl. adj.* **fyltered** tangled 1689 [OF *feltrer*].

fylþe *sb.* filth, impurity, sin(s) 6, 31, etc.; *pl.* filthiness, corruption 14 [OE *fŷlþ*].

fyn *adj.* fine, pleasing, perfect, worthy 721, etc. [OF *fin*].

fynde *v.* 3, etc.; *sg. pres. subj.* 466, 902; *sg. pa. t.* **fande** 133; *pl.* **fonde** 1212, **founden** 265; *pp.* **founde(n)** 547, 721, etc., **fonde(n)** 173, 356, **funde** 1735. find, discover 3, 996, etc., (fut. sense) 587, understand (them) 1726, come to 902, *1295*; *f. with his y3e* noticed 133 [OE *findan*].

fyned *sg. pa. t.* stopped 450, **fon** 369; *sg. imper.* **fyne** 929 [OF *finer*].

fyng(e)res *sb. pl.* fingers 1103, etc. [OE *finger*].

fynne *sb.* fin 531 [OE *fin(n)*].

fyoles *sb. pl.* phials, bowls for incense 1476, **vyoles** 1280 [OF *fiole*, AN *viole*].

fyr *sb.* fire 627, 954, 1011, fever 1095 [OE *fŷr*].

fyr(re) *adj. compar.* (more) remote 1680, final 1732 [OE *firra*, compar. of *feor*].

fyrmament *sb.* firmament 221 [OF *firmament*, L *firmamentum*].

fyrre. See **fer(re), fyr(re).**

fyrst(e) *adj.* first 205, etc., (as sb.) (first) moment 1069; *of f.* in the beginning 1714; *adv.* first(ly) 377, 1530, 1634, in the beginning 1718 [OE *fyrst*].

fysch *sb.* fish 288, 531 [OE *fisc*].

fyste *sb.* fist 1723, **fust** 1535 [OE *fȳst*].

fyþel *sb.* fiddle, viol, violin 1082 [OE *fiþele*].

fyþer *sb.* feather 1026, 1484; *pl.* wings 530 [OE *feþer*, pl. *fiþera, fiþru*].

fyue *adj.* five *1015*n., etc. [OE *fīf(e)*].

flayed *sg. pa. t.* frightened, dismayed 1723; *pp.* 960 [OE *flēgan*].

flakerande *pres. p.* fluttering 1410n. [cf. ON *flakka*].

flakes *sb. pl.* flakes, lumps 954 [cf. Norw. *flak*, ON *flakna*].

flaumbeande *ppl. adj.* flaming, brilliant 1468 [OF *flamber*].

flaunkes *sb. pl.* sparks 954 [cf. Sw. *flanka*].

fle *v.* flee 377, 914; *pl. pa. t.* **flowen** 945, 975 [OE *flēon*].

fleeȝ *sb. pl.* flying insects, butterflies 1476 [OE *flē(o)ge*].

fleme *v.* 287; 3 *sg. pres.* **flemeȝ** 596, **flemus** 31. drive, banish (*fro, (out) of* from) 31, etc. [OE *flēman*].

flesch(e) *sb.* flesh 202, etc., being(s), creature(s) 303, 356, 403, 560, (physical) being 975n., 1553; *adj.* **fleschlych** fleshly, sexual 265 [OE *flǣsc(lic)*].

flete *v.* 685, 1025; *sg. pa. t.* **flote** 421, 432; *pl.* **flette** 387. float 387, 1025, drift 421, swim 432, overflow, fill 685 [OE *flēotan*].

flyȝt *sb.* flight 377, 457, 530 [OE *flyht*].

flyt *sb.* brawling 421 [OE *flīt*].

flytande *pres. p.* contending 950 [OE *flītan*].

flod *sb.* flood, water 324, 369, etc. [OE *flōd*].

floȝed *sg. pa. t.* flowed, ran 397, **flowed** 428 [OE *flōwan*].

flokked *pl. pa. t.* flocked 386 [from next].

flokkes *sb. pl.* crowds 837, companies, armies 1767 [OE *flocc*].

flor *sb.* floor 133, 1397 [OE *flōr*].

flores *sb. pl.* flowers 1476 [OF *flor*].

flosed *sg. pa. t.* fell in strands 1689 [ON *flosna*].

flot *sb.* scum 1011 [ON *flot*].

flote *sb.* troop 1212 [OF *flote*].

flote, flowed, flowen. See **flete, floȝed, fle, flwe.**

flwe *sg. pa. t.* flew 432; *pl.* **flowen** 1010 [OE *flēogan*].

fo *sb.* foe 1219, 1767 [OE *gefā*].

fode *sb.* food 339, 1194, creature 466 [OE *fōda*].

fogge *sb.* coarse grass 1683 [cf. Norw. *fogg*].

fol. See **ful.**

fol *sb.* fool 202, 750, 996 [OF *fol*].

folde *sb.* earth, world, land 257, 287, etc.; (*vp)on f.* on earth 25, etc., (expletive or intensive) 403, 1147, 1175 [OE *fólde*].

folde *sg. imper.* place 1026 [OE *fáldan*].

fole *sb.* (appos.) horses' 1255 [OE *fole*].

foler *sb.* (ornamental) foliage 1410n. [see note].

foles. See **fowle** *sb.*

foles 3 *sg. pres.* becomes deranged 1422 [AN *foler*].

folȝes *v.* follow, attend 677, come next 1736, seek out, attack 918, look for 1212, follow, advance 974, serve 1165; *f. after* serves 6; *f. tylle* owed allegiance to 1752n.; *f. here face* went forward 978n.; *f. þe fet of* follow the footsteps of 1062; *ppl. adj.* **folwande** following, next 429 [OE *folgian*].

folyly *adv.* wantonly 696 [from OF *folie*].

folk(e) *sb.* folk, people 100, 386, etc., creatures 224, (as indef. pron.) one, a man 1129n.; *pl. gen.* (as adj.) **folken** human 271 [OE *folc*].

folmarde *sb.* polecat 534 [OE *fūl* + *mearþ*].

foman *sb.* enemy 1175 [OE *fāhman(n)*].

fon, fonde(n). See **fyned, fynde.**

fonded *sg. pa. t.* troubled 1103 [OE *fándian*].

fongeȝ *pres.* 457, 540; *sg. pa. t.* **feng** 377. assume 540; *f. to þe flyȝt* take flight 377, 457 [OE *fōn, fĕng*, ON *fanga*].

font *sb.* font 164 [OE *font*].

for, four (756) *cj.* for, because, since, in that 5, 28, 67, etc., (introd.) thus, now 205, 1025, 1633; *f. þat* in that, inasmuch as 279, 1144; *prep.* for, on account of, through 47, 177, etc., for (the sake of) 729, 754, 757, as, to be 275, 1087, 1163, 1368, to 75, 143, as regards 867, 1143, in 1550, in spite of 1332, to avoid 740, (in exchange) for 888, 1118 [OE *for þam(þe); for*].

forbedes 3 *sg. pres.* forbids 1147; *pp.* forboden 45, 826, (impers.) 998 [OE *forbēodan*].

forfare *v.* destroy 1168; *sg. pa. t.* forferde 571, fourferde perished 560 [OE *forfaran*; pa. t. from *forfēran*].

forfete *v.* forfeit 177; *pl. pres. subj.* were to be lost 743n. [OF *forfet*, pp. of *forfaire*].

forgart *pl. pa. t.* forfeited 240 [cf. ON *fyrirgöra*].

forged *pp.* built 343 [OF *forger*].

forgyue *v.* forgive 731 [*for-* + ME *give*, cf. OE *forgiefan*].

for3es *sb. pl.* furrows 1547 [OE *furh*].

for3ete *v.* 739, 1660; *sg. pa. t.* for3et(e) 203, 463; for3eten 1528. forget (about) 463, abandon 203, pardon 739 [OE *forgetan*].

foriusted *pp.* unhorsed (in jousting) 1216 [*for-* + OF *juster*].

forknowen *pp.* neglected 119n. [*for-* + OE *cnāwan*].

forloyne *v.* go astray 282, 750, stray from 1165; *ppl. adj.* forloyne erring 1155n. [OF *forloignier*, pp. *forloignie*].

forlote3 *pl. imper.* overlook 101 [*for-* + ON *láta*].

formast *adv.* foremost, first 494 [from next].

forme *adj.* first 257 [OE *forma*].

forme *sb.* appearance 174, shape 253, 1535, pattern, design (on cup) 1468, exemplar, example 3 [OF *forme*].

forme *v.* make 316, etc.; *f. out* drawn out, shaped 1462 [OF *former*].

fornes *sb.* furnace, cauldron 1011 [OF *fornais*].

forray *v.* forage 1200 [OF *forrier*].

forselet *sb.* fortress 1200 [AN *forcelet*].

forsette3 *pl. imper.* waylay 78n. [OE *forsettan*].

forsoke *sg. pa. t.* forsook, renounced 210; *pp.* forsaken (absol.) refused 75 [OE *forsacan*].

forst *sb.* frost 524 [OE *forst*].

forty. See faurty.

for-to *particle with infin.* (in order) to 91, 336, etc. [OE *for* + *tō*].

forþ(e), forth(e) *adv.* forth 77, etc.; *at f. na3tes* late in the night 1764n. [OE *forþ*].

forþer *v.* further, hasten, execute 304, 1051n.; *sb.* forþering furthering 3 [(from) OE *fyrþran*].

forbi *cj.* and so, therefore, on that account 33, 1175, etc. [OE *forþī*].

forþynke3 *impers. pres.* in *me f.* I repent 285; *sg. pa. t.* forþo3t (pers.) 557 [OE *forþencan*, infl. by *þyncan*].

forþrast *pp.* destroyed 249 [OE *forþrǣstan*].

forþwyth *prep.* before 304n. [from OE *forþ* + *wiþ*].

forward(e) *sb.* agreement 327, 1742 [OE *foreweard*].

fo(o)schip *sb.* enmity 918, 919 [from OE *gefá*].

foster *sb.* offspring 257 [OE *fōster*].

fote *sb.* 79, 88, etc.; *pl.* fete 156, 255, etc., fet 1062, fette 618, 802. foot 477, etc., foot's length 1200; *(vp)on f.* on foot 79n. etc.; *to f. and to honde* for the hands and feet 174 [OE *fōt*].

foul, foule, fouled, foule3, founde(n). See ful, fowle *adj.*, fowled, fowle *sb.*, fynde.

foundered *pp.* engulfed 1014n. [OF *fondrer*].

founde3 3 *sg. pres.* sets out 1764; *pl. imper.* go on 903 [OE *fúndian*].

founs *sb.* bottom 1026n. [AN *founz*].

four, fourferde, fourre. See for, forfare, faure.

fowle *adj.* foul 140, foule 462; *adv.* fowle vilely 1790 [OE *fúl(e)*].

fowle3 *sb.* bird 474, 530, 538; *pl.* foule3 56, foles 1410 [OE *fugol*].

fowled *sg. pa. t.* was defiled 269; *pp.* fouled defiled 1495 [OE *fúlian*].

fowre. See faure.

fox sb. fox 534 [OE fox].

frayes 3 sg. pres. terrifies 1553 [OF esfraer].

frayst v. seek, tell 1736n. [ON freista].

fraunchyse sb. generosity 750 [OF franchise].

fre adj. noble, gracious, good, true 203, etc., (as sb.) noble one 929; f. haldes hold dear 1062; of f. and of bonde bondmen and free 88 [OE frēo].

freke sb. man 1680 etc. [OE freca].

frely(ch) adj. splendid, fair 162, 173; adv. compar. freloker better 1106 [OE frēolic; frēolīce].

frende sb. friend 139, 399, etc.; fyn f. worthies 721 [OE frēond].

fresch adj. fresh 173 [OF fresche, f. of freis].

fretes 3 sg. pres. devours 1040; pp. freten 404 [OE fretan].

frette v. stock 339, decorate, inlay 1476 [OF freter].

fryst v. hold back 743 [cf. ON fresta].

fr(u)yt sb. fruit 245, etc. [OF fruit].

fryth sb. wood, wilderness 534, 1680 [OE fyrhþ(e)].

fro prep. from 31, 129, etc., above 920; cj. after, once 353, 833, 1325; f.(fyrst)þat from the (first) moment (that), after, once 1069, 1198 [ON frá].

frok sb. garment 136; pl. frokkes 1742 [OF froc].

froþande ppl. adj. frothing, festering 1721 [ON froða].

ful adj. full (of of) 1011, 1599, 1626; adv. (intensive) very, quite, most 20, 26, etc., fo(u)l 1458, 1754 [OE ful(l)].

fulfylle v. perform 264, bring (to completion) 1732 [OE fullfyllan].

fulȝed pp. baptised 164 [OE fulligian, fulwian].

fulle sb. whole amount; to þe f. completely, quite 343, unstintingly 120 [from OE ful(l)].

funde, fust. See fynde, fyste.

gay adj. merry 830, bright, fine 1315, 1444; gon. g. in gere be well-dressed 1811; adv. gaye richly 1568 [(from) OF gai].

gayn adj. good 259, 749; gaynly gracious 728 [(from) ON gegn].

gaynes pl. pres. have power 1608 [ON gegna].

galle sb. gall 1022 [ON gall].

gareȝ 3 sg. pres. order, cause, make 690; pa. t. gart 896, 1361, 1645 [ON göra].

garnyst pp. decorated (of with) 1277 [OF garniss-, garnir].

gate sb. way 676, 767, 931 [ON gate].

gauleȝ sb. pl. wretches 1525n. [? from OE gagol; see note].

gaȝafylace sb. treasury (in Temple) 1283 [OF gazophilace].

geder v. gather; g. hem samen (refl.) come together 1363 [OE gæderian].

gef. See giues.

gemmes sb. pl. gems 1441, 1468 [OF gemme].

gendered pp. begotten, born 300 [OF gendrer].

gendreȝ sb. pl. species 434 [OF gendre].

gent adj. splendid, beautiful 1495 [OF gent].

gentyl adj. gentile, heathen 76 [L gentilis].

gentyle adj. genteel, noble 1235, 1257, excellent, splendid 1309, respectful 1432, (as sb.) nobles 1216; superl. gentylest noblest 1180 [OF gentil].

gentylmen sb. pl. gentlemen 864 [prec. + OE man(n)].

gentryse sb. nobility 1159 [OF genterise].

g(u)ere sb. equipment, vessels 16n., 1505, clothes 1811 [ON gervi].

gered pp. adorned 1344, attired 1568, set 1444 [from prec.].

gest sb. guest 98, etc. [ON gestr].

geten. See ȝete.

gettes sb. pl. practices, fashions 1354 [OF jet].

gye v. rule, govern, command 1598, 1627, 1663 [OF gui(i)er].

gilde pp. gilded 1344 [OE gýldan].

gylt sb. sin 731, gult 690 [OE gylt].

gyn sb. vessel 491 [OF engin].

giues 3 sg. pres. 1528; sg. pa. t. gef 753, 1326; pp. geuen 259, 1627. give 259, etc., show, make clear 1326 [ON, cf. OI gefa, OSw. giva, ODa. give].

glad *adj.* glad, merry, cheerful 123 etc. [OE *glæd*].
glade *v.* gladden, cheer 499, 1083 [OE *gladian*].
glam *sb.* uproar 849, speech 499, 830 [ON *glam(m)*].
glede *sb.* kite 1696 [cf. OE *gli(o)da*].
glem *sb.* radiance 218 [OE *glæm*].
glent *sg. pa. t.* shone 218 [ON, cf. Sw. dial. *glänta*].
glette *sb.* filth, sin 306, 573 [OF *glette*].
glydes 3 *sg. pres.* glides, walks, moves, goes, comes 325, etc.; *sg. pa. t.* **glod** 499; *pres. p.* **glydande** 296 [OE *glīdan*].
glyfte *sg. pa. t.* was startled, winced (*with* at) 849 [uncertain].
gloped *sg. pa. t.* was aghast (*for* at) 849 [ON, cf. OI *glúpna*, Norw. dial. *glopa*].
glopnedly *adv.* in alarming fashion 896 [as prec.].
glori *sb.* glory 1337 [OF *glorie*].
gloryed *pl. pa. t.* gloried (*on* in) 1522 [L *gloriari*].
glorious *adj.* glorious 218 [AN *glori(o)us*].
glotounes *sb. pl.* gluttons, wretches 1505 [OF *gloton*].
go *v.* go 810; 3 *sg. pres.* **gos** 611, 1590, **goȝ** 325, 341; *pl. pres. subj.* **gon** 1811; *pl. imper.* **goȝ** 77; *pres. p.* **goande** 931 [OE *gān*].
gob(e)lotes *sb. pl.* goblets 1277, 1475 [OF *gobelet*].
god, God, God(d)e *sb.* god, God 16, 1730, etc.; *vnder G.* on God's earth 1077; *gen.* **Goddes, God(d)eȝ** 1799, etc.; *pl.* **goddes** 1165, 1608n. [OE *god*].
god(e), goud(e), gvd (639) *adj.* good, worthy 1619, etc., sweet 1447; **godlych** gracious 753; *superl.* **godelest** most excellent 1608n. [OE *gōd(lic)*].
go(u)d *sb.* goodness 1048, goods 1200, 1282, (coll. sense) 1315, (good) things 1326, 1528 [OE *gōd*].
godman, godmon, goodman *sb.* good man, master of the house 341, 611, 677, 849 [OE *gōd+man(n)*].
gold(e) *sb.* gold 1271, 1404, etc.; *adj.* **golden** golden 1525 [(from) OE *gōld*].

gome *sb.* man 137, 145, 1337, servant 77 [OE *guma*].
gorde *v.* plunge 911; *sg. pa. t.* beat (*to* on) 957 [uncertain].
gore *sb.* filth, vileness 306 [OE *gor*].
gorsteȝ *sb. pl.* (pieces of) land overgrown with gorse, scrubland(s) 99, 535 [OE *gorst*].
gost(e) *sb.* nature 729, spirit, breath 325, spiritual power 1598, 1627 [OE *gāst*].
goteȝ *sb. pl.* currents, swells 413 [? OE *gegot*].
gotȝ, goud(e). See **go, god(e), go(u)d.**
goun *sb.* gown, garment, vestment 145, 1315n., 1568 [OF *goune*].
gouernores *sb. pl.* rulers 1645 [OF *governeor*].
grace *sb.* grace, mercy 731, etc., favour asked, boon 1347 [OF *grace*].
gracyously *adv.* attractively, *also* by God's grace 488 [from OF *gracious*].
gray(e) *adj.* grey, dun-coloured 430, 1696 [OE *græg*].
grayþed *pp.* made ready 343, set 1485 [ON *greiða*].
grayþely *adv.* promptly 341 [ON *greiðliga*].
grattest. See **gret(e).**
graunt *adj.* great 765. See **mercy.** [AN *graunt*].
graunt *v.* agree, consent (absol.) 765; *g. hym* agreed (with him) 810 [OF *granter*].
grauen *pp.* buried 1332, engraved, inscribed 1324, 1475, 1544 [OE *grafan*].
grece *sb.* stairway 1590 [OF *grez, greis*, pl. of *gre*].
gredirne *sb.* gridiron 1277 [? OF *gredil*, altered by assoc. with *iron*, OE *īren*].
greme *sb.* anger 16, 947 [ON *gremi*].
gremen *v.* make angry 1347, be angry 138 [OE *gremian*].
grene *adj.* green 488, 602, 767; *sb.* grass 634, vegetation 1028 [OE *grēne*].
gresse *sb.* grass 1028 [OE *græs*].
gret(e) *adj.* great 12, 138, etc., broad, main 77, (as sb.) great men 1363; *superl.* **grattest** greatest 1645 [OE *grēat*].

gretyng *sb.* weeping 159 [from OE *grētan*].

greue *v.* anger 302, 306, 774, punish 138; *sb.* **greuing** wailing 159 [from OF *grever*].

greueȝ *sb. pl.* thickets 99 [OE *græfa*].

grymme *adj.* grim 1553, 1696; *adv.* **grymly** grimly 1534 [OE *grim(līce)*].

grysly *adj.* grisly 1534 [OE *grislic*].

gryspyng *sb.* gnashing 159n. [OE *gristbitung*].

grone *v.* groan (in childbirth) 1077 [OE *grānian*].

gropande *ppl. adj.* searching 591; *sb.* **gropyng** touching 1102 [(from) OE *grāpian*].

grounde *sb.* ground, earth 445, 798, etc., world 1324, 1663, foundations 911, source 591; *vpon g.* in the world 1363 [OE *grúnd*].

growe *v.* grow 1028, 1043; *pl. pa. t.* **grewen** increased 277 [OE *grōwan*].

gruchen *pl. pres. subj.* should refuse 1347; *pl. pa. t.* **gruȝt** 810 [OF *gruchier*].

gvd, guere, gult. See **god(e), g(u)ere, gylt.**

ȝark *v.* grant *652*, 758, 1708n. [OE *gearcian*].

ȝarm *sb.* clamour 971 [ON *jarmr*].

ȝat. See **ȝete.**

ȝate *sb.* gateway 796; *pl.* gates 785, etc., gateway 854 [OE *geat*].

ȝe *adv.* yes (indeed) 347 [OE *gē(a)*, *gæ*].

ȝe *pron.* 2 *pl.* you 352, 527, etc.; *acc. dat.* **yow** 357, 523, etc., (refl.) 352, 522; *gen.* (as poss. adj.) **yo(u)r** 94, 715, etc.; **yowself** you yourself 340; **yourseluen** yourselves 863 [OE *gē, ēow, ēower*].

ȝede *sg. pa. t.* went 432, 973 [OE *ēode*].

ȝederly *adv.* entirely 463 [from OE *ēdre, ǣdre*].

ȝeȝed *pl. pa. t.* shouted 846 [OE *gēgan*, cf. ON *geyja*].

ȝelde *v.* perform 665; *pp.* **ȝolden** restored, re-established 1708n. [OE *géldan*].

ȝellyng *sb.* yelling, shouting 971 [from OE *gellan*].

ȝemes *v.* rule, command 464, 1242, 1493 [OE *gēman*].

ȝender *adv.* yonder, (over) there 1617 [from OE *géond*].

ȝer *sb.* year 494, etc.; *pl.* **ȝer(e)** 1192, 1453 [OE *gē(a)r*].

ȝerneȝ *v.* desire 66, 758 [OE *géornan*].

ȝep(e) *adj.* bold, alert (or *adv.*) 881, (as *sb.*) alert man 796; *adv.* **ȝeply** quickly, soon 665, 1708 [OE *gēap(līce)*].

ȝestande *ppl. adj.* frothing, festering 846 [from OE **gest*, cf. *gist*].

ȝet, ȝette (867) *adv.* yet, nevertheless, at the same time 120, 230, etc., up to now 197, 815, 876, 1312, still, ever 1525, etc., even 754, 758, (with compars.) 50, 96, 97, also, as well 1158, 1232, 1803; *ȝ. er* before 648; *and ȝ.* but nevertheless 664 [OE *gēt*].

ȝete *sg. imper.* get, fetch, obtain 842; *pp.* **geten** 1505, **ȝat** 66n. [ON *geta*, OE *-gietan*].

ȝif *cj.* 613, etc., if 13, 36, etc., if 12, etc., though 914, 1665, whether, to see if 99, 607, *692; if þat if* 759 [OE *gif*, cf. ON *ef*].

ȝis *adv.* (contradicting implied negative) yes (we may) 1113 [OE *gīse*].

ȝisterdæg *gen.* yesterday's, of a short time before 463 [OE *gystran dæg*].

ȝokkeȝ *sb. pl.* yokes, pairs 66 [OE *geoc*].

ȝolden. See **ȝelde.**

ȝolped *pl. pa. t.* boasted 846 [OE *gielpan*].

ȝomerly *adj.* doleful 971 [OE *gēomorlic*].

ȝon *adj.* yonder, that (there) 751, 772 [OE *geon*].

ȝonde *adj.* yonder, that (there) 721 [from OE *géond*].

ȝong(e) *adj.* young 783, 842, 881 [OE *gēong*].

ȝore-whyle *adv.* recently 842 [OE *gēara + hwīl*].

ȝornen *pl. pa. t.* ran 881 [OE *(ge)éornan, geírnan*].

hach *sb.* hatch; *vnder h.* below deck, on shipboard 409 [OE *hæcc*].

haf *v.* 66, 972, etc., **haue** 164, 193, etc.; *2 sg. pres.* **hatȝ** 141, 328, etc.,

habbeȝ 95, **haueȝ** 171; 3 *sg.*
hatȝ 30, 306, etc., **hab(b)es** 308,
etc., *pl.* **han** 202, 693, etc., **haf**
95, 709, **habbe(ȝ)** 75, 105, **hatȝ**
517; *subj.* **haf** 616, 692, 1115,
haue 317, 590, 900; *sg. pa. t.*
had(e) 74, 248, etc.; *pl.* **hade(n)**
123, 831, etc.; *subj.* **had(e)** 424,
1484, etc.; *sg. imper.* **haf** 321, 349;
pp. **hade** 1443. have 325, etc.,
(auxil.) 95, etc., bring 941, 1443,
incur 183, partake of, share 164,
be engaged in 735, save 900; *h.*
(vp)on have on, wear, bear 30, 141,
1276 [OE *habban, haf-*].
hagherlych *adv.* fittingly, properly
18, **haȝerly** 1707 [from ON *hagr*,
cf. *hagliga*].
haylsed *pa. t.* greeted 612, 814 [ON
heilsa].
hayre. See **ayre** *sb.*[2]
halde *v.* 652, etc.; *sg. pa. t.* **helde**
1387; *sg. imper.* **halde** 335, **holde**
315; *pp.* **halden** 244, 276, 1078.
hold, have, keep, maintain 35, etc.,
allow 315, keep to 244, contain,
measure 1387, consider, reckon,
count 276, etc.; *h. of* owe allegiance
to 1162 [OE *háldan*].
halden. See **heldes.**
haleȝ 3 *sg. pres.* goes, soars (swiftly)
458; *sg. pa. t.* drank (*of*) from)
1520, **aled** hurried 380 [OF *haler*].
half *sb.* side 719; *on Godeȝ halue* on
God's behalf, in God's name 896;
pl. **halues** shores 1039, **half**
quarters 950 [OE *half*].
halȝed *sg. pa. t.* consecrated 506, set
apart 1163 [OE *hálgian*].
halyday *sb.* festival 134, 141, 166
[OE *háligdæg*].
halkeȝ *sb. pl.* corners; small rooms
321; *by h.* into the corners 104
[OE *heal(o)c*].
halle *sb.* hall 90, 129, etc., large room
321; *h. dore* hall-door 44; *h. flor*
hall-floor 1397 [OE *hall*].
halsed *pp.* greeted (him) 1621 [OE *hal-
sian* 'implore', cf. ON *heilsa* 'greet'].
halt *adj.* lame 102 [OE *halt*].
hamppred *sg. pa. t.* put in cases
1284 [from OF *hanepier*, *sb.*].
han, hande(s). See **haf, honde.**
hande-helm *sb.* helm, tiller 419 [OE

hánd + helma, cf. ME *handerother*].
hapeneȝ 3 *sg. pres.* fares; *h. ful fayre*
gains good fortune 27 [from ON
happ].
happe *sg. imper.* cover (*under* with)
626 [uncertain].
happeȝ *sb. pl.* blessed states 24 [ON
happ].
hard(e) *adj.* hard 1209, solid 1342,
difficult, dire, harsh, grievous 159,
562, etc.; *compar.* **harder** more
severe 50; *adv.* **harde(e)** harshly
44, 543, 596, badly 424, quickly
1204 [OE *heard(e)*].
hardy *adj.* bold; *watȝ h.* dared 143n.
[OF *hardi*].
hareȝ *sb. pl.* hares 391 [OE *hara*].
harlot *sb.* 39, etc.; *gen. pl.* **harlateȝ** 34;
gen. pl. **harloteȝ** 874. beggar 24,
39, 148, villain, lecher 860, 874,
rogue 1584; *sb.* **harlottrye** lewd-
ness 579 [(from) OF *harlot*].
harme *sb.* harm 166 [OE *hearm*].
harme *v.* harm 1503 [OE *hearmian*].
hasped *pp.* fastened 419 [OE *hæpsian*].
hast(e) *sb.* haste 39, 599, 1503; *vpon*
h. in haste 902 [OF *haste*].
hasted *pl. pa. t.* hurried 937 [OF
haster].
hasty(f)ly *adv.* precipitately 200; *h.*
sone very speedily 1150 [from OF
hasti(f)].
hate *sb.* hatred, anger 915, punishment 714 [from next and ON
hatr].
hate *v.* hate 168, (absol.) 1138, etc.
[OE *hatian*].
hat(te). See **hetes.**
hatel *adj.* hateful 227, (as *sb.*) hatred
200 [OE *hatol*].
hatereȝ *sb. pl.* (poor) clothes 33
[OE *hæteru*, pl.].
hatter, hatȝ. See **hot, haf.**
hattes *sb. pl.* hats; *hard h.* helmets
1209 [OE *hætt*].
haþel *sb.* man 27, 35, etc. [OE *hæleþ*,
infl. by *æþel(e)*].
haue(ȝ). See **haf.**
hauekes *sb. pl.* hawks 537 [OE
hafoc].
hauen *sb.* harbour 420 [OE *hæfen*].
he *pron.* 3 *sg. masc.* 3, 17, etc.; *acc.*
dat. **him** 6, 745, etc.; *gen.* (as *poss.*

adj.) **his(e)** 3, 8, 1216, etc., he 3, 6, etc., (refl.) 63, 124, etc., (absol.) 1140, 1163, 1219, 1573; **himself(e)**, **himseluen** him(self) 9, 924, etc., He Himself *584*; *bi h.* out of his own head, that was all his own 1426 [OE *hē, him, his*].

hede *sb.* 150, 1265, **heued** 876, 1707. head 150, etc.; *his h.* his person, he 1707n. [OE *hēafod*].

heȝe(st), heȝed. See **hyȝ(e), hyȝes.**

heȝþe *sb.* height 317; *vpon hyȝt* aloft 458 [OE *hēhþu*].

heyred, helde. See **he(y)red, herȝeȝ, elde, halde.**

heldes 3 *sg. pres.* 678, 1330; *sg. pa. t.* **heldet** 1681; *sg. pa. t. subj.* **helded** 39; *pp.* **halden** 42n. fall 1330, go 39, 678; *h. vnhole* became unsound 1681; *h. vtter* thrown out 42 [OE *héldan*].

hele *sb.* welfare, safety 920; *tourned to h.* became sound 1099 [OE *hǣlu*].

heled *sg. pa. t.* healed 1098 [OE *hǣlan*].

heles *sb. pl.* heels 1789 [OE *hēla*].

helle *sb.* Hell 168, 921, etc. [OE *hell*].

helle-hole *sb.* pit of Hell 223 [prec. + OE *hol*].

help *sb.* help 1345 [OE *help*].

helpe *v.* help 762; *sg. pa. t.* **help** (absol.) 1163 [OE *helpan*].

hem *pron.* 3 *pl. acc. dat.* 24, 67, etc., **hym** 130, 820, 843, **hom** 1715; *gen.* (as poss. adj.) **her(e)** 24, 978, etc., **hor** 1524. (to, for) them 24, etc., (refl.) 62, etc.; **hemself, hemseluen** themselves 15, 388, 702 [OE *heom, him, heora*].

hence *adv.* from here 944 [from OE *heonan*].

hende *adj.* gracious, pleasant 612, 1083n., 1172, **hynde** 1098 [OE *gehénde*].

hendelayk *sb.* courtesy 860 [from prec. + ON *-leikr*].

heng(e) *v.* hang 1584, be weighed 1734 [ON *hengja*].

hentteȝ *pl. pres.* 710; *pa. t.* **hent** 376, etc.; *sg. pa. t. subj.* **hent** 151. take, seize 376, etc., receive, come to 151, overtake 1150, (refl.) take to, adopt (for themselves) 710; *h. of* took away 1179 [OE *hentan*].

hepe *sb.* crowd, battalion 1775; *on a h.* together in a body 1211; *vpon h.* in ruins 912 [OE *hēap*].

her(e). See **ho, hem, ayre** *sb.*[2]

here *adv.* here 619, 622, etc.; *with preps.*: **her(e)after** hereafter, later, from now on 291, 1319; **hereaway** here, hither 647; **herbisyde** nearby 926; **hereinne** here(in), in this place 147, 1595; **herevtter** outside this place 927 [OE *hēr*].

here *sb.* company, household 409, 902 [OE *here*].

here *v.* hear (about), learn, find 1164; *sg. pa. t. and pp.* **herde** 193, 197, etc. [OE *hēran*].

he(y)red *pl. pa. t.* worshipped 1086, 1527n. [OE *herian*].

herȝeȝ *v.* 1179, 1294; *pp.* **heyred** 1786n. harry 1294, ransack 1786; *h. vp* ravaged 1179 [OE *hergian*].

heritage *sb.* heritage; *halde in h.* inherit 652 [OF *(h)eritage*].

herk(k)en *v.* 458, etc.; *pp.* **herkned** 193. hear, learn 193, attend to 1369, observe, see 980n.; *h. typyngeȝ* seek information, survey the scene 458 [OE *hercnian*].

herneȝ *sb. pl.* eagles 537 [OE *earn*].

hert *sg. pa. t.* hurt 1195 [OF *hurter*].

hert(t)e *sb.* heart 27, etc., intention 682, mind 1681; *at þe h.* inwardly 850 [OE *heorte*].

herttes *sb. pl.* harts 391, 535 [OE *heort*].

heruest *sb.* harvest 523 [OE *hærfest*].

hest(e) *sb.* command 94, 341, promise 1636 [from OE *hǣs*].

hete *sb.* heat 524, 604 [OE *hǣtu*].

heterly *adv.* cruelly 1222, with all speed 380 [? from MLG *hetter*].

hetes 3 *sg. pres.* 1346, **hat** 448, **hatte** 926; *sg. pa. t. and pp.* **hyȝt** 24, 714, etc.; *pp.* **hatte** 1322. promise 665, etc., make a promise 1636, assign 24, name, call 1322, be named, be called 299, 448, 926 [OE *hātan*].

heþe *sb.* heath 535 [OE *hǣþ*].

heþyng *sb.* contempt 579, 710 [ON *hæðing*].

heued. See **hede.**

heuen *sb.* Heaven 50n., 161, etc. [OE *heofon*].

heuened *sg. pa. t. and pp.* raised 506,

(*of* out of) 1601, raised up 1714, exalted 24, (*fro* above) 920 [OE *hafenian*, vowel from *hebban*, *hef-*].

heuen-glem *sb.* light in the sky, glimmer of dawn 946 [OE *heofon* + *glǣm*, cf. *heofonlēoma*].

heuen-kyng *sb.* king of Heaven 1628 [OE *heofoncyning*].

hyde *sb.* hide 630 [OE *hȳd*].

h(u)yde *v.* hide 682, (refl.) 915; *pp.* **hidde** 430; *ppl. adj.* **hid(d)e** hidden 1600, (as. sb.) hidden thing 1628 [OE *hȳdan*].

hider *adv.* here, to this place 100, 922 [OE *hider*].

hyȝ(e), heȝe (1391) *adj.* high (up), lofty 206, 379, etc., exalted, great 35, 50, etc., full, intense 604, fast 976, loud 1564, (as sb.) high ground 391; *h. dese* high dais 115; *on h.* on high 413; *superl.* **hyȝest, heȝest** (1749) highest 406, 451, worthiest 1749, (as sb.) Most High 1653; *adv.* **hyȝe** high (up) 1166n. etc., loud(ly) 1206, 1783, greatly 656; **hyȝly** specially 920, devoutly 1527 [OE *hēh, hēag-; hēhlīce*].

hyȝes *v.* 538 etc.; *sg. pa. t.* **heȝed** 1584; *sg. imper.* **hyȝ** 33. hasten 33, etc., desire strongly, threaten 1584 [OE *hīgian*].

hyȝeȝ *sb. pl.* servants 67 [OE *hīgan*, pl.].

hyȝt. See **heȝþe, hetes.**

hyȝtled *sg. pa. t.* embellished 1290 [uncertain].

hil(le) *sb.* hill 406, etc. [OE *hyll*].

hiled *pp.* covered 1397 [ON *hylja*].

him, hym, hynde. See **he, hem, hende.**

hyne *sb. pl.* fellows 822 [OE *hī(g)na*, gen. of *hīgan*, pl.].

hir. See **ho.**

hyrne *sb.* corner; outlying parts, hinterland 1294n. [OE *hyrne*].

his(e). See **he.**

hit *pron. 3 sg. neut.* it 1412n., 1514n. etc., (impers.) 808, 1125, etc., (as poss. adj.) 264, 956, etc.; *h. arn, h. wer(e)n* they are, there are (were) 112, 171, 253, 657n., etc.; *h. watȝ* there was 134n.; *h. one* by itself 927; **hitseluen** itself 281 [OE *hit*].

hitteȝ *3 sg. pres.* (absol.) comes upon it, finds it 479 [OE *hittan*, ON *hitta*].

hyue *sb.* hive 223 [OE *hȳf*].

ho *pron. 3 sg. fem.* she 2, 475, etc.; *acc. dat.* **hir** 1064 etc.; *gen.* (as poss. adj.) **her** 378, 477, etc., **hir** 487, 667; etc.; **hirself** herself 654, 822 [OE *hēo, hi(e)re, heore*].

ho-besteȝ *sb. pl.* she-animals 337 [prec. + OF *beste*].

hod *sb.* hood 34; *adj.* **hodleȝ** hoodless 643 [(from) OE *hōd*].

hofen. See **houen.**

hokyllen *pl. pres.* mow down 1267n. [from OE *hōc*].

hol *adj.* sound, strong 102, 594; *adv.* **holly** completely 104, 1140 [(from) OE *hāl*].

holde. See **halde.**

holde *sb.* kingdom 1597 [OE *háld*].

hole-foted *adj.* web-footed 538 [from OE *hāl* + *fōt*].

holȝe *adj.* hollow 1695 [OE *holg, holh*].

holy *adj.* holy 1602, 1625; *þat h. were maked* sanctified 1799 [OE *hālig*].

holkked *sg. pa. t.* gouged (*out* out) 1222 [cf. MLG *holken*].

holly, hom. See **hol, hem.**

home *sb.* home, dwelling 240, 1762 [OE *hām*].

hommes *sb. pl.* hams, legs 1541 [OE *ham(m)*].

honde, hande *sb.* hand 174, 941, etc.; *hade in h.* ruled 1704 [OE *hánd*].

hondel *pl. pres.* handle 11; *sb.* **hondelyng** handling 1101 [OE *handlian; handlung*].

honde-whyle *sb.* short (space of) time 1786 [OE *handhwīl*].

honest(e) *adj.* clean 14, 18n., 594, (in technical religious sense) 505, suitable, worthy 166, 638; *adv.* **honestly** worthily, properly, decently 134, 705, 1083 [(from) OF *honeste*].

honyseȝ *3 sg. pres.* spurns 596 [OF *honiss-, honir*].

honour *sb.* rank 35 [OF *hono(u)r*].

honour *v.* honour 594, 1340, 1714 [OF *hono(u)rer*].

hope *sb.* belief 1653; *for h. of* in expectation of 714 [OE *hopa*].

hope3 v. think, suppose 148, 663, 1681, hope 860 [OE *hopian*].

hor. See **hem.**

horce sb. horse 1684; *on hors* on horseback 79n., 1209 [OE *hors*].

hores sb. pl. hairs, (eye)lashes 1695n. [ON *hár*].

horyed pl. pa. t. urged, hurried 883 [? cf. MHG *hurren*].

hortyng sb. hurting 740 [from OF *hurter*].

horwed ppl. adj. (in technical religious sense) unclean 335 [OE *gehorwian*].

hot(e) adj. hot 626, fierce, violent 200, 1195, 1602; adv. hotly 707; adv. compar. **hatter** 1138 [OE *hāt(e)*].

hounde3 sb. pl. hounds 961 [OE *húnd*].

hous, hows sb. house, building 104, 1714, etc.; *h. dore* house-door 602 [OE *hūs*].

housholde sb. household, court 18 [prec. + OE *háld*, cf. MDu. *huushoud*].

houen pp. raised (up) 206, 413, 1451, **hofen** 1711 [OE *hóf*, pa. t. of *hebban*].

houe3 3 sg. pres. comes to rest, alights 485, stands 927 [uncertain].

how, hov adv. how 140, 143, etc.; *h. þat* how 496; cj. that 270 [OE *hū*].

how-so adv. however 1753 [OE *hū* + *swā*].

hues. See **hwe.**

huge adj. great 4, 1311, 1659 [OF *ahuge*].

huyde. See **h(u)yde.**

hundreth adj. and sb. hundred 442; pl. **hundred** 315 [OE *hundred*, ON *hundrað*].

hundreth adj. as sb. in *sex h.* six hundredth (year) 426 [from prec.].

hunger sb. hunger 1195, 1243 [OE *húngor*].

hurkele3 3 sg. pres. 150; sg. pa. t. **hurkled** 406. stand 406n.; *h. doun with his hede* hangs (down) his head 150 [cf. MLG *hurken*].

hurles v. rush, charge (forward) 1204, etc., fall precipitously, hurtle 223, push 44, ring 874n.; ppl. adj. **hurlande** surging 413 [prob. imit.].

hurrok sb. hurrock, rudder-band 419n. [cf. Norw. *hork* 'handle of a basket'].

hwe sb. shape 1707; pl. colouring 1119, **hues** colours 1483; adj. **hwed** coloured 1045 [(from) OE *hēow*].

I pron. 1 sg. I 64, 66, etc.; acc. dat. **me** 25, 68, etc., (refl.) 914, 915, (ethic dat.) 553; gen. (as poss. adj.) **my(n)** 55, 682, etc., (as disjunctive pron.) 1668; **myself, myseluen** (by, for) myself 194, etc., me 1572 [OE *ic*, *mē*, *mīn*].

ibrad sg. pa. t. overspread 1693 [OE *gebrǣdan*].

idolatrye sb. idolatry 1173 [OF *idolatrye*].

ydropike adj. dropsical 1096n. [OF *ydropike*].

if. See **3if.**

y3e sb. eye 133, 583, 768; pl. **y3en** 576, 588, etc. [OE *ēge*].

ilych(e) adv. alike, the same 228; *ay i.* ever onwards 975; *euer i.* on all sides 1386 [OE *gelīce*].

ilk(e) adj. same, very 105, etc., (as sb.) same man 511, same people 930 [OE *ilca*].

ille adj. vile, unbecoming 272, 864; adv. ill 73, 693, foully 955, with displeasure 1141; sb. evil 577; *tat3 to non i.* do not take it amiss 735 [(from) ON *illr; illa*].

image sb. image, statue 983 [OF *image*].

in adv. in 679, 1240, 1782; prep. **in(ne)** in(to), inside, on, at, amongst 3, 169, etc., (expr. manner) 301, 328, etc., in keeping with 215, 565, for, during 369, by (means of), through 686, 725, 1095, 1667, for 680, as 995 [OE *inn(e), in*].

ynde sb. indigo 1411 [OF *inde*].

inmydde(3) prep. in the middle of, during 125; *i. þe poynt of* at the height of 1677 [altered from OE *on middan*].

inmong(e3) prep. amongst 278, 1485 [altered from OE *onmáng*].

innogh(e), inogh, inno3e adj. enough 808, 1303, 1359, (as sb.) 1671, (as interj.) 669, in plenty 116; adv. well (enough) 297 [OE *genōh, genōg-*].

inobedyent adj. disobedient 237 [OF *inobedient*].

insy3t *sb.* opinion (*to* of) 1659 [? ON, cf. Sw. *insiht*].

inspranc *sg. pa. t.* sprang in 408 [*in-* + OE *springan*].

instrumentes *sb. pl.* instruments 1081 [OF *instrument*].

into *prep.* (in)to 129, 140, etc., up to 660 [OE *intō*].

inwith *adv.* inwardly 14 [OE *in* + *wiþ*].

ire *sb.* ire, anger 572, etc. [OF *ire*].

is 3 *sg. pres.* is 5, 17, etc. [OE *is*].

yþe3 *sb. pl.* waves *430* [OE *ȳþ*].

iwysse *adv.* indeed 84 [from OE *gewiss*].

iape3 *sb. pl.* (bawdy) games, antics, tricks 864, 877, **jape3** 272 [? from OF *gaber*, infl. by *japer*].

iaueles *sb. pl.* wretches, louts 1495 [uncertain].

ieaunte3 *sb. pl.* giants 272 [OF *geant*].

joy(e) *sb.* joy 491, merrymaking 128, **ioy** beauty 1309; *makes ioye* is delighted 1304 [OF *joie*].

ioyne *v.* be included (*to* in) 726, bring together 434n. [OF *joign-, joindre*].

ioyned *sg. pa. t.* ordered, despatched (*vnto* to) 1235, **joyned** appointed 877 [OF *enjoign-, enjoindre*].

ioyntes *sb. pl.* joints 1540 [OF *joint(e)*].

ioyst *adv.* closely, tightly 434n. [from OF *juste*].

iolyf *adj.* fair, worthy 864, **jolef** 300 [OF *jolif*].

iostyse *sb.* judge 877 [OF *justise*].

iueles *sb. pl.* precious objects, treasures 1441, 1495 [AN *juel*].

iuelrye *sb.* treasure 1309 [OF *juelerie*].

iuggement *sb.* judgement 726n. [OF *jugement*].

iuise *sb.* doom 726 [OF *juis(e)*].

iustised *sg. pa. t.* ruled 1170 [OF *justis(i)er*].

jumpred *ppl. adj.* (as. sb.) jumbled ones, motley company 491n. [uncertain].

kable *sb.* cable 418 [OF *cable*].

ka3t, kayre, kayser. See **cach(e), cayre, cayser.**

kake3 *sb. pl.* cakes, loaves 625 [ON *kaka*].

kare. See **care.**

kark *sb.* trouble 4 [AN *karke*].

karle. See **carle.**

kart *sb.* cart 1259 [ON *kartr*].

kast. See **kest** *v.*

keyes *sb. pl.* keys 1438 [OE *cǣg*].

kene *adj.* mighty, great 839, etc., sharp 1253, 1697; *superl.* **kennest** wisest 1575; *adv.* **kenely** swiftly 945 [OE *cēne; cēnlīce*].

kenne *v.* teach 865; *sg. pa. t.* **kende** 697; **kenned** knew 1702 [OE *cennan,* ON *kenna*].

kepe *v.* 264, etc.; *pp.* **keppte** 89. heed 1229, observe 292, recognise 508, receive 89, look for 234; *k. to* keep to 264; *bode k.* did as she was told 979 [OE *cēpan*].

kerue *v.* 1104, 1108, 1582; 3 *sg. pres.* **cerues** 1547; *pp.* **coruen** 1382, 1407, 1452. carve, cut, slice 1104, etc., tear 1582, fashion (by carving), cut ornamentally, figure 1382, 1407, 1452 [OE *ceorfan*].

kest *sb.* contrivance 1070; *cast of y3e* glance 768 [ON *kast*].

kest *v.* 634, 1455; *pl. pa. t.* **kesten** 951, 1515; *pp.* **kest** 234, etc., **kast** 460. throw, hurl 234, etc., throw away 1515, place 1744, scheme 1455 [ON *kasta*].

keuer *v.* 1605, 1700; *pp.* **couered** 1707. restore 1700, 1707, save (*of* from) 1605 [OE *acofrian*, OF *(re)covrer*, AN *-kevre*].

kydde. See **kyþe.**

kylle *v.* strike, knock (fut. sense) 876; *pp.* **kylde** killed 1252 [prob. OE **cyllan*].

kyn *sb.* kind; *what k.* . . . . *so* whatever 100; *orig. gen. sg.* in *alle kyne3* all kinds of 303; *orig. gen. pl.* in *fele kyn* various 1483 [OE *cynn*].

kyndam *sb.* kingdom 1700, 1731, **kyndom** 161 [OE *cynedōm*].

kynde *sb.* nature 263, 266, 1024, kind, species 334, etc.; *by (of) k.* according to nature 865, by its nature 1033, 1128; *adj.* lawful 697; *adv.* **kynd-(e)ly** appropriately 1n., exactly 319 [OE *(ge)cýnde; (ge)cýndelīce*].

kyng(e) *sb.* king 17, 1550, etc.; *gen.* **kynges** 1221 [OE *cyn(in)g*].

kynned *sg. pa. t.* was conceived 1072; *pp.* kindled 915 [OE *cennan*].

kyppe *pl. pres.* seize; *k. in honde* grasp 1510 [ON *kippa*].

kyryous. See **curious.**

kyrk(e) *sb.* church, temple 1270, 1431 [ON *kirkja*].

kyst(e) *sb.* chest 1438, Ark 346, 449, 464, 478 [ON *kista*].

kyte *gen.* kite's 1697 [OE *cȳta*].

kyþe *v.* 1368, etc.; *sg. pa. t.* **kydde** 23, 208. make clear, demonstrate 23, 1435, acknowledge 1368, practise, observe 851, offer, make 208 [OE *cȳþan*].

kyth(e) *sb.* land, country, kingdom, region, people 414, 901, etc.; *pl. gen.* (as adj.) **kythyn** of countries 1366 [OE *cȳþþu*].

klubbe *sb.* club 1348; *pl.* **clobbeȝ** 839 [ON *klubba*].

knaues *gen.* servant's 801; *pl.* bad men 855 [OE *cnafa*].

knawe *v.* 231, 1435, **know** 917; *sg. pa. t.* **knew** 281, 851, 1530; *pl.* **knewe(n)** 61, 827, 1087; *pp.* **knawen** 297, 1751, **knauen** 1575, **cnowen** 373. know, understand, perceive, realise, see 281, etc., acknowledge, recognise 231, 1087, know to be, recognise as 1575, know of, receive 61, make known 1751 [OE *cnāwan*].

knawlach *sb.* knowledge; *com to k.* came to his senses 1702 [from OE **cnāwlǣcan*, cf. *cnāwelācing*].

kne *sb.* knee 40; *pl.* **cnes** 1541 [OE *cnēo(w)*].

kneles 3 *sg. pres.* kneels 1345, 1591 [OE *cnēowlian*].

knyf *sb.* knife 1104 [OE *cnīf*].

knyȝtes *sb. pl.* knights 1397, 1431, 1519 [OE *cniht*].

knyt *sg. pa. t.* made (fast) 564 [OE *cnyttan*].

knokkes 3 *sg. pres.* knocks 1348 [OE *cnocian*].

know, koynt, koste. See **knawe, quoynt, cost(e).**

kote *sb.* cottage 801 [OE *cot(e)*].

kow *sb.* cow 1685; *pl.* **kuy** 1259 [OE *cū*, pl. *cȳ*].

kowpes, krakkes. See **cuppe, crak.**

lache *sg. pres. subj.* sustain 166; *pp.* 1186 [OE *læccan*].

ladde *sb.* fellow 36 [uncertain].

laddres *sb. pl.* ladders 1777 [OE *hlǣd(d)er*].

lady *sb.* lady 1059, 1084, 1589; *pl.* **ladis** 1352, 1370, **ladies** 1375, **ladyes** 1434 [OE *hlǣfdige*].

lafte. See **leue** *v.*[1]

laȝes *v.* laugh 661, etc.; *pl. pa. t.* **loȝen** 495 (OE *hlæhhan*).

lay *v.* place 1025, lay low 1650, assign 425, impose (*to* on) 263; *l. to þe grounde* laid low 1307 [OE *lecgan*, vowel from 2, 3 sg. pres. *legest*, *legeþ*].

lay(e). See **lygges.**

layk *sb.* conduct 1053, 1064, diversion 122, practice 274 [ON *leikr*].

laykeȝ *pl. imper.* play 872 [ON *leika*].

layteȝ *pl. imper.* search 97; *pp.* sought 1768 [ON *leita*].

lake *sb.* body of water, lake, sea, flood 1023, **llak** 438; *l. ryftes*? river valleys 536 [OE *lacu*].

lakked *pl. pa. t.* offended against 723 [cf. MDu. *laken*].

laled *sg. pa. t.* spoke 153, 913 [? cf. Da. *lalle*].

lamp *sb.* lamp 1273, 1485 [OF *lampe*].

langage *sb.* language 1556 [OF *langage*].

lanteȝ 2 *sg. pa. t.* gave 348 [OE *lǣnan*].

lape *v.* drink 1434 [OE *lapian*].

lapped *pp.* attired 175 [from OE *læppa*].

large *adj.* large, great, immense 438, etc., broad 1386; *sb.* breadth 314 [OF *large*].

lasched *sg. pa. t. subj.* might flare up 707 [imit.].

lasned *sg. pa. t.* subsided 438, 441 [from next].

lasse *adj. compar.* less 215, (as sb.) 1640. See **neuer.** [OE *lǣssa*].

last(e) *adj. superl.* last, final 608; *as sb.* in *at þe l., bi þe l.* finally, in the end 446 etc. [OE *lǣtest*].

last *v.* 894; 3 *sg. pres.* **lasteȝ** 568, **lasttes** 1124; *sg. subj.* **laste** 1594; *sg. pa. t.* **laste** 227, 1298. last, endure 568, etc., reach 227 [OE *lǣstan*].

lastes *sb. pl.* sins 1141 [ON cf. OI *lǫstr*].

lat *adj.* sluggish, remiss 1172 [OE *læt*].

late *adv.* late 1804n.; *compar.* **later** 1352. See **neuer**. [OE *late, lator*].

laþe *v.* invite, urge 900, etc.; *pl. imper.* **laþeȝ** 81 [OE *laþian*].

lauce *v.* open 1428, alleviate 1589, fly (*of* from) 966; *pa. t.* **laused** uttered 668, loosened, gave way 957 [from ON *lauss*].

launces *sb. pl.* branches *1485*n. [OF *la(u)nce*].

launde *sb.* field; *vpon l.* on the earth 1207; *on l. bestes* beasts of the earth 1000 [OF *la(u)nde*].

lauande *ppl. adj.* surging 366 [OE *lafian*].

law(e), laue (723) *sb.* law 188, 263, 723, religion 1167, 1174, 1307 [OE *lagu*].

lawe *sb.* hill 992 [OE *hlāw*].

laȝares *sb. pl.* sick people 1093 [ML *laȝarus*].

leaute *sb.* loyalty 1172 [OF *leaute*].

lebardeȝ *sb. pl.* leopards 536 [OF *lebard*].

lecherye *sb.* lechery 1350 [OF *lecherie*].

led *sb.*[1] lead 1025 [OE *lēad*].

led *sb.*[2] people, nation 691, **leede** 772 [OE *lēod*, f.].

lede *sb.* man, person, (in pl.) men, people 116, 261, 308n., 740, etc., servant 97, 614, prince, lord 1093, 1419, 1768; *l. of armes* men at arms 1773 [OE *lēod*, m.].

lederes *sb. pl.* leaders 1307 [OE *lǣdere*].

ledisch *adj.* 1556, **ludych** 73, **ludisch** 1375. of (a) people 1556, ? princely, noble 73n., 1375 [OE in *þiderlēodisc*].

le(e)f *sb.* love, dear one 939, 1066; *adj.* **lef** dear 772, **leue** 1622; **lefly** lovely 977 [OE *lēof(lic)*].

lege *sb.* sovereign, lord 1368; *adj.* sovereign 94; *watȝ l. tylle* owed allegiance to 1174 [OF *lege*].

legioun *sb.* legion 1293, 1773 [OF *legiun*].

leȝen, leyen. See **lygges.**

lel *adj.* true 1069, exact 425; *adv.* **lelly** truly 1066 [(from) AN *leel*].

lemed *sg. pa. t.* shone 1273, 1486 [from OE *lēoma*, cf. ON *ljóma*].

lemman *sb.* mistress 1352; *pl.* **lemanes** 1370 [OE **lēofman*].

lened *sg. pa. t.* (refl.) sat 784 [OE *hleonian*].

lenge *v.* stay, remain, lodge, dwell, live 412, 800, etc., be present 81, be seated 1419 [OE *léngan*].

lenger, lengest. See **long(e).**

lent *pp.*[1] placed, present 1084 [OE *léndan*].

lent *pp.*[2] granted (*in* to) 256 [OE *lǣnan*].

lenþe *sb.* 116, etc., **lencþe** 224; *pl.* **lenþe** 1383. length 314, 315, 1383, duration, length, space (of time) 568n. etc.; *on l.* lengthwise, i.e. down the hall 116; *þe l. of a terme* for a while 239 [OE *lengþu*].

lepes *pres.* leap, spring 966, 1209; *pp.* **lopen** rushed 990 [OE *hlēapan*].

lepre *adj.* leprous 1094 [from OF *lepre*].

lere *v.* teach 843 [OE *lǣran*].

leres *sb. pl.* cheeks, face *1542* [OE *hlēor*].

lerned *pp.* learned 693 [OE *léornian*].

lese *adj.* false 1719 [OE *lēas*].

lest *pl. pa. t.* failed 887; *pp.* **lorne** lost, ruined 932 [OE *lēosan*].

lest *cj.* lest, in case 151, 166, 943 [OE *þe lǣs þe*].

let *v.* 732; *pl. subj.* 670; *sg. pa. t.* **lette** 1174; *sg. imper.* **let** 1434; *pl. imper.* **leteȝ** 872; *pp.* **let** 1320. let, allow to 732, 1434; *l. we hit one* let it pass 670; *l. one* leave alone 872; *l. lyȝt bi (of)* set little store by 1174, 1320 [OE *lǣtan*].

letted *pp.* deprived 1803 [OE *lettan*].

letter *sb.* writing 1580; *pl.* **lettres** letters, writing(s) 1536, etc. [OF *lettre*].

leþe *v.* save 752; *sg. subj.* cease, be extinguished 648 [uncertain].

leþer *sb.* leather 1581 [OE *leþer*].

leue. See **le(e)f.**

leue *sb.* permission; *with your (þy) l.* by your leave 94, 347, 715; *his l. takeȝ* bids farewell 401 [OE *lēaf*].

leue *v.*[1] 378, 1233, 1678; *sg. pa. t. and pp.* **lafte** 1004, 1337. leave, abandon 378, etc., bequeath 1337 [OE *lǣfan*].

leue *v.*² believe, think, conclude 608, 752, 1703; *l. þou wel* be sure 1493 [OE *gelēfan*].

leues *sb. pl.* leaves 488, etc., (of book) 966 [OE *lēaf*].

lewed *adj.* ignorant, unenlightened 1580; *l. to rede* unable to interpret 1596 [OE *lǣwede*].

lyf, lyue *sb.* life 293, 308, etc., *gen.* **lyueȝ** 648; *on l.* alive 356, (intensive) 293; *his l.* for the rest of his life 1321 [OE *līf*].

lyflode *sb.* sustenance 561 [OE *līflād*].

lyft(e) *adj.* left 981, 1581 [OE *lyft*].

lyft(e) *sb.* sky, heavens 212, 366, etc., clear air 1761 [OE *lyft*].

lyft(e) *v.* 717, etc.; *pl. pa. t.* **lyfte** 1777. lift (up) 1649, 1777, make, pronounce 717, excite 586n.; *ppl adj.* **lyftande** heaving 443; **lyfte** high 1407 [ON *lypta*].

lygges *pres.* 99, 1126, 1792; *sg. pa. t.* **laye** 609, **lyȝe** 172; *pl.* **lay** 460, **leȝen** 936; *pp.* **leyen** 1003. lie, be 172, etc., lie hidden 99, 1126 [OE *licgan*].

lyȝt *adj.* light (in weight) 1026, eager, 987, light, little 1174, 1320; *adv.* **lyȝtly** quickly 817, 853 [OE *lēht(līce)*].

lyȝt *sb.* light 648, 1272; *pl.* 1486 [OE *lēht*].

lyȝt *v.* 476, etc.; *sg. pa. t.* 213, etc. alight 476, 1069, fall 213, 235, go down 691n., stop 800 [OE *līhtan*].

lyk *adj.* like 1436; *l. to* like 212, 790; *superl.* **lykkest** in *l. to* most like 261; *cj.* **like** as though 1008 [(from) ON *líkr*].

lik *v.* 1000; 3 *sg. pres.* **likkes** 1141n.; *pl. pa. t.* **likked** 1521. taste 1141, 1521; *l. on* lick 1000 [OE *liccian*].

lyke *v.* 36, etc.; *sg. subj.* 717; *sg. pa. t. subj.* 771. please (impers.) 539, etc., like it, approve 36, be pleased, desire 411, 435, permit 1726; *l. (ful) ille* displeases 693, was much displeased 73; *sb.* **lykyng** pleasure, delight 239, 1803, good disposition 172 [OE *līcian; līcung*].

lyknes 3 *sg. pres.* is like; *l. tylle* copies 1064 [from ON *líkr*, cf. MLG *līkenen*].

lykores *sb. pl.* liquors 1521 [OF *licor*].

lymeȝ *sb. pl.* limbs, parts (of the body) 175 [OE *lim*].

lyned *pp.* (of garment) lined 172n. [from OE *līn*].

lyouneȝ *sb. pl.* lions 536 [AN *liun*].

lyre *sb.* flesh 1687 [OE *līra*].

lysoun *sb.* ? opening 887n. [? OF *luision*; see note].

lyst *sb.*¹ practice 693 [OE *list*].

lyst *sb.*² edge 1761 [OE *līste*].

lyst *sb.*³ desire 843 [ON *lyst*].

lyst *impers. pres.* it pleases 872, 1000; *impers. subj.* 1766; *sg. pa. t.* **liste** pleased 415, was pleased 1356 [OE *lystan*].

lysten *sb.* power of hearing 586 [OE *hlyst*, infl. by ME *listenen*, v.].

lyte *adv.* little, by no means 119 [OE *lȳt*].

lyttel, little (1232) *adj.* little *233*, 965, 990, (as *sb.*) 617, of little account 1232; *set at l.* thought little of 1710; *a l.* (for) a little 451, 614, 736; *adv.* little 465, 935 [(from) OE *lȳtel*, ON *littill*].

lyþerly *adv.* badly 36 [OE *lȳþerlīce*].

lyue *v.* live 239, etc., **lyuy** 558; 2 *sg. pres.* **lyuyes** 1114; *sg. subj.* **lyuie** live as 581 [OE *lifian*].

lyue(ȝ), llak. See **lyf, lake.**

lo *interj.* lo, look 94, 541 [OE *lā*].

lodeȝmon *sb.* steersman 424 [cf. OE *lādman(n)*].

lodlych *adj.* hateful, loathsome 274, **loþelych** 1350, **lodly** (as *sb.*) loathsome people 1093; *adv.* **lodly** with loathing 1090 [OE *lāþlic; lāþlīce*].

lof *sb.* love 843, **luf** love, loved one 401 (twice), **loue** (coll. sense) loves 1419; *adj.* **lofly, louflych, luflych(e)** lovely, beautiful 939, 1486, courteous, gracious 809, 1804; *adv.* **luflyly** courteously 163 [OE *lufu; luflic; luflīce*].

loft(e) *sb.* air; *(vp)on l.* aloft, above, up, on high 206, 692, etc., on the upper part 1407, on top (of the altar) 1444, on the surface 1025, in Heaven 1803, upright 1342 [ON *(á) lopt*].

loge *sb.* house 800; *pl.* **logges** houses

(as dish covers) 1407; *l. dor* doorway of a lodge 784 [OF *loge*].

logge *v.* lodge 807; *sb.* **logging** house 887 [OF *logier*].

loghe *sb.* sea, flood 366, **loȝ(e)** 441, 1031 [OE (Nhb.) *luh*].

loȝ *adj.* low 1761, **loue** humble 28n.; *adv.* **loȝe** low 798; **loȝly** humbly 614, 745n. [(from) ON *lágr*].

loȝed *pp.* brought down 1650 [from ON *lágr*].

loȝen. See **laȝes**.

loke *v.* look, see 28, etc., (as interj.) 1069; *l. to* look to, pay heed to 263, 1059, see to it 317, 905, 944 [OE *lōcian*].

lome *adj.* lame 1094 [OE *lama*].

lome *sb.* vessel, Ark 314, 412, 443, 495 [OE *lōma*].

lomerande *ppl. adj.* stumbling 1094 [? from OE *lama*].

londe *sb.* land, country(side) 308, etc., world 568; *ouer l.* over the countryside 1293; *in l.* (merely intensive) 122 [OE *lánd*].

long(e) *adj.* long 1386, 1462, 1777; *þe l. naȝt* all night (long) 807; *vpon l.* after a long time 1193; *superl.* **lengest** (of time) longest 256; *adv.* **long(e)** (of time) long 809, etc.; *adv. compar.* **lenger** (of time) longer 810, 982 [OE *láng(e)*, *lengra*, *lengest*].

longed *pa. t.* pertained 1090, were subject 1747 [from OE *geláng*].

longing *sb.* anxiety 779, 1003 [OE *lángung*].

lopen. See **lepes**.

lorde *sb.* 28, 73, etc.; *gen.* **lordes** 1797. lord 73, 94, etc., (of God) 345, etc., husband 656 [OE *hláford*].

lordeschyp *sb.* lordship, power 1658 [OE *hláfordscipe*].

lore *sb.* lore 1556 [OE *lār*].

lorne. See **lest** *v.*

los *sb.* trouble 1589 [OE *los*].

loses *v.* 1141, etc.; *pp.* lost 1797. lose 586, etc., ruin 909; *l. hit ille* takes its loss badly 1141; *sb.* **losyng** perdition 1031 [OE *losian; losing*].

lot *sb.* speech, words 668 [ON *lát*].

lopelych. See **lodlych**.

loud(e) *adj.* loud 390, 1207; *adv.* loudly 153, 950 [OE *hlúd(e)*].

loue, louflych. See **loȝ, lof**.

louteȝ 3 *sg. pres.* bows 798 [OE *lūtan*].

loue. See **lof**.

loue *v.* praise, glorify, worship 1289, etc.; *sb.* **louyng** praising; *in l. hymseluen* in His praise 1448 [OE *lofian*].

loueȝ *sb. pl.* palms, hands 987 [ON *lófi*].

louy *v.* love, like 1066; 1 *sg. pres.* **luf** 1434; 2 *sg.* **louyeȝ** 841; 3 *sg.* **louies** 1052, etc.; *pl.* **loueȝ** 823; *pa. t. and pp.* **loued** 275, 723, 1059; *sg. pa. t. subj.* **louied** 21 [OE *lufian*].

lowkande *pres. p.* closing; *l. togeder* contracting (itself) 441n. [OE *lūcan*].

ludych, ludisch, luf, luflych(e), luflyly. See **ledisch, lof, louy**.

luf-lowe *sb.* fire of love 707 [OE *lufu*+ON *logi*].

luged *sg. pa. t.* lurched 443 [cf. Sw. *lugga*].

luly-whit *adj.* (as sb.) lily-white ones 977 [OE *lilie*+*hwīt*].

lulted *pp.* sounded 1207 [cf. LG, Du. *lul* 'pipe'].

lump *sb.* lump 1025 [cf. Da. *lump(e)*, Norw., Sw. dial. *lump*].

lumpen *pp.* happened; *impers. in hem had l. harde* they would have fared badly 424; *hym moȝt haf l. worse* he might have fared worse 1320 [OE *limpan*].

lust *sb.* lust 1350; *adj.* **lusty** worthy 981 [(from) OE *lust*].

luþer *adj.* wicked, worse 163, (as sb.) vileness 1090 [OE *lȳþre*].

ma. See **make** *v.*

mach *sb.* mate 695, (table-)companion 124 [OE *gemæcca*].

machches 3 *sg. pres.* strives 1512n. [from prec.].

mad(e). See **make** *v.*

madde *adj.* foolish 654 [OE *gemǣd(d)*].

maȝty *adj.* mighty 273, 279, **myȝty** 1237; *adv.* **maȝtyly** fiercely, ruthlessly 1267 [OE *mæhtig(līce)*, *mihtig*].

may *pres.* may, can, be able to, be allowed to 32, 843, etc.; *pa. t.*

myȝt 3, 530, etc., **moȝt** 22, 372, etc.; 2 *sg.* **moȝteȝ** 655 [OE. *mæg, mihte, muhte*].

mayden *sb.* maiden 248, 1267, etc. [OE *mægden*].

maynful *adj.* almighty 1730 [from OE *mægen*].

mayny-molde *sb.* (wide) world 514n. [OE *mægen + mólde*].

maynly *adv.* loudly 1427 [from OE *mægen*].

mayntnaunce *sb.* supporting 186 [OF *maintenance*].

mayster *sb.* master, lord, captain 125, 252, etc.; *adj.* **maysterful** imperious 1328 [(from) OF *maistre*].

maysterry *sb.* victory 1241 [OF *maistrie*].

make *sb.* mate, wife 331, 703, 994; equal, peer 248; *seuen m.* seven (of the same kind) 334 [OE *gemaca*].

make *v.* 373, 628, etc.; 3 *sg. pres.* **matȝ** 695; *pl. subj.* **make** 819; *sg. pa. t.* **mad(e)** 52, 641, etc.; *sg. imper.* **ma** 625, **make** 309, 314, 1067; *pp.* **mad(e)** 91, 247, 1720, **maked** 254, etc. prepare, create, make, contrive, cause 52, etc., play 1202, perform, carry out 247, 1238, do 1071, take as 695; *m. to þe* make for yourself 309 [OE *macian*].

male *sb.* male 337, 695, 703 [OF *male*].

malyce *sb.* evil 519, **malys** anger 250 [OF *malice*].

malscrande *ppl. adj.* charmed, deadly 991 [from OE *malscrung*].

malt(e) *v.* soften (it) 776n.; *m. wythinne* penetrate 1566 [OE *mæltan*].

man *sb.* 51, 180, etc., **mon** 124, 183, etc.; *gen.* **man(n)eȝ** 514, 520, 575; *pl.* **men** 119, 137, etc.; *pl. gen.* **manneȝ** 515, **monnes** 332, 1673. man, person 51, etc., servant 436, 613, 771, 818, 1512, mankind 285, etc., (as indef. pron.) one, a man 180, 183, 189, (in address) sir 581 [OE *man(n)*].

mancioun *sb.* house 309 [OF *mansion*].

mane *sb.* Mene 1727, 1730 [L *mane*].

maner *sb.* practice 701; *adv.* **manerly** courteously 91 [(from) AN *manere*].

mangerie *sb.* banquet 52, 1365 [OF *mangerie*].

mankynde *sb.* mankind 278, **monkynde** 564 [OE *mancynn*, with *cynn* repl. by *kynde*, OE *(ge)cýnd*].

manne *v.* be manned, be mastered 869n. [OE *mannian*].

mansed *ppl. adj.* accursed 774 [OE *-mánsod*].

mar(s)chal *sb.* marshal, officer in charge of feast 91, 118, 1427 [OF *mareschal*].

margerye-perle *sb.* pearl 556 [OF *margerie + perle*].

maryageȝ *sb. pl.* marriages 186 [OF *mariage*].

marie *v.* give in marriage, marry 52, 815 [OF *marier*].

marre *v.* corrupt 279, kill 991; *sb.* **marryng** in *m. of maryageȝ* adultery 186 [(from) OE *merran*, OF *marrir*].

mase *sb.* maze; *þe m.* delusion, vanity 395n. [cf. OE *āmasian*, v.].

maskle *sb.* spot 556 [OF *mascle*].

masse *sb.* gospel (read at mass) 51n. [OE *mæsse*].

mast *sb.* mast 417 [OE *mæst*].

mater *sb.* matter, sense 1566, 1617, 1635 [AN *matere*].

matȝ. See **make** *v.*

mawgre *sb.* hostility 250 [OF *maugre*].

me. See **I.**

med *adj.* appropriate (*to* to), in keeping (with) 1391n. [OE *gemēde*].

mede *sb.* reward 12, 24, 1632 [OE *mēd*].

medoes *sb. pl.* meadows 1761 [OE *mædwe*, obl. cases of *mæd*].

megre *adj.* thin 1198 [OF *megre*].

meyny *sb.* company 331, 454 [OF *mai(s)nee*].

meke *adj.* gentle 815, merciful 771, (as sb.) humble one 776; *adv.* **mekely** briskly 783n. [(from) ON **mēuk-*, cf. OI *mjúkr, mjúkliga*].

mekned 3 *sg. pa. t.* softened 1328 [from prec.].

mele *sb.* meal 226, 625 [OE *melu*].

mele *v.* speak 748, etc. [OE *mælan*].

menddyng *sb.* improvement 764 [from AN *mender*].

mene *adj.* poor 1241 [OE *(ge)mǽne*].

menes v. mean, signify 1567, 1733, explain 1635; m. als much as is as much as to say that 1730 [OE mǣnan].

meng(e) v. mix 625; m. with put in with 337 [OE méngan].

menscla3t sb. manslaughter 182 [cf. OE mannslæht].

mensk adj. (as sb.) polite matters; of m. speken made polite conversation 646n.; sb. **menske** honours 121, grace 522, noble estate 1740 [ON mennskr; mennska].

menske3 3 sg. pres. honours 141; pp. 118 [from ON mennska].

mercy sb. mercy 395, **mersy** 776; graunt m. thank you 765; adj. **mercyable** merciful 1113; **mercyles** merciless 250 [(from) OF merci; merciable].

mere sb.¹ sea 991 [OE mere].

mere sb.² border 778 [OE mǣre].

mery, merþe. See **myry, myrþe.**

merit sb. reward 613 [OF merite].

merk adj. dark, obscure 1617; sb. darkness 894 [ON myrkr].

merkke3 3 sg. pres. 637; sg. pa. t. and pp. **merk(k)ed** 558, etc., place 637, figure, decorate 1487, write 1617, 1727; m. to lyuy appointed to live, gave life to 558 [OE mearcian].

meruayl(e) sb. marvel, wonder 22, 586, 1164 [OF merveille].

meschef sb. misfortune, evil 708, 1164, the worst 373 [OF meschef].

mese v. moderate 764 [OF amesir].

message sb. messenger 454 [OF message].

messe3 sb. pl. dishes 637 [OF mes].

mester sb. need 67 [OF mester].

mesure sb. moderation 215, 247, 565; adj. **mesurable** moderate 859 [OF mesure; mesurable].

metalles sb. pl. metals 1513 [OF metal, L metallum].

mete adj. appropriate, right, suitable 337, 637, equal 1662 [OE gemǣte].

mete sb. food 121, 466, etc., meal 118, 125, dish 1354 [OE mete].

mete v. meet 797; sg. pa. t. **mette** 371; pl. **metten** 86, 1394 [OE mētan].

mette3 sb. pl. measures 625 [OE met].

met3 sb. blow 215n. [OF mes].

meth sb. mildness, mercy 436, **meþe** 247, 565; adj. **meþele3** immoderate, violent 273 [OE mǣþ(lēas)].

meue3 v. move 303, 783 [OF moev-, moveir].

my. See **I.**

myddes sb. midst; in þe m. in the middle 1388 [altered from OE on middan].

mydny3t sb. midnight, middle of the night 894 [OE midniht].

my3t. See **may.**

my3t sb. power 644, etc.; of m. powerful 1656 [OE miht].

my3ty. See **ma3ty.**

myke sb. crutch (for mast when lowered) 417 [MDu. micke].

mylde adj. gentle, merciful 728 [OE milde].

myle(3) sb. pl. miles 674, 1387 [OE mīl].

mylke sb. milk 637 [OE milc].

mylke v. milk 1259 [OE milcan].

myn. See **I.**

mynde sb. mind 518, etc., purpose 1328, 1502 [OE gemýnd].

mynystred sg. pa. t. served 644 [OF ministrer].

mynne v. (with on) remember, think of 436, 771; impers. pres. **myne3** in me m. on I remember 25 [ON minna].

mynstrasy sb. minstrelsy 121 [OF menestralsie].

myntes 3 sg. pres. intends, has in mind 1628 [OE myntan].

myre sb. mire 1114 [ON mýrr].

myry, mery (1760) adj. merry 130, bright, clear 804, 1760, fine, worthy, goodly, excellent 331, 934, etc.; superl. **myriest** most pleasant, most excellent 254, 701; adv. **myry** merrily 1516; **myryly** happily 493 [OE myrge; myriglīce].

myrþe, merþe sb. pleasure, bliss 189, 703, sport 1519; talkede m. talked pleasantly 132 [OE myrgþ].

misschapen ppl. adj. misshapen, evil 1355 [OE mis-+scapen, pp.].

mysse v. 189, 551; pp. **myst** 994, 1198. forfeit 189; m. of forfeit 551; wat3 m. was missing 994, was lacking 1198 [OE missan].

mysseleue sb. wrong faith 1230 [OE mis-+lēafa].

myst *sb.* mist 1760 [OE *mist*].

mistrauþe *sb.* bad faith; *founde in m.* found to be faithless 996 [OE *mis-+trēowþ*].

mo *adj. compar.* more (in number) 98, etc. [OE *mā*].

mod(e) *sb.* mood, outlook 713, nature 215, 565, anger 764, thought, inner meaning 1635n. [OE *mōd*].

modey *adj.* proud 1303 [OE *mōdig*].

moder *gen.* mother's; *m. chylde* man 1303 [OE *mōdor*].

moȝt(eȝ). See **may.**

mold(e) *sb.* earth 279, 708, etc., land (sg. sense) 454 [OE *mólde*].

mon. See **man.**

moni(e), mony(e) *adj.* many 96, 193, etc., (as *sb.*) 521, 572, etc., many a 43, 1299, 1439, 1602, 1687; *m. a* many a 659, 1286, etc. [OE *manig*].

monyfolde *adv.* many times 278 [OE *manigféalde*].

monyth *sb.* month 427, 493, 1030 [OE *mōnaþ*].

monkynde, monnes. See **man, mankynde.**

monsworne *sb.* perjury 182 [from OE *mānsworen*, pp. of *mānswerian*].

moon *sb.* moaning, lamentation 373 [OE **mān*].

mor *sb.* moor 1673; *on m.* on earth 385 [OE *mōr*].

more *adj. compar.* more, greater, further 96, etc.; *no m.* no more, no further, no longer 385, 513, etc.; *adv. compar.* more 76, 168, etc.; *neuer m.* never(more) 191 [(from) OE *māra*].

morn(e) *sb.* morning 493, next morning 1001, 1793 [OE *morne*, dat. of *morgen*].

mornande *pres. p.* mourning, grieving 778n. [OE *múrnan*].

mornyng *sb.* morning 804 [from OE *morne*, dat. of *morgen*].

morsel *sb.* morsel 620 [OF *morsel*].

morteres *sb. pl.* mortars, bowls of wax with floating wicks 1487 [AN *morter*].

most(e) *adj. superl.* greatest, mightiest 254, 385 [OE (Nhb.) *māst*].

most 2 *sg. pres.* 1673; 3 *sg.* **mot** 580; *pa. t.* **most(e)** 407, 1031, 1331.

shall 580, must 407, etc. [OE *mōt, mōste*].

mote *sb.* blemish 556 [OE *mot*].

mount(e) *sb.* mountain, hill 447, 994 [OF *(mo(u)nt*, OE *munt*].

mourkenes 3 *sg. pres.* darkens 1760 [ON *myrkna*].

mourkne *v.* rot 407 [ON *morkna*].

mowþe *sb.* mouth 1669 [OE *mūþ*].

much *adj.* much, great 22, 182, etc.; *adv.* much, greatly 189, 285, etc. [shortened from OE *mycel*].

mudde *sb.* mud 407 [MLG *mudde*].

mukel *adj.* great 52, etc. [OE *mycel*, infl. by ON *mikill*].

mul *sb.* dust 736n. [OE *myl*].

multyplyed *pl. pa. t.* multiplied 278; *pl. imper.* **multyplyeȝ** 522 [OF *multiplier*].

munster *sb.* church, temple 1267 [OE *mynster*].

nade *sg. pa. t.* had not 404 [OE *nabban*].

naȝt *sb.* 484, etc., **nyȝt** 526, 779, etc., **niyȝt** 359, 1779; *gen.* **naȝtes** 1764n. night 359, etc., nightfall 1779; *on n.* by night 578 [OE *næht, niht*].

nay *adv.* no 729, 743, 758 [ON *nei*].

nayed *sg. pa. t.* refused 65; *pl.* **nay** said . . . not 805n. [OF *nier*].

nayte *v.* use 531 [ON *neyta*].

naytly *adv.* well 480 [from ON *neytr*].

nakeryn *pl. gen.* (as adj.) of horns 1413n. [cf. OF *nacaire*].

name *sb.* name 410, etc., **nome** 297n. [OE *nama*].

nas *sg. pa. t.* was not 983n., etc.; *sg. pa. t. subj.* **nere** 21 [OE *nis, næs, nēre*].

nature *sb.* nature 1087, **natwre** 709 [OF *nature*].

nauþer *adv.* (prec. by *ne*) either 1226, 1556, **nawþer** 1028; *cj.* (correl. with *ne*) neither 1104, 1336 [OE *nāwþer*].

ne *adv.* not 152, 178, etc., (pleonastic) 225, 1205; *cj.* nor 34, 48, etc. [OE *ne*].

nede *sb.* need 1163; *adj.* meagre 146n.; **nedleȝ** useless 381; *adv.* **nede(s)** necessarily 407, 1331 [(from) OE *nēd; nēde(s)*].

neȝ(e) *v.* come near, go near, approach

143, etc.; *sg. pres. subj.* **neȝe** *32*n. [from OE *nēh*].

neȝe *prep.* near, with 803 [OE *nēh*].

nekke *sb.* neck 1638 [OE *hnecca*].

nel 1 *sg. pres.* will not 513; 3 *sg.* **nyl** 1261; *pa. t.* **nolde** 805, 1091 etc. [OE **nyllan, nolde*].

nem. See **nymmes.**

ner *adv.* almost 1558; *wel n.* almost 1585; *prep.* **nere** near 414 [(from) ON *nær*, OE *nēr*].

nere. See **nas.**

neue *sb.* fist 1537 [ON *hnefi*].

neuen *v.* call on 410, 1525, state 1376 [ON *nefna*].

neuer *adv.* never 48, etc., not (at all) 587, 615, etc.; *n. on* never a one, no one 1555; *n. so* never so 1330; *n. þe lasse, n. þe later* nevertheless 215, 1352 [OE *nǣfre*; cf. *nā þȳ lǣs*].

newe. See **nwe.**

next *adv.* next; *n. after* immediately afterwards 261 [OE *nĕxt*].

nice *adj.* extravagant 1354, (as sb.) wanton (man) 1359, **nyse** ignorant, ill-bred 824 [OF *nice*].

nye *sb.* 1376, **niye** 1002, **nwy** 301; *pl.* **nyes** 1754. trouble 1376, 1754, anguish 1002, fury 301 [OF *anui*].

nif *cj.* if not, unless 21, 424 [OE *ne + gif*].

nyȝe *adv.* almost 484 [OE *nēh*].

n(i)yȝt, nyl. See **naȝt, nel.**

nymmes 3 *sg. pres.* 480, 481; *sg. pa. t.* **nem** 505, **nome** 1613; *pp.* **nomen** *1002*, 1281, **nummen** *1291.* take, capture 480, etc., undergo, endure *1002*n.; *n. out* picked out 505 [OE *niman*].

nyteled *pl. pa. t.* blundered (in ignorance, helplessly) 888n. [see note].

no *adj.* no, not any 136, etc., **non(e)** 21, etc.; *n. oþer* nothing else 342n., 742, 1681, no other kind 508; *adv.* **no** (with compars.) no 234, 385, etc. [OE *nān*].

noble *adj.* noble, excellent 121, 167, etc., (as. sb.) nobles 1226 [OF *noble*].

nobleye *sb.* nobility 1091 [OF *nobleie*].

no-bot *adv.* only, just 1127 [next + *būtan, būte*].

noȝt *sb.* nothing 209, etc.; *adv.* not (at all), by no means 84, 106, 1245, **not** 22, 32, etc.; *adj.* **noȝty** vile 1359 [(from) OE *nāht, nōht*].

noye *v.* trouble, anger, distress, harass 1236; 3 *sg. pres.* **nuyeȝ** 578; *sg. pa. t.* **nuyed** 1176; *pp.* **nyed** 1603, **nwyed** 306 [OF *in anuier, anoier*].

noyse *sb.* noise 849, etc. [OF *noise*].

nolde, nome, nome(n), non(e). See **nel, name, nymmes, no.**

non(e) *pron.* none, no one 72, 101, etc.; *n. oþer* þen none other than 1704 [OE *nān*].

norne *v.* ask 803; *sg. pa. t.* **nurned** declared 669, offered 65 [cf. Sw. dial. *norna, nyrna* 'inform secretly'].

norture *sb.* nurture, breeding 1091 [OF *norture*].

not. See **noȝt.**

note *sb.* course of action 1233, activity, effort 381, way, practice 727, 1651 [OE *notu*].

notes *sb. pl.* notes 1413 [OF *note*].

noted *pp.* noted, famed 1651; *sb.* **notyng** noting, appreciation 1354 [(from) OF *noter*].

now, nov *adv.* now, at this time 1008, etc., now (in weakened sense, introd. clause or with imper.) 301, etc.; *cj.* since, now that 1111, 1305, if now 721 [OE *nū*].

noumbre *sb.* number 737, 1376, amount, sum 1283; *bi a clene n.* in a full reckoning 1731 [AN *numbre*].

nuyeȝ, nuyed, nummen, nurned. See **noye, nymmes, norne.**

n(e)we *adj.* new 1354, succeeding, successive 526 [OE *nēowe*].

nwy, nwyed. See **nye, noye.**

obeched *sg. pa. t.* did homage to, bowed to 745 [OF *obeiss-, obeir*].

odde *adj.* odd, extra 426, (as sb.) (single) one 505; *adv.* **oddely** exceptionally 698, absolutely 923 [(from) ON *odda-*].

of *prep.* of, (away) from, out of 287, 596, 901, etc., by (means of), with 892, 1253, etc., (agent) by 243, on account of 1728, (made, consisting) of 954, 1081, 1276, 1279, etc., about, concerning 26, 51, etc., with respect to, in terms of 27, 253, 425, 1019, etc., concerned with *1579*n., (objective) 295, 1565, etc., (of quality) 1389, 1390 (twice), etc., (partitive) 42, 88 (twice), 640, etc.; (poss.) 622, 690, etc.; *adv.* off 440n., 630, 876, 1179, 1191, 1265 [OE *of*].

ofte *adv.* often 410, 423, etc. [OE *oft*].

oȝt *sb.* anything 663, 1092 [OE *ā(wi)ht, ō(wi)ht*].

oke *sb.* oak 602 [OE *āc*].

olde *adj.* old 601, 1123; *superl.* **aldest** 1333 [OE *áld*].

olipraunce *sb.* arrogance, ostentation 1349 [cf. OF *olibrieux*, adj., from *Olibrius* (name of tyrant)].

olyue *sb.* olive 487 [OF *olive*].

on. See **a.**

on *prep.* on, upon, at, in, by *1460*, etc.; *adv.* on(wards) 380, 905, on him 30 [OE *on*].

on *adj.* one, a single 152, etc., (one and) the same 716, 718, (intensifying superl.) very 144, 892, (as adv.) first(ly) 997; *pron.* **on(e)** one (person, thing) 25, 42, 63, 1555; (*þat*) *o.* (contrasted with *oþer*) the first (one) 299, 999 [OE *ān*].

one *adv.* alone 178, 670, 731, 872; *þyn o.*, *hit o.* on your (its) own, the only one 923, 927 [OE *āna*].

onelych *adv.* only 1749 [OE **ānlīce*, cf. *ānlic*, adj., *ǣnlīce*, adv.].

ones *adv.* once (upon a time), formerly 23, etc., once, one time 982, on a certain occasion 1357, once more 761; (*alle*) *at o.* (all) at once, together 1672, etc.; *at þis o.* for this once 624, 801 [OE *ānes*].

onhede *sb.* oneness; *in o.* as a unity, as one 612 [OE *ān* + **-hǣde*, cf. *-hād*].

on-yȝed *adj.* one-eyed 102 [OE *ānēgede*].

onsware *sb.* answer 753 [OE *andswaru*].

oo *interj.* o 861.

open *v.* reveal 1600; *ppl. adj.* **vponande** in *wyd v.* that opens wide *318*n. [OE *openian* (infl. by *up*)].

ordaynt *pp.* ordained, appointed 237 [AN *ordeiner*].

ordenaunce *sb.* ordinance, plan (of Creation) 698 [OF *ordenance*].

ordure *sb.* filth 1092, filthy thing 1101 [OF *ordure*].

orenge *sb.* orange 1044 [OF *orenge*].

organes *sb. pl.* organs 1081 [OF *organe*].

ornementes *sb. pl.* ornaments, furnishings 1799, **vrnmentes** 1284 [OF *ornement*].

orppedly *adv.* quickly 623 [OE *orpedlīce*].

oste *sb.* host 1204 [OF *ost*].

oþer *adj.* other 175, etc.; *pron.* other (one, thing) 1227, etc., second 299, 999; *pl.* **oþer** others, rest 332, etc., latter 1511n.; *of (alle) o.* (intensifying superl.) of all 256, 701, 1749 [OE *ōþer*].

oþer *cj.* or 42, 417, etc. [as prec.].

oþerwayeȝ *adv.* otherwise, alternatively 448 [from OE *ōþer*, adj. + *weg*].

our(e). See we.

oure *sb.* hour 1779 [AN *ure*].

out, oute (41, 1046), *adv.* out 98, 353, etc., on the outside 1046, out of shape 41, finished, over 442; *o. of* out of, (away) from 287, 289, etc., (of material) out of 1342, 1408, apart from, untouched by 923; *o. of age* over age, advanced in years 656 [OE *ūt(e)*].

outborst *pl. pa. t.* burst out 1251 [OE *ūt(ā)berstan*].

outcomlyng *sb.* alien 876 [from OE *ūtācumen, ūtcymen(e)*, etc.].

outkast *pp.* cast out 1679 [OE *ūt* + ON *kasta*].

outtaken *pp.* excepted, except for 357, 1573 [OE *ūt* + ON *taka*].

ouþer *pron.* either (of them) 795 [OE *āwþer*].

ouer *prep.* over, across 133, 472, etc., above 406, surpassing 1314 [OE *ofer*].

ouerbrawden *pp.* covered over (with plumage) 1698n. [OE **oferbrogden*, pp. of *oferbregdan*].

ouerȝede *sg. pa. t.* passed away 1753 [OE *oferēode*].

ouerseyed *pp.* passed away 1686 [OE *ofer* + *sīgan, sǣgan*].

ouertok *pl. pa. t.* overtook 1213 [OE *ofer* + ON *taka*].

ouertorned *pl. pa. t.* went by 1192 [OE *ofer* + *túrnian*].

ouerþwert *adj.* crosswise, horizontal 1384; *adv.* across 316 [OE *ofer* + ON *þvert*, neut. of *þverr*].

ouerwalteȝ 3 *sg. pres.* rolls over 370 [OE *ofer* + *gewæltan*].

owne. See **aune.**

ox(e) *sb.* ox 1086, 1682; *pl.* **oxen** 66 [OE *oxa*].

payne *sb.* penalty 244, 716, pain 190, torment, torture 1227; *on p. of* on pain of 46 [OF *peine*].

payre *sb.* pair 335, 338 (twice) [OF *paire*].

payres 3 *sg. pres.* deteriorates 1124 [OF *empeirier*].

pakked *pp.* packed (up) 1282 [MDu., MLG *pakken*].

palays *sb.* palace 83, etc., **palayce** 1389 [OF *palais*].

palle *sb.*[1] (rich) material 1637 [OE *pæll*].

palle *sb.*[2] paling 1384n. [OF *pal*].

papeiays *sb. pl.* parrots 1465 [AN *papejaye*].

paper *sb.* paper 1408n. [AN *papir*, OF *papier*].

paradis *sb.* Paradise 195, 704, (earthly) paradise 238, 1007 [OF *paradis*].

parage *sb.* rank 167 [OF *parage*].

paramoreȝ *sb. pl.* lovers 700n. [from OF *par amurs*].

parchmen *sb.* parchment 1134 [OF *parchemin*].

pared *sg. pa. t.* carved 1536; *pp.* cut 1408 [OF *parer*].

parformed *sg. pa. t.* inflicted 542 [OF *parformer*].

parget *sb.* plaster 1536 [cf. OF *porget*, sb., *pargeter*, v.].

parlatyk *adj.* palsied 1095 [OF *paralytique*, L *paralyticus*].

part *v.* divide 1007, descend 242 [OF *partir*].

partrykeȝ *sb. pl.* partridges 57 [OF *perdriz*, *pertriz*].

passe *v.* 942, etc.; *sg. pa. t.* **past** 1654; *sg. pa. t. subj.* **passed** 856; *pp.* **past** 1672. pass, move, go 72, etc., pass by 844, pass through 856n., surpass 1389, pass away, end 395, 1672; *p. out of* came from 1654; *p. fro* leave 615 [OF *passer*].

paume *sb.* hand, fist 1533, 1542, claw, talon 1697n. [OF *paume*].

peces *sb. pl.* pieces 1348 [OF *pece*].

penaunce *sb.* penance 1116, 1131 [OF *penance*].

peneȝ *sb. pl.* pens 322 [OE *penn*].

penies *sb. pl.* pennies, money 1118 [OE *penig*].

penitotes *sb. pl.* peridots, green gems 1472n. [OF *peritot*, *peridot*].

penne *sb.* pen 1546, 1724 [OF *penne*].

penne-fed *adj.* fed in a pen 57 [OE *penn* + *fēd(d)*, pp. of *fēdan*].

pented *sg. pa. t.* belonged 1270 [OF *apendre*].

peple *sb.* people, race 242, etc., persons 111 [AN *people*].

per(e) *sb.* peer, equal 1336, opposite number, opponent 1214 [OF *per*].

peraunter *adv.* perhaps 43 [OF *par aventure*].

peril(e) *sb.* peril 856n., 942 [OF *peril*].

perle *sb.* pearl 1068, etc. [OF *perle*].

perre *sb.* (coll. sense) jewels 1117 [OF *perr(er)ie*].

pertly *adv.* manifestly 244 [from OF *apert*].

phares *sb.* Peres 1727, 1736, 1737 [L *phares*].

pich *sb.* pitch 1008 [OE *pic*].

pyche *v.* 477; *pp.* **pyȝt** 83, etc. set, place 477, 1463, fill 83n.; *p. to* attached to, next to 785 [OE *picc(e)an*].

pyes *sb. pl.* magpies 1465 [OF *pie*].

pyese *sb.* piece; *in p.* (intensive) still 1124n. [OF *en piece*].

piked *pp.* picked, pecked; *p. of* partaken of 1466n. [OE *pīc(i)an*, cf. *pīcung*].

pyled *pl. pa. t.* pillaged 1270; *pp.* 1282 [OE *pilian*, *pylian*].

pyleres *sb. pl.* pillars 1271, 1479 [AN *piler*].

pinacles *sb. pl.* pinnacles 1463 [OF *pinacle*].

pyned *pp.* afflicted, consumed (*in* by) 1095 [OE *pīnian*].

pynkardines *sb. pl.* gems of some kind 1472 [uncertain].

pipes *sb. pl.* pipes 1081, 1413 [OE *pīpe*].

pit *sb.* pit 1008 [OE *pytt*].

pite *sb.* pity 232, 396 [OF *pite*].

place sb. place 1317, area 1385, dwelling-place 238, house 72, 146, 1282, city 785, 1013; hade into p. brought to its place 1443 [OF place].

play sb. play, sport, revelry, dalliance 700, 1494, 1502 [OE plega].

played pl. pa. t. came and went 787 [OE pleg(i)an]

playn adj. smooth 1068, 1134, bare 1531; sb. plain 1216, 1379 [OF plain].

planed pp. planed 310 [OF planer].

plantted sg. pa. t. established, created 1007 [OE plantian].

plaster sb. plaster 1549 [OE plaster, OF plastre].

plat adj. level 1379; **platful** cram-full, filled to overflowing 83n. [(from) OF plat].

plat pl. pa. t. struck 1265; sb. **plattyng** beating 1542 [(from) OE plættan].

plater sb. platter 638 [AN plater].

plek sb. spot, place 1379 [cf. MDu. plecke].

plese v. please 338 [OF plaisir].

plyes v. bend; enclose 1385n.; p. to inclines to, has to do with 196 [OF pl(e)ier].

plyt sb. condition, kind 111, setting 1494 [AN plit, OF ploit].

plow sb. plough 68 [OE plōg, plōh].

plunged pp. plunged 1008 [OF plungier].

poynt(e) sb. point; vch a p. every-thing 196; in(mydde) þe p. of at the height of 1502, 1677; at þis ilke p. at this very moment, now 628 [OF point].

poynted pp. painted (over), decorated (of with) 1408n. [OF point, pp. of poindre].

poyntel sb. pointed instrument (for writing), stylus 1533 [OF pointel].

poysened ppl. adj. poisoned 1095 [from OF poisonner].

polyce v. polish, cleanse 1131; pp. 1068, **polysed** 1134 [OF poliss-, polir].

polyle sb. poultry 57 [OF polaille].

polle sb. crown (of the head) 1265 [cf. Du., LG polle].

polment sb. soup, stew 628, 638 [L pulmentum].

pomgarnades sb. pl. pomegranates 1466 [OF pome garnate, pome grenade].

porche sb. porch, gatehouse 785 [OF porche].

porpor, porpre sb. purple (material) 1568, 1743, (as adj.) 1637 [OE purpure, OF porpre].

port sb. gate 856 [OF porte].

portrayed sg. pa. t. 700, **purtrayed** 1536; pp. **pourtrayd** 1271, **pur-trayed** 1465. form, devise 700n., 1536, depict 1465, paint (over), decorate (in with) 1271n. [OF portraire].

poruayes 3 sg. pres. formulates 1502 [AN porveier].

postes sb. pl. pillars 1278 [OE post].

potage sb. pottage 638 [OF potage].

pouer sb. power 1654, **power** 1660 [AN poer].

pouer(e) adj. poor 127n., 146, 1074, lowly 773, (as sb.) lowly one 615n. [OF povre].

pray sb. prey, booty; in p. token captured as booty 1297 [OF preie].

pray v. entreat 72, 232, 615 [OF preier].

prayed sg. pa. t. ravaged 1624 [OF pre(i)er].

prayse v. value, deem 146, 1117, (as pass. infin.) be valued, be prized 189, praise, admire 148, 642, 1479, glorify 1313 [OF preisier].

prece sb. press, throng 880 [OF presse].

prechande pres. p. preaching, insist-ing on 942 [OF prechier].

precious adj. worthy of respect, worshipful, holy 1282n., **presyous** 1496 [OF precios].

prelates sb. pl. prelates 1249 [OF prelat].

presed pl. pa. t. pressed (in torture) 1249 [OF presser].

presens sb. presence 8, 147, 1496 [OF presence].

presented sg. pa. t. presented 1297, pp. 1217 [OF presenter].

presoner(e)s sb. pl. prisoners 1217, 1297, 1308 [AN prisoner].

prest sb. priest 8, 1131, 1249 [OE prēost].

prest adj. quick 147; adv. **prestly** promptly 328 [(from) OF prest].

preue *v.* 704; *pp.* 1748, **proued** 1158,
1496. prove, show 1158, turn out to
be 754, establish as, recognise as
1496, 1748 [AN *prev-*, OF *prover*].

pryce *sb.* prize; (*þe*) *p. of* the best of
(in) 1308, 1614 [OF *pris*].

pr(i)yde *sb.* pride 179, 1349, 1657,
glory 1227, 1677, ceremony 1450;
of p. noble 1389 [OE *prȳde*].

prymate *sb.* primate, leader 1570 [OF
primat].

prynce *sb.* prince 49, 1215, etc. [OF
prince].

pryncipal(e) *adj.* royal 1531, 1781
[OF *principal*].

pryncipalte *sb.* sovereignty 1672,
principality 1738 [OF *principalte*].

prys *adj.* precious 1117n. [OF *de pris*].

pryuyest *adj. superl.* most intimate,
most important 1748n.; *adv.*
pryuyly delicately, cleanly 1107n.,
pryuely apart, specially 238 [(from)
OF *prive*].

profert *pl. pa. t.* projected 1463 [OF
proferer].

profete *sb.* prophet 1624, **prophete**
1614; *pl.* **prophetes** 1492; *pl. gen.*
prophetes 1300 [OF *prophete*].

profetie *sb.* (company of) prophets
1308; *pl.* **profecies** prophecies
1158n. [OF *profetie, profecie*].

proper *adj.* excellent 195 [OF *propre*].

proud(e), prowde *adj.* proud, self-
opinionated 232, proud, noble,
valiant 1177, 1772; *superl.* **pruddest**
noblest 1300; *adv.* **prudly** proudly,
splendidly 1379, 1466 [(from) OE
prūd, OF *prud*].

proued. See preue.

prouince *sb.* province, country 1300,
1614, 1624 [OF *province*].

pulle *v.* pull 68; *pl. pa. t.* **pulden** 1265
[OE *pullian*].

pure *adj.* pure 1570, fair, noble 1271,
(intensive) itself 704; *adv.* **purely**
completely 1660. See **clergye**.
[(from) OF *pur*].

pure *v.* purify 1116 [OF *purer*].

puryte *sb.* purity 1074 [OF *purite*].

pursaunt *sb.* surrounding wall 1385n.
[OF *po(u)rceint*].

pursued *sg. pa. t.* advanced 1177 [AN
pursuer].

purtrayed. See portrayed.

put *pp.* put 244, 1214; *sb.* **puttyng**
putting 46 [(from) OE *pūtian*].

quayntyse, quat. See **quoyntis,
what.**

quauende *ppl. adj.* surging 324 [? OE
cwafian].

qued *sb.* evil, mischief 567 [OE
cwēad].

quelle *v.* kill 324, 567 [OE *cwellan*].

quen. See **when.**

quene *sb.* queen 1351, etc. [OE *cwēn*].

quik *adj.* quick 624, alive 324; *sb. pl.*
quyke3 living things 567 [OE *cwic*].

quyl(e), quite. See **whyl(e), whit.**

quyte *v.* (shall) pay 1632 [OF *quiter*].

quoynt, koynt (1382) *adj.* skilfully-
made 1382, 1459, attractive 871,
well-dressed (*also* polite *and* wise)
160 [OF *cointe*].

quoyntis *sb.* 54, **quayntyse** 1632,
coyntyse 1287, 1809. wisdom, skill
1287, 1632, fine clothes 54, refine-
ment (? *and* fine clothes) 1809 [OF
cointise, queintise].

quos, quo-so. See **who.**

quoþ *pa. t.* said 139, 621, etc. [OE
cweþan].

rac *sb.* storm(-cloud) 433 [cf. OI *reki*].

rachche *v.* go (*after* for, to get) 619
[OE *ræc(c)an, reccan*].

rad *adj.* frightened 1543 [ON *hræddr*].

radly *adv.* quickly 671, 797 [OE
hrædlīce].

rafte *sg. pa. t.* took away by force,
carried off 1431; *pp.* 1142, 1739
[OE *rēafian*].

ra3t, ran, rank. See **reche** *v.*, **renne,
ronk.**

rayke *v.* go 671, (refl.) 465; *ppl. adj.*
raykande advancing 382 [ON
reika].

rayn *sb.* rain 440, 953, 959; *r. ryfte*
cataract 368n. [OE *regn*].

rayne *v.* rain 354; *ppl. adj.* **raynande**
in *r. ryg* rain-storm 382 [OE
regnian].

rankor *sb.* rancour 756 [OF *rancor*].

rape *sb.* fall, ruin 233n. [ON *hrap*].

rasped *sg. pa. t.* rasped, scratched
1724; *pp.* 1545 [OF *rasper*].

rasse *sb.* cleft, crevice 446n. [OF
ras(s)e].

ratted adj. ragged 144 [uncertain].

rauen sb. raven 455, 465 [OE hræfn].

raw adj. raw 790 [OE hrēaw].

rawþe sb. pity 972, remorse 233 [from OE hrēowan, cf. ON hryg̊ð].

reames. See **reme**.

rebaudeȝ sb. pl. scoundrels 873 [OF rebaud].

rebel adj. disobedient 455 [OFı rebelle].

rebounde sg. pa. t. rebounded 422 [OF rebonder].

reche sb. (pall of) smoke 1009 [OE rēc].

reche v. 890, 1369; pl. pres. 906; sg. pres. subj. 1766; sg. pa. t. and pp. **raȝt** 561, etc. reach, extend 1691, give 561, 1739, offer, pay 1369, get, take 890, 1766, go 766; r. to reach 906 [OE rǣcan, pa. t. rǎhte].

reches 3 sg. pres. cares 465 [OE *rēcan, reccan].

recordeȝ 3 sg. pres. records 25 [OF recorder].

recouerer sb. relief 394 [AN recoverer].

red adj. red 1045 [OE rēad].

rede v. 1555, etc.; sg. pres. subj. 1642; pl. subj. **reden** 1346; pp. **red** 194. read 194, read in church 7, read, understand, interpret, make out 1555, etc., guide 1642, deal with 1346n. [OE rēdan].

redy adj. ready 345, 869, eager, zealous 294, 724 [from OE rǣde].

redles adj. in despair 1197, **rydelles** 969; as sb. in for r. for lack of counsel, in despair 1595 [OE rǎdlēas].

reflayr sb. scent 1079 [OF reflair].

refrayne v. refrain from 756 [OF refrener].

regioun sb. region 760, 964 [OF region].

reȝtful adj. righteous 724 [OE *rehtful, cf. rihtful].

rehayte v. encourage, pay one's compliments to 127 [OF rehaiter].

reynyeȝ sb. pl. 'reins', seat of affections, primarily kidneys, loins; r. and hert innermost being 592n. [OF reins].

reysoun. See **re(y)soun**.

reken adj. honest 738, 756, noble 1082; adv. suitably 10; **rekenly** suitably 1318, courteously 127 [OE recen(e), recenlice].

rekken v. reckon (vp up) 2 [OE gerecenian].

relece v. absolve (of from) 760 [OF relesser].

relygioun sb. religion, faith 7, 1156 [OF religion].

relykes sb. pl. sacred objects 1156, 1269 [OF relique].

reme sb. realm 1572; pl. **reames** 1316 [OF reaume].

remnaunt sb. remnant; þe r. all that remained 433, (all) the rest 738 [OF remenant].

remued pp. removed 646, banished 1673 [OF remuer].

renayed pp. refused 105 [OF reneier].

rended pp. torn 1595; ppl. adj. **rent** 40, 144 [OE réndan].

rengne sb. kingdom 1334, etc., reign 1734 [OF regne].

rengned sg. pa. t. and pp. 328, 1169, 1321; pl. imper. **rengneȝ** 527. reign, hold sway 527, etc.; r. in lived in (a state of) 328n. [OF regner].

renischche adj. strange, outlandish 96n., **runisch** 1545; adv. **renyschly** harshly (? and outlandishly) 1724 [see note].

renk sb. man 766, **ring** 592; gen. **renkes** 786; pl. **renkeȝ** men, people 7, 96, 105, renkkes 969, 1514 [OE rinc, cf. OI rekkr].

renne v. 527, etc.; pa. t. **ran** 797, etc.; pl. pa. t. **runnen** 391. run 391, etc., continue 527 [ON renna, OE rinnan].

rent. See **rended**.

reres v. rear, rise (high) 366, 423, 1461; pl. pa. t. **rerd** raised, sent up 873 [OE rǣran].

res sb. rush 1782 [OE rǣs].

reset sb. refuge 906 [OF recet].

re(y)soun sb. 328, 1633; pl. **resoun(e)ȝ** 2, 184, 194. reason 328, discourse, writing 194, statement 184, justification 2; to r. brynges make sense of 1633 [OF re(i)sun].

resounable adj. reasonable, law-abiding 724 [OF resonable].

rest sb. rest, sleep 890, 1208, 1766 [OE rest].

restes 3 *sg. pres.* 738; *sg. pa. t.* **rest** 446; *pl. imper.* **rest** 906, **rette3** 619; *pp.* **restted** 616. rest 446, etc., stand 738 [OE *restan*].

restle3 *adj.* restless, changing 527 [OE *restlēas*].

restored *pp.* restored 1705 [OF *restorer*].

reuel *sb.* revels 1369 [OF *revel*].

reuerence *sb.* reverence, respect 10, **reuerens** 1318; *reche hym r.* pay him their respects 1369 [OF *reverence*].

reward(e) *sb.* reward 1346; *kydde a r.* made return, responded 208 [AN *reward*].

rewled *sg. pa. t.* (refl.) conducted himself 294 [OF *reuler*].

rial *adj.* splendid, rich 786, 1082, **royl** 790; *adv.* **ryally** splendidly 812 [(from) OF *rial, roial*].

rialte *sb.* (royal) splendour 1321, **rialty** 1371 [OF *rialte*].

riboudrye *sb.* loose living 184 [OF *ribauderie*].

rych(e) *adj.* rich, noble, well-born, splendid, great, mighty 37, 127, 1299, etc., (as *sb.*) mighty king 1321, noblemen 1208; *superl.* **rychest** most mighty 1217, worthiest 1572; *adv.* **ryche** richly 1411; **rychely** richly 1045 [OE *rīce*, OF *riche*; OE *rīclīce*].

rychen *pl. pres.* prepare 10n. [? OE **ryccan*, cf. ON *rykkja*].

ryde *v.* ride 1293, 1572 [OE *rīdan*].

rydelles. See **redles.**

ridlande *pres. p.* falling (as from a sieve), sifting 953 [from OE *hriddel*].

ryfte *sb.* rift 368, 536, 964. See **lake, rayn.** [ON *ript* 'breach of contract'].

ryg(e) *sb.* storm 354, 382 [cf. ON *hregg, hrið*, OE *hrīþ*].

ry3t *sb.* right; *as he r. hade* as was proper for him to do 1318; *by r.* correctly 1633, as of right 2; *of r.* true 194; *on r.* indeed 1513; *adj.* true, correct 283; *adv.* favourably, well 1346, (intensive) right, just 59n., 1061, 1754; *r. now* swiftly 1754; **ry3te3** precisely 427 [OE *riht(e), rihtes*].

ry3twys *adj.* righteous 294, 328 [OE *rihtwīs*].

ring. See **renk.**

ryngande *ppl. adj.* resonant 1082; *sb.* **rynging** ringing 1513 [(from) OE *hringan*].

rypande *pres. p.* probing 592 [OE *rȳpan*].

ripe *adj.* ripe 869, 1045 [OE *rīpe*].

ryse *v.* 363, etc.; *pa. t.* **ros** 797, etc. rise (up), arise 363, etc., (of sun, dawn) 893, 932, (from sleep) 1766, 1793, stand (up) 671, 853 [OE *rīsan*].

ryth *sb.* bull 1543 [OE in *hrīþfald, hrīþheorde*].

robbed *sg. pa. t.* robbed, plundered 1156; *pp.* 1142 [OF *rob(b)er*].

robbors *sb. pl.* robbers 1269 [AN *rob(b)ere*].

robe *sb.* robe, garment 144, 1595 [OF *robe*].

roborrye *sb.* robbery 184 [OF *rob(b)erie*].

roche3 *sb. pl.* rocks, crags 537 [OF *roche*].

ro3(e) *adj.* rough 1545, 1724, furious 382; **ro3ly** (as *sb.*) troubled vessel 433n. [OE *rūh, rūg-, rūw-*; see note].

royl. See **rial.**

rok *sb.*[1] rock 446 [OF *roque*, cf. OE *stānrocc*].

rok *sb.*[2] crowd, company 1514n. [? ON *hroki* 'heap above brim of full vessel'].

roled *sg. pa. t.* rolled, spun 423; *ppl. adj.* **rollande** flowing 790 [OF *rol(l)er*].

romyes 3 *sg. pres.* bellows 1543 [OF *rumier, rungier*].

ronk *adj.* wilful, vile 455, 760, 873, grown, adult 869, **rank** great 233 [OE *ranc*].

rore3 *v.* roar 390, 1543 [OE *rārian*].

ros. See **ryse.**

rose *sb.* (attrib.) of the rose 1079 [OF *rose*].

rose *v.* praise 1371 [ON *hrósa*].

rost(t)ed *pp.* roasted 59, 959 [OF *rostir*].

rote *sb.*[1] root 619 [OE *rōt*].

rote *sb.*[2] rottenness, corruption 1079 [from OE *rotian*].

rotes *sb. pl.* stringed instruments 1082 [OF *rote*].

roþeled *v.*[1] *pp.* ? heated, broiled 59n. [see note].

roþeled v.[2], sg. pa. t. ? reeled to and
fro, staggered 890. See note to l. 59.
[cf. ON riðlask].

roþer sb. rudder 419 [OE roþer].

roþum sb. redness 1009n. [ON
roðmi].

roum sb. room, space 96 [OE rŭm].

rounde adj. round 927, 1121; sb. on on
r. about 423 [OF ro(u)nd-, ro(o)nt].

rowtande ppl. adj. violent 354 [OE
hrūtan].

rowtes sb. pl. crowds, hordes 969,
1197, 1782 [OF route].

rubies sb. pl. rubies 1471 [OF rubi].

ruddon sb. redness, red light 893n.
[see note].

rueled sg. pa. t. tumbled, poured
953n. [OF rueler].

runisch, runnen. See renischche,
renne.

rurd sb. noise 390 [OE réord].

rusched sg. pa. t. rushed, poured
368 [AN russher].

ruþen v. rouse 895n., (of from) 1208
[? ON (h)ryðja].

rweȝ v. impers. as in me r. I repent,
I regret 290, 561 [OE hrēowan].

rwly adv. pitifully 390 [OE hrēowlīce].

sacrafyce sb. sacrifice 1497, sacrafyse 510, sacrefyce 1447, sakerfyse 507 [OF sacrifice].

sadde adj. solemn, dignified 595, 640,
dismal 525, long 1286, advanced
657 [OE sæd].

sade. See say.

sadeles sb. pl. saddles 1213 [OE
sadol].

saf prep. except (for) 1749, saue 409
[AN sa(u)f].

safyres sb. pl. sapphires 1469 [OF
safir].

sage adj. learned 1576 [OF sage].

saȝe sb. 1670, sawe 109; pl. saȝes
1599, 1737, saueȝ 1545, sawes
1609. saying, word 1545, etc.,
command 109, 1670 [OE sagu].

saȝtled v.[1], sg. pa. t. settled, came to
rest 445 [OE setlan, infl. by next].

saȝtled v.[2], sg. pa. t. made his peace
230; pp. reconciled (to to) 1139; sb.
saȝtlyng reconciliation 490, peace
1795 [(from) OE sahtlian, sæhtlian].

say v. say, tell 53, 1112, 1552; 2 sg.

pres. seggeȝ 621; 3 sg. says 657,
saytȝ 29, 75; sg. subj. say 868; sg.
pa. t. sayd (refl.) 853, sayde 63, 97,
etc., sade 210; pl. sayden 93, 645,
647; sg. imper. say 139; as so s. that
is to say 29n. [OE secgan].

sayl sb. sail 420 [OE segl].

sayned pl. pa. t. blessed 986; pp.
746 [OE segnian].

sake sb. sake 922 [OE sacu].

sakerfyse. See sacrafyce.

sakles adj. innocent 716 [OE sacléas].

sakred pp. sacred, consecrated 1139
[OF sacrer].

sale sb. hall 107, 120, etc. [OE sæl].

salt sb. salt 820, 823, etc.; adj. 984,
995 [OE s(e)alt].

same adj. same, very 660 [ON samr].

samen adv. together 645, 1363;
al(le) s. (all) together, all at once
400, 468, 1291 [OE æt samne, ON
saman].

samen v. 870, samne 53; pp.
samned 126, 361. assemble, gather
53, etc.; s. wyth consort with 870
[OE samnian].

samen-feres sb. pl. companions 985
[prec. + OE gefēra].

samples sb. pl. examples, parables
1326n. [AN assample].

sancta sanctorum sb. Holy of Holies
1274, 1491.

sapyence sb. wisdom 1626 [OF
sapience].

sardiners sb. pl. sardines, red gems
1469n. [OF sardine].

sarre(st), sat. See sore, sitte.

sathrapas sb. pl. wise men, sages
1576n. [OF satrape, L satrapa].

sauce sb. sauce 823 [OF sauce].

saudan sb. sultan, emperor 1323; gen.
saudans 1364, 1388 [OF soudan].

saule sb. soul 290, 575, 1135, sawele
1139, sawle 1130, 1599, 1626; pl.
sauleȝ 332n. [OE sāwol].

saundyuer sb. glass-gall, acid scum
formed in glass-making 1036 [OF
suin de verre].

saueȝ. See saȝe.

sauteray sb. psaltery, stringed instrument 1517 [OF sauterie].

saue. See saf.

saue v. save 332, etc., (of from) 988
[OF sa(u)ver].

sauement *sb.* safety 940 [OF *sa(u)vement*].

saueour *sb.* Saviour 576, **sauio(u)r** 176, 746 [OF *sauveour*].

sauere3 3 *sg. pres.* seasons 825; *sg. imper.* **sauour** consider *581*n. [OF *savourer*].

sauyte *sb.* safety, salvation 489 [OF *sauvete*].

sauor *sb.* smell 510, 1447n., taste 995 [OF *savour*].

sauour, sawe(s), saw(e)le. See **sauere3, sa3e, saule.**

scaled *pl. pa. t.* scaled *1776*n. [OF *escaler*].

scape *v.* escape 62, 529, 928 [AN *ascaper*].

scarre3 *v.* take alarm 598, startle 838, fly (*on* into, up to) 1784n. [ON *skirra*, OF *escarrir*].

scaþe, skaþe *sb.* harm, injury 151, 1186, disaster 600, wrong, sin 21, etc. [ON *skaði*].

scelt *sg. pa. t.* in *s. in scorne* mocked in scorn, scorned 827n., **skelt** broke out 1186; *pl.* **skelten** came hurrying 1554; *pp.* **skelt** raised 1206 [see note].

schad *sg. pa. t.* came down 1690 [OE *scēadan*].

schadow *sb.* shade 605 [OE *scead(u)we*, obl. cases of *sceadu*].

schal, schale (553) *v.* shall, will, must 354, etc.; 2 *sg. pres.* **schalt** 742; *pl.* **schul** 107, **schin** 1435, 1810; *pa. t.* **schuld(e)** 249, etc.; *pl. pa. t. subj.* **schulde** 108 [OE *sceal, scylon, scolde*].

schalke *sb.* man 1029; *pl.* **schalkke3** 762 [OE *scealc*].

schame *sb.* shame, baseness 597, 850, **schome** 1115 [OE *sceamu*].

schame3 3 *sg. pres.* is ashamed 580 [OE *sceamian*].

schap *sb.* shape 1121; *pl.* **schappes** 1460 [OE *gesceap*].

schape *v.* endeavour 762; *s. non oper* have it no other way 743 [formed on OE *scapen*. pp. of **sceppan*].

scharp(e) *adj.* sharp, piercing 840, deep, great 850, 1310, swift 475 [OE *scearp*].

schauen *ppl. adj.* shaved 1134 [OE *sceafan*].

schawe *v.* 1599, 1626, **schewe** 122, 170, 553; *pl. pres.* **schewe** 840; *sg. pa. t.* **schewed** 662, **scheweed** 791; *pp.* **schewed** 600, etc., **scheued** 250. show, display, disclose, demonstrate 250, etc., explain 1599, 1626, utter 840, provide 122, be revealed 791, make an appearance 553n., (refl.) look 170 [OE *scēawian*].

schelde3 *sb. pl.* shoulders (of boar) 58 [OE *scéld*].

schende *v.* punish, destroy, kill 519, 742; *pp.* **schent** 47, 580, 1029 [OE *scéndan*].

schene *adj.* bright, beautiful 170, 1076, 1310 [OE *scēne*].

schepon *sb.* cow-shed 1076 [OE *scypen*].

schin. See **schal.**

schyne *v.* shine 1115, 1121, 1532 [OE *scīnan*].

schyre *adj.* bright, beautiful 553, 605, 1278; *adv.* **schyr** brightly 1121 [OE *scīr(e)*].

schyre-wykes *sb. pl.* groin, middle of the body 1690n. [OE *scyru, scearu* + ON in *munnvik*, etc.].

schome. See **schame.**

schonied *sg. pa. t.* shunned, fled from 1101 [OE *scunian*].

schor *sb.* shower 227 [OE *scūr*].

schortly *adv.* soon, directly 600, 742; *s. at ones* decisively 519 [OE *sceortlīce*].

schot *sg. pa. t.* shot; *s. to* came over 850 [OE *scēotan*].

schout *sb.* shout 840 [uncertain].

schowued *pp.* shoved, thrust 44, 1029, driven (*of* from) 1740 [OE *scūfan*].

schrank *sg. pa. t.* recoiled 850 [OE *scrincan*].

schrewedschyp *sb.* depravity 580 [from next].

schrewe3 *sb. pl.* evildoers 186 [OE *scrēawa*].

schryfte *sb.* shrift, confession 1115, 1130, 1133 [OE *scrift*].

schrylle *adj.* shrill 840 [cf. OE *scyl*, LG *schrell*].

schroude-hous *sb.* vestry, sacristy 1076 [next + OE *hūs*, cf. OE *scrūdelshūs*].

schrowde *sb.* clothes 47, 170 [OE *scrūd*].

schul, schuld(e). See **schal.**

schulderes *sb. pl.* shoulders *1690* [OE *sculdor*].

schunt *pp.* moved aside, retreated 605 [? from OE *scunian*].

scylle *sb.* 151, s̡kyl 569, etc., **skyly** 62n. reason, wits 151, meaning 1554, intention, purpose 569, 709, 827, pretext, excuse 62n.; *hit no s. were* it would not be reasonable 823; *adj.* **scylful** reasonable, righteous 1148; **skylly** clear 529n. [(from) ON *skil; -skilligr*].

scla3t *sb.* slaughter 56 [OE *slæht*].

scoymus *adj.* 21, 1148, **skoymos** 598. fastidious 21; *s. of* revolted by 598, 1148 [OF *esco(y)mos*].

scole *sb.* cup 1145 [ON *skál*].

scoleres *sb. pl.* scholars 1554 [OF *escoler*].

scomfyted *pl. pa. t.* 1784; *pp.* **scoumfit** 151. be thrown into confusion 1784; *s. of his scylle* scared out of his wits 151 [formed on OF *desconfit*, pp. of *desconfire*].

scorne *sb.* scorn 827 [OF *escarn*].

scorned *pp.* scorned 709 [OF *escharnir*].

scowte-wach *sb.* sentry-patrol 838n. [OF *escoute* + OE *wæcce*].

scraped *pp.* scraped 1546 [ON *skrapa*].

scrypture *sb.* writing 1546 [L *scriptura*].

scrof *adj.* rough *1546* [from OE *scruf, scurf*].

scue. See **skwe.**

se(e) *sb.* sea 984, 1015, 1020; *gen.* **se** 1039n. [OE *sǣ*].

se(e) *v.* 68, 126, etc.; *sg. pres. subj.* 178, 576; *sg. pa. t.* **se3** 209, 398, 1710, **sy3e** 788; *pl.* **sy3e** 985, **se3en** 1529; *sg. imper.* **se** (as interj.) 661, 1225; *pp.* **sen** 1169. see 68, etc., look after 988 [OE *sēon*].

seche *v.* 454, etc.; *sg. pres. subj.* 1130; *pa. t.* **so3t** 201, etc.; *pl. pa. t.* **so3tten** 1371. seek (out), look for 454, etc., (as pass. infin.) 1559, be concerned, strive (with infin.) 201, 1286, come 1371; *s. after* seek out 420; *s. to* come to, go to, reach, touch 29, etc., resort to 1130n. [OE *sēcan, sōhte*].

secounde *adj.* second 427 [OF *second*].

sed(e) *sb.* seed, breeding stock 336, 358, offspring 660, seed-time 523n. [OE *sēd*].

seete. See **se(e)te.**

sege *sb.* siege 1185 [OF *sege*].

segg(e) *sb.* 681, etc.; *pl. gen.* **segge3** *515*n. man 117, etc., servant 93 [OE *secg*].

segge3, se3(en). See **say, se(e)** *v.*

seyed *pp.* passed 353 [OE *sǣgan, sīgan*].

seknesse *sb.* sickness 1078 [OE *sēocness*].

selcouth *sb.* marvellous event 1274 [OE *sel(d)cūþ*].

self(e), selue(n) *adj.* (self-)same, very 660, 1418, 1769, (foll. sb.) himself, itself 243, etc., (foll. sb. in gen.) 786, (as sb.) oneself, one's person 579n. [OE *self(a), selfan*].

sely *adj.* innocent 490 [OE *(ge)sēlig*].

sellen *pl. pres.* sell 1038 [OE *sellan*].

sem *sb.* seam 555 [OE *sēam*].

semblaunt *sb.* bearing 640, friendly manner, friendliness 131 [OF *semblant*].

semble *sb.* assembly 126 [AN *semblee*].

seme *adj.* seemly 549, 1810 [ON *sœmr*].

semed *sg. pa. t.* suited 793, seemed (to be), looked 117, 416 [ON *sœma*].

sem(e)ly, semlych (1247) *adj.* seemly, fair, attractive 209, etc., (as sb.) seemly one 1055, pretty ones 870; *compar.* **semloker** prettier 868; *adv.* **semely** attractively 1442 [ON *sœmiligr, sœmiliga*].

sen. See **se(e)** *v.*

sende *v.* 353, etc.; *sg. subj.* 1811; *sg. pa. t. and pp.* **sende** 53, 781, etc.; *sg. imper.* **sende** 1615. send, give 53, etc., (fut. sense) 353, send messengers 780, 1615; *s. agayn* gone back, returned 1705 [OE *sēndan*].

ser(e) *adj.* various, different 336, etc. [ON *sér*].

sergaunte3 *sb. pl.* servants 109 [OF *serjant*].

serges *sb. pl.* candles 1489 [OF *cerge*].

seruage *sb.* servitude 1257 [OF *servage*].

seruaunt *sb.* servant 631, 733, 988 [OF *servant*].

serue *v.* serve 18, 724, etc., (absol.) 1812, (at table) 38, 120, etc., give oneself to 1115, officiate (in religious house) 1264, serve, avail 530, (absol.) 750 [OF *servir*].

seruyse *sb.* service 1152, (at table) 1401 [OF *servise*].

sese *v.* cease 523 [OF *cesser*].

seses *v.* seize, take possession of 1313, 1795 [OF *seisir*].

sesoune3 *sb. pl.* seasons 523 [OF *seson*].

set(e). See **sette3, sitte.**

se(e)te *sb.* seat, throne 37, etc., abode 1388, place (at table) 92, 1395, sitting down (at table) 59n. [ON *sæti*].

seten. See **sitte.**

sette3 *3 sg. pres.* 469, 636; *sg. pa. t.* **set, set(t)e** 290, 507, 1453, 1710; *pl.* **setten** 672; *pp.* **set(te)** 37, 1015, etc. set, place, situate 290, etc., (absol.) 636, arrive 986, lay 1185, seat 37, 1401, deal out, take 1225, direct, turn 672, (refl.) apply oneself 1453; *s. on* settles on, chooses 469; *ppl. adj.* **set** set, given 1364 [OE *settan*].

sepe *sg. pres. subj.* boil, cook 631 [OE *sēoþan*].

seve *sb.* stew, sauce 108; *pl.* **seue3** 825, **seves** *1406* [OF *seve*, cf. OE *sēaw*].

seuen *adj.* seven 334, *1453*, etc. [OE *seofon*].

seuentepe *adj.* seventeenth *427*n. [OE *seofontēoþa*].

seuenpe *adj.* seventh 361 [from OE *seofon*].

sewer *sb.* servant (responsible for service at table) 639 [AN *asseour*].

sex *adj.* six 426 [OE *sex*].

syde *sb.* side 144, etc., environs, outskirts 956, 968; *on vche a s.* on every side, everywhere 78, 555, 1380 [OE *sīde*].

side-bordes *sb. pl.* side tables 1398 [OE *sīd-* + *bord*].

syence *sb.* 1454, 1599; *pl.* **ciences** 1289. art, skill 1289, 1454, wisdom 1599 [OF *science*].

sy3e. See **se(e)** *v.*

sy3t(e) *sb.* sight 29, etc., apparition 1722, (eye)sight 706, appearance 1406; *s. of y3en* glance 1005; *in his s.* before his eyes 1221; *hade s. of* caught sight of 610; *see with s.* see 192, 576, 1710; *setten her s.* turned their eyes 672 [OE *gesihþ, -siht*].

sykande *pres. p.* sighing 715 [OE *sīcan*].

syled *sg. pa. t.* passed (on) 131 [cf. Norw., Sw. dial. *sila* 'flow'].

sylk *sb.* silk 790 [OE *sioloc*].

syluer *sb.* silver 1277, 1344; *adj.* **sylueren** silver 1406 [OE *siolfor; silfren*].

symbales *sb. pl.* cymbals 1415 [OF *symbale*].

symple *adj.* gentle, mild 746n.; *superl.* **symplest** most lowly 120 [OF *simple*].

synful *adj.* sinful 15, 716, 1111 [OE *synnful*].

syngen *pl. pres.* 7; *sg. pa. t.* **songe** 1516; *pl.* **songen** 1763, sing 7, 1763, ring out 1516 [OE *singan*].

syngne *sb.* sign, token 489, miraculous event 1710n. [OF *signe*].

synk *v.* 398, 910; *3 sg. pres.* **synkke3** 689, 1026; *pl. pa. t.* **sunkken** 968; *pres. p.* **synkande** 445; *pp.* **sonkken** 1014. sink 398, etc., cause to sink 1014; *s. in* penetrates, assails 689n. [OE *sincan*].

synne *sb.* sin 520n., 1019n., etc. [OE *synn*].

synned *pp.* sinned 679 [from prec., cf. OE *syngian*].

sir *sb.* (in address) sir 715, 1622, (as title) 900 [unstressed form of next].

syre *sb.* sire, lord 661, etc.; *gen.* 1299 [OF *sire*].

syt(e) *sb.* sorrow 1257, evil 566 [ON *sȳt*, cf. OI *sút*].

sitte *v.* 91, etc.; *sg. pa. t.* **sat** 992, **sete** 661, 1171; *pl.* **sete(n)** 645, 829, etc.; *pp.* **seten** 833. sit 479, 601, etc., (absol.) 833, (at table) 91, 107, etc., (on throne) 552, 1498, sit as 1260, be situated 992, remain 550, live, dwell 773, 1257; *s. at* sit down to 829, 1763 [OE *sittan*].

syþe *sb.* time, period 1169, 1453; *pl.*
syþe 1188, 1417, **syþeʒ** 1686 [OE
sīþ].

syþen *adv.* then, afterwards, next 116,
175, etc., after that time 262; *cj.*
since 684 [OE *siþþan*].

siue *sb.* sieve 226 [OE *sife*].

skarmoch *sb.* skirmishing 1186 [OF
escar(a)muche].

skaþe. See **scaþe.**

skeles *sb. pl.* platters 1405 [OF
escuele].

skelt(en). See **scelt.**

skete *adj.* quickly 1186 [ON *skēot*,
cf. OI *skjótt*].

skewes. See **skwe.**

skyfted *pp.* altered 709 [ON *skipta*].

skyg *adj.* particular 21 [cf. Norw., Sw.
dial. *skygg*].

skyl(y). See **scylle.**

skyre *adj.* bright 1776 [ON *skírr*].

skyrmeʒ 3 *sg. pres.* moves swiftly
about 483 [OF *eskirmir*].

skyualde *sb.* splitting-up 529n. [see
note].

skoymos. See **scoymus.**

skowteʒ 3 *sg. pres.* scouts 483 [OF
escouter].

skwe *sb.* sky, heaven, cloud 483, **scue**
1784; *pl.* **sk(e)wes** 1206, 1759 [ON
skiw-, sḱ].

slayne. See **slow.**

slauþe *sb.* sloth 178 [from OE
slāw].

sleke *v.* extinguish 708 [OE *sleacian*].

slepande *pres. p.* sleeping 1785 [OE
slēpan].

slyʒt *sb.* cunning 1289 [ON *slœgð*].

slyp *sb.* ? quick movement, stroke
1264 [? from next].

slyppe *v.* slip, pass 985, escape 1785
[MLG *slippen*].

slow *sg. pa. t.* slew, killed 1221; *pl.*
slouen 1264, **slowen** 1247; *pp.*
slayne 55, 1785 [OE *slēan*].

smach *sb.* smell 461n., savour 1019
[OE *smæc*].

smachande *pres. p.* smelling 955 [OE
smæccan].

smal *adj.* fine 226 [OE *smæl*].

smart *adj.* bitter 1019; *adv.* **smartly**
sharply 711 [(from) OE *smeart*].

smelle *sb.* smell; *hade þe s. of* smelt
461 [? from OE **smyllan*].

smylt *adj.* refined 226n. [? cf. MDu.,
MLG *smilten*].

smyte *v.* smite, strike down 711 [OE
smītan].

smod *sb.* filth 711 [cf. LG *smaddern*,
v.].

smoke *sb.* smoke 955 [OE *smoca*].

smokeʒ 3 *sg. pres.* smokes 226 [OE
smocian].

smolderande *ppl. adj.* smothering
955 [cf. LG *smöln*, MDu. *smölen*].

smolt *v.* go 461n., 732 [see note].

smoþely *adv.* quietly, in peace 732
[from OE *smōþ*].

snaw *sb.* snow 222 [OE *snāw*].

so *adv.* so, to such an extent 262, 1148,
etc., such 850, (intensive) 552, 557,
etc., thus, in this way 29n., 69, 118,
etc., as 1550, (reinforcing indef.
prons.) 100, 819, 1648, (correl. with
as cj.) 198, 519, etc., (correl. with
þat cj.) 269, 279, etc.; *s. þat* so that
83; *s. watʒ* as was 786; *is s.* is so, is
the case 669; *s. . . . to* so as to 685,
904 [OE *swā*].

soberly *adj.* dignified 117n.; *adv.*
solemnly 1497, earnestly 799 [from
OF *sobre*].

sodenly *adv.* suddenly, swiftly 910,
1769, urgently 201 [from AN
sodein].

soffered. See **suffer.**

softe *adj.* pleasant 445; *adv.* **softely**
softly 822 [(from) OE *sŏfte*].

soʒt(ten). See **seche.**

soyle *sb.* earth 1039; *vpon s.* along the
ground 1387 [AN *soil*].

solace *sb.* comfort(s), joy, delight,
bliss 870, 1080, etc. [OF *solas*].

solased *sg. pa. t.* cheered 131 [OF
solacier].

solem(p)ne *adj.* solemn, dignified
1171, 1447; *adv.* **solempnely**
solemnly 37 [(from) OF *solem(p)ne*].

solem(p)nete *sb.* high estate 1678,
festivity 1757, reverence, respect
1313n. [OF *solem(p)nete*].

solie *sb.* seat, throne 1171, **soly** 1678
[L *solium*].

somer *sb.* summer 525, 1686 [OE
sumor].

somones *sb.* command 1498 [OF
somonce].

sonde *sb.* embassy, messengers 53;

pl. (sg. sense) embassy 781 [OE *sánd*].

sonde3mon *sb.* messenger 469 [gen. of prec. + OE *man(n)*].

sone *adv.* soon, quickly, at once, without delay 361, 461, etc.; *as s. as, s. so* as soon as 219, 1550 [OE *sōna*].

sonet *sb.* music 1516; *pl.* bells 1415 [OF *sonet*].

songe *sb.* song 1080 [OE *sáng*].

songe(n), sonkken, sonne. See **syngen, synk, sunne.**

sope *sb.* mouthful 108 [OE *sopa*].

soper *sb.* supper 107, etc. [OF *soper*].

sore *adj.* vile 1111n., 1136; *superl.* **sarrest** most severe 1078; *adv.* **sore** sorely, deeply 290, 557; *adv. compar.* **sarre** more severely 1195 [OE *sār(e)*].

sor3(e), sorewe (778n.) *sb.* sorrow 563, 778, 1080, muck, filth 846n.; *for her s.* to their sorrow 75 [OE *sorg*].

sorsers *sb. pl.* sorcerers 1579n. [OF *sorcier*].

sorsory *sb.* sorcery 1576 [OF *sorcerie*].

sotyly *adv.* slyly 654n. [from OF *so(u)til*].

sotte *sb.* idiot 581 [OE *sott*, OF *sot*].

soth(e) *adj.* true 515, 1643; *adv.* **sothely** truly, indeed 666, **soþ(e)ly** 299, 657 [OE *sōþ(līce)*].

soþe *sb.* truth 1598, 1626; *for s.* in truth, indeed 1737 [OE *sōþ*].

soþefast *adj.* (of God) true 1491 [OE *sōþfæst*].

soufre *sb.* sulphur 954, 1036 [OF *soufre*].

sovly *adj.* filthy 1111, **sowle** 168n. [see note].

soun. See **s(o)un.**

soun *sb.* sound, clamour 689, 973 [AN *s(o)un*].

sounde *adj.* healed 1078, perfect 555; *adv.* safely, securely 1795 [(from) OE *gesúnd*].

souned *sg. pa. t.* sounded 1670 [AN *suner*].

souped *pp.* eaten supper 833 [OF *super*].

sour *adj.* bitter, acid 1036, vile 192n. [OE *sūr*].

sour *sb.* leaven 820 [from prec.].

souerayn *sb.* sovereign, lord 93, *1225*,

etc.; *gen.* 1670; *adj.* sovereign 1454 [OF *so(u)verain*].

sowle. See **sovly.**

space *sb.* opportunity 1774, (wide) extent, generosity 755n.; *in s.* in course of time 1606 [OF *espace*].

spakly *adv.* readily, willingly 755 [ON *spakliga*].

spare *v.* spare 776, (absol.) 1245; *s. of* refrain from 755 [OE *sparian*].

spec *sb.* speck 551 [OE *specca*].

speche *sb.* speech, discourse, words 3, 26, etc., language 1565 [OE *spēc*].

special *adj.* chosen 1492n. [OF *especial*].

sped *sb.* power 1607 [OE *spēd*].

spede *v.* succeed (*of* with) 1058, (absol.) be enough 551; *s. and spylle3* makes and mars 511; *ppl. adj.* **sped** in *s. whyle* short time 1285n. [OE *spēdan*].

spedly *adv.* without delay 1729 [OE *spēdlīce*].

speke *v.* speak 301, 511; *sg. pa. t.* 1220; *pl.* **speken** 646, 845; *pp.* **spoken** 1671 [OE *sp(r)ecan*].

spere *sb.* (attrib.) spear 1383 [OE *spere*].

spye *v.* spy 1774, (absol.) 780 [OF *espier*].

spylle3 3 *sg. pres.* destroys, kills 511; *sg. pa. t.* **spylt** (absol.) 1220; *pl.* **spylled** spilt 1248 [OE *spillan*].

spyrakle *sb.* breath (of life), spirit 408n. [OF *spiracle*, L. *spiraculum*].

spyryt *sb.* spirit 1607 [AN *spirit*].

spiritually *adv.* spiritually 1492 [from OF *spirituel*].

spysere3 *sb. pl.* apothecaries 1038 [OF *espicier*].

spyt *sb.* anger 755 [OF *despit*].

spitous *adj.* shameful 845; *adv.* **spitously** contemptuously 1220, 1285 [(from) OF *despito(u)s*].

spoyle *v.* plunder, ravage 1285, 1774 [from OF *espoillier*].

spote *sb.* spot 551 [OE *spot*].

sprawlyng *sb.* convulsive movement, death-throes 408 [from OE *spreawlian*].

spredes 3 *sg. pres.* is expressed 1565; *sg. pa. t.* **sprad** was present 1607 [OE *-sprædan*].

spryng *v.* spring, go out 1362 [OE *springan*].

spumande *ppl. adj.* foaming *1038* [OF *espumer*].

spured *sg. pa. t.* asked 1606 [OE *spyrian*].

sputen *pl. pa. t.* disputed, talked together 845 [OF *desputer*].

stabled *sg. pa. t. and pp.* set in place, placed 1667, governed 1334, 1652 [OF *establir*].

stac. See **steke**.

stad(de) *pp.* placed, set (up) 1506, given a place 90, transfixed as, turned into 983n.; *as þay s. wern* as they found themselves 806 [ON *staddr*, pp. of *steðja*].

stayred. See **sta(y)red**.

stal *sb.* place 1506 [OE *steall*].

stalle *v.* (bring to a) halt 1184, situate 1378, install 1334 [from prec., cf. OF *estaler, installer*].

stalworth *adj.* strong 884, solid 983; *superl.* **stalworþest** most stalwart 255 [OE *stǽlwyrþe*].

stamyn *sb.* prow 486 [ON *stamn*].

stanc *sb.* pool 1018; *pl.* **stangeȝ** floodgates, cataracts 439n. [OF *estanc*].

standes. See **stonde** *v.*

stare *sb.* gaze, power of sight 583 [from next].

sta(y)red *pa. t.* stared, looked 389, 787, shone, gleamed 1396, 1506n. [OE *starian*].

state *sb.* high estate 1708 [OF *estat*].

statue *sb.* statue 995 [OF *statue*].

staueȝ 3 *sg. pres.* stows, lodges, houses 480; *pp.* **staued** 352, 357, **stawed** 360, **stowed** seated (at table) 113 [from OE *stōw*].

steke *v.* 754; *sg. pa. t.* **stac** 439; *pl.* **steken** 884; *pl. imper.* **stekeȝ** 157, 352; *pp.* **stoken** 360, 1199, 1524. shut up, confine 157, etc., (refl.) 352, 439, fasten 884, stick fast 1524, restrain 754; *s. vp* closed (up) 439 [OE *stecan*].

stel(en) *pl. pa. t.* stole, slipped 1203, took, captured (by surprise) 1778; *ppl. adj.* **stollen** secret, private 706 [OE *stelan*].

stemme 2 *pl. pres. subj.* stop; *s. no stepe* stop 905 [ON *stemma*].

stepe *sb.* step 905 [OE *stepe*].

steppe *adj.* bright 583; *adv.* **stepe** brightly 1396 [(from) OE *stēap*].

sterreȝ *sb. pl.* stars 1378 [OE *steorra*].

steuen *sb.*[1] voice 770, outcry, clamour 1203, 1402, 1778, sound 1524 [OE *stefn*, f.].

steuen *sb.*[2] command 360, 463, (appointed) meeting 706 [OE *stefn*, m., ON *stefna*].

stewarde *sb.* steward 90 [OE *stīweard*].

stiffe *adj.* hard 983; *superl.* **styfest** strongest 255; *adv.* **stifly** fast, firmly, securely 157, 352, 1652 [(from) OE *stīf*].

styȝe *pl. pa. t.* climbed 389 [OE *stīgan*].

styȝtled *pp.* looked after 90 [OE **stihtlian*, cf. *stihtan*].

stykked *sg. pa. t.* put 583; *pl. imper.* **stik** 157 [OE *stician*].

stylle *adj.* still, calm 1203, quiet, secluded 706, secretive 589, silent 1523; *adv.* still, quietly 486, etc.; **stylly** quietly 806, 1778 [OE *stille*; *stillīce*].

styngande *ppl. adj.* stinging, venomous 225 [OE *stingan*].

stynkkeȝ 3 *sg. pres.* stinks 577; *pl.* **stynkes** 847; *ppl. adj.* **stynkande** 1018 [OE *stincan*].

stynt *v.* cease, abate, pause 225, etc. [OE *styntan*].

styry *v.* stir, move 403, 1720 [OE *styrian*].

stod. See **stonde** *v.*

stoffed *pp.* stuffed 1184 [OF *estoffer*].

stoken. See **steke**.

stokkes, stok(k)eȝ *sb. pl.* the stocks 46, 157; *s. and stones* stocks and stones 1343, 1523, 1720 [OE *stocc* 'post'].

stollen. See **stel(en)**.

ston *sb.* stone 983, 1720, etc., precious stone, gem 1120, etc. [OE *stān*].

stonde *sb.* blow 1540; *pl.* **stoundes** times 1716; *in s.* at times 1603 [OE *stúnd*].

stonde *v.* 1490; 3 *sg. pres.* **stondes** 984, 999, **standes** *1618*; *pa. t.* **stod** 255, 486. stand 255, etc., perch 486 [OE *stándan*].

stonen *adj.* (made of) stone 995 [from OE *stān*, cf. *stǽnen*].

ston-harde *adv.* very firmly 884 [OE *stān + héarde*].

stoped *sg. pa. t.* stopped up 439 [OE in *forstoppian*].

storme *sb.* storm 225 [OE *storm*].

stoundes. See **stonde** *sb.*

stout(e) *adj.* bold, worthy 787, 1184, great, mighty 1343, 1396 [AN *stout*].

stowed. See **staueȝ.**

stray *v.* stray 1199 [OF *estraier*].

strayned *sg. pa. t.* strained, afflicted 1540 [OF *estrei(g)n-, estreindre*].

strayt *adv.* securely 1199, severely 880 [OF *estreit*].

strake *sb.* blast (of trumpet) 1402n. [uncertain].

stra(u)nge, stronge (1494n.) *adj.* extraordinary 409, alien, unnatural 861, 1494; *wyȝe s.* foreigner 875 [OF *estrange*].

strecheȝ *pl. imper.* hasten, move 905 [OE *streccan*].

stremeȝ *sb. pl.* streams 364, 374 [OE *strēam*].

strenkle *v.* sprinkle, scatter, put forth 307n. [? ME *sprinklen*, infl. by *strewen*].

stren(k)þe *sb.* violence 880, might 1430; *in s. of* by the strength of 1667n.; *wyth s.* by force 1155 [OE *strengþu*].

strete *sb.* road, highway 787, 806; *pl.* **streeteȝ** 77n. [OE *strēt*].

strye *v.* destroy 307, 1768; *sg. pa. t.* **stryed(e)** 375, 1018 [OF *destruire*].

strok *sb.* stroke, impact 1540 [OE *strāc*].

strong(e) *adj.* strong, mighty, cruel 1034, etc.; *compar.* **stronger** stronger 835 [OE *stráng*].

stronge. See **stra(u)nge.**

stud *sb.* place 1378, standpoint, high place 389; *in his s.* as his successor 1334 [OE *styde, stede*].

sturne *adj.* loud 1402n. [OE *stýrne*].

such(e) *adj.* 190, 541, etc., such, so great, of the same kind 190, etc., (absol.) 1039, 1061; *s. a* such a (foll. by *as* cj.) 748, 1009, (foll. by *þat* cj.) 873, 1365, (with *þat* omitted) 971, (intensive) a most 354, 1588; *pron.* such 1036; *s. as* such as, what 640 [OE *swylc*].

sued *sg. pa. t.* followed; *s. after* fol-

lowed, attended 681 [AN *suer, siwer*].

suffer *v.* suffer, endure, experience 716, 718, 1256; *pp.* **suffred** 892, **soffered** 1701 [AN *suffrir*, OF *soffrir*].

sulp *v.* pollute, corrupt 15, 1130, (*in* by, with) 550, 1135 [uncertain].

sum *adj.* some, a 628; *pron.* **summe** some 388, etc. [OE *sum*].

sumquat *sb.* something 627n. [prec. + OE *hwæt*].

sumtyme *adv.* once, formerly 1157, 1257, 1260, for once 582; *s. byfore* formerly 1152 [OE *sum + tīma*].

sumwhyle *adv.* formerly 1496 [OE *sum + hwīl*].

s(o)un *sb.* son 649, 666, 1299; *pl.* **suneȝ, sun(n)es** 1673, etc. [OE *sunu*].

sunkken. See **synk.**

sunne *sb.* sun 1758, **sonne** 932; *vnder s.* under the sun 549 [OE *sunne*].

suppe *v.* sup, swallow 108 [OE *sūpan*, Nhb. pa. t. *gesupede*].

surely *adv.* surely, indeed 1643 [from OF *sur*].

sustnaunce *sb.* sustenance 340 [AN *sustenaunce*].

sute *sb.* suit; *of s.* to match 1457 [OF *siute*].

swayf *sb.* sweeping blow, sweep 1268 [from ON *sveifa* 'sweep', cf. *sveif* 'tiller'].

swaynes *sb. pl.* servants 1509 [ON *sveinn*].

swaneȝ *sb. pl.* swans 58 [OE *swan*].

swap *sb.* blow 222 [imit.].

sware *adj.* square 319, 1386 [OF *esquarre*].

sware *pl. pres.* answer 1415 [ON *svara*].

swarmeȝ 3 *sg. pres.* swarms 223 [from OE *swearm*].

swengen *v.* rush, go swiftly 109, 667 [OE *swéngan*].

swey *v.* move 788; *sg. pa. t.* **swe** fell 956; *pl.* **swyed** sped, came 87; *ppl. adj.* **sweande** speeding 420 [OE *swēgan*].

swelt *v.* die 108, destroy 332 [OE *sweltan*].

swemande *ppl. adj.* afflicting, painful 563 [OE *āswǣman*].

swepen *pl. pres.* rush 1509 [? formed on OE *swēop*, pa. t. of *swāpan*].

swer *sg. pa. t.* swore 667 [OE *swerian*].

swete *adj.* sweet, fair, pleasant, comely 640, etc.; *superl.* **swettest** 1006; *of s.* the sweetest of 1247 [OE *swēte*].

swetnesse *sb.* sweetness 525 [OE *swētness*].

sweued *pl. pa. t.* subsided, fell 222n. [OE *swebban, swefan, geswefian*].

swyed. See **swey.**

swyere3 *sb. pl.* squires 87 [OF *esquier*].

swyfte *adj.* swift, nimble 1509; *adv.* **swyftly** swiftly 87 [OE *swift(līce)*].

swymmed *pl. pa. t.* swam 388 [OE *swimman*].

swyn *sb. pl.* swine 58 [OE *swīn*].

swypped *pl. pa. t.* escaped 1253 [OE *swipian*, ON *svipa*].

swyre *sb.* neck 1744 [OE *swīra*].

swyþe, swyþee (1211) *adv.* greatly; heavily 354, severely 1176, devoutly 987, quickly, with all speed 1211, 1509, very 816, 1283, 1299; *as s.* at once 1619 [OE *swīþe*].

swol3ed *sg. pa. t.* devoured 1268 [OE *swelgan*].

sworde *sb.* sword 1253, 1268 [OE *swurd*].

tabarde *sb.* tabard, sleeveless upper garment 41 [OF *tabart*].

table *sb.* table 39, 832, etc. [OF *table*].

tabornes *sb. pl.* drums 1414n. [OF *taborne, tabor*].

tayt *adj.* lively, agreeable 871 [ON *teitr*].

tayt *sb.* pleasure 889, game, joke 935n. [ON *teiti*].

take *v.* 804, etc.; *pl. pa. t.* **tok(en)** 935, 1192, 1297; *pl. imper.* **take3** 154, **tat3** 735; *pp.* **taken** 943, 1131, **tan** 763. take, capture 836, etc., catch (up) 943, bring 330, receive 935, 1131, (refl.) take, come to 1201, include 1232; *t. to non ille* do not take it amiss 735; *his leue t.* bids farewell 401; *your waye t.* go on your way 804; *t. in* found engaged in 763 [ON *taka*].

tale *sb.* tale 587, conversation 676, matter 662, 1437, meaning 1557 [OE *talu*].

talke *sb.* talk, conversation 735 [from next].

talke3 3 *sg. pres.* talks 154; *sg. pa. t.* **talkede** 132 [from base of OE *talu*].

talle *sb.* general (bodily) appearance 48n. [OF *ta(i)lle*].

tame *adj.* (as sb. pl.) tame animals 311, 362 [OE *tam*].

tan, tat3. See **take.**

techal *sb.* Tekel 1727, 1733 [L *thecel*].

teche *sb.* sin 943, 1230, sign 1049 [OF *teche*].

teche *v.* teach, instruct 160, 1733, show 676 [OE *tǣcan*].

tede *adj.* divinely ordained, fated 1634n. [OE *getēod(e)*; see note].

teen *pl. pres.* go 9; *sg. pres. subj.* **tee** 1262 [OE *tēon*].

.telde *sb.* house 866 [OE *téld*].

telde *v.* 211, 1342; *pp.* **telled** 1808n. raise, set 211, 1342; *t. vp* aroused 1808 [OE *téldian*].

telle *v.* tell (of) 687, 1153, 1634; *pp.* **tolde** 1623 [OE *tellan*].

teme *v.* conceive, become pregnant 655n.; *pl. pres.* **temen** in *t. to* attach themselves to 9 [OE *tēman*].

tem(m)ple, tempple *sb.* temple 9, Temple (in Jerusalem) 1151, 1262, 1490 [OE *temp(e)l*, OF *temple*].

tempre *sg. imper.* temper 775 [OE *temprian*].

temptande *ppl. adj.* trying, distressing 283 [OF *tempter*].

ten *adj.* ten 763 [OE *tēn*].

tender *adj.* tender 630 [OF *tendre*].

tene *adj.* angry 1808 [from next].

tene *sb.* anger, hostility 283, 687, 1232 [OE *tēona*].

tene *v.* be angry 1137n., harm 759 [OE *tēonian*].

tenfully *adv.* in anguish 160 [from OE *tēonful*].

tent *v.* heed 935; *t. him with tale* engage Him in conversation 676 [OF *atendre*, infl. by *atent*, sb].

terme *sb.* time, period 239, 568n., word 1733; *t. of þe tyde* appointed time 1393 [OF *terme*].

terne *sb.* tarn, lake 1041 [ON **tarnu*, cf. OI *tjorn*].

teþe sb. pl. teeth 160 [OE *tōþ*].

teueled laboured 1189 [OE *tæfl(i)an*, ON *tefla*].

tid adv. quickly 901; *als(o) t., as t.* at once, immediately 64, 1099, 1213 [ON *titt*, ? infl. by OE *tīd(līce)*].

tyde sb. (appointed) time 1393 [OE *tīd*].

ty3ed pp. joined 702 [OE *tīgan*].

ty3t v. contrive, manage 1108, grant 1153; pl. pa. t. (refl.) went away 889n. [OE *tyhtan*, infl. by *dihtan*].

tykle sb. wantonness 655n. [? formed on ME *tick*].

til cj. until 484, 906, etc., to the extent that 548 [as next].

tylle prep. (postponed) to 882, etc. [OE (Nhb.) *til*, ON *til*].

tylt. See **tult.**

tymbres sb. pl. tambourines 1414 [OF *timbre*].

tyme sb. time 106, 660, etc.; *on a t.* once, one day 1657 [OE *tima*].

tyne v. strike down, overthrow 907; 2 sg. pres. **tyne3** (fut. sense) 775; sg. pa. t. **tynt** 216 [ON *týna*].

tyned sg. pa. t. confined 498 [OE *tȳnan*].

tyraunte3 sb. pl. evil men 943 [OF *tyrant*].

tyrauntyre sb. tyranny 187 [from prec.].

tyrue v. strip (*of* off) 630n., overturn, overthrow *1234* [see note].

type adj. tenth 216 [OE *tē(o)þa*].

typyng sb. message, word 498, 1557; pl. information 458 [OE *tīdung*, infl. by ON *tīðindi*].

tyxte sb. text, wording 1634 [ONF *tixte*].

to adv. too 22, 182, 861, 1231, 1376 [as next].

to prep. to 97, 154, etc., (implying motion) 39, 44, etc., until 1032, for 204, 309, 340, 808, 1716, with respect to, for 174, 315, 844, 1659, towards 1172, against 832, 1230; adv. to 162, near 1551; *particle with infin.* (in order) to 45, 64, etc. [OE *tō*].

tocleues 3 sg. pres. sticks (*in* in) 1806n. [*to-* + OE *cléofian*].

tocoruen. See **tokerue.**

togeder(e) adv. together 160, etc.,

at the same time 307, 1290 [OE *tōgædere*].

to3e adj. tough 630 [OE *tōh*].

tok(en). See **take.**

tokened pl. pa. t. represented 1557 [OE *tācnian*].

tokenes sb. pl. tokens 1049 [OE *tācen*].

tokerue v. destroy 1700; pl. pa. t. **tocoruen** cut open 1250 [OE *tōceorfan*].

tolde, toles. See **telle, tool.**

tolk(e) sb. man 687, 757, 889, (of God) 498; pl. **tulk(k)es** 1189, 1262, 1623 [ON *túlkr*].

tom sb. (space of) time, opportunity 1153 [ON *tóm*].

tomarred ppl. adj. (utterly) astray 1114n. [*to-* + OE *merran*, OF *marrir*].

tonge sb. tongue 1524 [OE *tunge*].

tool sb. tool(s) 1342; pl. **toles** 1108 [OE *tōl*].

topace sb. topaz 1469 [OF *topace*].

torent sg. pa. t. burst open 368 [OE *tōréndan*].

tormenttoure3 sb. pl. torturers 154 [OF *tormentour*].

torne v. turn round 976, **turne** go 64n.; sg. pa. t. **tourned** turned 1099 [OE *turnian*, OF *to(u)rner*].

torne pp. torn 1234 [OE *teran*].

torof sg. pa. t. broke up 964 [*to-* + ON *rífa*].

torres sb. pl. tors, hill-like masses (of cloud) 951n. [OE *torr*].

tos sb. pl. toes 1691 [OE *tā*].

tote3 sb. pl. toes of shoes 41 [MDu. *tote*].

totorne ppl. adj. torn 33, 41 [OE *tōteran*].

toun(e) sb. town 721, 751, etc., property, estate 64 [OE *tūn*].

tour sb. entourage, retinue 216n. [OF *atour*].

toures sb. pl. towers 1189, 1383 [AN *tur*].

tourned. See **torne** v.

tourne3 sb. pl. tricks, doings 192 [AN *tourn*].

tow. See **two.**

towalten pl. pa. t. burst out 428 [*to-* + OE *-wæltan*].

toward(e) prep. towards, to 672, etc. [OE *tōweard*].

towche v. touch 245, etc., make known 1437; wat3 t. arrived 1393 [OF toucher].

trayled ppl. adj. decorated with trailing designs 1473 [OF traillier, MLG, MFlem. treilen].

traysoun sb. treason 187 [AN treisoun].

traytoures sb. pl. evildoers 1041 [OF traitour].

trayþ(e)ly adv. pitilessly, violently 907n., 1137 [from ON tregða; see note].

tramountayne sb. north 211n. [OF tramontaine].

trasche3 sb. pl. old shoes 40n. [uncertain].

traw(e), trow(e) v. 655, 1049, etc.; sg. imper. **trave** 587. believe, think 587, etc., think to 388; t. vpon take note of 1049; I t. (intensive) as I believe 1686, 1803 [OE trēow(i)an].

trawþe, trauþe (723, 1490) sb. truth 723, 1604, 1736, true faith 1490, loyalty, obedience 236; by hys (hir) t. on his (her) honour 63n., 667; in t. truly 1703 [OE trēowþ].

tre sb. tree 622, 1041, wood 1342, board 310 [OE trēo(w)].

treso(u)r sb. treasure 866, treasurer 1437 [OF treso(u)r].

tresorye sb. treasury 1317 [OF tresorie].

trespas sg. pres. subj. should offend 48; pp. **trespast** (to against) 1230 [OF trespasser].

trestes sb. pl. trestles 832 [OF treste].

trichcherye sb. treachery 187 [OF tricherie].

tryed ppl. adj. (specially) chosen, special 1317 [OF trier].

tryfled adj. ornamented with trefoils 1473n. [from AN triffle, trefle].

trysty adj. (as sb.) true men 763 [? from OE *tryst, cf. ON traust].

troched adj. provided with tines; pinnacled 1383 [from OF troche].

tron sg. pa. t. went 132; pres. p. **trynande** 976 [uncertain].

trone. See **throne.**

trot sb. trot, pace 976 [OF trot].

trow(e), true. See **traw, trwe.**

trumpen pl. gen. (as adj.) of trumpets 1402n. [OF trumpe].

trussed sg. pa. t. packed 1317 [OF trusser].

trwe adj. true, virtuous, worthy 682, 759, etc., **true** (as sb.) virtuous people 702; adv. **trwly** as was proper 1490 [OE trēowe; trēowlīce].

tuch sb. detail (of dress) 48n. [OF touche].

tulk(k)es. See **tolk(e).**

tulket pl. pa. t. sounded 1414n. [cf. ONF toquer].

tult pl. pa. t. tipped 1213; pp. **tylt** tilted (to against) 832n. [? OE *tyltan, cf. tealt(r)ian].

turne. See **torne** v.

tweyne adj. two 674, etc. [OE twēgen].

twenty adj. twenty 757, 759, 1383 [OE twentig].

twentyfolde adv. twenty times, many times 1691n. [OE *twentigfáld, twentigfeald].

twynande pres. p. twisting round 1691 [from OE twīn].

twynne adj. twofold; in t. in two 1047, apart 966 [OE (ge)twinn].

twynne v. part 402 [from prec.].

two, tow (866) adj. two 155, 702 etc. [OE twā, tū].

þa3 cj. though, even if 48, 72, etc. [OE þæh, þǎh].

þay, thay (9) pron. 3 pl. they 9, 53n., etc.; gen. **þayres** (disjunctive) theirs 1527 [ON þeir, þeira].

þare. See **þer(e).**

þat, that (433) adj. demonstr. that, the 433, etc.; pl. **þo(se)** 97, 332, etc.; pron. **þat** that, it 251, 309, etc.; pron. pl. **þo(se)** 173n., 261, etc. [OE þæt, þā, þās].

þat cj. that 53, 126, etc., (prec. by so, such) 152, 269, 874, etc., so that, in such a way that, in order that 72, 178, 914, etc., in that 694, 1090 [OE þæt].

þat pron. rel. that, which, who(m) 2, 5, 6, 7, 694, etc., in which (used loosely) 996, when 1069, that which, what, those who(m), etc. 286, 376, 553, 580, 652, 898, 1144, 1445, etc.; þ. . . . hit, his, þay, hem which, whose, who 274, 448, 926, 952, 1109, 1532 [OE þæt, for þe].

þe. See þou.

þe adv. with compar. (so much) the 296 [OE þĕ, þȳ].

þe def. art. the 2, 4, etc., (generalising) 288, 374, 1616 (1st), etc. [OE þĕ, for sĕ].

þede sb. (coll. sense) vessels 1717n. [uncertain].

þeder. See þider.

þefte sb. theft 183 [OE þēoft].

þen(ne), þenn, thenne adv. then, afterwards, in that case, and so 53, 73, 77, 349, etc., now, thus 178, if then 39, 1141 [OE *þenne, þænne].

þen, þenne (1108) cj. than 76, 168, etc. [as prec.].

þenk 1 sg. pres. 304, 711, 1729; 3 sg. þynke3 749; sg. pa. t. and pp. þo3t 138, 590; pl. imper. þenkke3 819. think of, conceive 590, consider 749, decide 138, intend (to) 304, etc.; þ. on take care 819 [OE þencan, þōhte].

þer(e), þare (1076) adv. there, in that place, on it, on them 11, 126, etc., thither 1677, then, on that occasion, in that case, in this 203, 216, 1319, (indef.) there 263, 375, 926, etc., (there) where, the place where, wherever, when 158, 379, 1004, 1015, 1027, 1419, etc.; þ. as where 24, 769; with preps.: þerabof above (them) 1481; þeraboute round about 1796; þerafter afterwards 93, 157, etc.; þeranvnder underneath (it) 1012; þeratte at that 1554; þerbi, þerby there 1034, on them 1404; þerbysyde nearby 673; þerinne, þerin (993) there(in), in it 311, 321, etc.; þerof of it 306, 604, 1752, with it 972, from it, from them 1499, 1507n.; þeron on(to) it, on(to) them, there 244, 386, etc., with them 1719; þeroute out(side) 44, 109, etc., in the open 807; þerouer over them 1407; þerto thither, there 1394, in that regard 701; þertylle to it 1509; þervpone on it 1665; þerwyth with them 1406, at that, on that account 138, 1501, thereupon 528 [OE þēr].

þerue-kake3 sb. pl. unleavened loaves 635 [OE þe(o)rf + ON kaka].

þese. See þis.

þester sb. darkness 1775 [OE þēostru].

þewed adj. gracious 733 [from next].

þewe3 sb. pl. ways 203, good nature, goodwill, grace, favour 544n., 755, 1436 [OE þeawas, pl.].

þewes sb. pl. thieves 1142 [OE þēof].

þi, þy. See þou.

þider adv. thither, to that place 45, etc., þeder 64, 461, 1775 [OE þider].

thy3e sb. thigh 1687 [OE þēh].

þik(ke) adj. thick, solid 1687, thick, dense 222, teeming 220, abundant, ever-present 952; as sb. in for þ. on account of being dense, thickly 226; adv. þikke thickly, heavily 953, tightly 504, rapidly 1416; adv. compar. þiker at closer intervals 1384 [OE þicce].

þyn. See þou.

þyng sb. thing 1600, etc., þynk 819; pl. þinke3 916, þink practices 1359 [OE þing].

þynk impers. pres. subj. it seem 744; impers. pa. t. þo3t 1504, (pers.) seemed 562 [OE þyncan, þūhte].

þink(e3), þynke3. See þyng, þenk.

þirled sg. pa. t. pierced 952 [OE þirlian, þyrlian].

þis, þyse (1802) adj. demonstr. this, the 65, 106, etc.; pl. þise 84, 105, etc., þis 822, þese 1710; pron. þis this 229, 1013, 1751; pron. pl. þyse 42, 1049 [OE þis].

þo, þo3t. See þat adj. demonstr., þenk, þynk.

þo3t sb. thought, desire 516 [OE þōht].

þole v. endure 190 [OE þolian].

þonkkes 3 sg. pres. thanks 745 [OE þancian].

þor3. See þur3.

þorpes sb. pl. villages 1178 [OE þorp, þrop].

þose. See þat adj. demonstr.

þou, þow pron. 2 sg. 95, 145, etc.; acc. dat. þe 169, 1616 (2nd), etc.; gen. (as poss. adj.) þi, þy(n) 95, 143, 165, etc., you 95, etc., (refl.) 169, 333, etc.; þyself yourself 581, 582 [OE þū, þē, þīn].

þowsande3 sb. pl. thousands 220 [OE þūsend].

þrad pp. punished 751 [OE þrēa(ga)n].

þral sb. fellow 135 [OE þrǽl, ON þræll].

þratten. See þretes.

þrawe3 3 sg. pres. 590; sg. pa. t. þrwe 635, 879; pl. þrwen 220; pp. þrawen 516, þrowen 504, 1384. fly 590, place swiftly 635, be flung 220, turn 516, press (together), crowd 504, 879, set 1384; ppl. adj. þrawen close-packed 1775 [OE þrāwan].

þre adj. three 298 (twice) etc. [OE þrēo].

þrefte adj. unleavened 819 [? based on metathesised form of OE þe(o)rf].

þrenge. See þrynges.

þrep sb. debate, question 350 [from OE þrēapian, cf. ON þrap].

þrepyng sb. quarrelling 183 [OE þrēapung].

þretes pres. threaten 680, 1728; pl. pa. t. þratten 937 [OE þrēatian].

þretty adj. thirty 751, 754, þrette 317 [OE þrittig].

þreuenest. See þryue.

þryd(de) adj. third 69, 249n., 1571, etc. [OE þridda].

þrye3 adv. thrice 429 [from OE þria].

þryftyly adv. with propriety 635 [from ON þrift].

þry3t sg. pa. t. crowded 1687; ppl. adj. in þ. in in the midst of 135 [OE þryccan].

þrynges 3 sg. pres. 180, 1639; pl. pres. þrenge 930; pl. pa. t. þrong(en) 879, 1775. rush, hurtle 180, 1775, push 879; þ. after follow, owe allegiance to 930n., 1639 [OE þringan].

þrynne adj. three 606, 645, 1805; in þ. as three words 1727 [ON þrinnr].

þryue v. flourish, have life 250; ppl. adj. þryuande (as sb.) worthy men 751; ppl. adj. þryuen grown 298; superl. þryuenest noblest, most worthy 1639, þreuenest 1571 [ON þrífask, þrífinn].

þro adv. in earnest, clearly 1805, eagerly, swiftly 590, violently 220 [from ON þrár].

þro sb. wrath 754 [ON þrá].

þrobled pl. pa. t. crowded, jostled 879; pres. p. þrublande 504n. [see note].

þroly adv. violently 180, urgently, impatiently 504 [ON þráliga].

throne sb. throne 1112, 1396, trone 211, 1794 [OF t(h)rone].

þrong(e) sb. throng, crowd 135, 504, 754 [ON þrong, OE geþráng].

þrong(en). See þrynges.

þrote sb. throat 180, 1569 [OE þrote].

þrowen, þrublande, þrwe(n). See þrawe3, þrobled.

þunder-þrast sb. (bolt ðf) lightning 952n. [from OE þunor + þrǽstan].

þur3, þor3 (1761) prep. through 1204, 1761, throughout 1361, 1362, by (means of) 731, etc., on account of 236, 241, 1325 [OE þurh].

þur3out prep. throughout 1559 [OE þurhūt].

þus, thus (161) adv. thus, so, in this way 26, 47, 577n., etc., as follows 314, 681, 1733 [OE þus].

vch(e), vuche (378) adj. each, every 31, 228, etc.; v. a every 78, 196, etc.; pron. vchon(e) each one 71, 497, 1111, etc.; v. on oþer one on another 267 [OE ylc (+ān(a))].

vglokest adj. superl. ugliest, worst 892 [ON uggligr].

v3ten sb. the part of the night immediately before the dawn; vpon v. at daybreak 893 [OE ūhte, on ūhtan].

vmbe prep. about, around 879, 1474, etc. [OE umbe, ymbe].

vmbebrayde sg. pa. t. embraced 1622n. [umbe- + OE bregdan].

vmbegrouen pp. 'grown round', covered 488 [umbe- + OE grōwan].

vmbekeste3 3 sg. pres. circles (round) 478 [umbe- + ON kasta].

vmbely3e v. surround 836 [OE ymblicgan].

vmbesweyed pp. surrounded 1380 [umbe- + OE swēgan].

vmbeþour adv. round about 1384 [umbe- + OE þori 'main part'].

vmbewalt sg. pa. t. surrounded 1181 [umbe- + OE wæltan].

vmbre sb. ? dull weather 524 [OF ombre].

vnblyþe adj. unpleasant 1017 [OE unblīþe].

vnbrosten ppl. adj. unbroken 365 [un- + OE berstan, ON bresta].

vncheryst *ppl. adj.* uncared for 1125 [*un-*+OF *cheriss-, cherir*].

vnclannes(se) *sb.* uncleanness 30, 1800, 1806 [OE *unclǣnness*].

vnclene *adj.* unclean, foul 710, 1144, 1713, uncleansed, unpurged 550 [OE *unclǣne*].

vncloses 3 *sg. pres.* opens 1438, sets forth 26 [*un-*+OF *clos-, clore*].

vncowþe *adj.* unknown, strange 1600, 1722, **vncouþe** 414 [OE *uncūþ*].

vnder *prep.* under 226, 483, etc. [OE *under*].

vnderȝede *sg. pa. t.* realised 796 [OE *undergān*].

vndyd *sg. pa. t.* destroyed 562 [OE *undōn*].

vnfayre *adj.* unseemly 1801 [OE *unfæger*].

vnfolded *sg. pa. t.* opened 962; *sg. imper.* **vnfolde** make known 1563 [*un-*+OE *fáldan*].

vnfre *adj.* base, evil 1129 [*un-*+OE *frēo*].

vngarnyst *ppl. adj.* not suitably dressed 137 [*un-*+OF *garniss-, garnir*].

vngoderly *adj.* bad, vile 145n., 1092 [see note].

vnhap *sb.* misfortune, disaster 892, 1150; *for þyn v.* to your misfortune 143 [ON *úhapp*].

vnhappen *ppl. adj.* accursed 573 [*un-*+ON *heppinn*, infl. by *happ*].

vnhaspe *v.* disclose 688 [*un-*+OE *hæpsian*].

vnhyles 2 *sg. pres.* uncover 1628; *pp.* **vnhuled** 451 [cf. ON *hylja*].

vnhole *adj.* unsound 1681 [OE *unhāl*].

vnhonest *adj.* unclean 579 [*un-*+OF *honeste*].

vnhuled. See **vnhyles.**

vnkyndely *adv.* ungratefully 208 [from OE *uncýnde*].

vnknawen *ppl. adj.* unknown 1679 [*un-*+OE *cnāwan*].

vnmard *adj.* undefiled 867 [from *un-*+OE *merran*, OF *marrir*].

vnneuened *ppl. adj.* unsaid, retracted 727n. [ON *únefndr*].

vnryȝt *sb.* wrong; *wyth v.* wrongfully 1142 [OE *unriht*].

vnsauere *adj.* unseasoned 822 [*un-*+OF *savoure*].

unsmyten *adj.* unharmed 732 [*un-*+OE *smītan*].

vnsounde *adj.* unsound, corrupt 575; *adv.* **vnsoundely** with disastrous effect 201n. [*un-*+OE *gesund(līce)*].

vnstered *ppl. adj.* ungoverned; *v. wyth syȝt* not overlooked, with none to see 706 [*un-*+OE *stēoran*].

vnswolȝed *ppl. adj.* undevoured (*of* by) 1253 [*un-*+OE *swelgan*].

vnto *prep.* to 9, 1235 [OE **untō*].

vntrwe *adj.* untrue, false 184, etc. [OE *untrēowe*].

vntwyneȝ 3 *sg. pres.* destroy 757 [from *un-*+OE *twīn*].

vnþeweȝ *sb. pl.* sins 190 [OE *unþēaw*].

vnþonk *sb.* displeasure 183 [OE *unþanc*].

vnþryfte *sb.* wickedness, folly 516, 1728; *adv.* **vnþryftyly** wantonly 267 [(from) *un-*+ON *þrift*].

vnþryuandely *adv.* poorly 135 [from *un-*+ON *þrífask*].

vnwaschen *ppl. adj.* unwashed 34 [OE *unwæscen*].

vnwelcum *adj.* unwelcome 49 [from *un-*+OE *wilcuma*, ON *velkominn*].

vnworþelych *adj.* unworthy, shameful 305 [OE *unwurþlic*].

vp, vpe (1010), **vppe** (1421) *adv.* up 2, 211, etc., aroused 834, out of bed 1001 [OE *up, upp(e)*].

vpbraydeȝ 3 *sg. pres.* throws up 848 [prec.+OE *bregdan*].

vpcaste *pp.* proclaimed, uttered 1574 [*up*+ON *kasta*].

vpfolden *ppl. adj.* uplifted (in prayer) 643n. [*up*+OE *fáldan*].

vplyfte *ppl. adj.* uplifted (in prayer) 987 [*up*+ON *lypta*].

vpon *adv.* open 453, 501, 882 [OE *open*, infl. by *up*].

vpon, upon (268, 1112) *prep.* upon, on, at, in 416, 719, etc.; *adv.* on (you, it) 141, 1276 [*up*+OE *on*].

vponande, vppe. See **open, vp.**

vprerde *sg. pa. t.* raised up 561 [*up*+OE *rǣran*].

vpryse *v.* get up (from bed) 896 [*up*+OE *rīsan*].

vpwafte *pl. pa. t.* rose (up) 949 [*up*+OE **wǣfan*].

vrnmentes, vrþe. See **ornementes, erþe.**

vrþly adj. earthly 35 [OE eorþlic].

vsage sb. practice 710 [OF usage].

vse v. practise, indulge in 267n., etc., pass 295, partake of (sacramentally) 11 [OF user].

vsle sb. ash(es) 747; pl. **vselleȝ** cinders, sparks 1010 [OE ysl].

vtter adv. out(side) 42 [OE ŭtter, ūtor].

vtwyth adv. outwardly 14 [OE ūt + wiþ].

vuche, vus. See **vch(e), we.**

vayled pl. pa. t. were used 1151, were valued 1311n. [OF vail, valoir].

vayneglorie sb. vainglory 1358 [OF vaine glorie].

vale sb. valley 673 [OF val].

vanist sg. pa. t. vanished 1548 [OF e(s)vaniss-, e(s)vanir].

vanyte sb. presumption 1713 [OF vanite].

veng(i)aunce, uengaunce sb. vengeance 247, 744, 1013 [OF vengeance].

venged, uenged. See **weng.**

venym sb. venom, wickedness 754 [OF venim].

venkquyst sg. pa. t. overcame 544; pp. **venkkyst** 1071 [formed on OF venquis, pa. t. of veintre].

verayly adv. (intensive) emphatically 664, utterly 1548 [from OF verai].

vergynyte sb. virginity 1071 [OF virginite].

vertuous adj. of special power (of gems) 1280 [OF vertuo(u)s].

vessel sb. (coll.) vessels 1311, 1429, 1451, **vessayl** 1791; pl. **vesselles** 1151, 1315, **vessayles** 1713 [AN vessel(e)].

vesselment sb. vessels 1280, 1288 [OF vesselement].

vestures sb. pl. vestments 1288 [OF vesture].

vice sb. vice 199 [OF vice].

vycios adj. vicious, vile 574 [OF vicious].

vyl adj. disgusting; me v. þynk I am disgusted 744 [OF vil].

vyla(y)nye sb. evil 544, 574, disgrace 863n. [OF vilanie, vilenie].

vylen pl. pres. degrade 863 [OF viler].

vilte sb. vileness, abomination 199 [OF vilte].

vyolence sb. violence 1071 [OF violence].

violent adj. violent 1013 [OF violent].

vyoles. See **fyoles**

voyde v. lay waste 1013; v. away forego 744; v. of syȝt disappeared (from sight) 1548 [AN voider].

vouche v. offer, give 1358 [OF voucher].

wach(e) sb. state of wakefulness; (coll. sense) watch, sentries 1205; leyen in a w. lain awake 1003 [OE wæcce].

waft(e) sg. pa. t. moved to and fro, surged 422n., swung 857n., (vpon open) 453 [OE *wæfan; see note to line 422].

waged pp. fluttered 1484 [OE wagian].

waȝeȝ sb. pl. waves 404, **waweȝ** 382 [OE wæg, infl. by wagian].

way(e) sb. way, road, path 282, etc.; by þe w. along the road 974 [OE weg].

wayferande ppl. adj. wayfaring; w. frekeȝ travellers 79 [OE wegfērende].

waykned sg. pa. t. was enfeebled 1422n. [from ON veikr].

wayne v. send, give 1504, 1616, 1701 [OE in bewægnan].

wayte v. examine 1552, look 1423, try 292, search 99 [ONF waitier].

waked pl. pa. t. roused 85n. [OE wacian].

waken v. 323, **wakan** 948; sg. pa. t. and pp. **wak(e)ned** 437, etc. waken (from sleep) 891, 933, awaken, arouse, raise (up), call (up) 323, etc. [OE wæcn(i)an].

wakker adj. compar. weaker 835 [OE wăccra, compar. of wāc].

wale adj. choice 1716, noble 1734 [from ON val].

wale sg. imper. choose (refl.) 921; pp. **walt** marked out 1734 [as prec., cf. ON velja].

walk v. walk 1674; pl. pres. **walkeȝ** 503 [OE walcan].

walkyries sb. pl. enchanters 1577n. [OE wælcyri(g)e, from ON valkyrja].

walle sb. wall 1181, etc. [OE wall].

walled ppl. adj. walled 1390n. [OE geweallod].

walle-heued sb. well-head, spring

364n.; *pl.* **welle-hede3** 428 [OE
wælla, wella + *hēafod*].

walt. See **wale** *v.*, **waltes.**

walter *v.* roll, toss about 415, flow
1027 [MLG *walteren*].

waltes 3 *sg. pres.* 364, 1037; *sg. pa. t.*
walt 501. burst, gush 364, be flung
1037; *w. vpon* swung open 501 [OE
wæltan].

wan. See **wynne.**

wapped *pl. pa. t.* flung 882 [? ON
vappa].

war *adj.* careful 292, 589; *be w. by* take
warning by 712; *wat3 (wern) w. of*
became aware of 606, 970 [OE *wær*].

war *sg. imper.* in *w. þe* take care, look
out 165, etc. [OE *warian*].

wary *v.* curse 513; *ppl. adj.* **waryed**
accursed 1716 [OE *wærgan, w(i)er-
gan*].

warisch *v.* protect 921 [ONF *wariss-,
warir*].

warla3es *sb. pl.* sorcerers 1560 [OE
wǣrloga].

warmed *sg. pa. t.* warmed 1420 [OE
werman].

warnyng *sb.* warning 1504 [OE
warnung].

warp *v.* say, speak, utter 152; *sg. pa. t.*
warp 213, **werp** 284n.; *pl.* **warpen**
drove 444 [OE *weorpan*, ON *varpa*].

was. See **wat3.**

wasch(e) *v.* 323, etc.; *pp.*
waschen(e) 618, etc. wash, cleanse
618n., etc., (absol.) wash (oneself)
831n., 1138 [OE *wascan*].

wassayl *interj.* wassail! your health!
1508 [ON *ves heill*].

wast *v.* 326, 431, 1489; *sg. pa. t.* 1178.
destroy 326, etc., waste 1489 [ONF
waster].

wasturne *sb.* wilderness 1674 [OE
wēstern, infl. by ONF *wast*].

water *sb.* water, flood, deluge 323,
371, etc.; *pl.* **wattere3** 437, 496,
wat(t)eres rivers 1380, 1776 [OE
wæter].

wat3 2 *sg. pa. t.* were 143, **were**
1623; 3 *sg.* **wat3** 92, 120, etc., **was**
126, etc.; *pl.* **wer(n), were(n)**
385n. etc.; *sg. pa. t. subj.* **wer(e)**
22, 1029, etc., **wore** 928; *pl. subj.*
wer(e) 82, 618n., etc., **wern** 113
[OE *wæs, wēron, wēre*].

wawe3. See **wa3e3.**

wax *sb.* wax 1487 [OE *wæx*].

wax *sg. pres. subj.* 1123; *sg. pa. t.*
wax(ed) 375, 397, **wex** 204, 235;
pl. **wexen** 1198; *pl. imper.* **waxe3**
521. grow, become 204, etc., rise
397, prosper 521, take place 235
[OE *waxan*].

waxlokes *sb. pl.* wax-like curls
1037n. [OE *waex* + *locc*].

we *pron.* 1 *pl.* we 95, 622, etc.; *acc.
dat.* **vus** 246, 1507n., etc.; *gen.* (as
poss. adj.) **our(e)** 28, 345, 986, etc.
[OE *wē, ūs, ūre*].

wed *sg. pa. t.* was mad 1585 [OE
wēdan].

wedde *v.* wed 69, 330, 934 [OE
weddian].

wede *sb.* (coll. sense) clothes 793; *pl.*
clothes 20, 1208, etc. [OE *wǣd(e)*].

weder *sb.* weather 444, storm 948, air,
sky 475, 847, 1760 [OE *weder*].

we3tes *sb. pl.* scales, balance 1734
[OE *wiht*, infl. by prec. and ON
weht, vétt].

weye *v.* 719; *pl. pa. t.* **we3ed** 1420;
pl. imper. **we3e** 1508. bring 1420,
1508, weigh 719 [OE *wegan*].

wekked. See **wykked.**

wel *adv.* well, properly 113, 320, etc.,
much 1100, 1132, 1138; *ful w.* fully
1699; *sb.* good fortune 1647 [OE
wel].

wela *adv.* most 831 [OE *wellā*].

welcom *adj.* (made) welcome 813
[from OE *wilcuma*, ON *velkominn*].

welde *v.* wield 644, 835, use, enjoy
705, 1351, rule, govern 17, 1646n.,
etc. [OE *wéldan*].

wele *sb.* blessedness 651 [OE *wela*].

welgest *adj. superl.* ? strongest 1244
[? cf. OE *welig*].

welkyn *sb.* sky 371 [OE *welcn, weol-
cen*].

welle-hede3. See **walle-heued.**

welle3 *sb. pl.* wells, springs 439n.
[OE *wella*].

wel-ne3e *adv.* almost 1422, **wel-
ny3e** 704 [OE *wel-nēh*].

wen. See **when.**

wenches *sb. pl.* girls 974, 1250,
women, concubines 1423, 1716
[shortened from OE *wencel*].

wende3 3 *sg. pres.* goes 675, 777; *pa.*

t. **went** 415, 501, 857; *sg. imper.*
wende 471; *pl. imper.* **wende3** 521
[OE *wéndan*].

wene 1 *sg. pres.* think, fancy 821 [OE
wēnan].

weng *v.* take vengeance, exact re-
tribution 201; *sg. pa. t.* **venged** 199,
uenged 559 [OF *venger*].

wepande *pres. p.* weeping 778 [OE
wēpan].

weppen *sb.* weapon 835 [OE *wĕpn*].

wer *sg. pa. t.* (refl.) excused himself
69n. [OE *werian*[1]].

wer(e). See **wat3**.

were3 3 *sg. pres.* wears, has 287; *sb.*
weryng wearing, being worn 1123
[(from) OE *werian*[2]].

werk *sb.* 305, 589, etc.; *pl.* **werk(k)es**
136, 171, 1258, etc. work, act,
action, deed 171, etc., labour(s)
136n., 1258, activity, behaviour 305,
658, 1050, structure (sg. sense)
1480; *w. þat he made* His creation
198; *of w.* elaborate 1390n.; *withoute w.* more without more ado 1725
[OE *we(o)rc*].

wern, werp. See **wat3, warp**.

werre *sb.* warfare 1178 [ONF *werre*].

wers *adj.* worse 80; *worþy oþer w.*
worthy or not so worthy 113;
superl. **werst** worst 694; *adv.* **worse**
worse 1320 [OE *wyrsa, wyrsta*;
wyrs].

wete *v.* wet 1027 [OE *wētan*].

weþer, wex(en), wham. See
wheþer, wax *v.*, **who**.

what *adj. interrog.* 35, etc., **whatt** 845,
quat 741, 1119. what (sort of) 35,
100, 1556, 1557; *w. . . . so* whatever
819; *pron.* 752, 913, 1119, (ellipt.)
what shall you do 757; *w. if* what if
737, 741, 751; *pron. rel.* that which,
what 152, 1567, 1587; *interj.* look,
listen, lo 487, 845, etc. [OE *hwæt*].

what-so *pron.* whatever 1099 [OE
(*swā*) *hwæt swā*].

wheder *adv.*[1] whither, where (to go)
917; **whederwarde-so** wherever
422 [OE *hweder, hwider*; *hwider
swā+weard*].

wheder *adv.*[2] yet 570 [OE *hweþre,
hwæþere*].

when *adv.* 61, 89, etc., **quen** 529, etc.,
wen 343. when(ever) 37, etc., by

which time 361; *w. þat* when 961,
1537 [OE *hwenne, hwænne*].

wher(e) *adv. rel.* where 491, 1079,
1080, wherever 444; **where-so**
where 675, wherever 791 [OE
hwǣr; *swā hwǣr swā*].

wheþer *cj.* whether 918, (correl. with
oþer or) 113; *w. . . . 3if* that if 583;
adv. **weþer** (introd. dir. question)
717 [OE *hweþer, hwæþer*].

why *adv. interrog.* why 828, 1595 [OE
hwī].

whichche *sb.* chest, Ark 362 [OE
hwicce].

whyl(e), whil *cj.* while, as long as
206, 1124, etc., **whil** 1298, **quyl**
627; *prep.* **quyle** until 1686 [OE
þā hwīle þe].

whyle *sb.* short while 833; *in a (sped)
w.* in a short while, soon 1285, 1620;
3et a w. still 743 [OE *hwīl*].

whit *adj.* white 793, **whyte** 1120,
quite 1440 [OE *hwīt*].

who *pron. interrog.* who 875, 1699;
acc. dat. **wham** (as rel.) 259; *gen.*
quos in *q. . . . so* (the man) whose
1648; **who-so** whoever 1, 1647,
1649, **quo-so** 1650 [OE *hwā*; *swā
hwā swā*].

wich *pron. interrog.* which, what 169;
pron. rel. 1060 (2nd); *adj.* 1060 (1st),
1074 [OE *hwilc*].

wychecrafte *sb.* witchcraft 1560 [OE
wiccecræft].

wyche3 *sb. pl.* wizards 1577n. [OE
wicca].

wyde *adj.* wide, open 370; *on w.*
around 1423n. *adv.* **wyd** wide 318
[OE *wīd(e)*].

wydoe3 *sb. pl.* widows 185 [OE
widewe].

wif *sb.* wife, woman 69, 330, etc.; *pl.*
wyues 112, 1250, etc. [OE *wíf*].

wy3(e) *sb.* man 235, 1181, etc., (of
God) 5, 230, 280, 284, servant 899,
1587, (in address) sir 545 [OE
wiga].

wy3t *adv.* quickly, in a moment 617;
wy3tly 908 [(from) ON *vigt*].

wy3t *sb.* creature 471 [OE *wiht*].

wyk(ke) *adj.* evil 908, hostile 1063n.
[from OE *wicca*].

wyk(k)et *sb.* wicket, door 501, wicket
(gate) 857, 882 [AN *wiket*].

wykked *adj.* wicked, evil 570, etc., **wekked** 855 [from OE *wicca*].

wyl 1 *sg. pres.* 358; 2 *sg.* **wylt** 165, 764, 930; *pl.* **wyl** 517; *sg. subj.* **wyl** 1065; *pa. t.* **wolde** 928, etc. *Pres.* will, wish (for), want (to) 360, 930, 1065, etc., (as fut. auxil.) 517, etc.; *Pa. t.* wished (to), would (like to) 231, 928, etc., required 360, (ellipt.) wanted (to say), meant 1552 [OE *willan, wolde*].

wylde *adj.* (of animals) wild 58, 533, 1676, wild, furious 302, etc., (as sb. pl.) (wild) animals, (wild) creatures 311, etc. [OE *wílde*].

wylger *adj. compar.* ? wilder 375n. [see note].

wyly *adv.* cunningly, artfully 1452 [from OE *wíl*, ONF *wile*].

wylle *sb.* will, desire, purpose, mind, heart 200, 309, etc., wilfulness 76n.; *in his w.* as he wishes 1646 [OE *will(a)*].

wylnesful *adj.* wilful; as *sb.* in *for w.* for wilfulness 231n. [from OE *gewilnes*].

wylsfully *adv.* wilfully 268 [from OE *willes*, gen. of *will*].

wyn(e) *sb.* wine 1127, etc. [OE *wín*].

wynd(e) *sb.* wind 847, etc.; *vpon w.* in the wind 1484 [OE *wind*].

wynde₃ *pl. pres.* turn, go 534 [OE *wíndan*].

wyndow(e) *sb.* window 318, 453 [ON *vindauga*].

wyndowande *ppl. adj.* winnowing, swirling 1048n. [OE *windwian*].

wynge *sb.* wing 475, 1484 [first in pl., ON *vængir*].

wynne *v.* 617, etc.; *sg. pa. t.* **wan** 140; *pl.* **won(n)en** 882, etc.; *pp.* **won(n)en** 112, 1004, 1669, **wunnen** 1305. win, gain 1120, 1305, find 1550, bring 617, make one's way, go 882, etc., come 140, issue 1669, prevail on 1616, beget 112, 650n. [OE *winnan*].

wynnelych *adj.* gracious 1807; *adv.* **wynnely** excellently 831 [OE *wynlic; wynlíce*].

wynter *sb.* winter 525 [OE *winter*].

wyrdes *sb. pl.* fate (sg. sense) 1224, 1605 [OE *wýrd*].

wyrke *v.* 1287, **work** 663; 2 *sg. pa. t.*

wro₃te₃ 720; *pa. t. and pp.* **wro₃t** 5, 171, 725, etc.; *sg. imper.* **wyrk** 311. work, fashion, construct 311, etc., make, create 5, etc., do, perform 171, etc., act 1063, 1319; *ppl. adj.* **wro₃t** constructed 1381 [OE *wyrcan, wrohte*].

wyrles 3 *sg. pres.* whirls, flies 475 [ON *hvirfla*].

wys(e) *adj.* wise, learned 1555, (*of* in) 1560, prudent 1592, (as *sb.*) wise man 1319, 1741 [OE *wís*].

wyse *sb.* 268, 271, etc.; *pl.* **wyse(s)** 1728, 1805. manner, fashion, way 268, etc., form 1187; *on þis w.* as follows 327 [OE *wíse*].

wysed *sg. pa. t.* directed, sent 453 [OE *wísian*].

wysses 3 *sg. pres.* instructs 1564 [OE *wissian*].

wyt *v.* 1052, etc.; 2 *sg. pres.* **wost** 875; *sg. subj.* **wyt** 1360; *pa. t.* **wyst(e)** 152, etc. know understand, see 152, etc., know of 1204, 1360; *w. of* be aware of 1770 [OE *witan, wát, wiste*].

wyt(te) *sb.* reason 1422, 1701, mind 515, meaning 1630, skill 348 [OE *wit(t)*].

wyte *v.* blame, be blamed 76 [OE *wítan*].

wyter *adv.* plainly 1552; **wyterly** plainly 1567, to be sure 171 [from ON *vitr; vitrliga*].

wytered *pp.* informed 1587 [ON *vitra*].

wytles *adj.* distracted 1585 [OE *witléas*].

wittnesse *sb.* evidence 1050 [OE *witnes*].

with *prep.* (together) with 58, 124, etc., by (means of) 19, 516, 1495, etc., in anticipation of, for 56n., at (the same time as) 213; *w. þat* thereupon 671 [OE *wiþ*].

wythal *adv.* as well 636 [from prec. + OE *al(l)*].

wyþerly *adv.* fiercely 198 [from OE *wiþer*].

wythhalde *v.* restrain 740 [from OE *wiþ + háldan*].

withinne *adv.* (on the) inside 312, 883, etc., inside them 1195, amongst them 1465, inwardly, at heart 20,

305, 593; *prep.* in(side) 431, 434, etc., (of time) within 1779, 1786; *hym w.* in his heart, in him, inwardly 284, 1607 [OE *wiþinnan*].

withoute(n) *adv.* (on the) outside 313, 1205, 1487, outwardly 20; *prep.* without 252, 350, etc. [OE *wiþūtan*].

wytte(3), wyues. See **wyt(te), wyf.**

wlates 3 *sg. pres.* is disgusted 1501, (impers.) it is disgusting 305 [OE *wlătian*].

wlatsum *adj.* loathsome 541 [from OE *wlătta + -sum*].

wlonk, wlonc (889), *adj.* lordly, polite 606, 831, rich 793, fair 899, 933; as *sb.* in *þe wlonk* what is clean 1052 [OE *wlanc*].

wo *sb.* sorrow, adversity 1701, misfortune 541; *adj.* anguished 284 [(from) OE *wā*].

wod(e) *adj.* mad 828, 1558, furiously eager, furious 204n., wild, raging 364 [OE *wōd*].

wod(e) *sb.* wood, trees 370, 387, 1028 [OE *wudu*].

wo3e, wowe *sb.* wall 832, 839, etc. [OE *wāg*].

wolde. See **wyl.**

wolfes *sb. pl.* wolves 1676 [OE *wulf*].

wombe *sb.* stomach, belly 462, 1250, 1255 [OE *wámb*].

won *sb.* custom 720 [OE *(ge)wuna*].

won *v.* 1676; 2 *sg. pres.* **wone3** 875; 3 *sg.* **wonies** 1340, 1807, **wons** 326; *pa. t.* **wonyed** 252, 431, 675, **woned** 362; *pres. p.* **wonyande** 293. live, dwell 252, etc., live as 875 [OE *wunian*].

won(e) *sb.* dwelling, house 140, 375, 533, place 1489, 1508, (sg. sense) 841, territory, site 1178, place to live, abode (sg. sense) 471, town, city 891, 928, 1770, (sg. sense) 1197, room 311; *in w.* at home 779 [ON *ván*].

wonded *sg. pa. t.* feared 855 [OE *wándian*].

wonder, wunder *sb.* wonder 584, 1310; *of w.* wonderful 1390n.; *þat w. hem þo3t* which amazed them 1504; *adv.* **wonder** wonderfully 1381, very 5, 153, 880; **wonderly** exceedingly 570 [OE *wundor(líce)*].

woned *pp.* diminished 496 [OE *wanian*].

won(n)en. See **wynne.**

wonnyng *sb.* (dwelling-)place 921 [OE *wunung*].

wont *pl. pres.* lack 13; *pl. subj.* be wanting 739 [ON *vanta*].

wonte *ppl. adj.* accustomed 1489 [OE *gewunod*, pp. of *(ge)wunian*].

worcher *sb.* creator 1501 [from OE *wyrcan*].

worde *sb.* word 149, 152, etc., speech 213, 840, 1669, command 348 [OE *wórd*].

wore, work. See **wat3, wyrke.**

worlde *sb.* world, earth 252, 293, etc., universe 228n., prosperity 1298; *w. withouten ende* for all time 712; *in þe w.* (intensive) in the world, at all 548, 1123; *gen.* **worldes** 1802, (intensive) in the world, at all 1048 [OE *wor(u)ld*].

worme3 *sb. pl.* snakes 533 [OE *wurm*].

worre *adj.* worse, wrong 719 [ON *verri*, infl. by ME *worse*].

worschyp wo(u)rchyp *sb.* honour, respect 545, etc.; *with (þe) w.* with due respect, respectfully 1127, 1616 [OE *wurþscipe*].

worse. See **wers.**

worþe *adj.* worth 1244 [OE *wurþ*].

worþe *v.* become, be 60, etc.; *w. to monye* turn into many, increase in numbers 521n. [OE *wurþan*].

worþy *adj.* worthy 84, 113, 718, worshipful, glorious 231 [from OE *wurþ*].

worþ(e)ly, worþ(e)lych *adj.* worthy, noble, of noble rank 49n., etc. [OE *wurþlic*].

wost. See **wyt.**

woþe *sb.* danger, harm 855, 988 [ON *váði*].

wowe(s). See **wo3e.**

wrak, wrek *sg. pa. t.* took vengeance; *w. on* punished 198, 570 [OE *wrecan*].

wrake *sb.* 213, etc., **wrache** 204, 229. (act of) vengeance, revenge, punishment 204, etc., hostility 1808; *adj.* **wrakful** vengeful, bitter 302, 541 [(from) OE *wracu, wræc*].

wrange *sb.* wrongdoing 76; *adj.* perverted 268 [OE *wráng*].

wrappe3 *sg. pres.* (refl.) dress (yourself) 169 [uncertain].

wrast *sg. pa. t.* wrought up, worked up 1166n.; *pl.* **wrasten** burst out 1403n.; *pp.* **wrast** cast (*out of* out from) 1802 [OE *wrǣstan*].

wrastled *pl. pa. t.* wrestled 949 [OE **wrǣstlian*].

wrath *sb.* anger 204, etc. [OE *wrǣþþu*].

wrath *v.* anger 719, 828, become angry 230, 690 [from prec.].

wrech *sb.* wretch 84, etc. [OE *wrecca*].

wrek. See **wrak.**

wrenchез *sb. pl.* tricks 292 [OE *wrenc*].

wryste *sb.* wrist 1535 [OE *wrist*].

wryt *sb.* writing 1552, 1567, 1630, Holy Writ, Bible 657 [OE *writ*].

wrytes 3 *sg. pres.* writes 1534; *pp.* **wryten** 1725 [OE *wrītan*].

wryþeз *pl. pres.* 533; *sg. pa. t.* **wroth** 821. writhe, slither 533; *w. to dyspyt* took it amiss 821n. [OE *wrīþan*].

wroзt(eз). See **wyrke.**

wroþe *adj.* fierce 1676, **wroth** angry 5; *adv.* **wroþ(e)ly** angrily, fiercely 280, 949 [OE *wrāþ(līce)*].

wruxeled *pp.* ? built up (with alternating courses of masonry) 1381n. [OE *wrixlan*].

wunder, wunnen. See **wonder, wynne.**

yo(u)r, yow. See **зe.**

INDEX OF NAMES